STAGGER LEE™

OCT   2006

Written by
DEREK McCULLOCH

Drawn by
SHEPHERD HENDRIX

Lettering by
RICHARD STARKINGS &
COMICRAFT'S JIMMY BETANCOURT

Design by
JOHN ROSHELL OF COMICRAFT

Derek says:
Like everything else I do,
this is for Tara and Pearl.

Shepherd says:
For You!
(You know who you are!)

"When the legend becomes fact,
print the legend"

—James Warner Bellah and Willis Goldbeck,
The Man Who Shot Liberty Valance

"Come all you sporty fellows
And listen unto me,
I will tell to you the awful tale
Of that bad man Stackalee.
That bad, that bad man Stackalee"

—Unknown

Stagger Lee 101

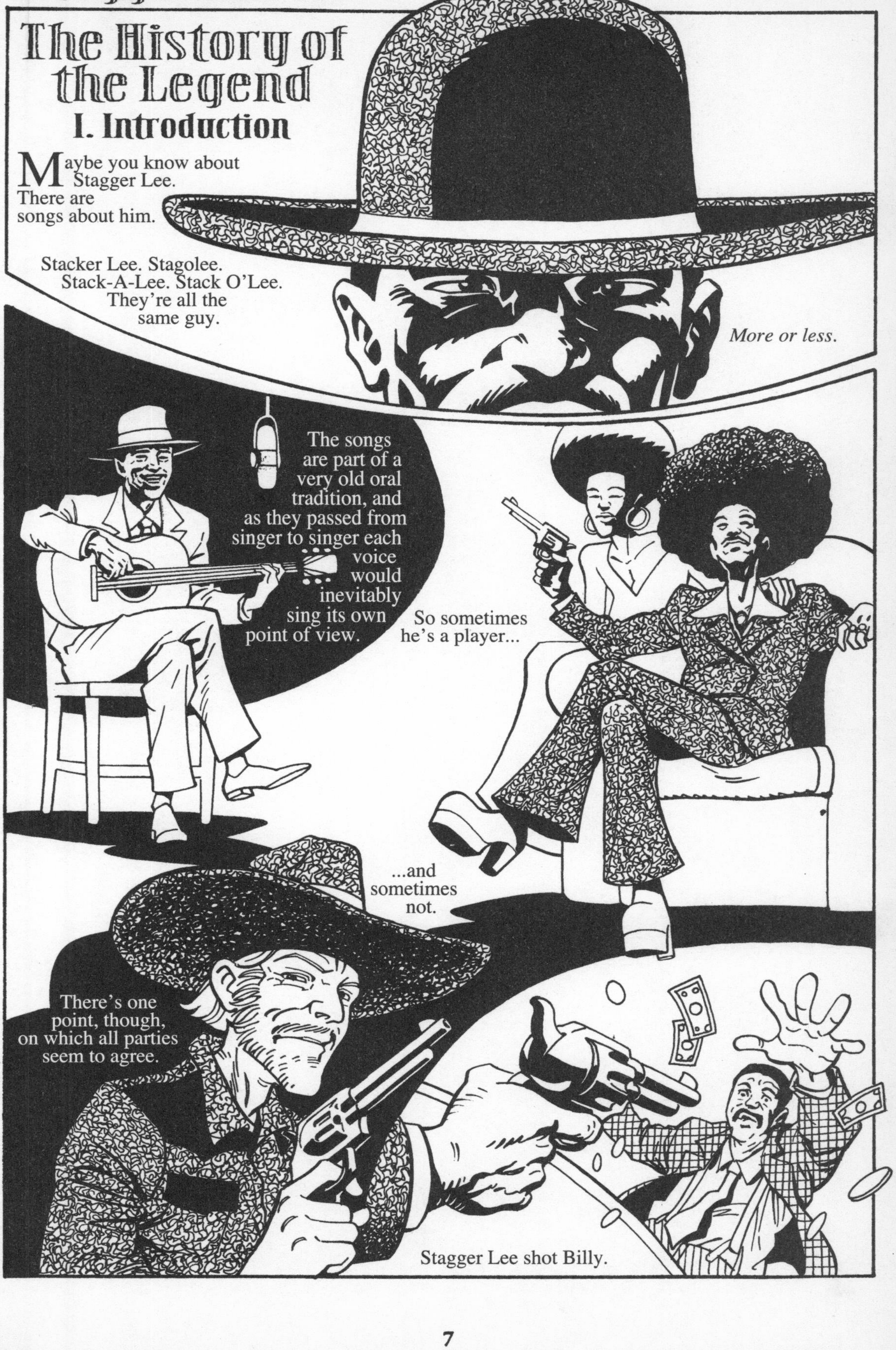
The History of the Legend
I. Introduction
Maybe you know about Stagger Lee. There are songs about him.
Stacker Lee. Stagolee. Stack-A-Lee. Stack O'Lee. They're all the same guy.
More or less.
The songs are part of a very old oral tradition, and as they passed from singer to singer each voice would inevitably sing its own point of view.
So sometimes he's a player...
...and sometimes not.
There's one point, though, on which all parties seem to agree.
Stagger Lee shot Billy.

PROLOGUE

,The BAD MAN

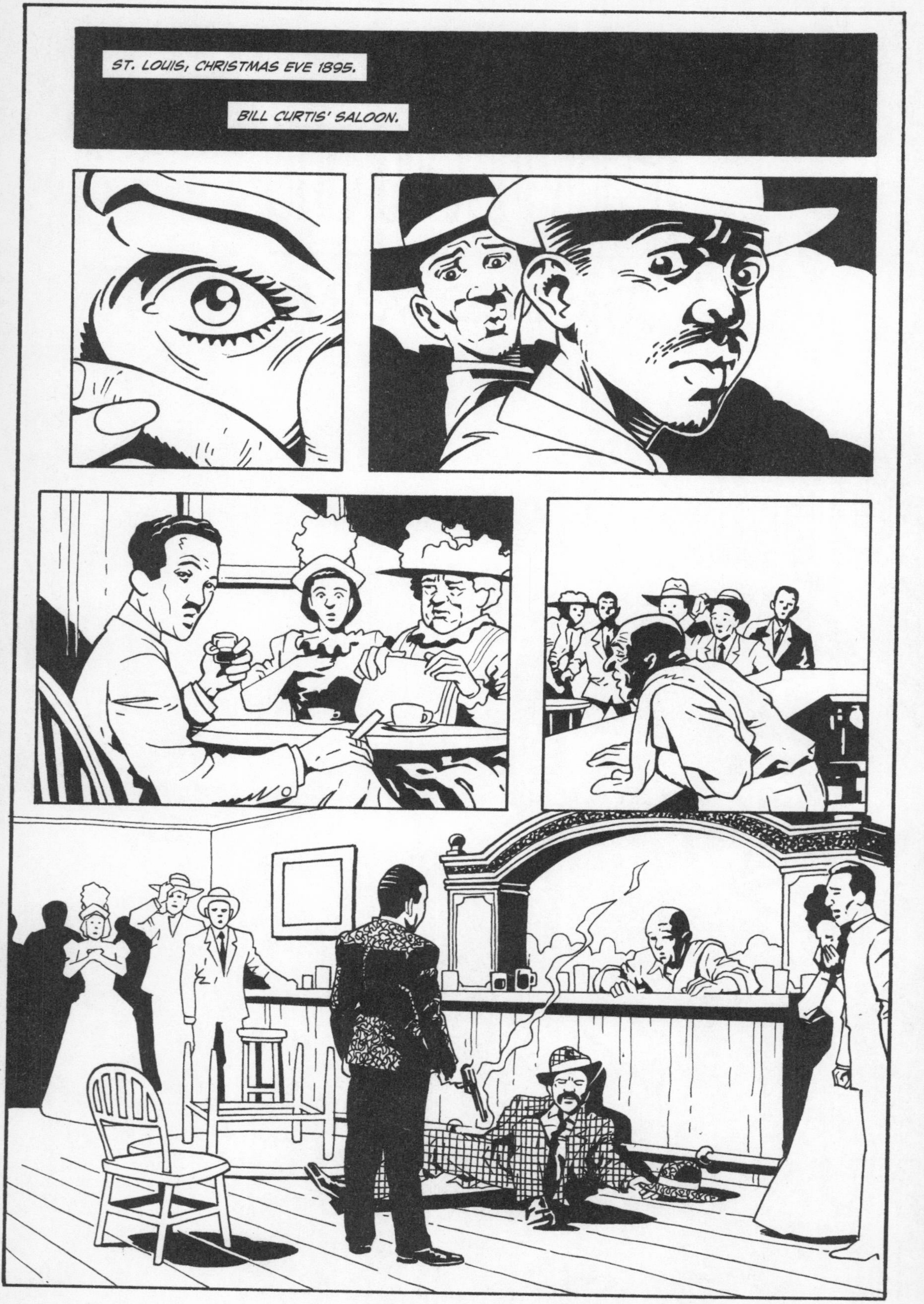
ST. LOUIS, CHRISTMAS EVE 1895.
BILL CURTIS' SALOON.

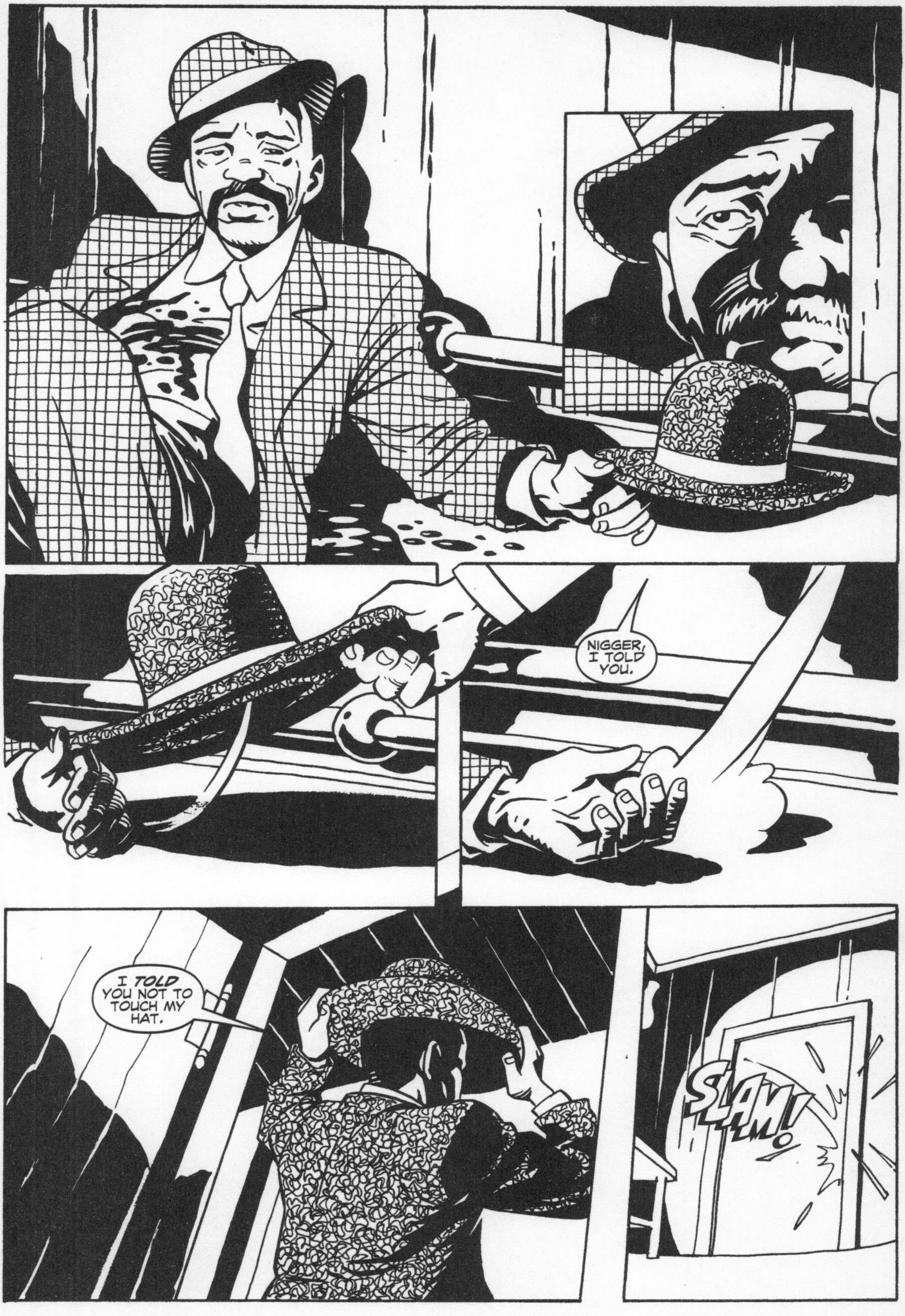
NIGGER, I TOLD YOU.
I *TOLD* YOU NOT TO TOUCH MY HAT.
SLAM!

PART ONE

,The HAT

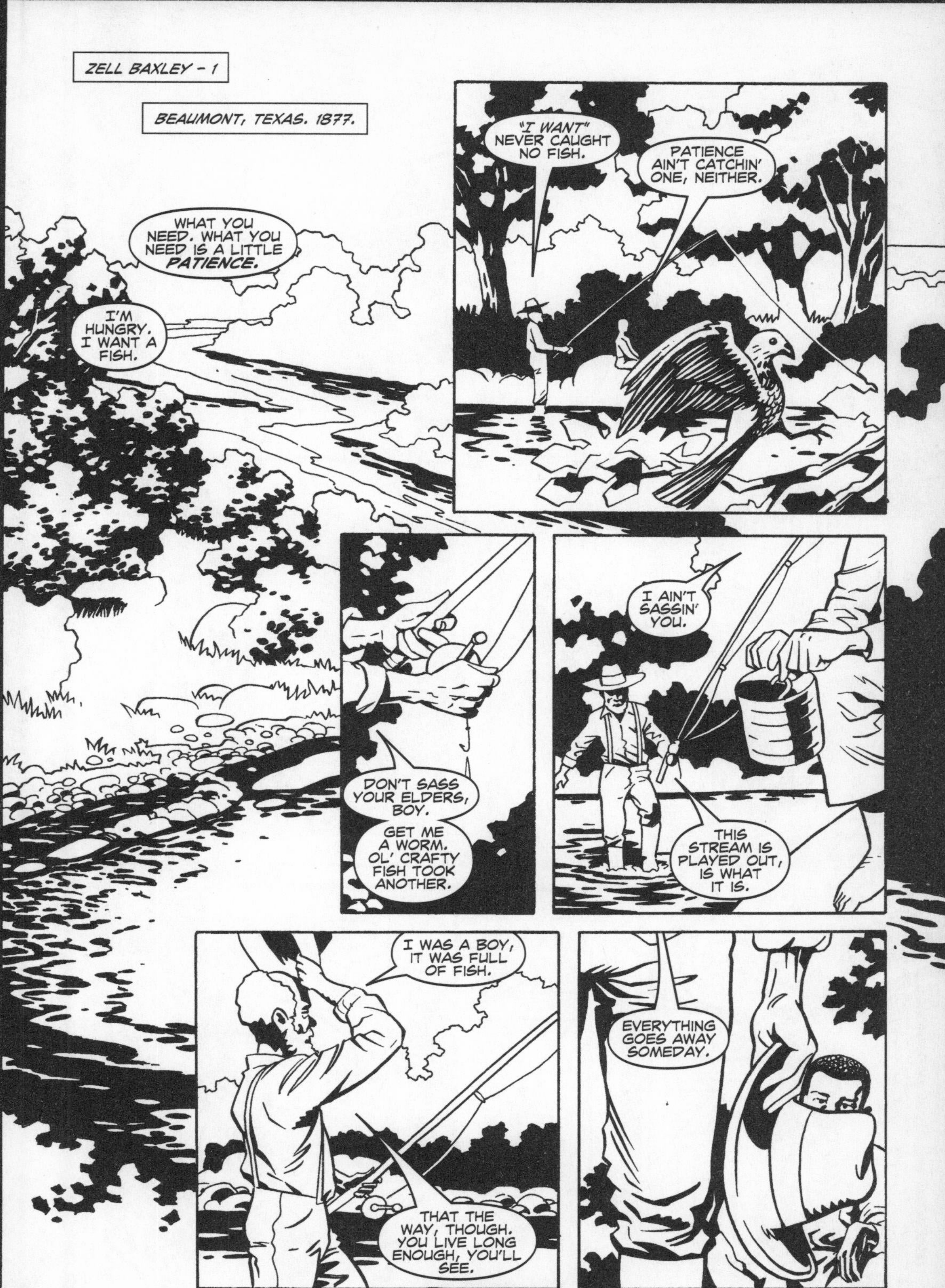
ZELL BAXLEY – 1
BEAUMONT, TEXAS. 1877.
I'M HUNGRY. I WANT A FISH.
WHAT YOU NEED. WHAT YOU NEED IS A LITTLE PATIENCE.
"I WANT" NEVER CAUGHT NO FISH.
PATIENCE AIN'T CATCHIN' ONE, NEITHER.
DON'T SASS YOUR ELDERS, BOY.
GET ME A WORM. OL' CRAFTY FISH TOOK ANOTHER.
I AIN'T SASSIN' YOU.
THIS STREAM IS PLAYED OUT, IS WHAT IT IS.
I WAS A BOY, IT WAS FULL OF FISH.
THAT THE WAY, THOUGH. YOU LIVE LONG ENOUGH, YOU'LL SEE.
EVERYTHING GOES AWAY SOMEDAY.

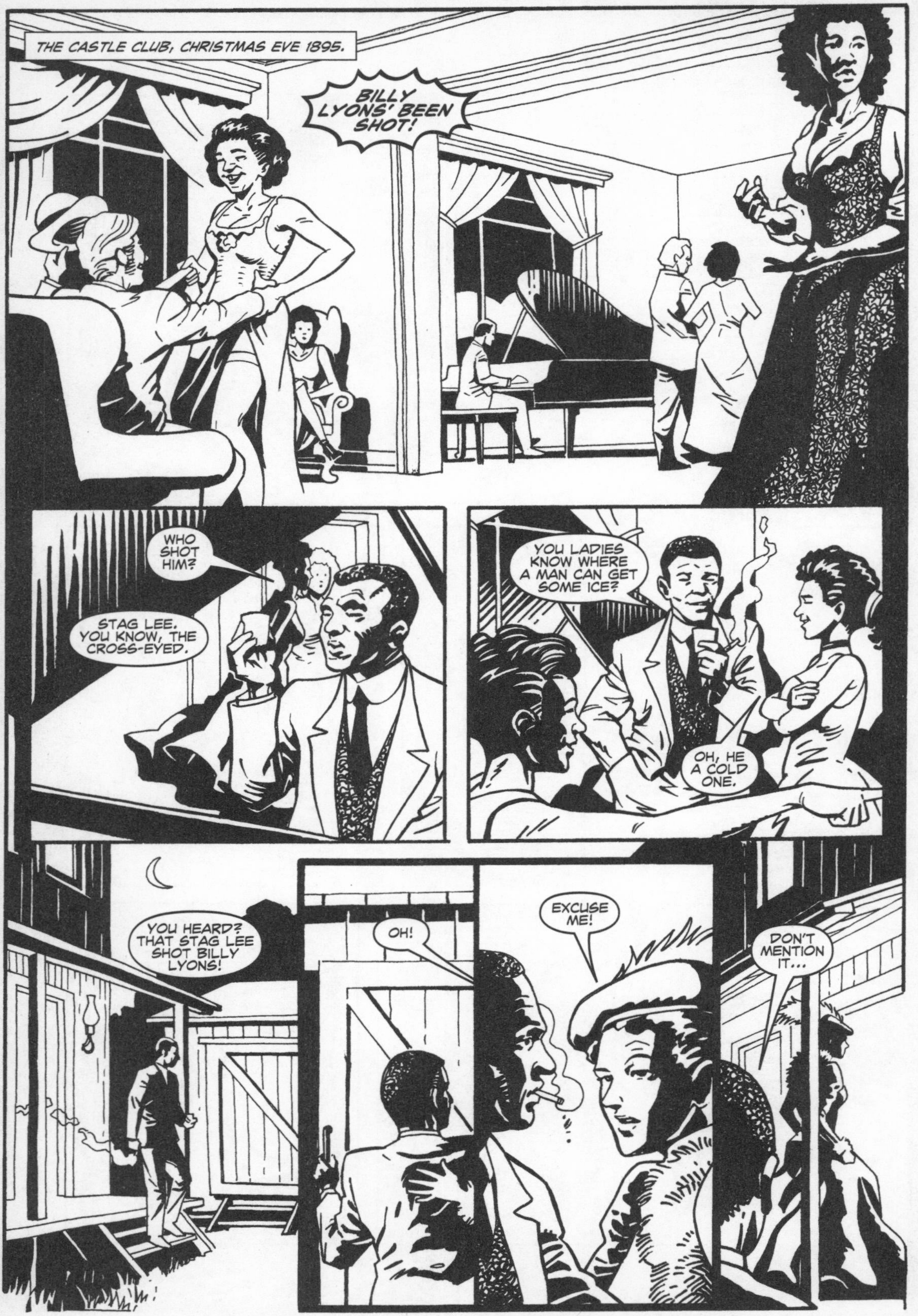

THE CASTLE CLUB, CHRISTMAS EVE 1895.
BILLY LYONS' BEEN SHOT!
WHO SHOT HIM?
STAG LEE. YOU KNOW, THE CROSS-EYED.
YOU LADIES KNOW WHERE A MAN CAN GET SOME ICE?
OH, HE A COLD ONE.
YOU HEARD? THAT STAG LEE SHOT BILLY LYONS!
OH!
EXCUSE ME!
DON'T MENTION IT...

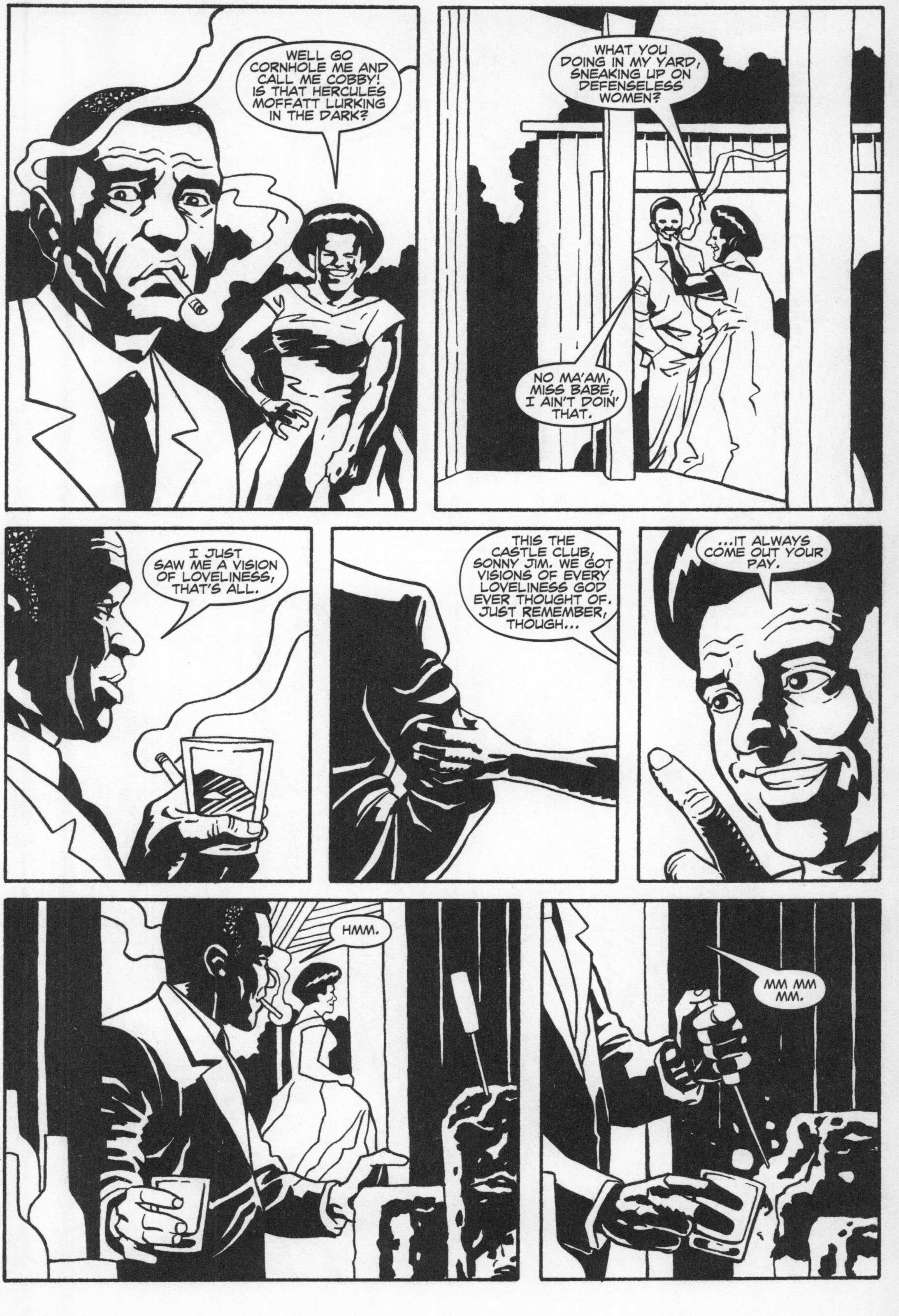
WELL GO CORNHOLE ME AND CALL ME COBBY! IS THAT HERCULES MOFFATT LURKING IN THE DARK?
WHAT YOU DOING IN MY YARD, SNEAKING UP ON DEFENSELESS WOMEN?
NO MA'AM, MISS BABE, I AIN'T DOIN' THAT.
I JUST SAW ME A VISION OF LOVELINESS, THAT'S ALL.
THIS THE CASTLE CLUB, SONNY JIM. WE GOT VISIONS OF EVERY LOVELINESS GOD EVER THOUGHT OF. JUST REMEMBER, THOUGH...
...IT ALWAYS COME OUT YOUR PAY.
HMM.
MM MM MM.

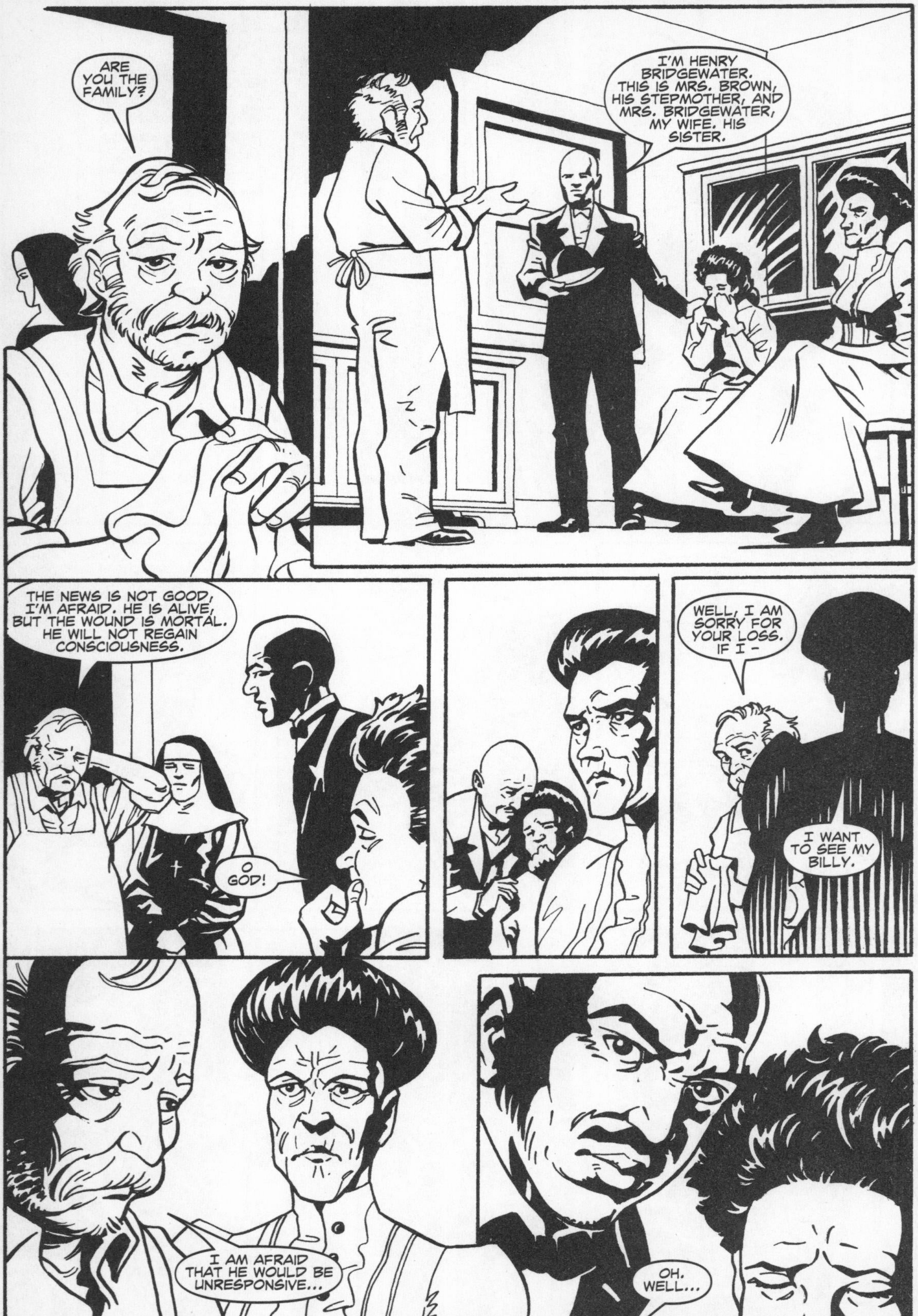
ARE YOU THE FAMILY?
I'M HENRY BRIDGEWATER. THIS IS MRS. BROWN, HIS STEPMOTHER, AND MRS. BRIDGEWATER, MY WIFE. HIS SISTER.
THE NEWS IS NOT GOOD, I'M AFRAID. HE IS ALIVE, BUT THE WOUND IS MORTAL. HE WILL NOT REGAIN CONSCIOUSNESS.
O GOD!
WELL, I AM SORRY FOR YOUR LOSS. IF I –
I WANT TO SEE MY BILLY.
I AM AFRAID THAT HE WOULD BE UNRESPONSIVE...
OH. WELL...

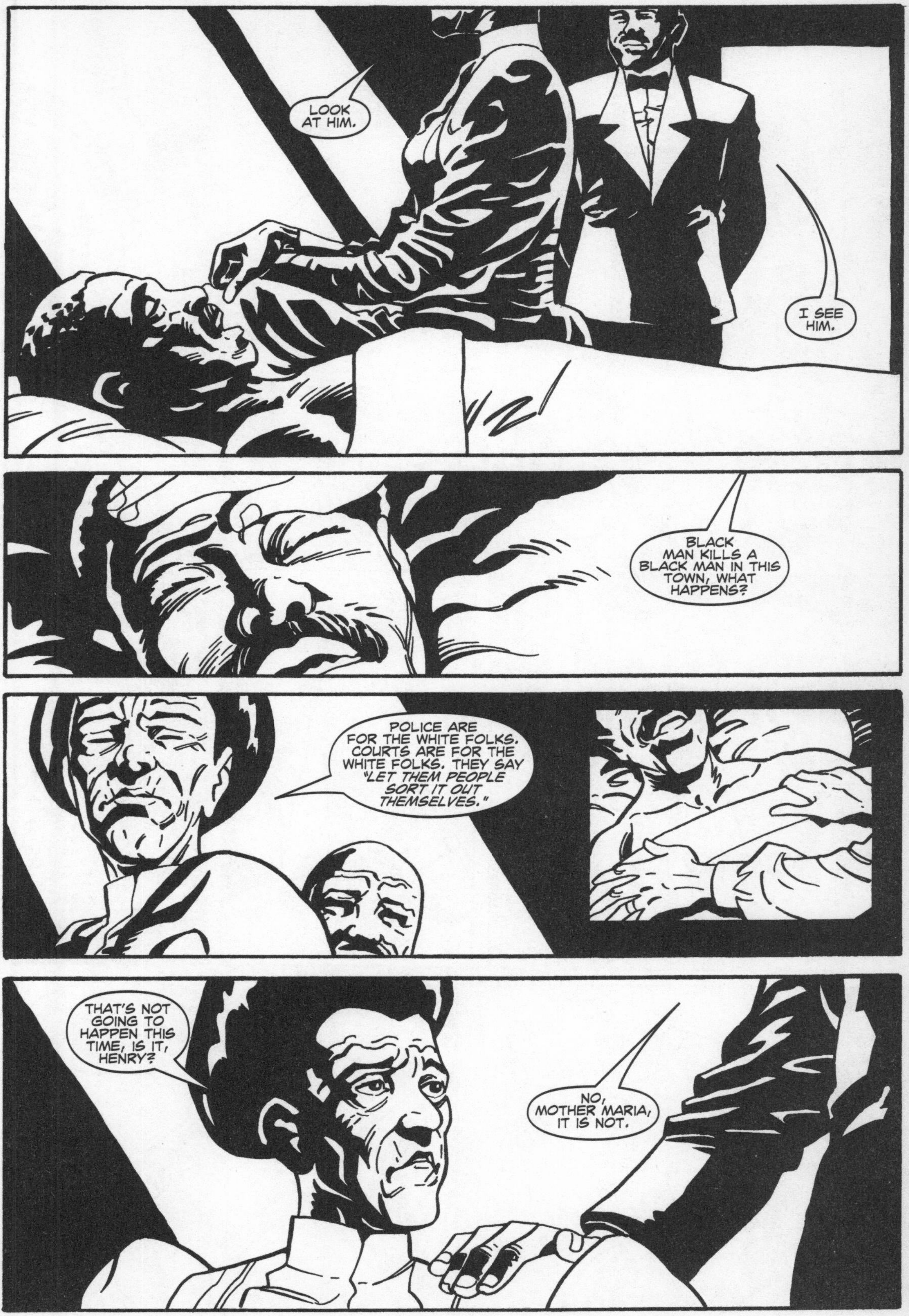
LOOK AT HIM.
I SEE HIM.
BLACK MAN KILLS A BLACK MAN IN THIS TOWN, WHAT HAPPENS?
POLICE ARE FOR THE WHITE FOLKS. COURTS ARE FOR THE WHITE FOLKS. THEY SAY *"LET THEM PEOPLE SORT IT OUT THEMSELVES."*
THAT'S NOT GOING TO HAPPEN THIS TIME, IS IT, HENRY?
NO, MOTHER MARIA, IT IS NOT.

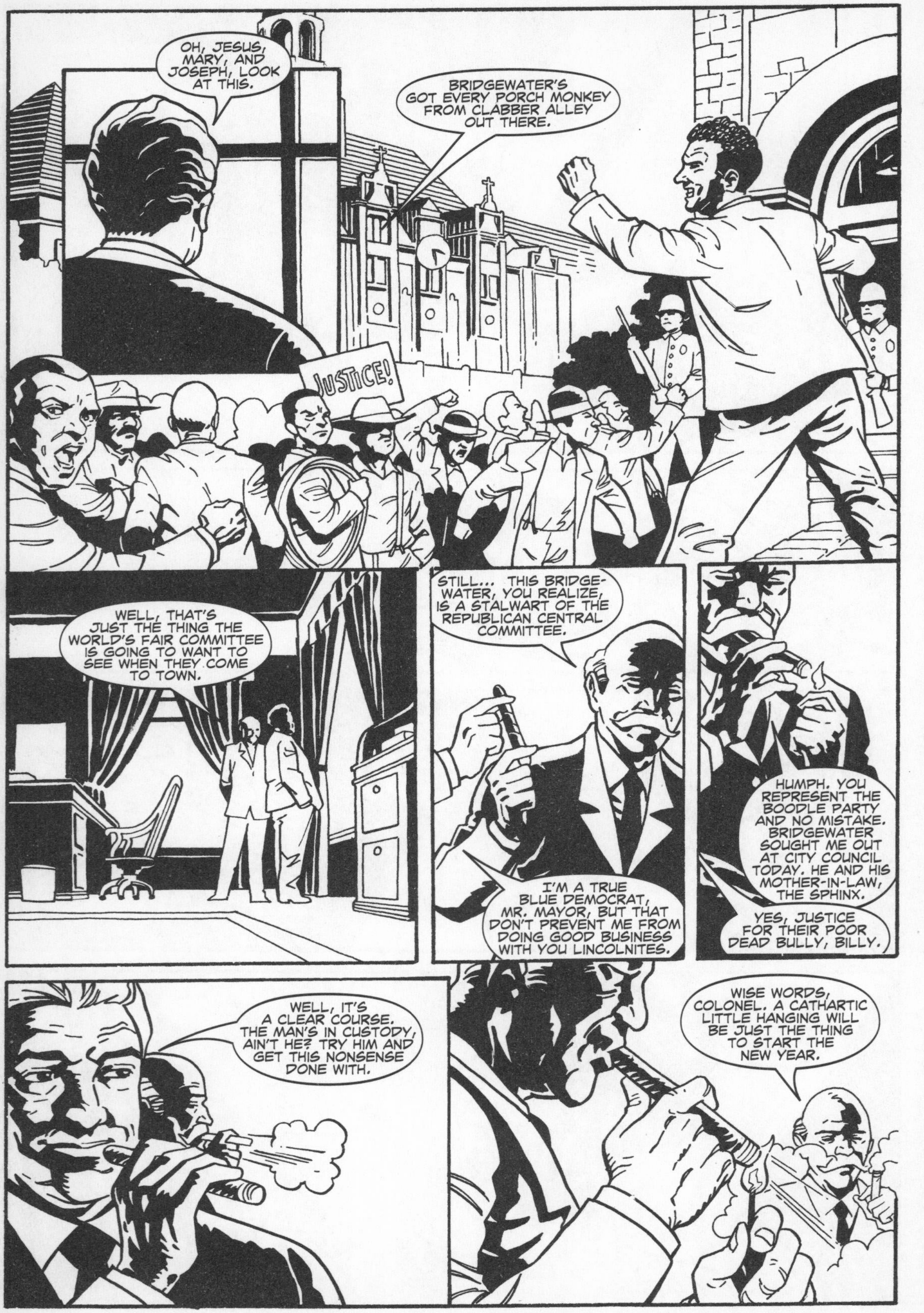
OH, JESUS, MARY, AND JOSEPH, LOOK AT THIS.
BRIDGEWATER'S GOT EVERY PORCH MONKEY FROM CLABBER ALLEY OUT THERE.
JUSTICE!
WELL, THAT'S JUST THE THING THE WORLD'S FAIR COMMITTEE IS GOING TO WANT TO SEE WHEN THEY COME TO TOWN.
STILL... THIS BRIDGE-WATER, YOU REALIZE, IS A STALWART OF THE REPUBLICAN CENTRAL COMMITTEE.
I'M A TRUE BLUE DEMOCRAT, MR. MAYOR, BUT THAT DON'T PREVENT ME FROM DOING GOOD BUSINESS WITH YOU LINCOLNITES.
HUMPH. YOU REPRESENT THE BOODLE PARTY AND NO MISTAKE. BRIDGEWATER SOUGHT ME OUT AT CITY COUNCIL TODAY. HE AND HIS MOTHER-IN-LAW, THE SPHINX.
YES, JUSTICE FOR THEIR POOR DEAD BULLY, BILLY.
WELL, IT'S A CLEAR COURSE. THE MAN'S IN CUSTODY, AIN'T HE? TRY HIM AND GET THIS NONSENSE DONE WITH.
WISE WORDS, COLONEL. A CATHARTIC LITTLE HANGING WILL BE JUST THE THING TO START THE NEW YEAR.

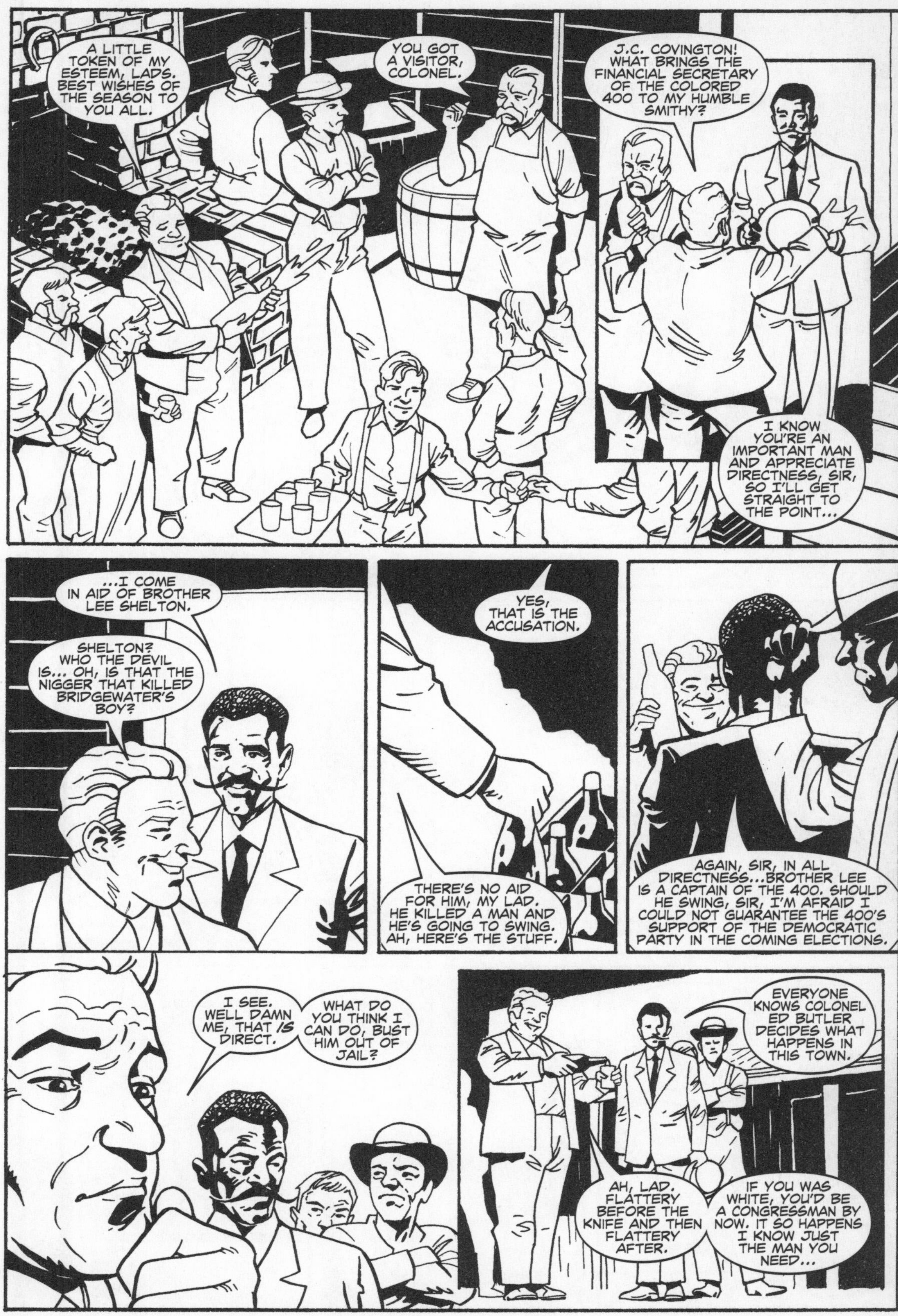
A LITTLE TOKEN OF MY ESTEEM, LADS. BEST WISHES OF THE SEASON TO YOU ALL.
YOU GOT A VISITOR, COLONEL.
J.C. COVINGTON! WHAT BRINGS THE FINANCIAL SECRETARY OF THE COLORED 400 TO MY HUMBLE SMITHY?
I KNOW YOU'RE AN IMPORTANT MAN AND APPRECIATE DIRECTNESS, SIR, SO I'LL GET STRAIGHT TO THE POINT...
...I COME IN AID OF BROTHER LEE SHELTON.
SHELTON? WHO THE DEVIL IS... OH, IS THAT THE NIGGER THAT KILLED BRIDGEWATER'S BOY?
YES, THAT IS THE ACCUSATION.
THERE'S NO AID FOR HIM, MY LAD. HE KILLED A MAN AND HE'S GOING TO SWING. AH, HERE'S THE STUFF.
AGAIN, SIR, IN ALL DIRECTNESS...BROTHER LEE IS A CAPTAIN OF THE 400. SHOULD HE SWING, SIR, I'M AFRAID I COULD NOT GUARANTEE THE 400'S SUPPORT OF THE DEMOCRATIC PARTY IN THE COMING ELECTIONS.
I SEE. WELL DAMN ME, THAT *IS* DIRECT.
WHAT DO YOU THINK I CAN DO, BUST HIM OUT OF JAIL?
EVERYONE KNOWS COLONEL ED BUTLER DECIDES WHAT HAPPENS IN THIS TOWN.
AH, LAD. FLATTERY BEFORE THE KNIFE AND THEN FLATTERY AFTER.
IF YOU WAS WHITE, YOU'D BE A CONGRESSMAN BY NOW. IT SO HAPPENS I KNOW JUST THE MAN YOU NEED...

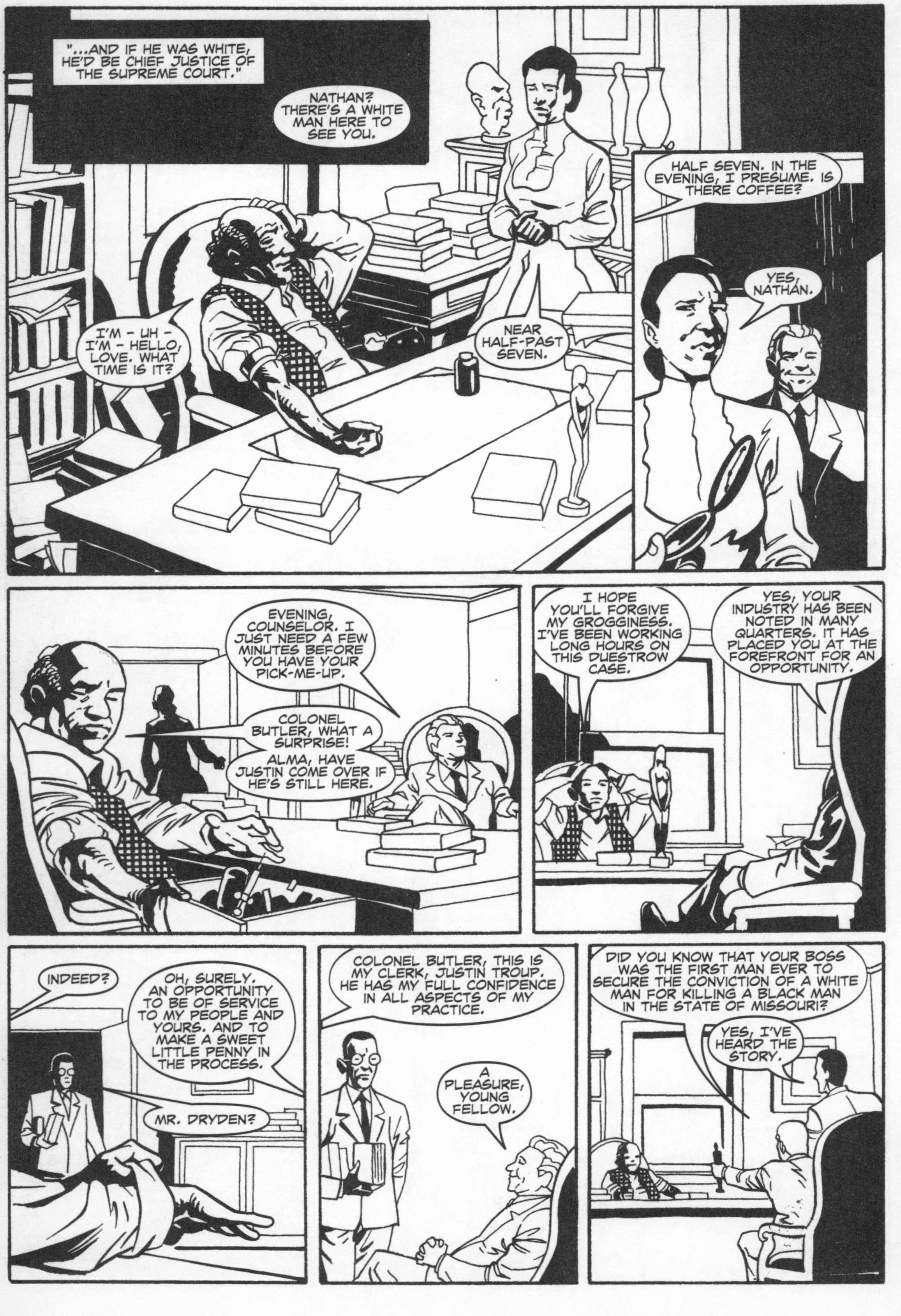
"...AND IF HE WAS WHITE, HE'D BE CHIEF JUSTICE OF THE SUPREME COURT."
NATHAN? THERE'S A WHITE MAN HERE TO SEE YOU.
I'M - UH - I'M - HELLO, LOVE. WHAT TIME IS IT?
NEAR HALF-PAST SEVEN.
HALF SEVEN. IN THE EVENING, I PRESUME. IS THERE COFFEE?
YES, NATHAN.
EVENING, COUNSELOR. I JUST NEED A FEW MINUTES BEFORE YOU HAVE YOUR PICK-ME-UP.
COLONEL BUTLER, WHAT A SURPRISE!
ALMA, HAVE JUSTIN COME OVER IF HE'S STILL HERE.
I HOPE YOU'LL FORGIVE MY GROGGINESS. I'VE BEEN WORKING LONG HOURS ON THIS DUESTROW CASE.
YES, YOUR INDUSTRY HAS BEEN NOTED IN MANY QUARTERS. IT HAS PLACED YOU AT THE FOREFRONT FOR AN OPPORTUNITY.
INDEED?
OH, SURELY. AN OPPORTUNITY TO BE OF SERVICE TO MY PEOPLE AND YOURS. AND TO MAKE A SWEET LITTLE PENNY IN THE PROCESS.
MR. DRYDEN?
COLONEL BUTLER, THIS IS MY CLERK, JUSTIN TROUP. HE HAS MY FULL CONFIDENCE IN ALL ASPECTS OF MY PRACTICE.
A PLEASURE, YOUNG FELLOW.
DID YOU KNOW THAT YOUR BOSS WAS THE FIRST MAN EVER TO SECURE THE CONVICTION OF A WHITE MAN FOR KILLING A BLACK MAN IN THE STATE OF MISSOURI?
YES, I'VE HEARD THE STORY.

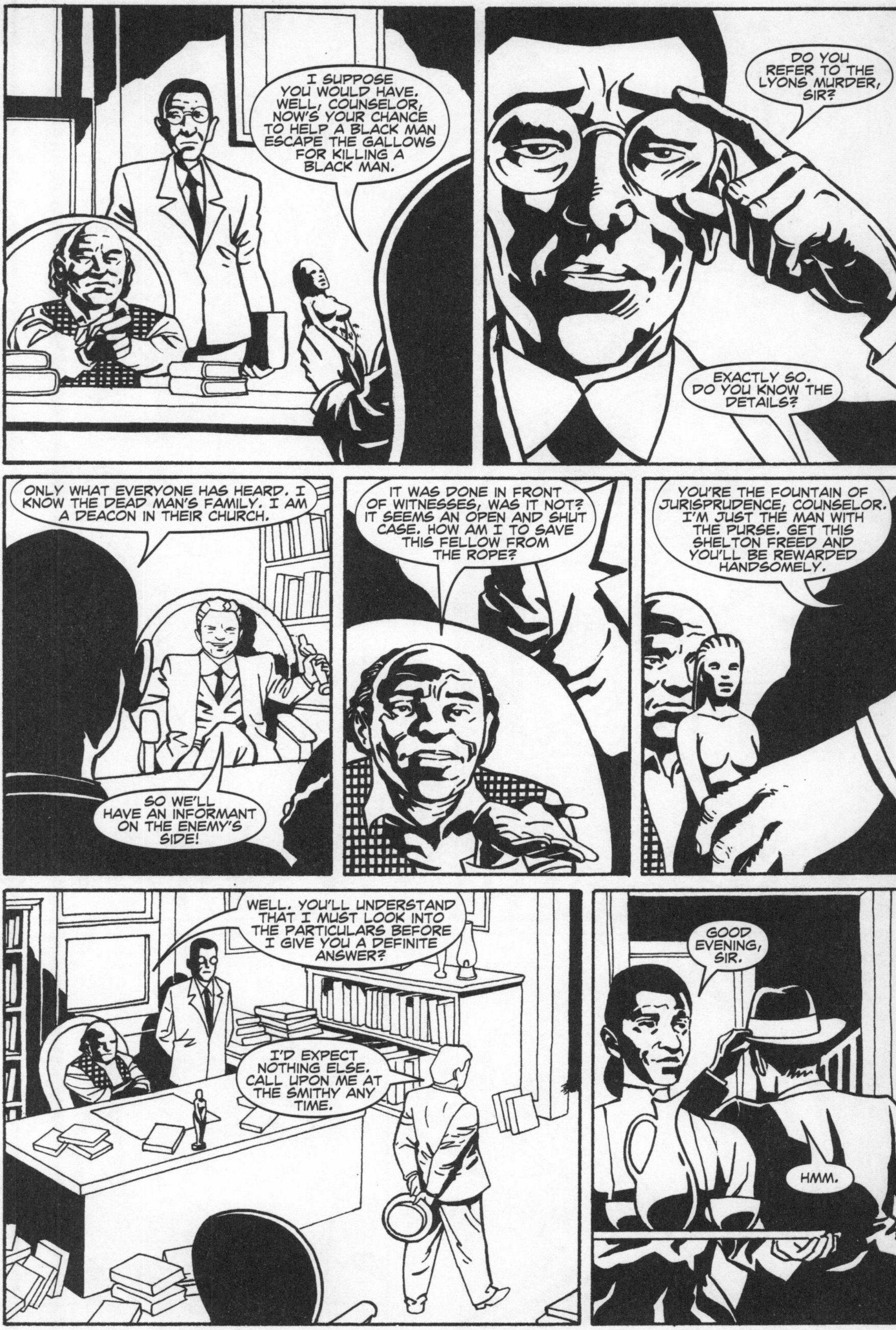
I SUPPOSE YOU WOULD HAVE. WELL, COUNSELOR, NOW'S YOUR CHANCE TO HELP A BLACK MAN ESCAPE THE GALLOWS FOR KILLING A BLACK MAN.
DO YOU REFER TO THE LYONS MURDER, SIR?
EXACTLY SO. DO YOU KNOW THE DETAILS?
ONLY WHAT EVERYONE HAS HEARD. I KNOW THE DEAD MAN'S FAMILY. I AM A DEACON IN THEIR CHURCH.
SO WE'LL HAVE AN INFORMANT ON THE ENEMY'S SIDE!
IT WAS DONE IN FRONT OF WITNESSES, WAS IT NOT? IT SEEMS AN OPEN AND SHUT CASE. HOW AM I TO SAVE THIS FELLOW FROM THE ROPE?
YOU'RE THE FOUNTAIN OF JURISPRUDENCE, COUNSELOR. I'M JUST THE MAN WITH THE PURSE. GET THIS SHELTON FREED AND YOU'LL BE REWARDED HANDSOMELY.
WELL. YOU'LL UNDERSTAND THAT I MUST LOOK INTO THE PARTICULARS BEFORE I GIVE YOU A DEFINITE ANSWER?
I'D EXPECT NOTHING ELSE. CALL UPON ME AT THE SMITHY ANY TIME.
GOOD EVENING, SIR.
HMM.

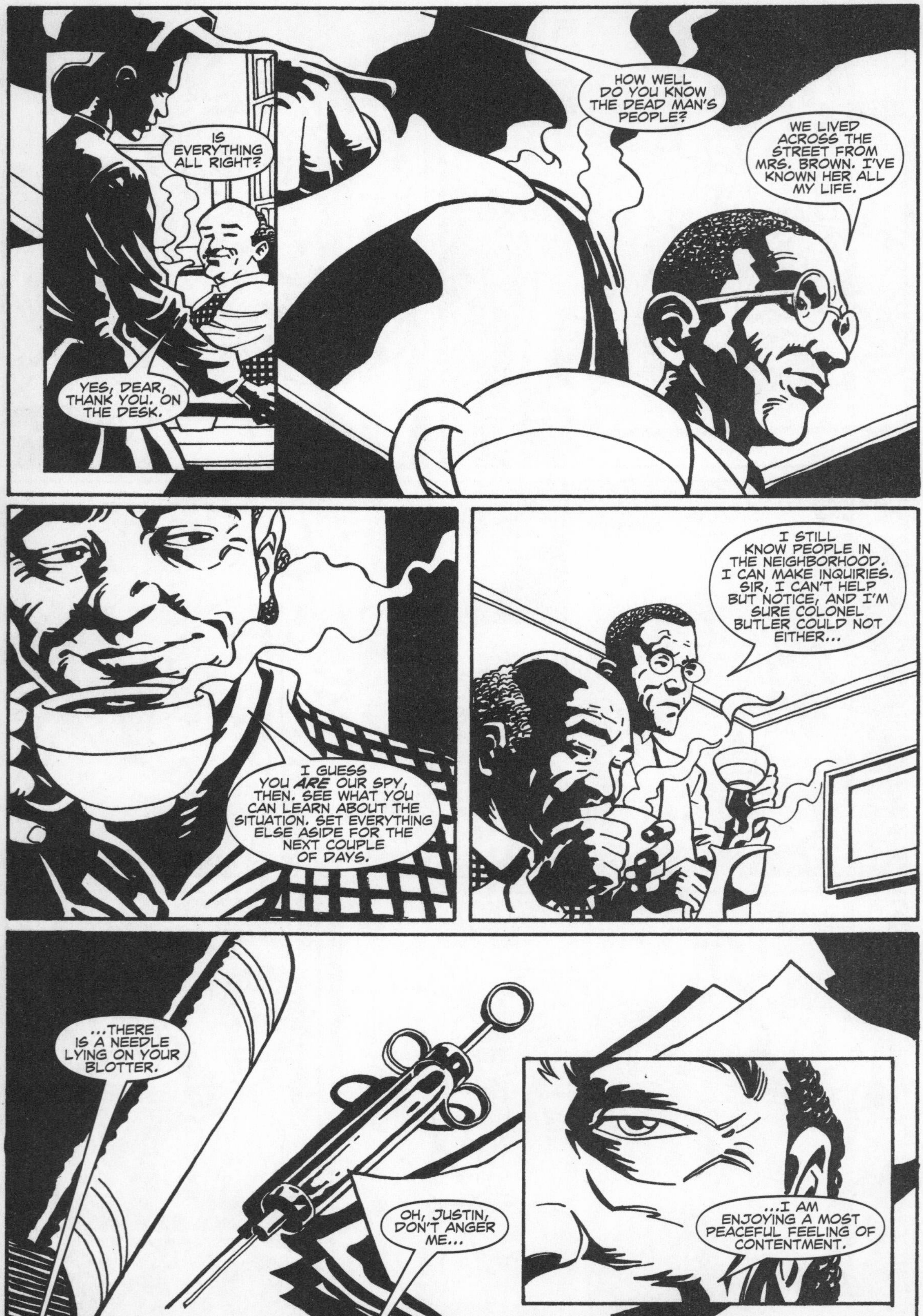
HOW WELL DO YOU KNOW THE DEAD MAN'S PEOPLE?
IS EVERYTHING ALL RIGHT?
YES, DEAR, THANK YOU. ON THE DESK.
WE LIVED ACROSS THE STREET FROM MRS. BROWN. I'VE KNOWN HER ALL MY LIFE.
I GUESS YOU ARE OUR SPY, THEN. SEE WHAT YOU CAN LEARN ABOUT THE SITUATION. SET EVERYTHING ELSE ASIDE FOR THE NEXT COUPLE OF DAYS.
I STILL KNOW PEOPLE IN THE NEIGHBORHOOD. I CAN MAKE INQUIRIES. SIR, I CAN'T HELP BUT NOTICE, AND I'M SURE COLONEL BUTLER COULD NOT EITHER...
...THERE IS A NEEDLE LYING ON YOUR BLOTTER.
OH, JUSTIN, DON'T ANGER ME...
...I AM ENJOYING A MOST PEACEFUL FEELING OF CONTENTMENT.

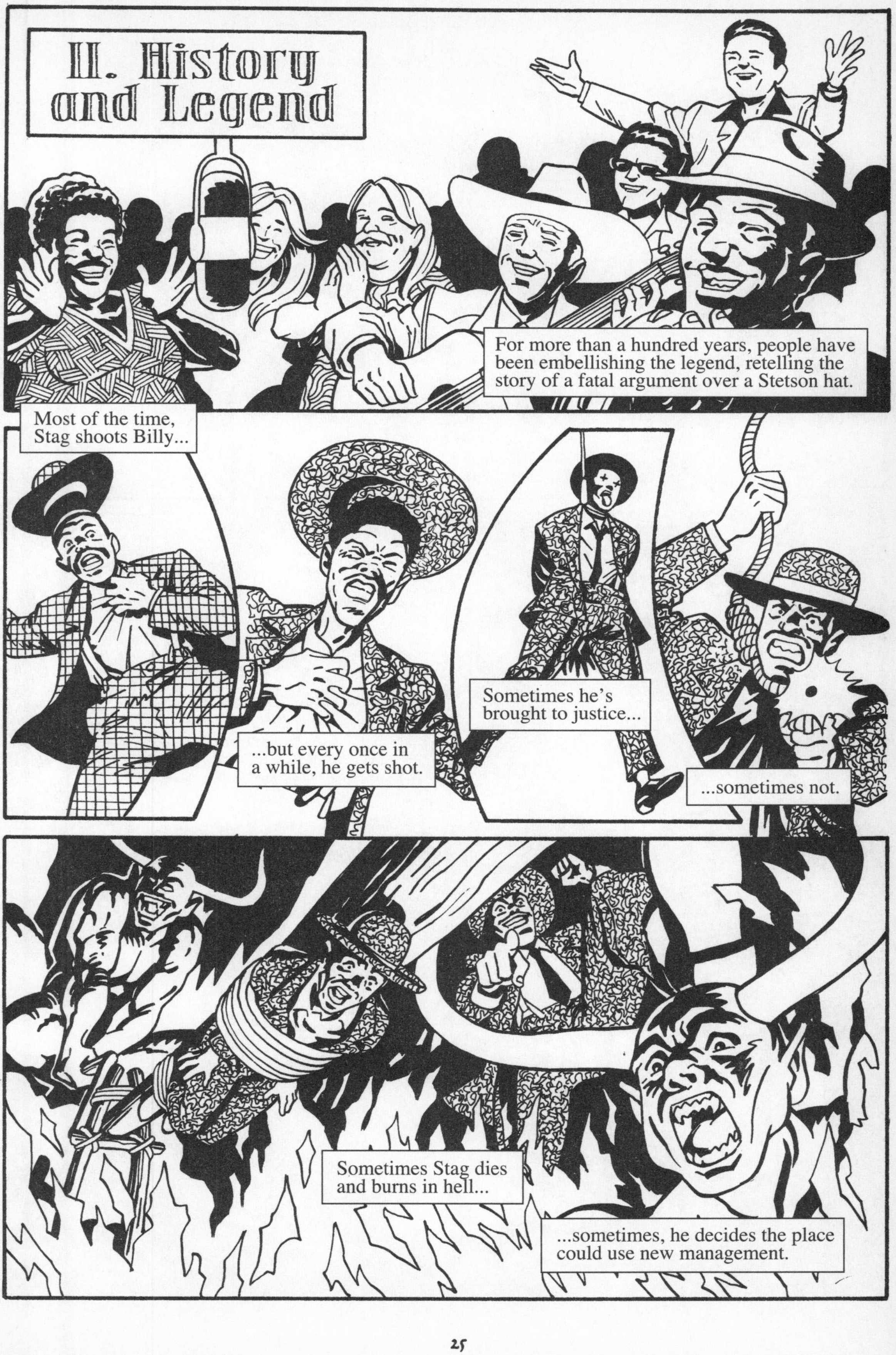
II. History and Legend
For more than a hundred years, people have been embellishing the legend, retelling the story of a fatal argument over a Stetson hat.
Most of the time, Stag shoots Billy...
...but every once in a while, he gets shot.
Sometimes he's brought to justice...
...sometimes not.
Sometimes Stag dies and burns in hell...
...sometimes, he decides the place could use new management.

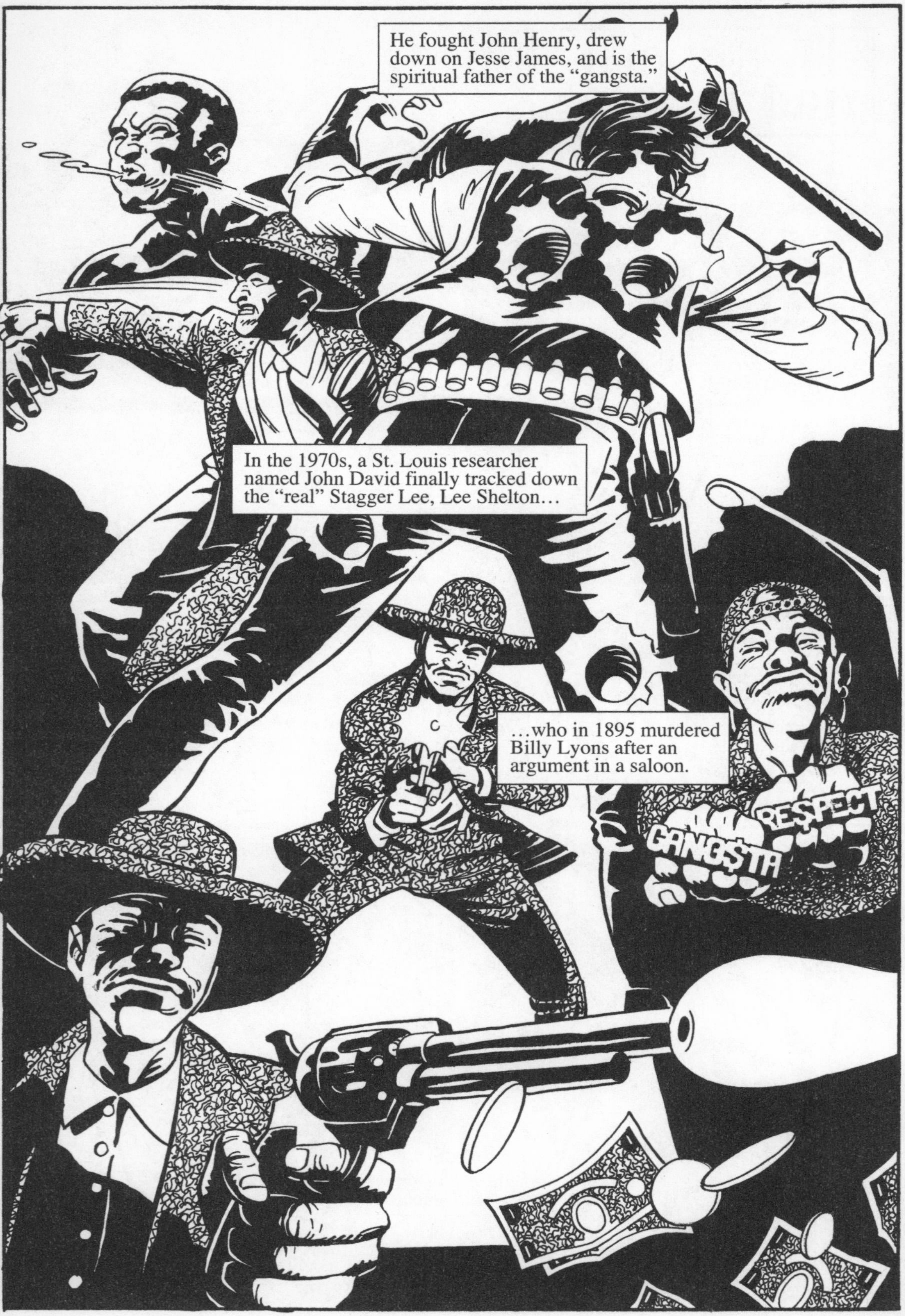
He fought John Henry, drew down on Jesse James, and is the spiritual father of the "gangsta."
In the 1970s, a St. Louis researcher named John David finally tracked down the "real" Stagger Lee, Lee Shelton…
…who in 1895 murdered Billy Lyons after an argument in a saloon.
RE$PECT
GANG$TA

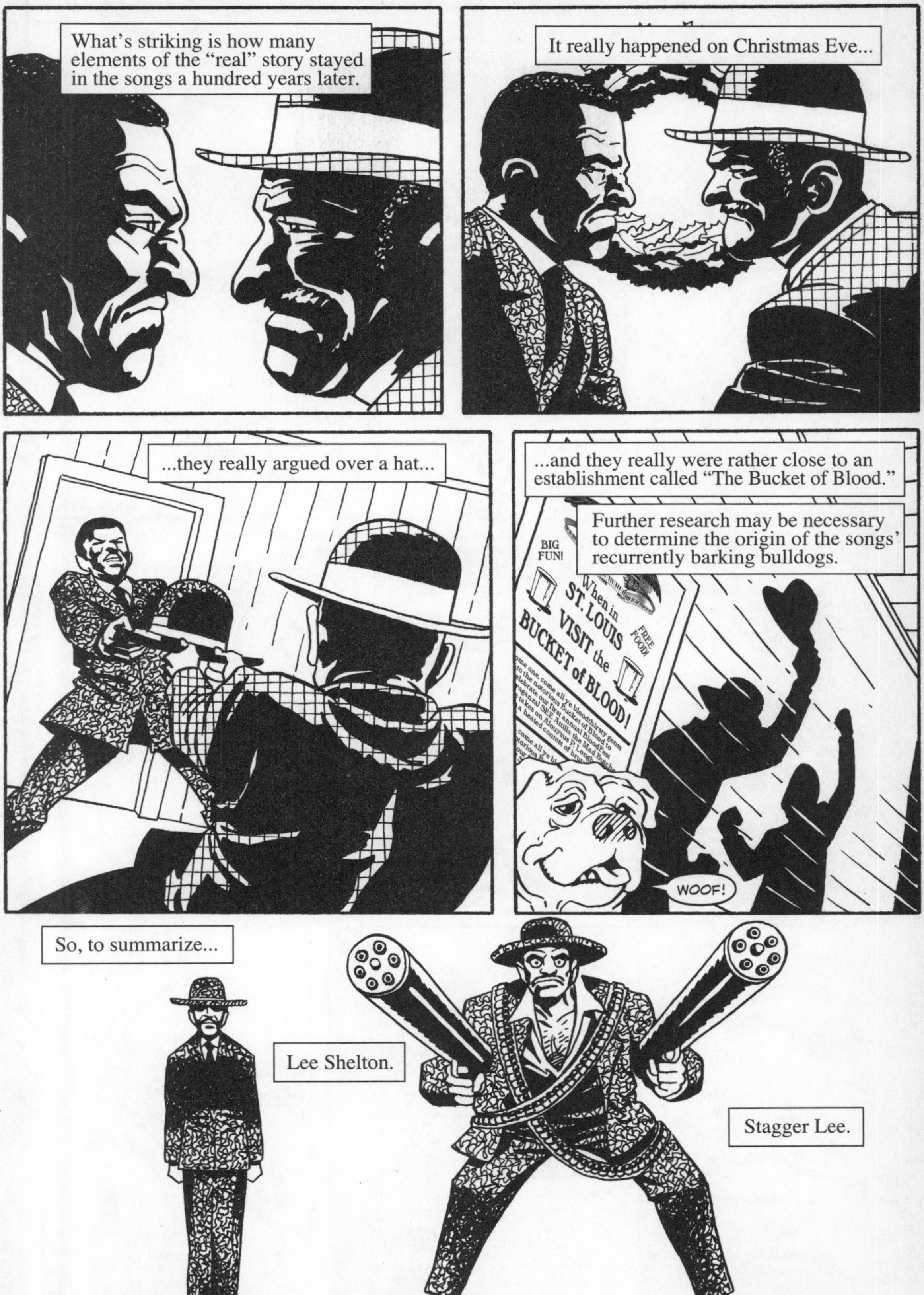
What's striking is how many elements of the "real" story stayed in the songs a hundred years later.
It really happened on Christmas Eve...
...they really argued over a hat...
...and they really were rather close to an establishment called "The Bucket of Blood."
Further research may be necessary to determine the origin of the songs' recurrently barking bulldogs.
BIG FUN!
When in ST. LOUIS VISIT the BUCKET of BLOOD!
FREE FOOD!
WOOF!
So, to summarize...
Lee Shelton.
Stagger Lee.

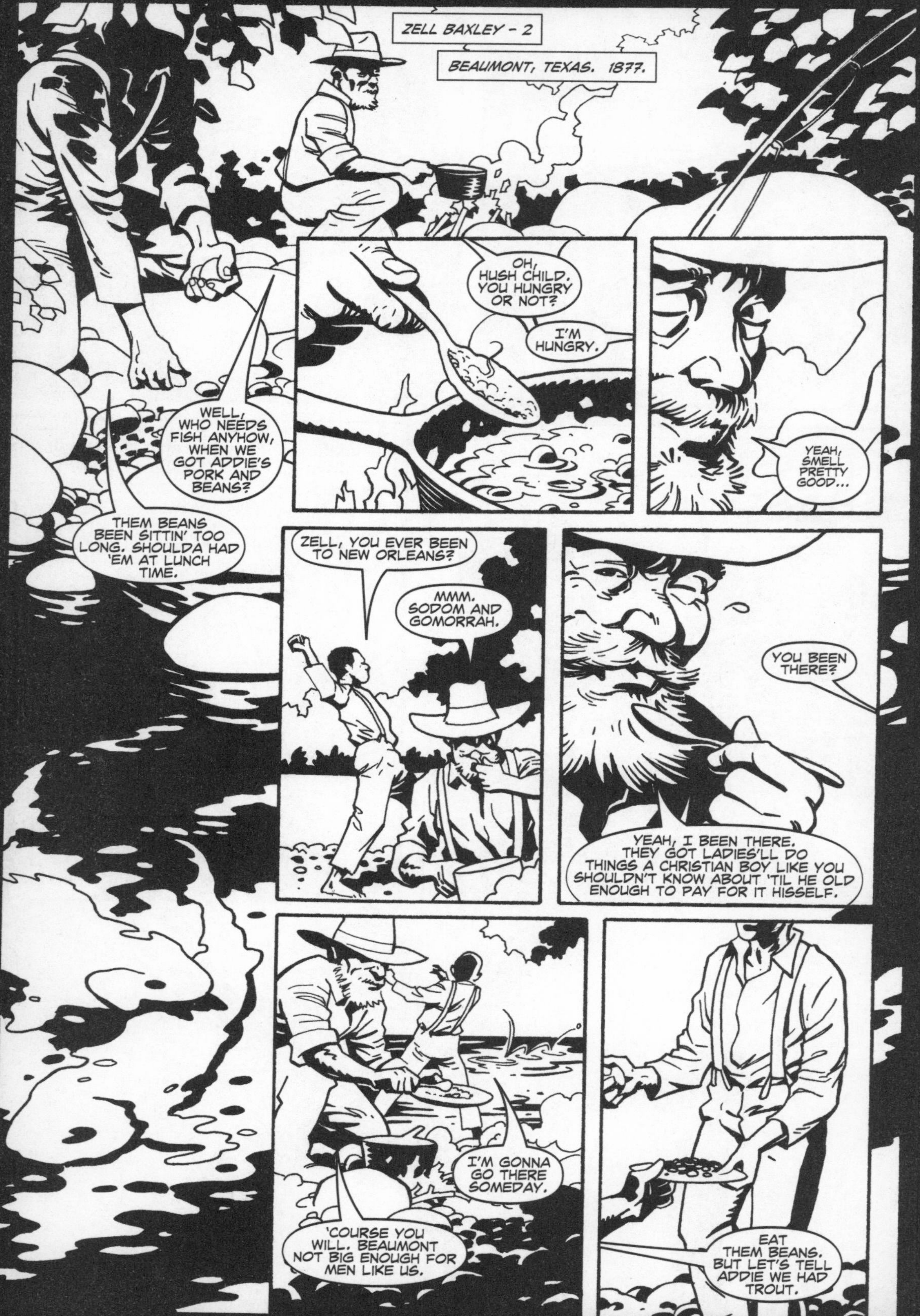
ZELL BAXLEY - 2
BEAUMONT, TEXAS. 1877.
WELL, WHO NEEDS FISH ANYHOW, WHEN WE GOT ADDIE'S PORK AND BEANS?
THEM BEANS BEEN SITTIN' TOO LONG. SHOULDA HAD 'EM AT LUNCH TIME.
OH, HUSH CHILD. YOU HUNGRY OR NOT?
I'M HUNGRY.
YEAH, SMELL PRETTY GOOD...
ZELL, YOU EVER BEEN TO NEW ORLEANS?
MMM. SODOM AND GOMORRAH.
YOU BEEN THERE?
YEAH, I BEEN THERE. THEY GOT LADIES'LL DO THINGS A CHRISTIAN BOY LIKE YOU SHOULDN'T KNOW ABOUT 'TIL HE OLD ENOUGH TO PAY FOR IT HISSELF.
I'M GONNA GO THERE SOMEDAY.
'COURSE YOU WILL. BEAUMONT NOT BIG ENOUGH FOR MEN LIKE US.
EAT THEM BEANS. BUT LET'S TELL ADDIE WE HAD TROUT.

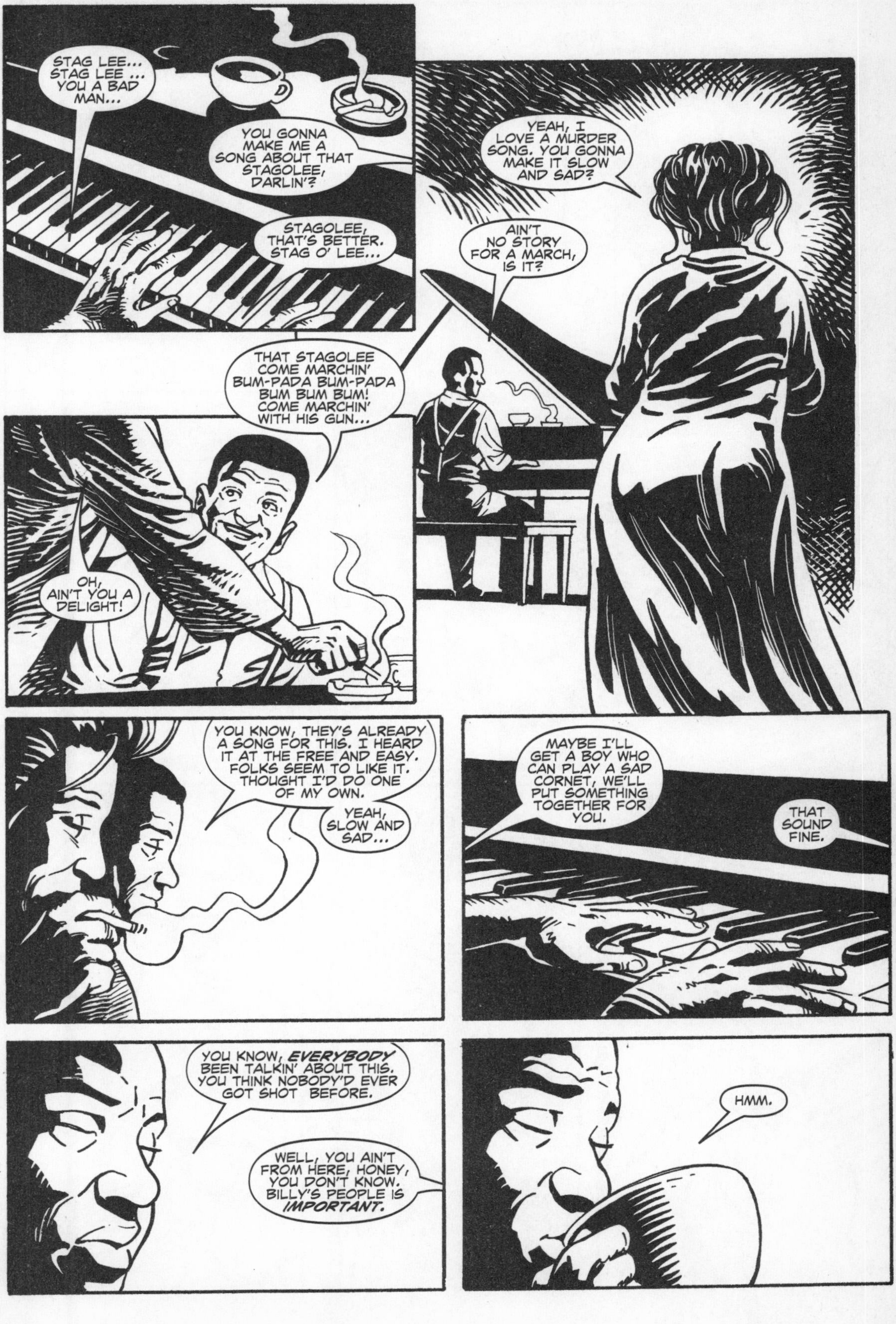
STAG LEE... STAG LEE... YOU A BAD MAN...
YOU GONNA MAKE ME A SONG ABOUT THAT STAGOLEE, DARLIN'?
STAGOLEE, THAT'S BETTER. STAG O' LEE...
YEAH, I LOVE A MURDER SONG. YOU GONNA MAKE IT SLOW AND SAD?
AIN'T NO STORY FOR A MARCH, IS IT?
THAT STAGOLEE COME MARCHIN' BUM-PADA BUM-PADA BUM BUM BUM! COME MARCHIN' WITH HIS GUN...
OH, AIN'T YOU A DELIGHT!
YOU KNOW, THEY'S ALREADY A SONG FOR THIS. I HEARD IT AT THE FREE AND EASY. FOLKS SEEM TO LIKE IT. THOUGHT I'D DO ONE OF MY OWN.
YEAH, SLOW AND SAD...
MAYBE I'LL GET A BOY WHO CAN PLAY A SAD CORNET, WE'LL PUT SOMETHING TOGETHER FOR YOU.
THAT SOUND FINE.
YOU KNOW, EVERYBODY BEEN TALKIN' ABOUT THIS. YOU THINK NOBODY'D EVER GOT SHOT BEFORE.
WELL, YOU AIN'T FROM HERE, HONEY, YOU DON'T KNOW. BILLY'S PEOPLE IS IMPORTANT.
HMM.

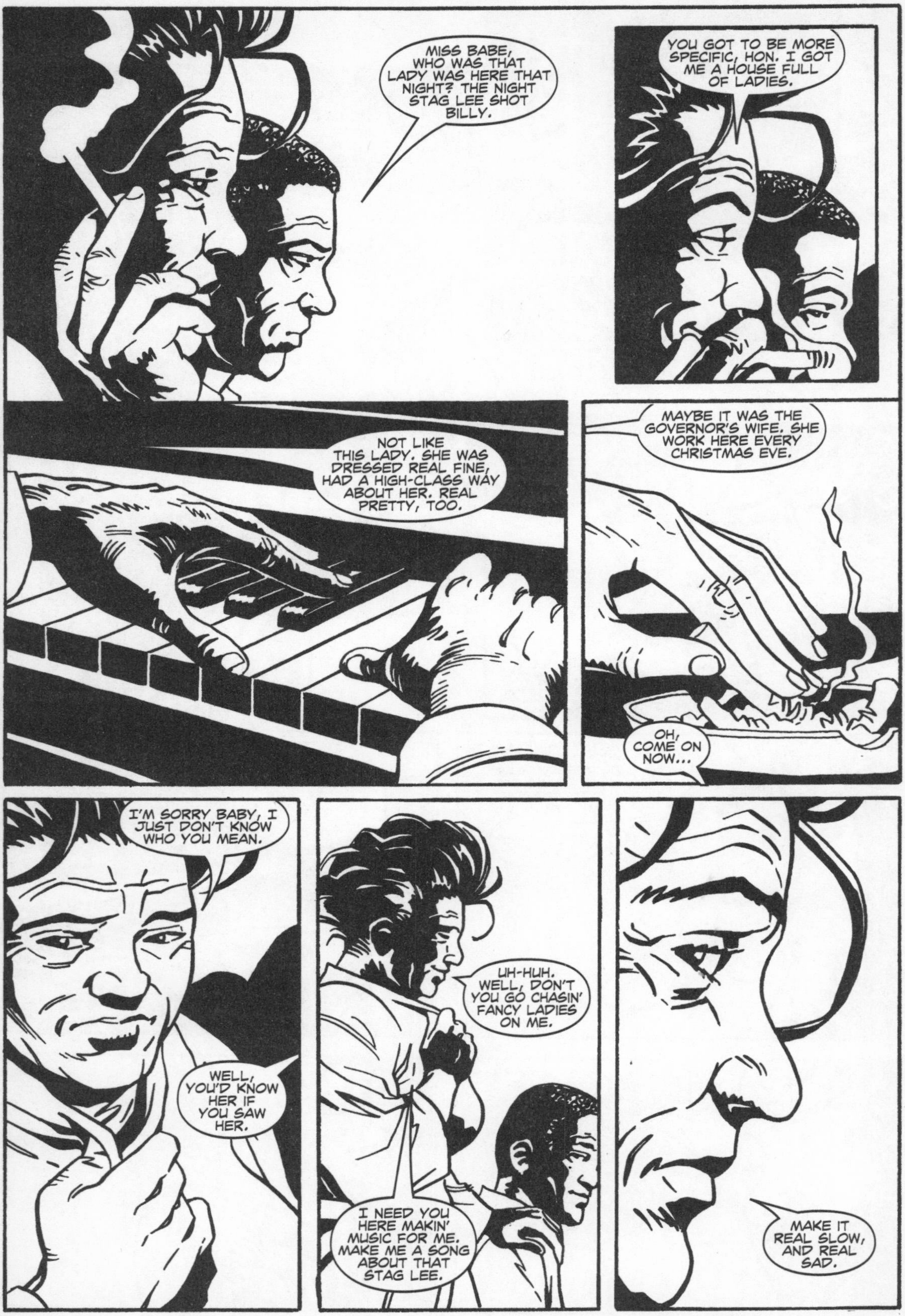
MISS BABE, WHO WAS THAT LADY WAS HERE THAT NIGHT? THE NIGHT STAG LEE SHOT BILLY.
YOU GOT TO BE MORE SPECIFIC, HON. I GOT ME A HOUSE FULL OF LADIES.
NOT LIKE THIS LADY. SHE WAS DRESSED REAL FINE, HAD A HIGH-CLASS WAY ABOUT HER. REAL PRETTY, TOO.
MAYBE IT WAS THE GOVERNOR'S WIFE. SHE WORK HERE EVERY CHRISTMAS EVE.
OH, COME ON NOW...
I'M SORRY BABY, I JUST DON'T KNOW WHO YOU MEAN.
WELL, YOU'D KNOW HER IF YOU SAW HER.
UH-HUH. WELL, DON'T YOU GO CHASIN' FANCY LADIES ON ME.
I NEED YOU HERE MAKIN' MUSIC FOR ME. MAKE ME A SONG ABOUT THAT STAG LEE.
MAKE IT REAL SLOW, AND REAL SAD.

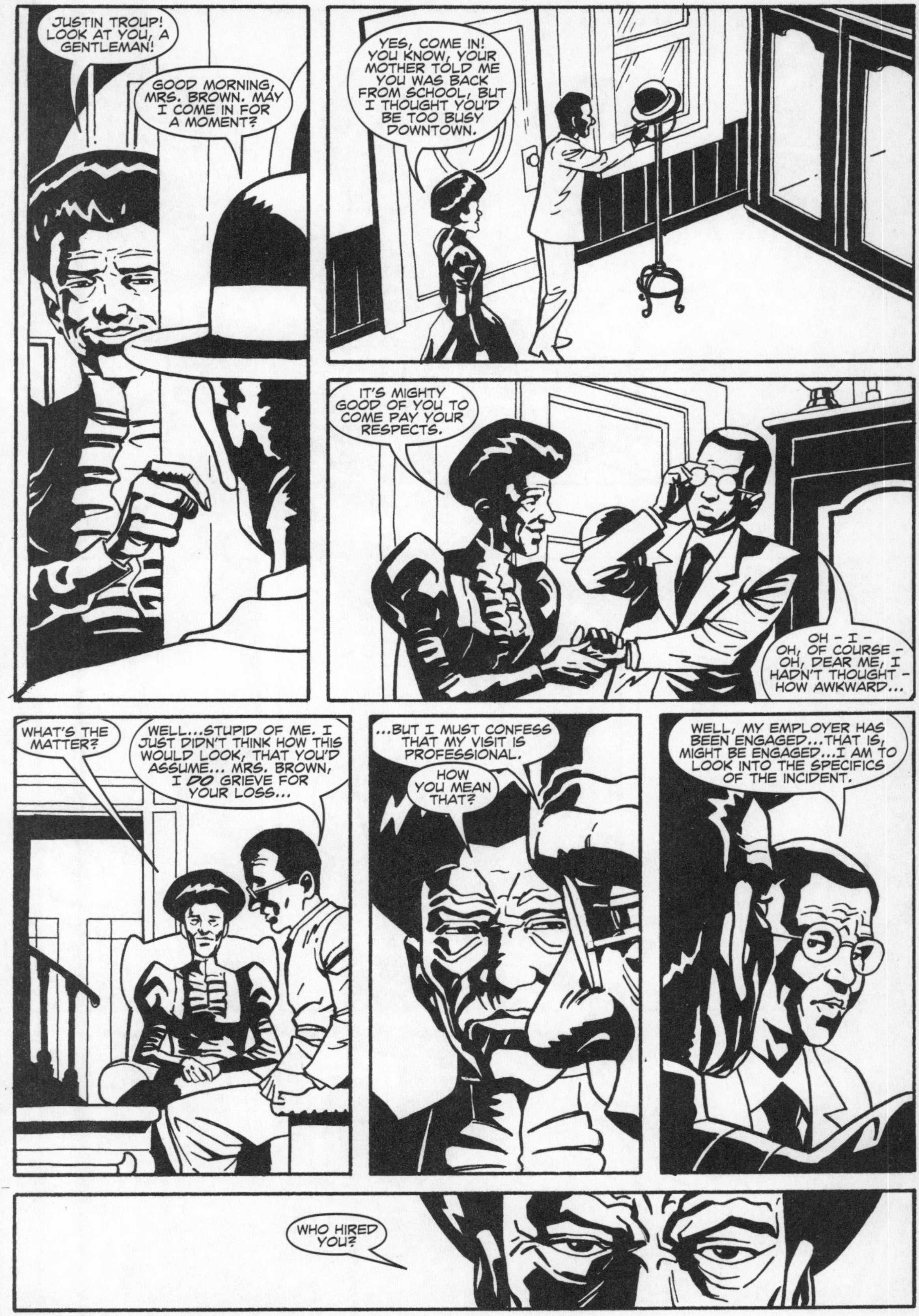
JUSTIN TROUP! LOOK AT YOU, A GENTLEMAN!
GOOD MORNING, MRS. BROWN. MAY I COME IN FOR A MOMENT?
YES, COME IN! YOU KNOW, YOUR MOTHER TOLD ME YOU WAS BACK FROM SCHOOL, BUT I THOUGHT YOU'D BE TOO BUSY DOWNTOWN.
IT'S MIGHTY GOOD OF YOU TO COME PAY YOUR RESPECTS.
OH - I - OH, OF COURSE - OH, DEAR ME, I HADN'T THOUGHT - HOW AWKWARD...
WHAT'S THE MATTER?
WELL...STUPID OF ME. I JUST DIDN'T THINK HOW THIS WOULD LOOK, THAT YOU'D ASSUME... MRS. BROWN, I *DO* GRIEVE FOR YOUR LOSS...
...BUT I MUST CONFESS THAT MY VISIT IS PROFESSIONAL.
HOW YOU MEAN THAT?
WELL, MY EMPLOYER HAS BEEN ENGAGED...THAT IS, MIGHT BE ENGAGED...I AM TO LOOK INTO THE SPECIFICS OF THE INCIDENT.
WHO HIRED YOU?

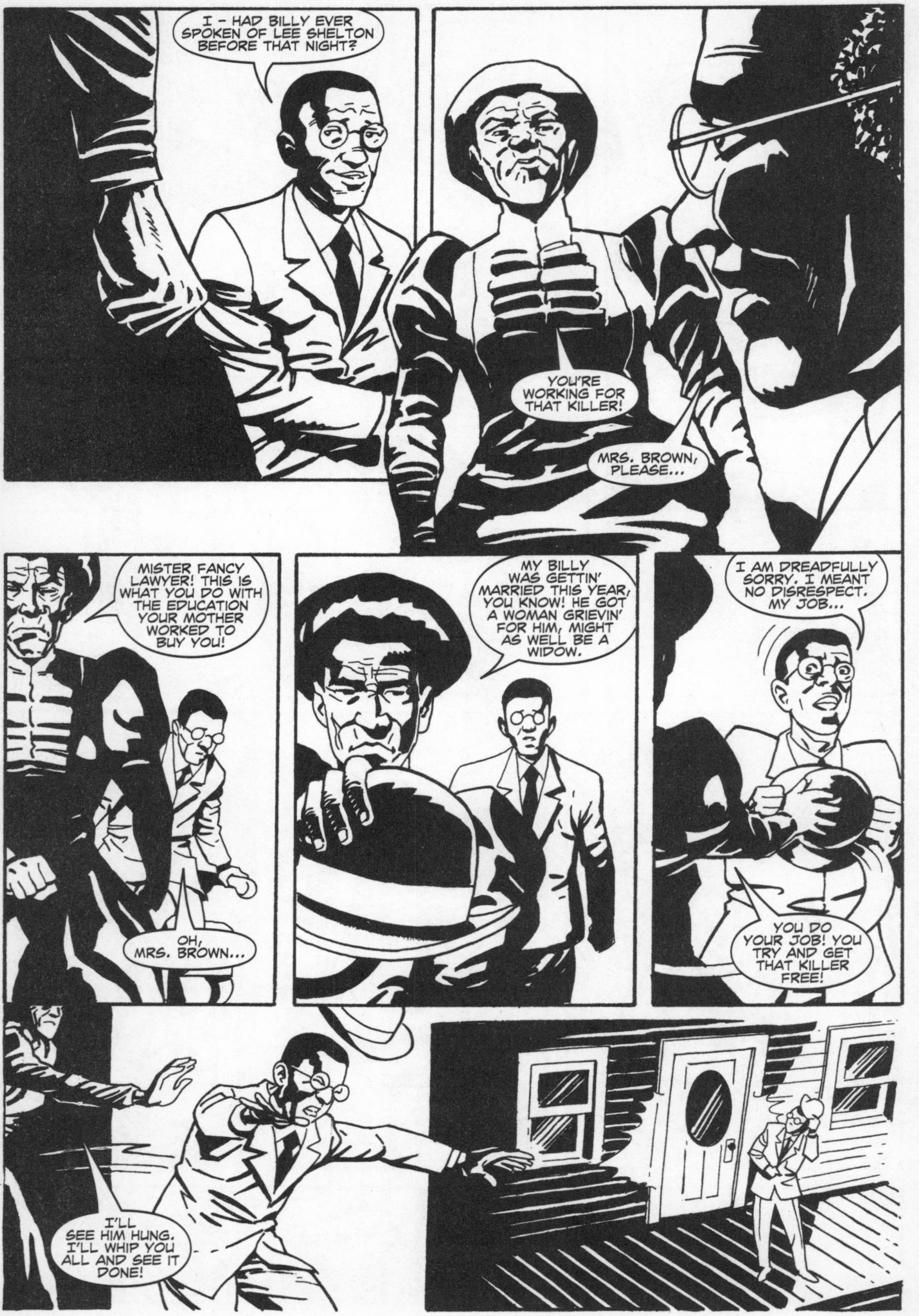
I - HAD BILLY EVER SPOKEN OF LEE SHELTON BEFORE THAT NIGHT?
YOU'RE WORKING FOR THAT KILLER!
MRS. BROWN, PLEASE...
MISTER FANCY LAWYER! THIS IS WHAT YOU DO WITH THE EDUCATION YOUR MOTHER WORKED TO BUY YOU!
OH, MRS. BROWN...
MY BILLY WAS GETTIN' MARRIED THIS YEAR, YOU KNOW! HE GOT A WOMAN GRIEVIN' FOR HIM, MIGHT AS WELL BE A WIDOW.
I AM DREADFULLY SORRY. I MEANT NO DISRESPECT. MY JOB...
YOU DO YOUR JOB! YOU TRY AND GET THAT KILLER FREE!
I'LL SEE HIM HUNG. I'LL WHIP YOU ALL AND SEE IT DONE!

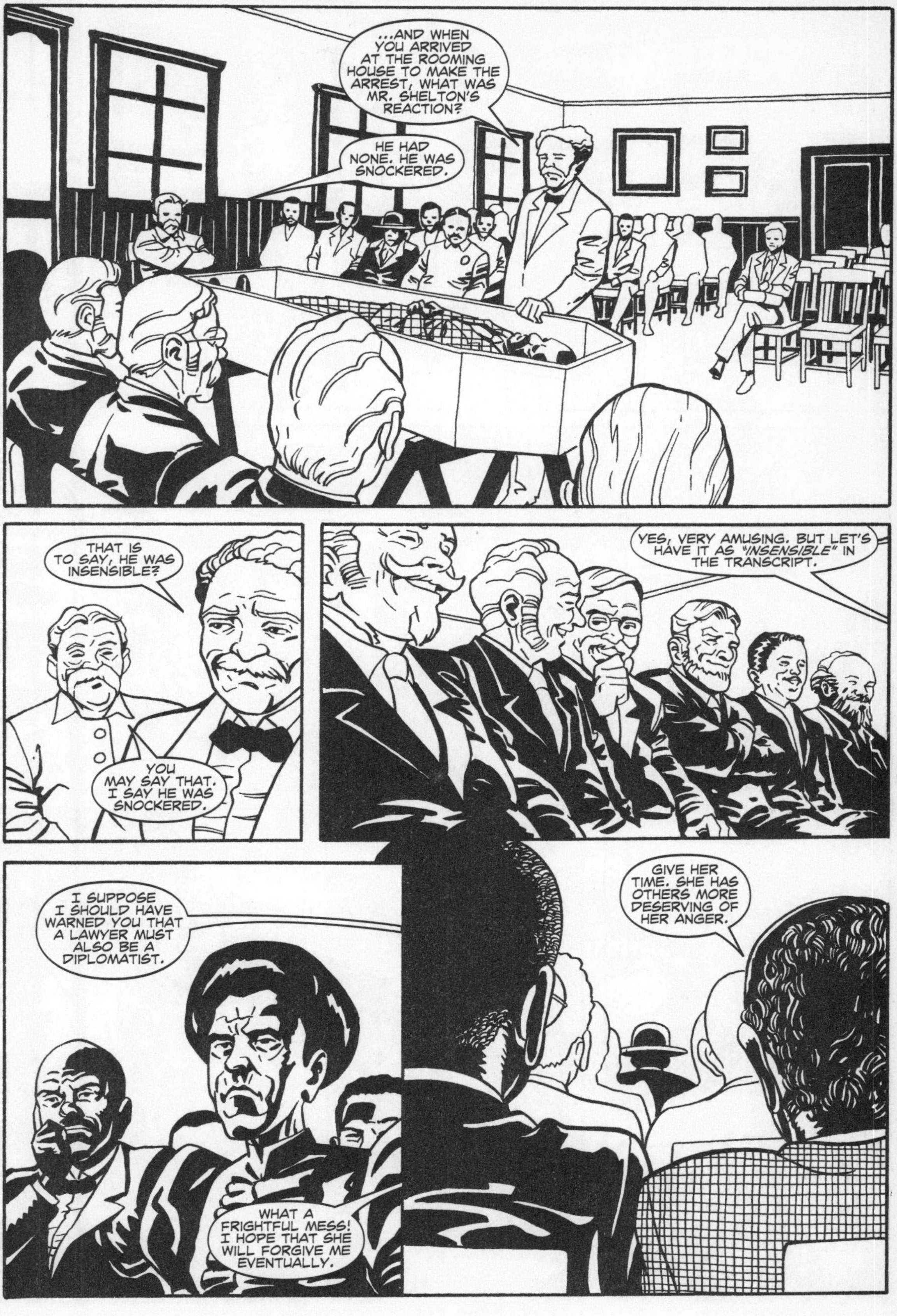
...AND WHEN YOU ARRIVED AT THE ROOMING HOUSE TO MAKE THE ARREST, WHAT WAS MR. SHELTON'S REACTION?
HE HAD NONE. HE WAS SNOCKERED.
THAT IS TO SAY, HE WAS INSENSIBLE?
YOU MAY SAY THAT. I SAY HE WAS SNOCKERED.
YES, VERY AMUSING. BUT LET'S HAVE IT AS "INSENSIBLE" IN THE TRANSCRIPT.
I SUPPOSE I SHOULD HAVE WARNED YOU THAT A LAWYER MUST ALSO BE A DIPLOMATIST.
WHAT A FRIGHTFUL MESS! I HOPE THAT SHE WILL FORGIVE ME EVENTUALLY.
GIVE HER TIME. SHE HAS OTHERS MORE DESERVING OF HER ANGER.

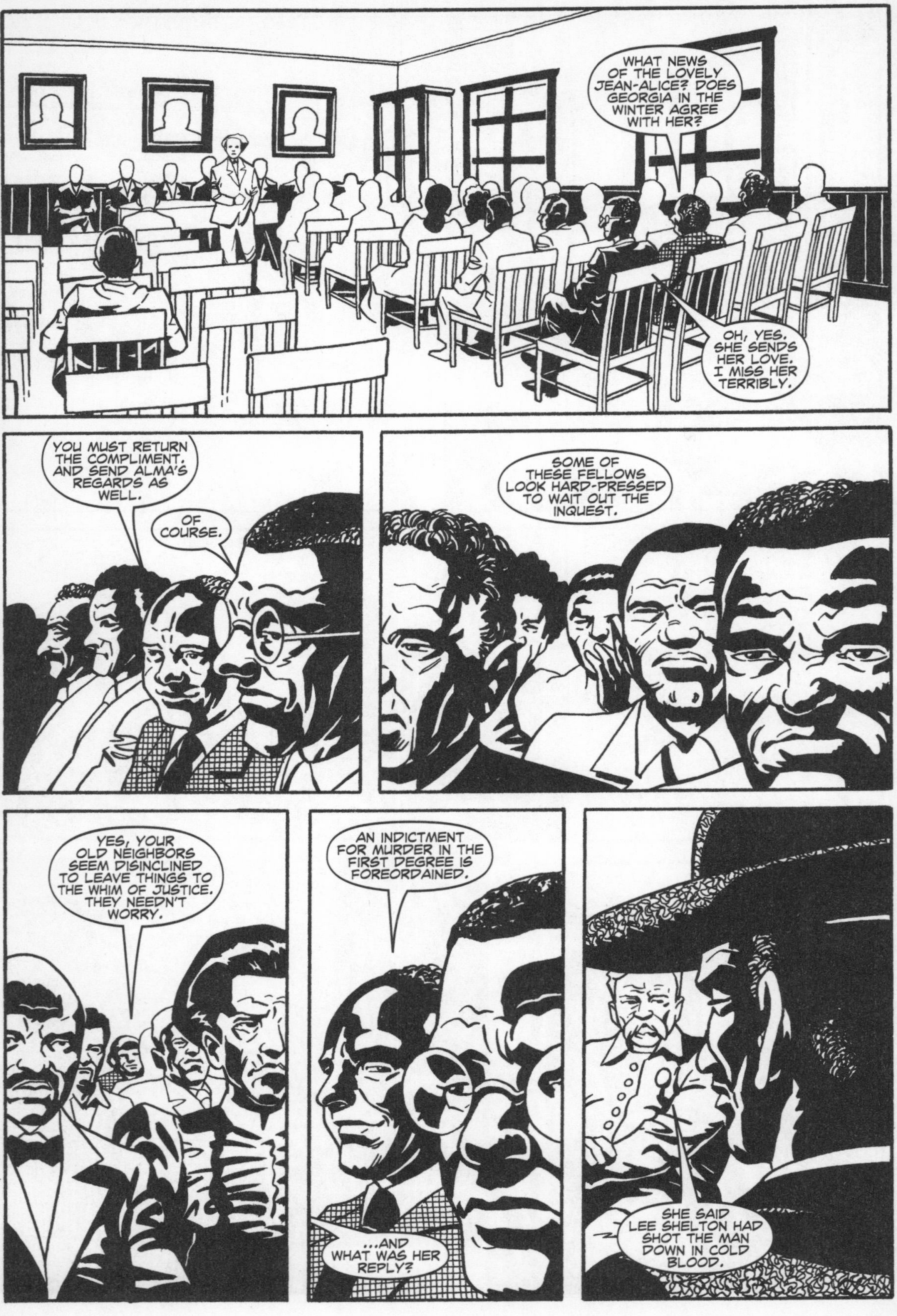
WHAT NEWS OF THE LOVELY JEAN-ALICE? DOES GEORGIA IN THE WINTER AGREE WITH HER?
OH, YES. SHE SENDS HER LOVE. I MISS HER TERRIBLY.
YOU MUST RETURN THE COMPLIMENT. AND SEND ALMA'S REGARDS AS WELL.
OF COURSE.
SOME OF THESE FELLOWS LOOK HARD-PRESSED TO WAIT OUT THE INQUEST.
YES, YOUR OLD NEIGHBORS SEEM DISINCLINED TO LEAVE THINGS TO THE WHIM OF JUSTICE. THEY NEEDN'T WORRY.
AN INDICTMENT FOR MURDER IN THE FIRST DEGREE IS FOREORDAINED.
...AND WHAT WAS HER REPLY?
SHE SAID LEE SHELTON HAD SHOT THE MAN DOWN IN COLD BLOOD.

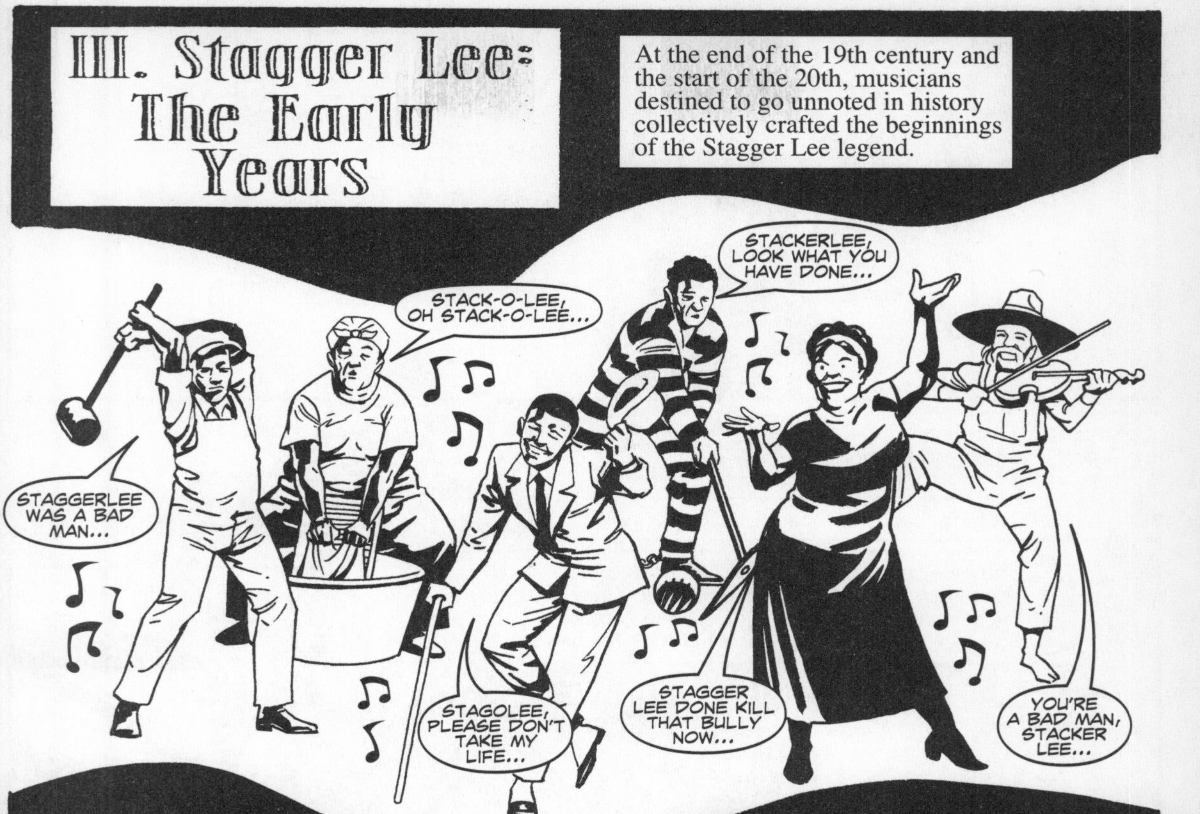
III. Stagger Lee: The Early Years
At the end of the 19th century and the start of the 20th, musicians destined to go unnoted in history collectively crafted the beginnings of the Stagger Lee legend.
STAGGERLEE WAS A BAD MAN...
STACK-O-LEE, OH STACK-O-LEE...
STAGOLEE, PLEASE DON'T TAKE MY LIFE...
STACKERLEE, LOOK WHAT YOU HAVE DONE...
STAGGER LEE DONE KILL THAT BULLY NOW...
YOU'RE A BAD MAN, STACKER LEE...

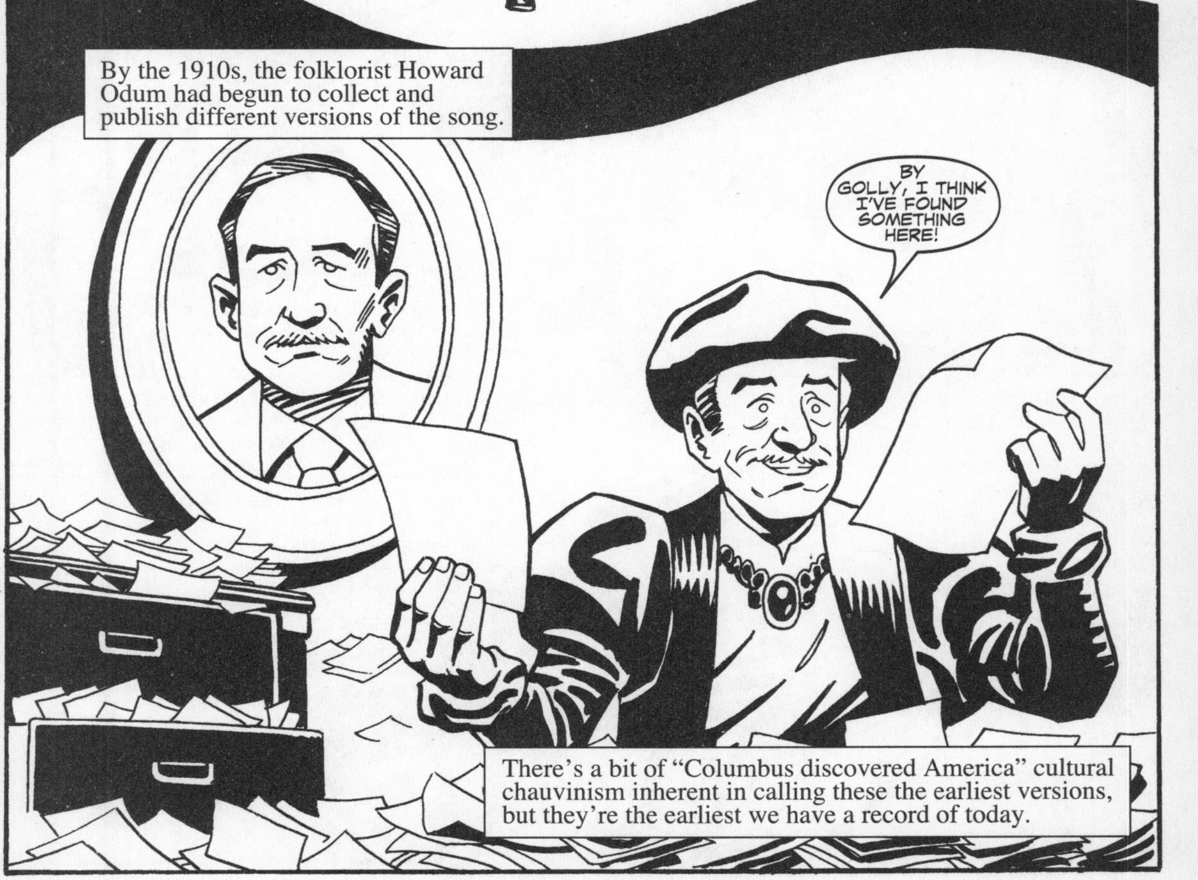
By the 1910s, the folklorist Howard Odum had begun to collect and publish different versions of the song.
BY GOLLY, I THINK I'VE FOUND SOMETHING HERE!
There's a bit of "Columbus discovered America" cultural chauvinism inherent in calling these the earliest versions, but they're the earliest we have a record of today.

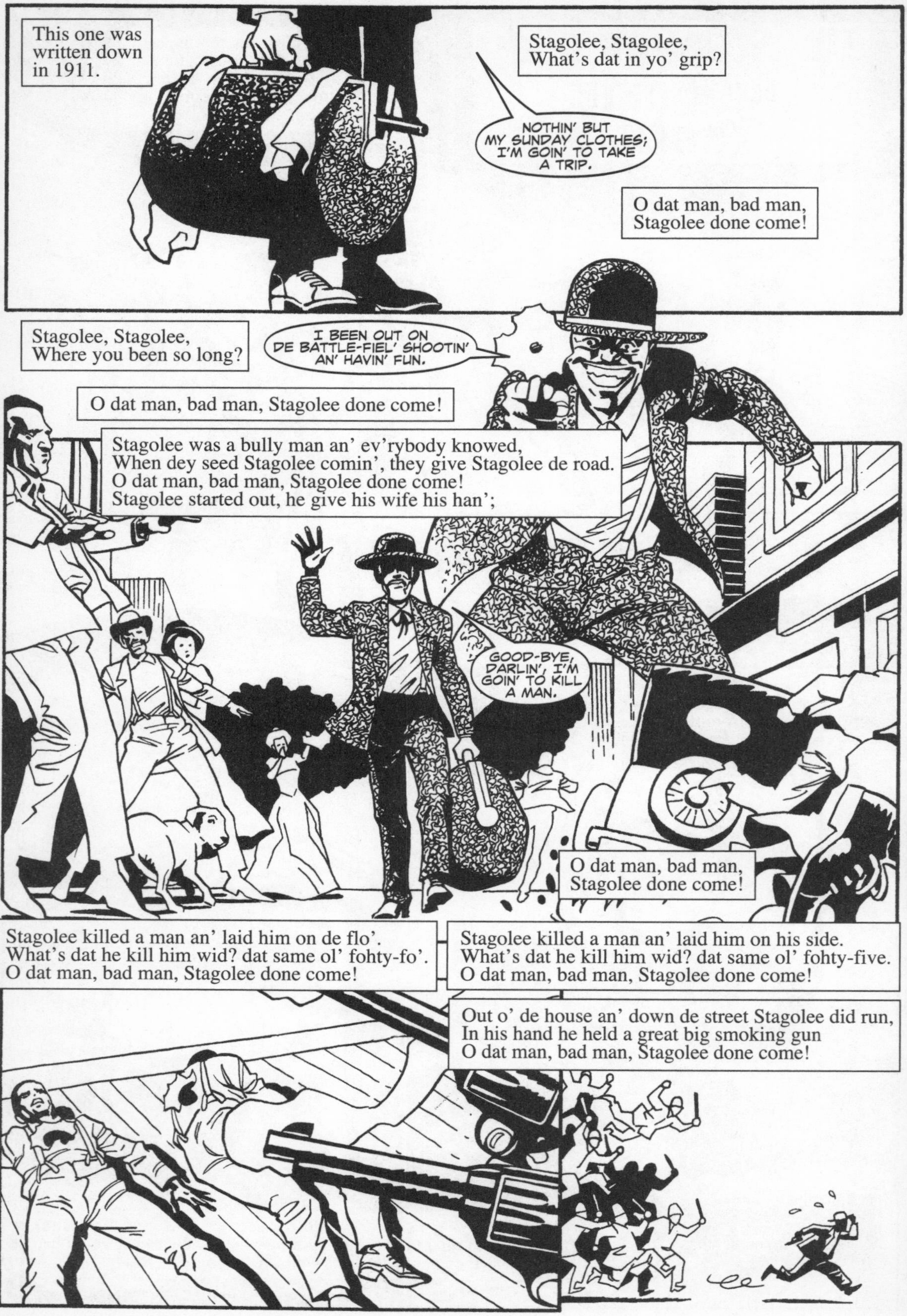

This one was written down in 1911.
Stagolee, Stagolee, What's dat in yo' grip?
NOTHIN' BUT MY SUNDAY CLOTHES; I'M GOIN' TO TAKE A TRIP.
O dat man, bad man, Stagolee done come!
Stagolee, Stagolee, Where you been so long?
I BEEN OUT ON DE BATTLE-FIEL' SHOOTIN' AN' HAVIN' FUN.
O dat man, bad man, Stagolee done come!
Stagolee was a bully man an' ev'rybody knowed,
When dey seed Stagolee comin', they give Stagolee de road.
O dat man, bad man, Stagolee done come!
Stagolee started out, he give his wife his han';
GOOD-BYE, DARLIN', I'M GOIN' TO KILL A MAN.
O dat man, bad man, Stagolee done come!
Stagolee killed a man an' laid him on de flo'.
What's dat he kill him wid? dat same ol' fohty-fo'.
O dat man, bad man, Stagolee done come!
Stagolee killed a man an' laid him on his side.
What's dat he kill him wid? dat same ol' fohty-five.
O dat man, bad man, Stagolee done come!
Out o' de house an' down de street Stagolee did run,
In his hand he held a great big smoking gun
O dat man, bad man, Stagolee done come!

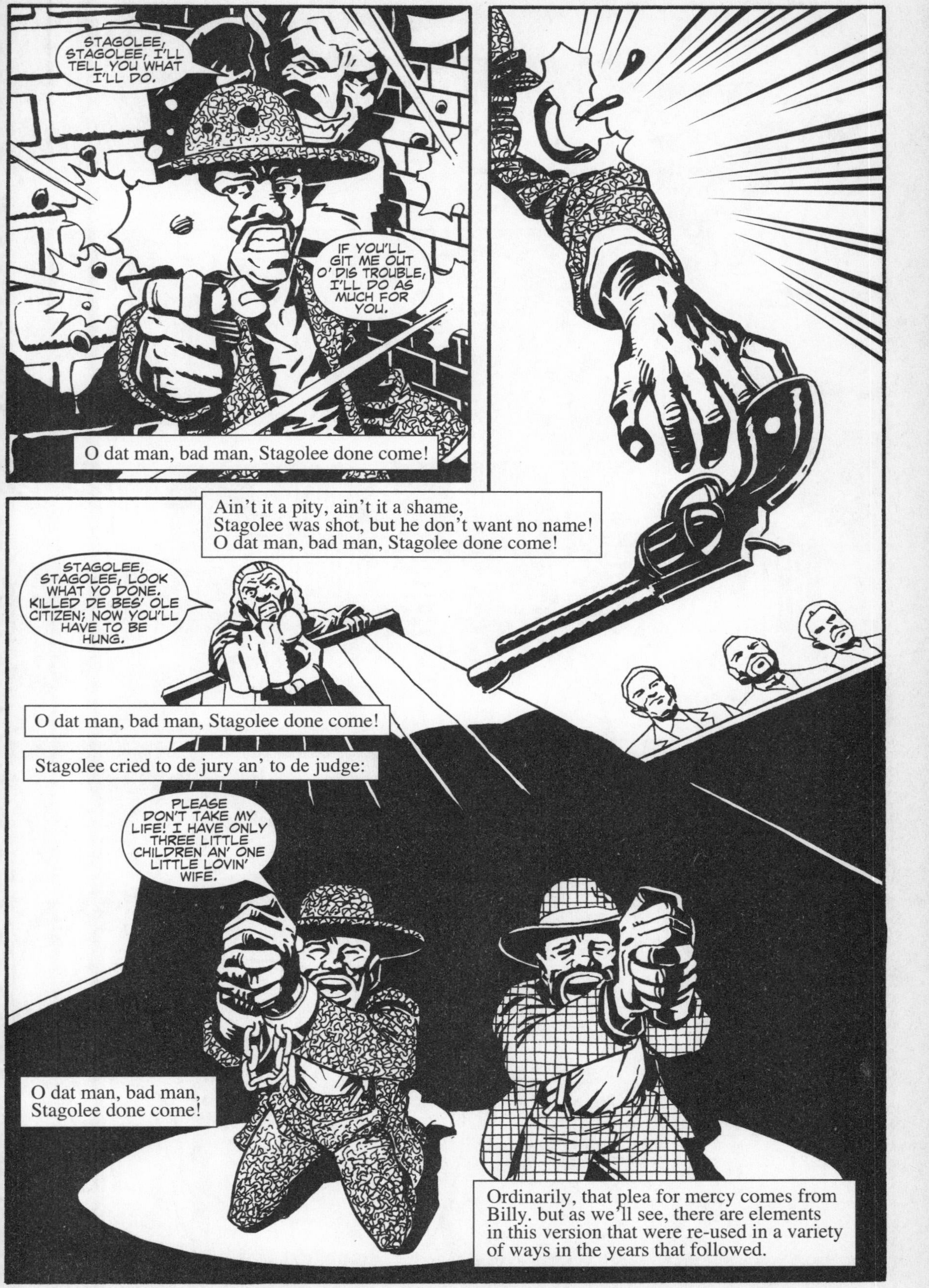

STAGOLEE, STAGOLEE, I'LL TELL YOU WHAT I'LL DO.
IF YOU'LL GIT ME OUT O' DIS TROUBLE, I'LL DO AS MUCH FOR YOU.
O dat man, bad man, Stagolee done come!
Ain't it a pity, ain't it a shame,
Stagolee was shot, but he don't want no name!
O dat man, bad man, Stagolee done come!
STAGOLEE, STAGOLEE, LOOK WHAT YO DONE. KILLED DE BES' OLE CITIZEN; NOW YOU'LL HAVE TO BE HUNG.
O dat man, bad man, Stagolee done come!
Stagolee cried to de jury an' to de judge:
PLEASE DON'T TAKE MY LIFE! I HAVE ONLY THREE LITTLE CHILDREN AN' ONE LITTLE LOVIN' WIFE.
O dat man, bad man, Stagolee done come!
Ordinarily, that plea for mercy comes from Billy. but as we'll see, there are elements in this version that were re-used in a variety of ways in the years that followed.

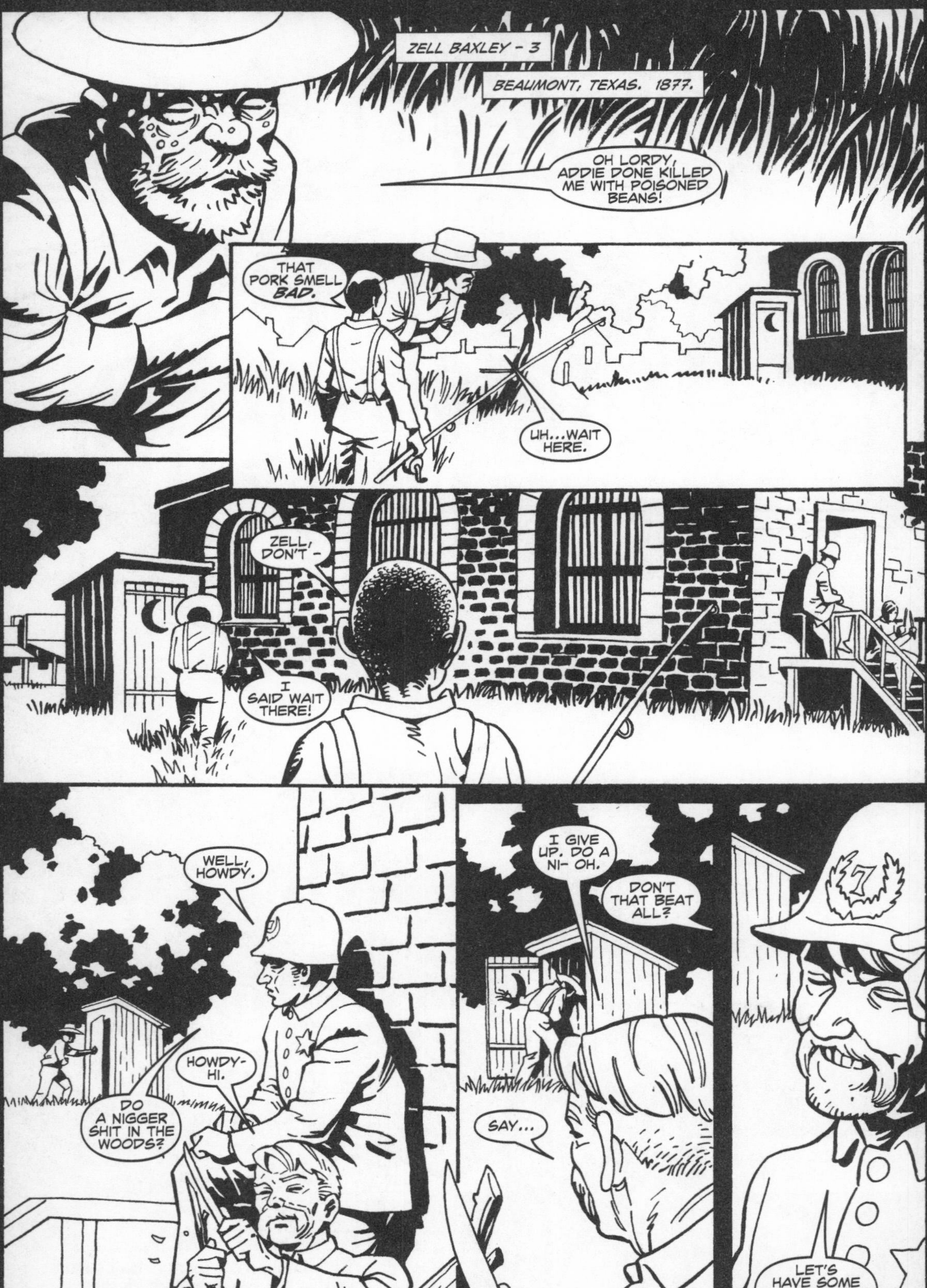
ZELL BAXLEY - 3
BEAUMONT, TEXAS. 1877.
OH LORDY, ADDIE DONE KILLED ME WITH POISONED BEANS!
THAT PORK SMELL BAD.
UH...WAIT HERE.
ZELL, DON'T -
I SAID WAIT THERE!
WELL, HOWDY.
HOWDY-HI.
DO A NIGGER SHIT IN THE WOODS?
I GIVE UP. DO A NI- OH.
DON'T THAT BEAT ALL?
SAY...
LET'S HAVE SOME FUN! GET THE SHOTGUN...

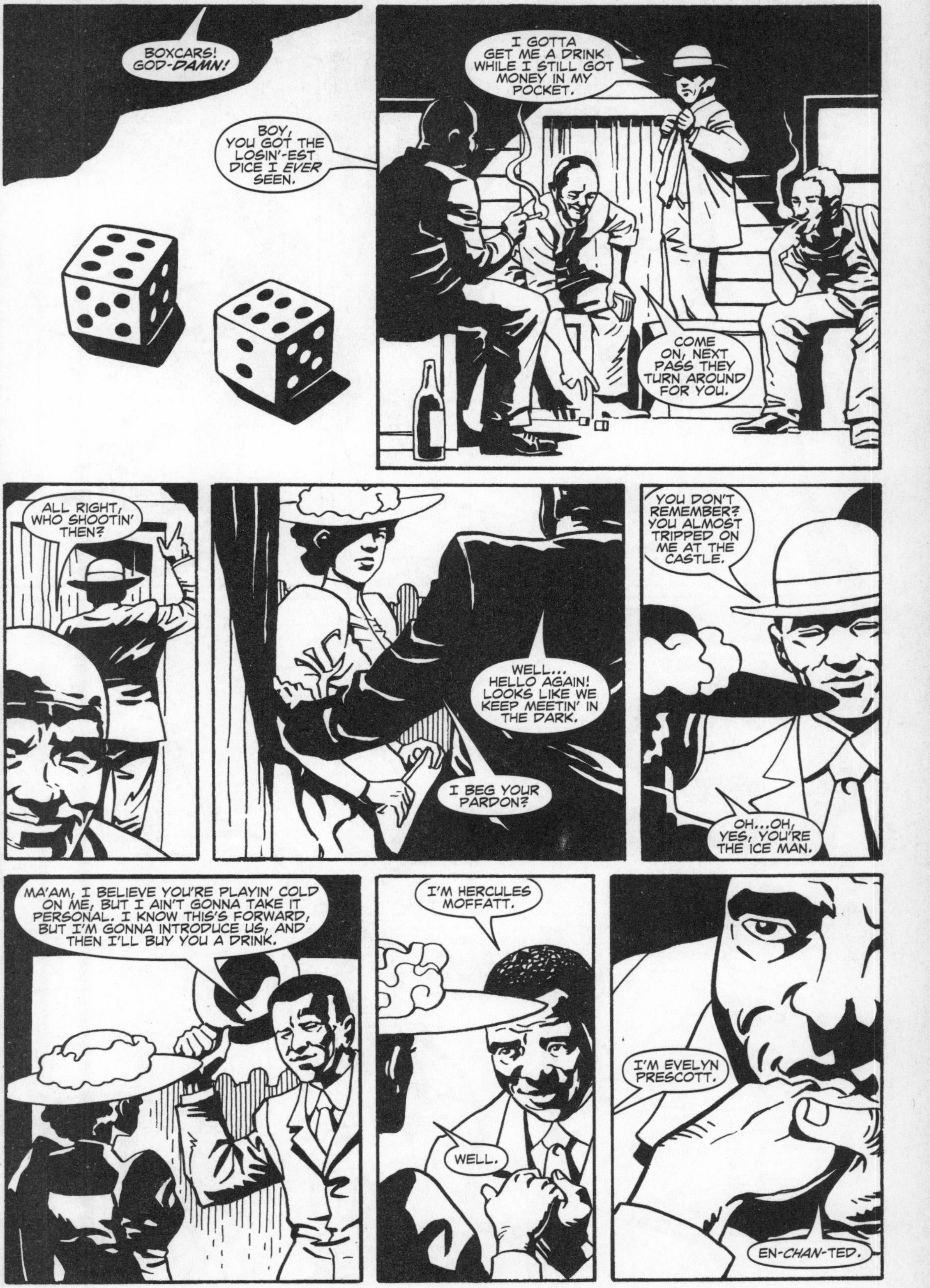
BOXCARS! GOD-*DAMN!*
I GOTTA GET ME A DRINK WHILE I STILL GOT MONEY IN MY POCKET.
BOY, YOU GOT THE LOSIN'-EST DICE I *EVER* SEEN.
COME ON, NEXT PASS THEY TURN AROUND FOR YOU.
ALL RIGHT, WHO SHOOTIN' THEN?
WELL... HELLO AGAIN! LOOKS LIKE WE KEEP MEETIN' IN THE DARK.
I BEG YOUR PARDON?
YOU DON'T REMEMBER? YOU ALMOST TRIPPED ON ME AT THE CASTLE.
OH...OH, YES, YOU'RE THE ICE MAN.
MA'AM, I BELIEVE YOU'RE PLAYIN' COLD ON ME, BUT I AIN'T GONNA TAKE IT PERSONAL. I KNOW THIS'S FORWARD, BUT I'M GONNA INTRODUCE US, AND THEN I'LL BUY YOU A DRINK.
I'M HERCULES MOFFATT.
WELL.
I'M EVELYN PRESCOTT.
EN-*CHAN*-TED.

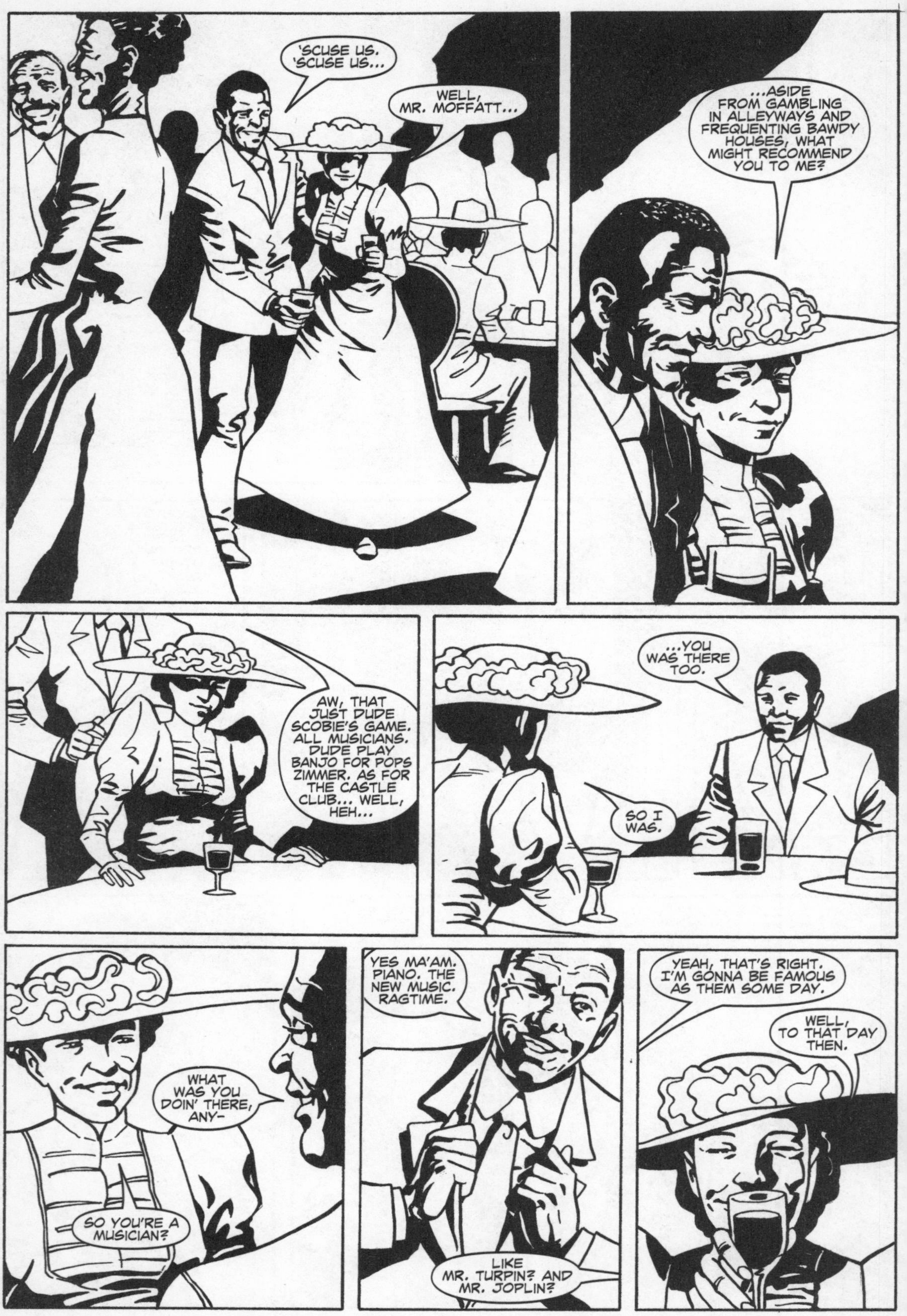

'SCUSE US. 'SCUSE US...
WELL, MR. MOFFATT...
...ASIDE FROM GAMBLING IN ALLEYWAYS AND FREQUENTING BAWDY HOUSES, WHAT MIGHT RECOMMEND YOU TO ME?
AW, THAT JUST DUDE SCOBIE'S GAME. ALL MUSICIANS. DUDE PLAY BANJO FOR POPS ZIMMER. AS FOR THE CASTLE CLUB... WELL, HEH...
...YOU WAS THERE TOO.
SO I WAS.
WHAT WAS YOU DOIN' THERE, ANY-
SO YOU'RE A MUSICIAN?
YES MA'AM. PIANO. THE NEW MUSIC. RAGTIME.
LIKE MR. TURPIN? AND MR. JOPLIN?
YEAH, THAT'S RIGHT. I'M GONNA BE FAMOUS AS THEM SOME DAY.
WELL, TO THAT DAY THEN.

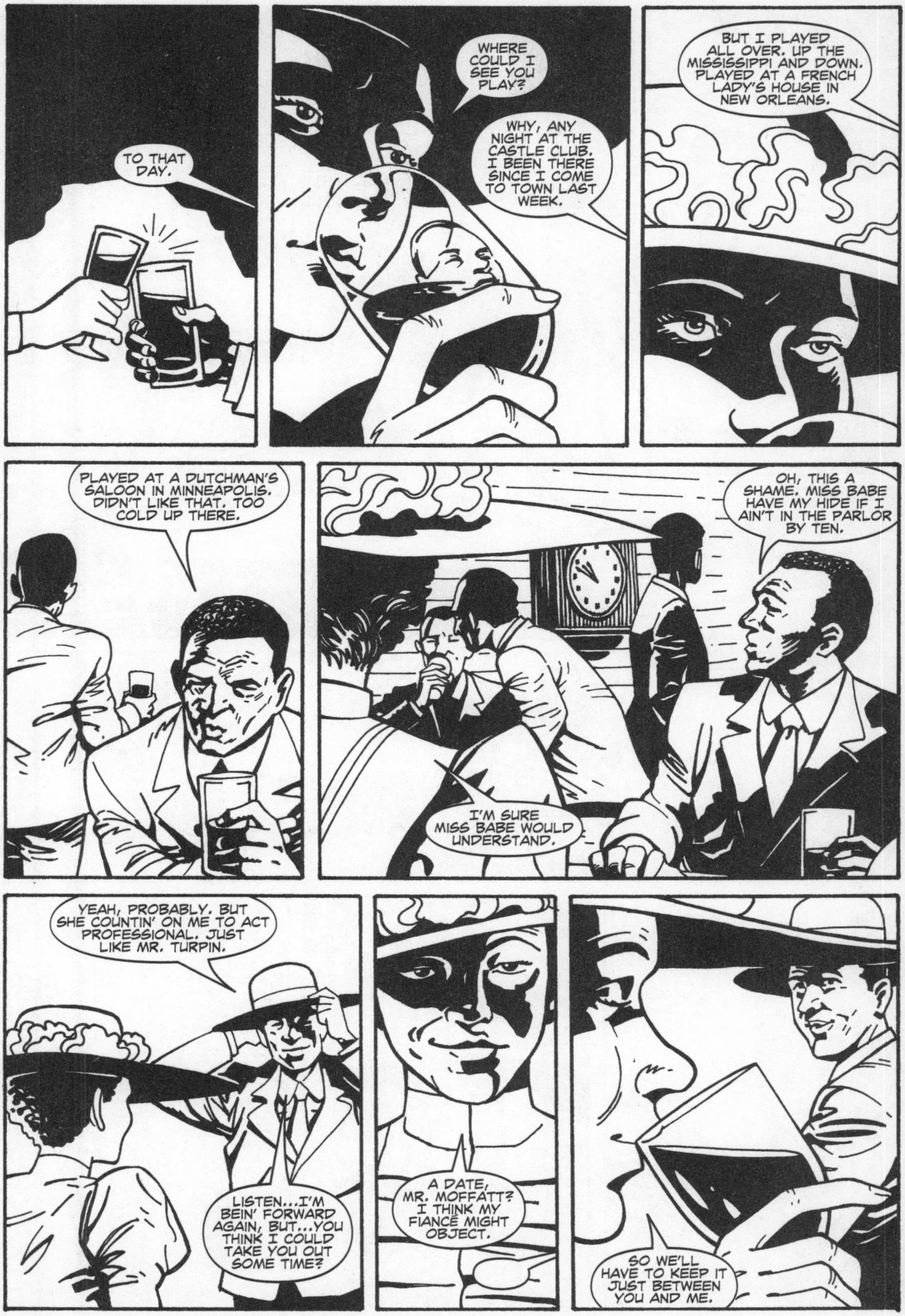
TO THAT DAY.
WHERE COULD I SEE YOU PLAY?
WHY, ANY NIGHT AT THE CASTLE CLUB. I BEEN THERE SINCE I COME TO TOWN LAST WEEK.
BUT I PLAYED ALL OVER. UP THE MISSISSIPPI AND DOWN. PLAYED AT A FRENCH LADY'S HOUSE IN NEW ORLEANS.
PLAYED AT A DUTCHMAN'S SALOON IN MINNEAPOLIS. DIDN'T LIKE THAT. TOO COLD UP THERE.
OH, THIS A SHAME. MISS BABE HAVE MY HIDE IF I AIN'T IN THE PARLOR BY TEN.
I'M SURE MISS BABE WOULD UNDERSTAND.
YEAH, PROBABLY. BUT SHE COUNTIN' ON ME TO ACT PROFESSIONAL. JUST LIKE MR. TURPIN.
LISTEN...I'M BEIN' FORWARD AGAIN, BUT...YOU THINK I COULD TAKE YOU OUT SOME TIME?
A DATE, MR. MOFFATT? I THINK MY FIANCÉ MIGHT OBJECT.
SO WE'LL HAVE TO KEEP IT JUST BETWEEN YOU AND ME.

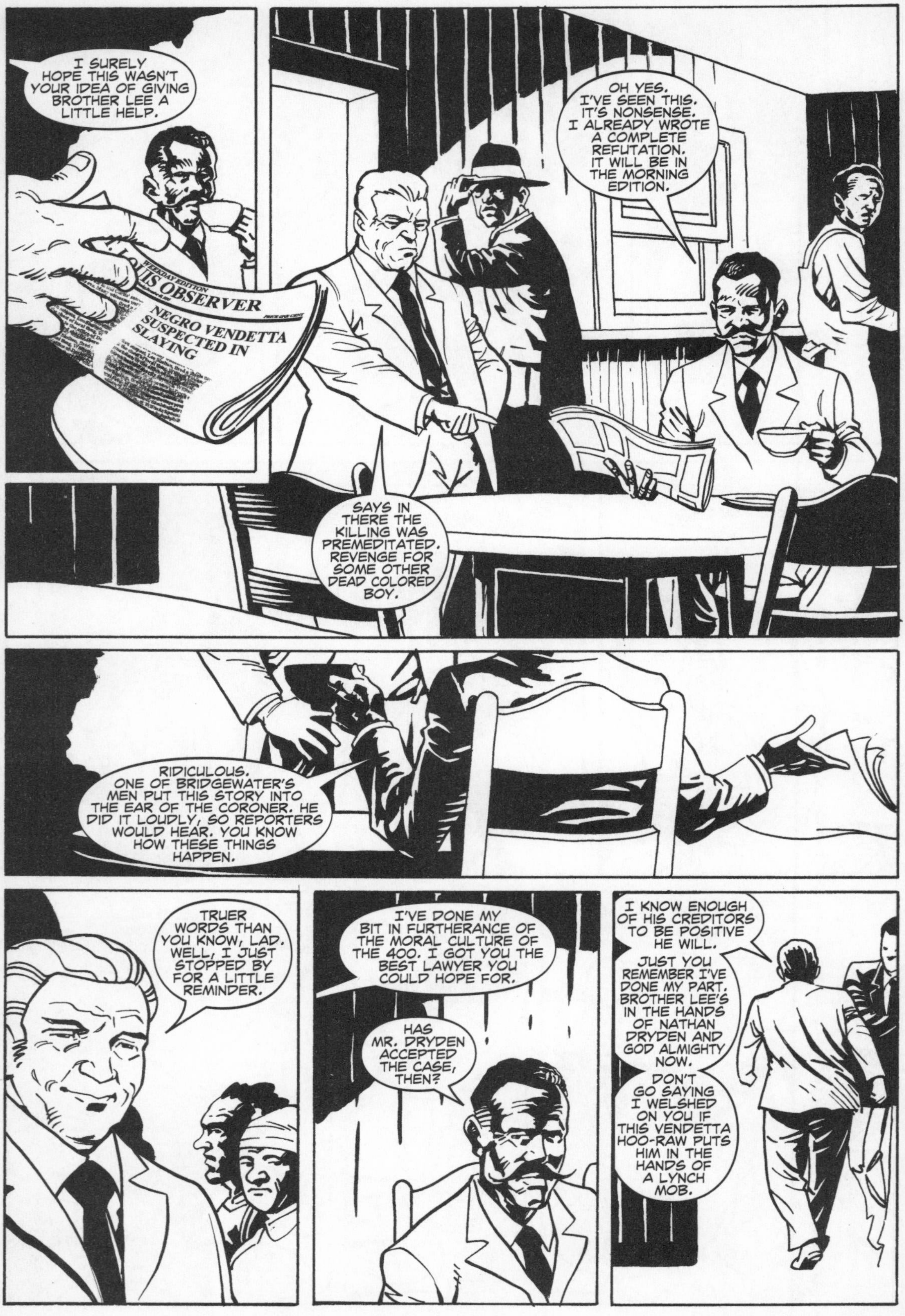
I SURELY HOPE THIS WASN'T YOUR IDEA OF GIVING BROTHER LEE A LITTLE HELP.
WEEKDAY EDITION
LOUIS OBSERVER
NEGRO VENDETTA SUSPECTED IN SLAYING
OH YES. I'VE SEEN THIS. IT'S NONSENSE. I ALREADY WROTE A COMPLETE REFUTATION. IT WILL BE IN THE MORNING EDITION.
SAYS IN THERE THE KILLING WAS PREMEDITATED. REVENGE FOR SOME OTHER DEAD COLORED BOY.
RIDICULOUS. ONE OF BRIDGEWATER'S MEN PUT THIS STORY INTO THE EAR OF THE CORONER. HE DID IT LOUDLY, SO REPORTERS WOULD HEAR. YOU KNOW HOW THESE THINGS HAPPEN.
TRUER WORDS THAN YOU KNOW, LAD. WELL, I JUST STOPPED BY FOR A LITTLE REMINDER.
I'VE DONE MY BIT IN FURTHERANCE OF THE MORAL CULTURE OF THE 400. I GOT YOU THE BEST LAWYER YOU COULD HOPE FOR.
HAS MR. DRYDEN ACCEPTED THE CASE, THEN?
I KNOW ENOUGH OF HIS CREDITORS TO BE POSITIVE HE WILL.
JUST YOU REMEMBER I'VE DONE MY PART. BROTHER LEE'S IN THE HANDS OF NATHAN DRYDEN AND GOD ALMIGHTY NOW.
DON'T GO SAYING I WELSHED ON YOU IF THIS VENDETTA HOO-RAW PUTS HIM IN THE HANDS OF A LYNCH MOB.

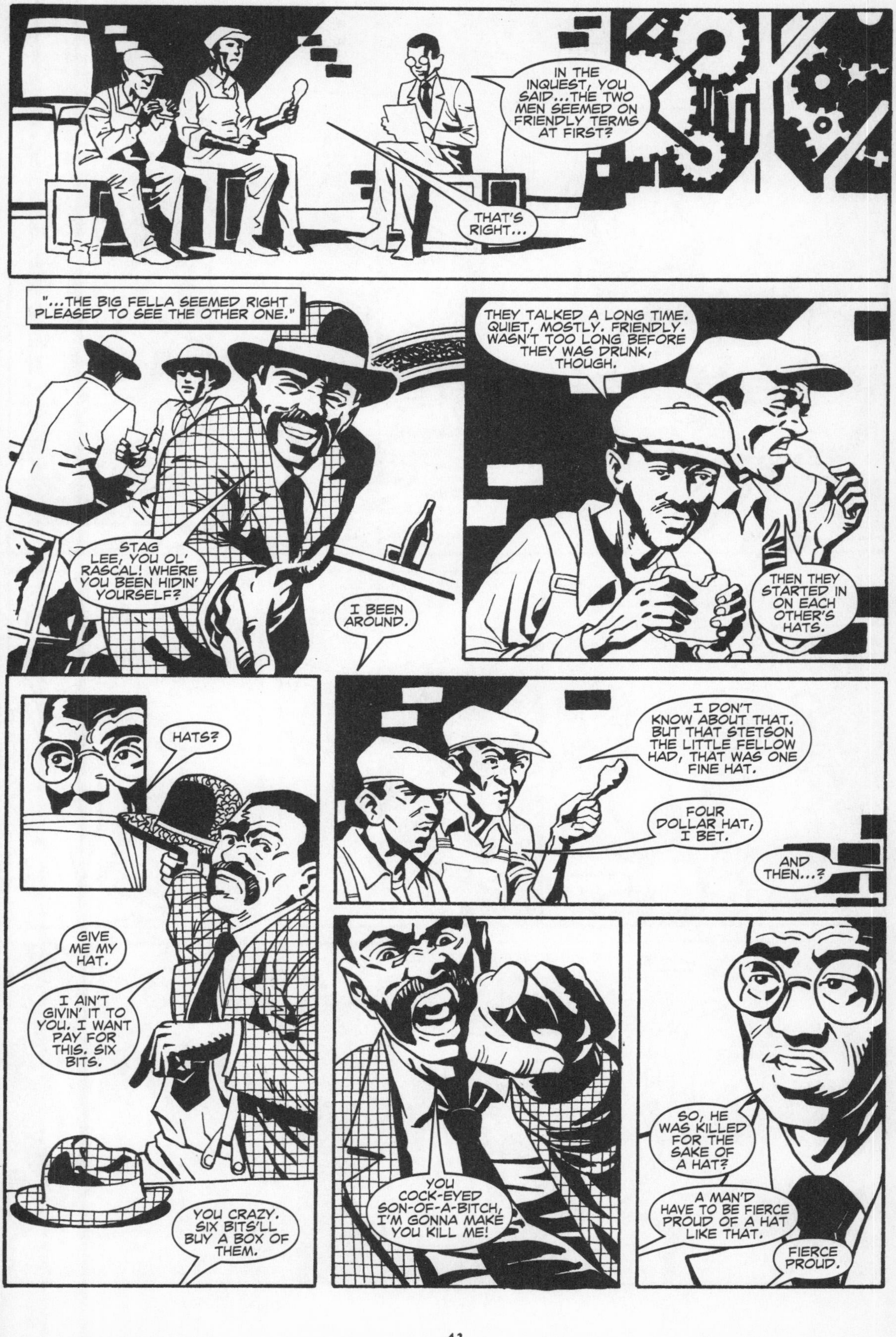
IN THE INQUEST, YOU SAID...THE TWO MEN SEEMED ON FRIENDLY TERMS AT FIRST?
THAT'S RIGHT...
"...THE BIG FELLA SEEMED RIGHT PLEASED TO SEE THE OTHER ONE."
STAG LEE, YOU OL' RASCAL! WHERE YOU BEEN HIDIN' YOURSELF?
I BEEN AROUND.
THEY TALKED A LONG TIME. QUIET, MOSTLY. FRIENDLY. WASN'T TOO LONG BEFORE THEY WAS DRUNK, THOUGH.
THEN THEY STARTED IN ON EACH OTHER'S HATS.
HATS?
GIVE ME MY HAT.
I AIN'T GIVIN' IT TO YOU. I WANT PAY FOR THIS. SIX BITS.
YOU CRAZY. SIX BITS'LL BUY A BOX OF THEM.
I DON'T KNOW ABOUT THAT. BUT THAT STETSON THE LITTLE FELLOW HAD, THAT WAS ONE FINE HAT.
FOUR DOLLAR HAT, I BET.
AND THEN...?
YOU COCK-EYED SON-OF-A-BITCH, I'M GONNA MAKE YOU KILL ME!
SO, HE WAS KILLED FOR THE SAKE OF A HAT?
A MAN'D HAVE TO BE FIERCE PROUD OF A HAT LIKE THAT.
FIERCE PROUD.

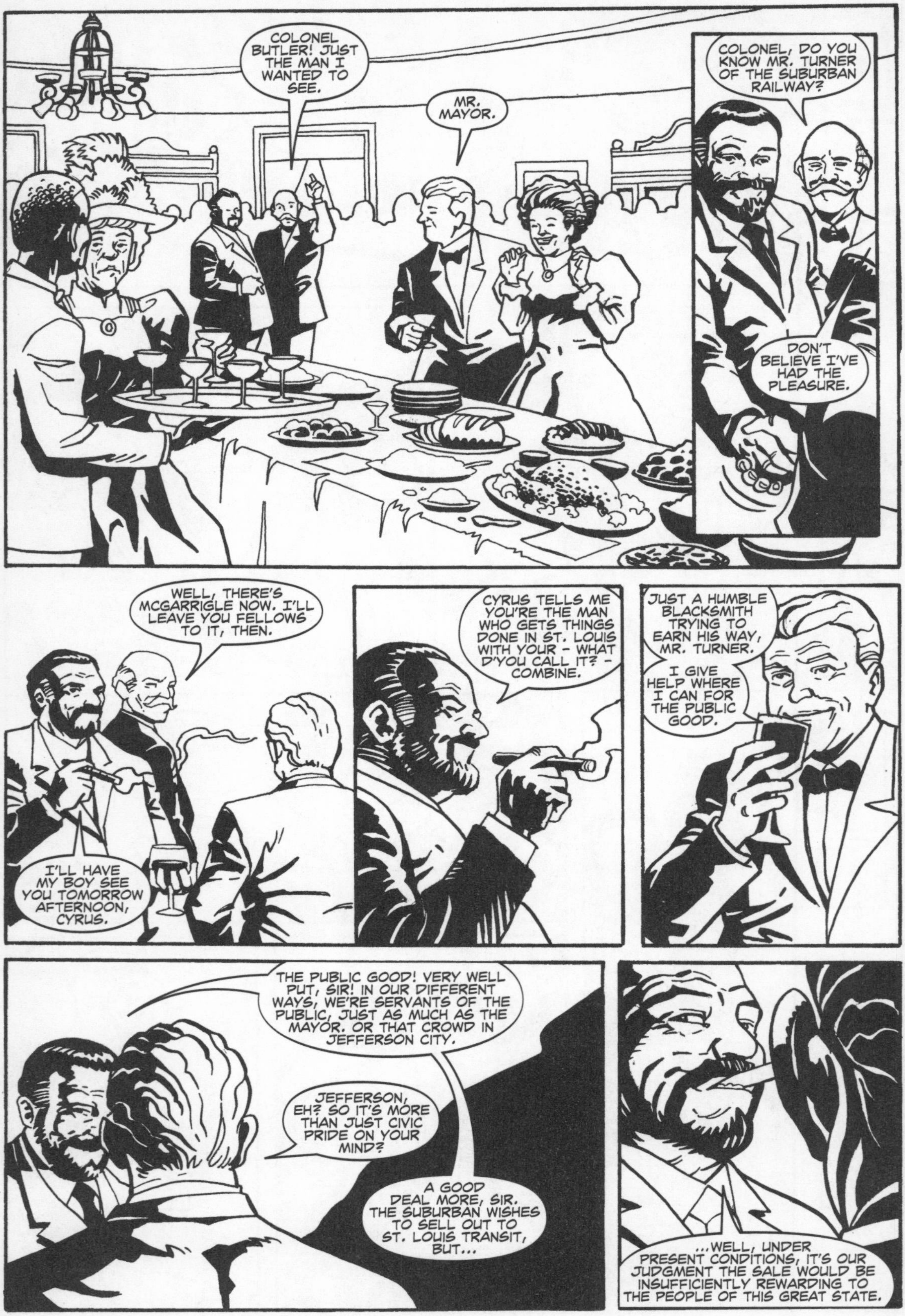
COLONEL BUTLER! JUST THE MAN I WANTED TO SEE.
MR. MAYOR.
COLONEL, DO YOU KNOW MR. TURNER OF THE SUBURBAN RAILWAY?
DON'T BELIEVE I'VE HAD THE PLEASURE.
WELL, THERE'S MCGARRIGLE NOW. I'LL LEAVE YOU FELLOWS TO IT, THEN.
I'LL HAVE MY BOY SEE YOU TOMORROW AFTERNOON, CYRUS.
CYRUS TELLS ME YOU'RE THE MAN WHO GETS THINGS DONE IN ST. LOUIS WITH YOUR - WHAT D'YOU CALL IT? - COMBINE.
JUST A HUMBLE BLACKSMITH TRYING TO EARN HIS WAY, MR. TURNER.
I GIVE HELP WHERE I CAN FOR THE PUBLIC GOOD.
THE PUBLIC GOOD! VERY WELL PUT, SIR! IN OUR DIFFERENT WAYS, WE'RE SERVANTS OF THE PUBLIC, JUST AS MUCH AS THE MAYOR. OR THAT CROWD IN JEFFERSON CITY.
JEFFERSON, EH? SO IT'S MORE THAN JUST CIVIC PRIDE ON YOUR MIND?
A GOOD DEAL MORE, SIR. THE SUBURBAN WISHES TO SELL OUT TO ST. LOUIS TRANSIT, BUT...
...WELL, UNDER PRESENT CONDITIONS, IT'S OUR JUDGMENT THE SALE WOULD BE INSUFFICIENTLY REWARDING TO THE PEOPLE OF THIS GREAT STATE.

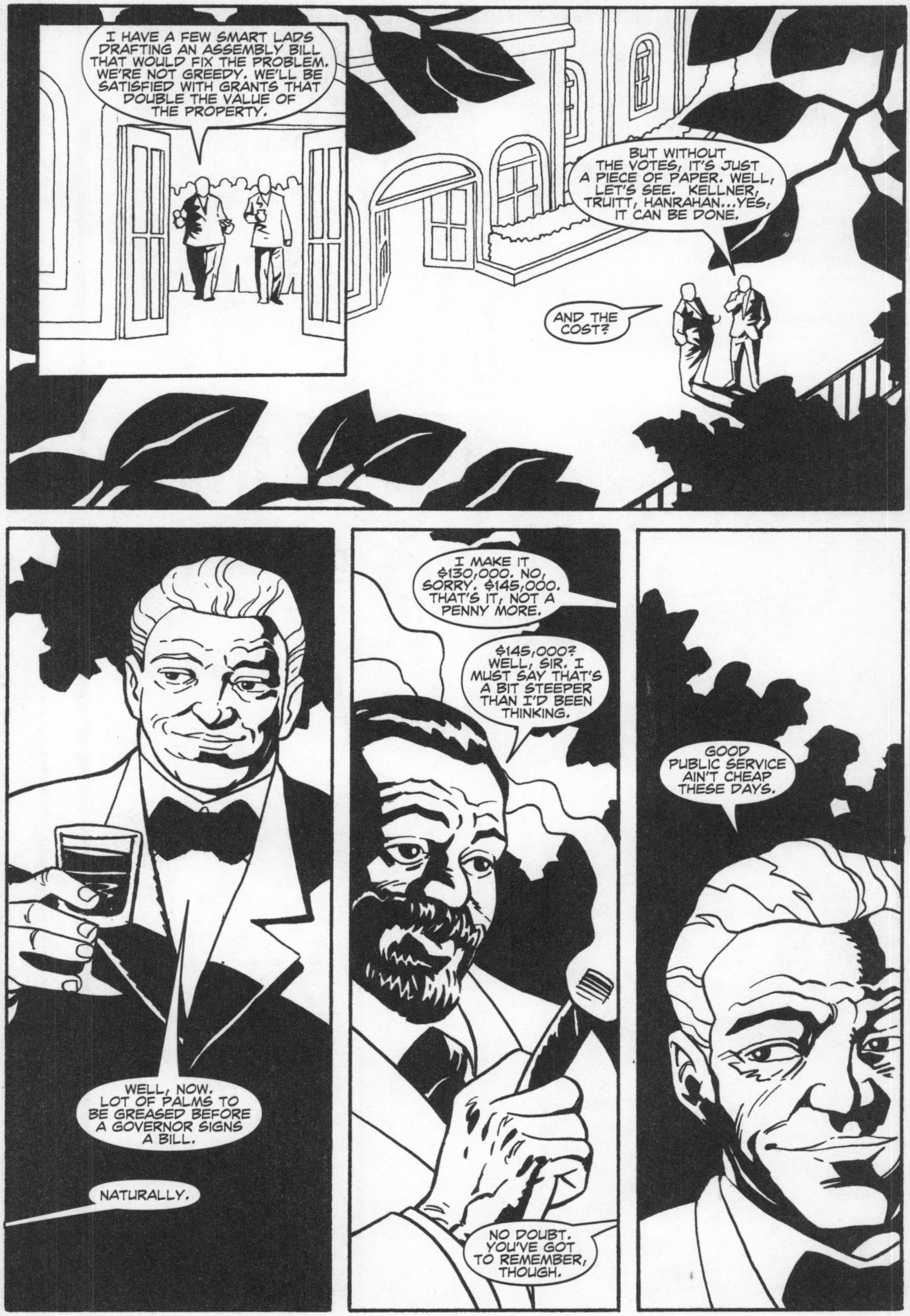
I HAVE A FEW SMART LADS DRAFTING AN ASSEMBLY BILL THAT WOULD FIX THE PROBLEM. WE'RE NOT GREEDY. WE'LL BE SATISFIED WITH GRANTS THAT DOUBLE THE VALUE OF THE PROPERTY.
BUT WITHOUT THE VOTES, IT'S JUST A PIECE OF PAPER. WELL, LET'S SEE. KELLNER, TRUITT, HANRAHAN...YES, IT CAN BE DONE.
AND THE COST?
WELL, NOW. LOT OF PALMS TO BE GREASED BEFORE A GOVERNOR SIGNS A BILL.
NATURALLY.
I MAKE IT $130,000. NO, SORRY. $145,000. THAT'S IT, NOT A PENNY MORE.
$145,000? WELL, SIR. I MUST SAY THAT'S A BIT STEEPER THAN I'D BEEN THINKING.
NO DOUBT. YOU'VE GOT TO REMEMBER, THOUGH.
GOOD PUBLIC SERVICE AIN'T CHEAP THESE DAYS.

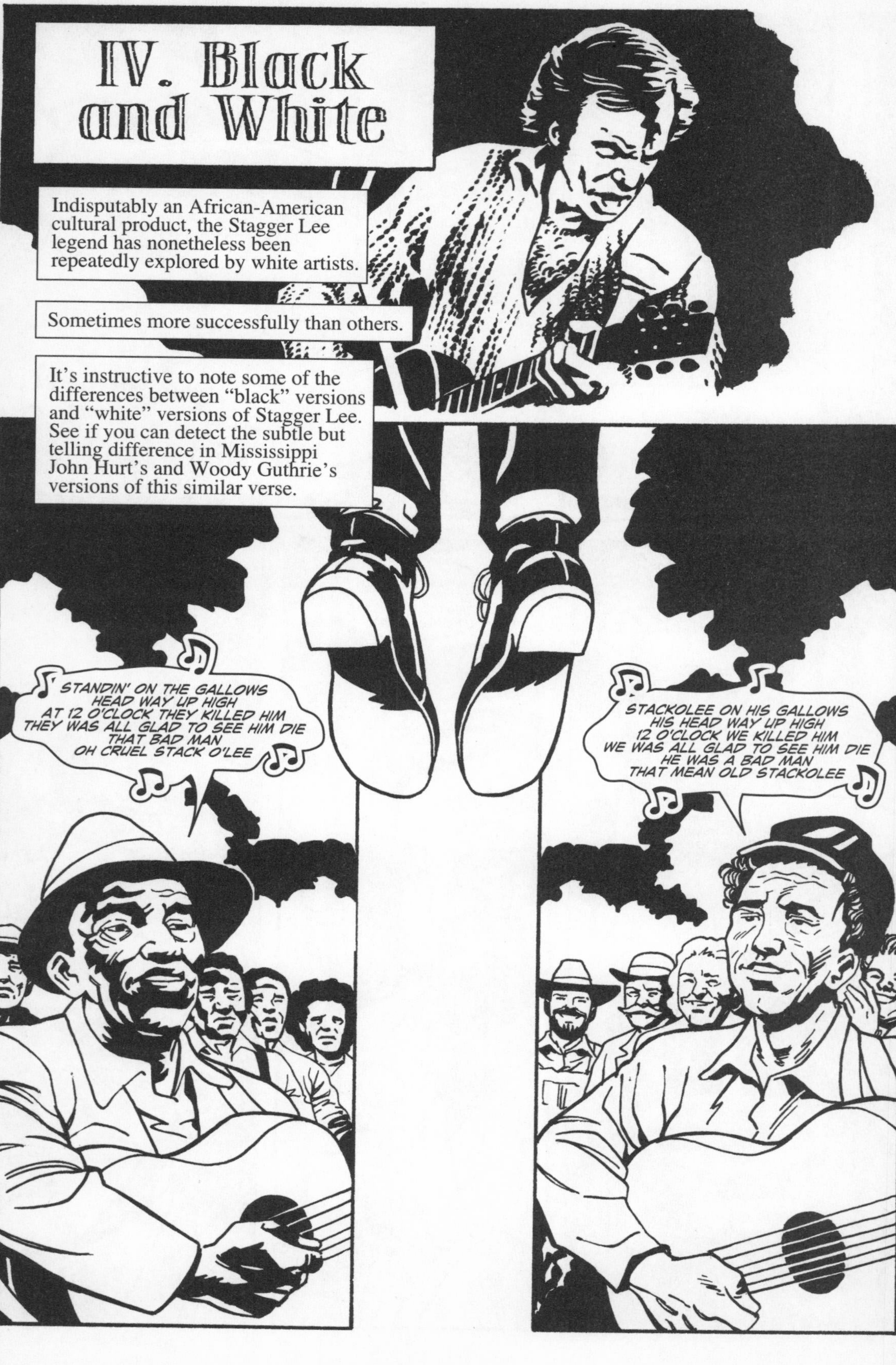
IV. Black and White
Indisputably an African-American cultural product, the Stagger Lee legend has nonetheless been repeatedly explored by white artists.
Sometimes more successfully than others.
It's instructive to note some of the differences between "black" versions and "white" versions of Stagger Lee. See if you can detect the subtle but telling difference in Mississippi John Hurt's and Woody Guthrie's versions of this similar verse.
STANDIN' ON THE GALLOWS HEAD WAY UP HIGH AT 12 O'CLOCK THEY KILLED HIM THEY WAS ALL GLAD TO SEE HIM DIE THAT BAD MAN OH CRUEL STACK O'LEE
STACKOLEE ON HIS GALLOWS HIS HEAD WAY UP HIGH 12 O'CLOCK WE KILLED HIM WE WAS ALL GLAD TO SEE HIM DIE HE WAS A BAD MAN THAT MEAN OLD STACKOLEE

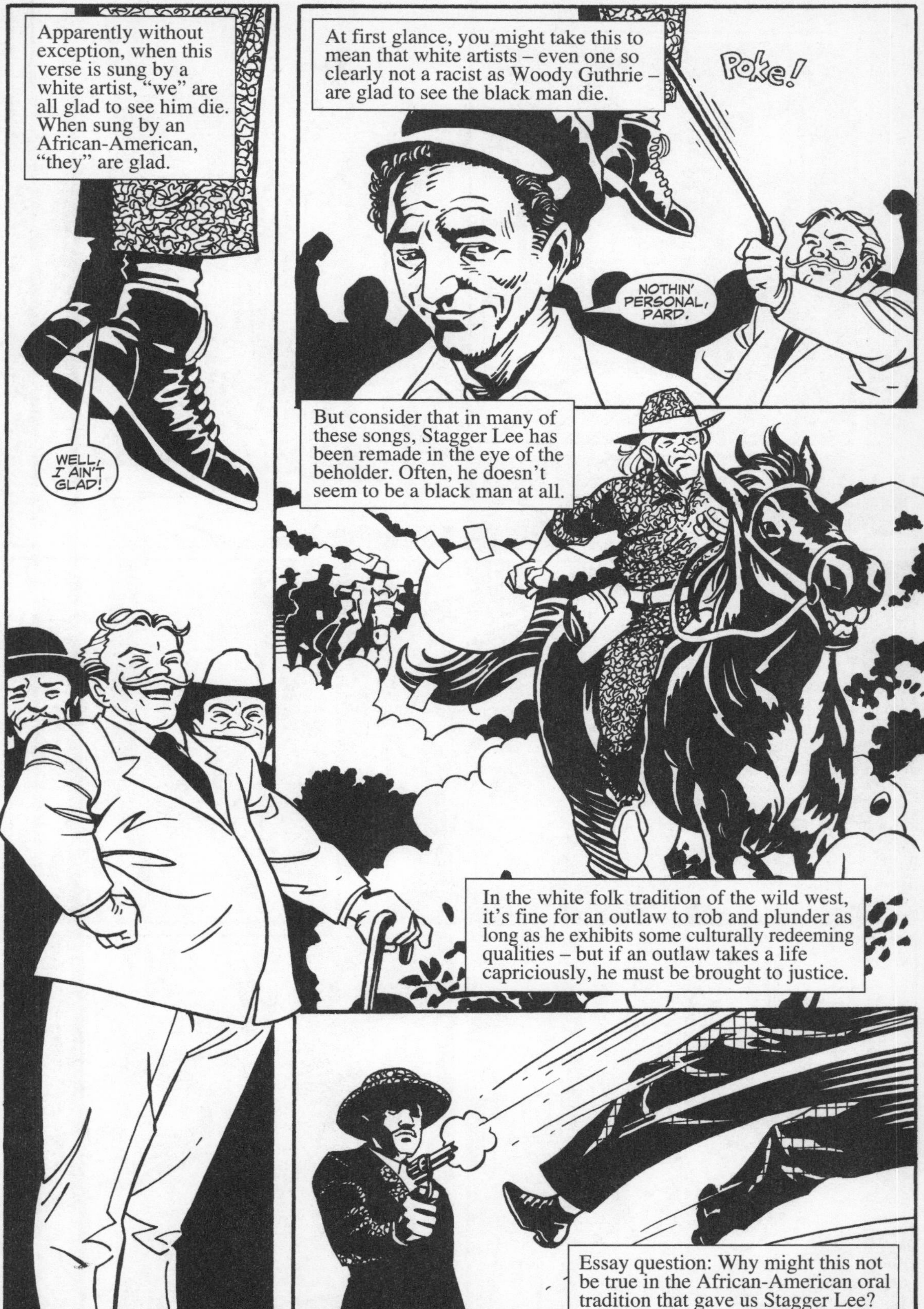
Apparently without exception, when this verse is sung by a white artist, "we" are all glad to see him die. When sung by an African-American, "they" are glad.
WELL, I AIN'T GLAD!
At first glance, you might take this to mean that white artists – even one so clearly not a racist as Woody Guthrie – are glad to see the black man die.
Poke!
NOTHIN' PERSONAL, PARD.
But consider that in many of these songs, Stagger Lee has been remade in the eye of the beholder. Often, he doesn't seem to be a black man at all.
In the white folk tradition of the wild west, it's fine for an outlaw to rob and plunder as long as he exhibits some culturally redeeming qualities – but if an outlaw takes a life capriciously, he must be brought to justice.
Essay question: Why might this not be true in the African-American oral tradition that gave us Stagger Lee?

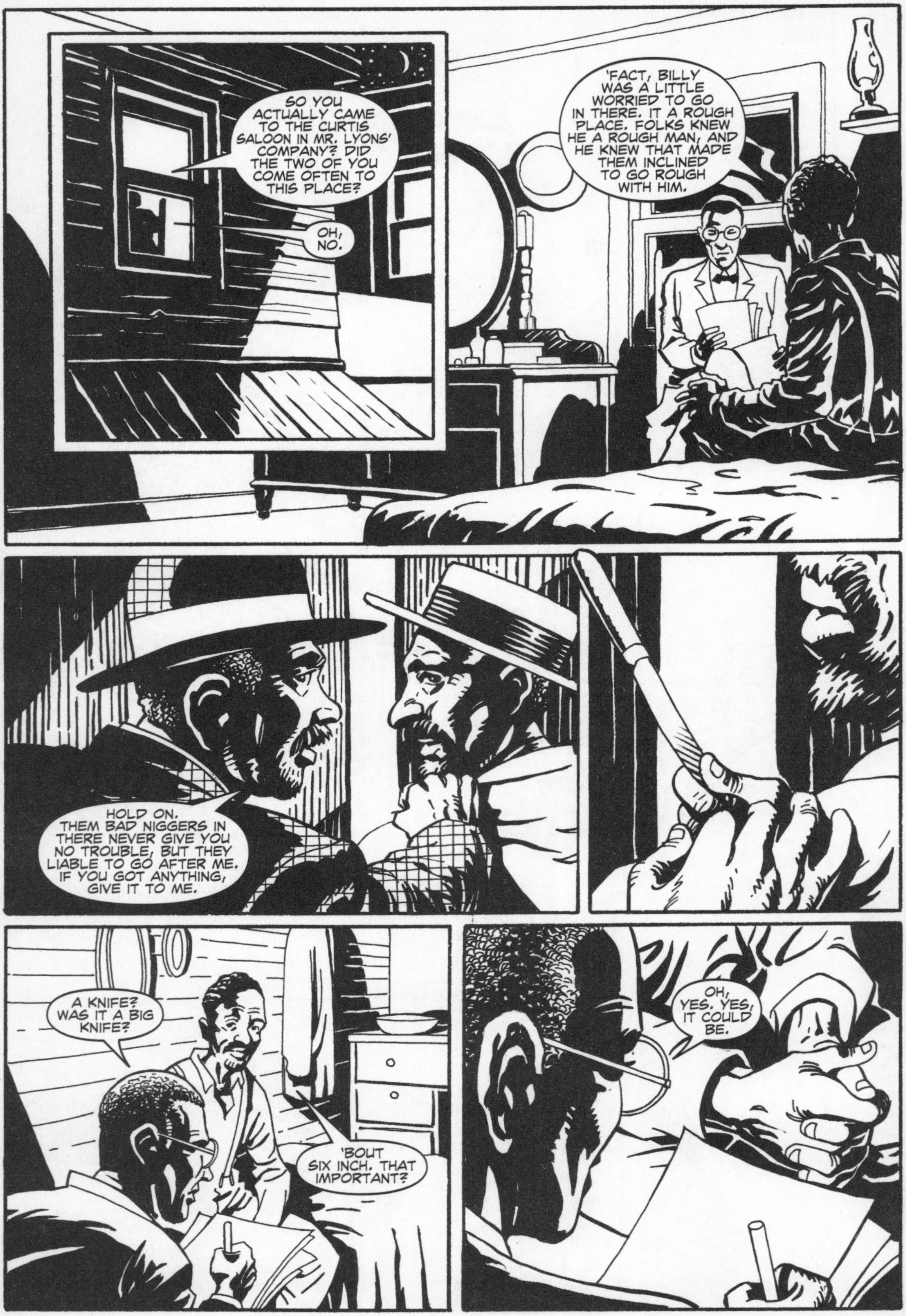
SO YOU ACTUALLY CAME TO THE CURTIS SALOON IN MR. LYONS' COMPANY? DID THE TWO OF YOU COME OFTEN TO THIS PLACE?
OH, NO.
'FACT, BILLY WAS A LITTLE WORRIED TO GO IN THERE. IT A ROUGH PLACE. FOLKS KNEW HE A ROUGH MAN, AND HE KNEW THAT MADE THEM INCLINED TO GO ROUGH WITH HIM.
HOLD ON. THEM BAD NIGGERS IN THERE NEVER GIVE YOU NO TROUBLE, BUT THEY LIABLE TO GO AFTER ME. IF YOU GOT ANYTHING, GIVE IT TO ME.
A KNIFE? WAS IT A BIG KNIFE?
'BOUT SIX INCH. THAT IMPORTANT?
OH, YES. YES, IT COULD BE.

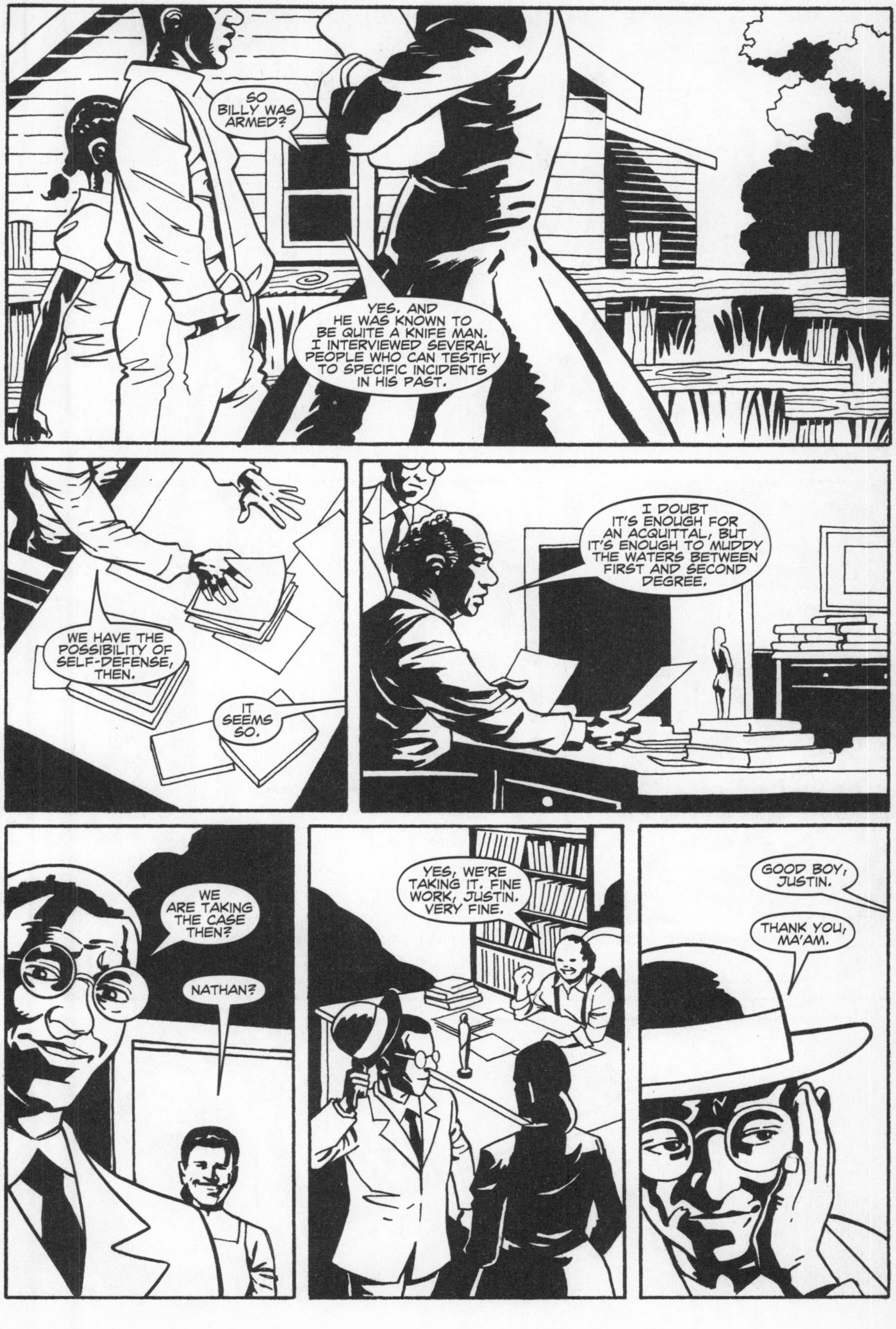
SO BILLY WAS ARMED?
YES. AND HE WAS KNOWN TO BE QUITE A KNIFE MAN. I INTERVIEWED SEVERAL PEOPLE WHO CAN TESTIFY TO SPECIFIC INCIDENTS IN HIS PAST.
WE HAVE THE POSSIBILITY OF SELF-DEFENSE, THEN.
IT SEEMS SO.
I DOUBT IT'S ENOUGH FOR AN ACQUITTAL, BUT IT'S ENOUGH TO MUDDY THE WATERS BETWEEN FIRST AND SECOND DEGREE.
WE ARE TAKING THE CASE THEN?
NATHAN?
YES, WE'RE TAKING IT. FINE WORK, JUSTIN. VERY FINE.
GOOD BOY, JUSTIN.
THANK YOU, MA'AM.

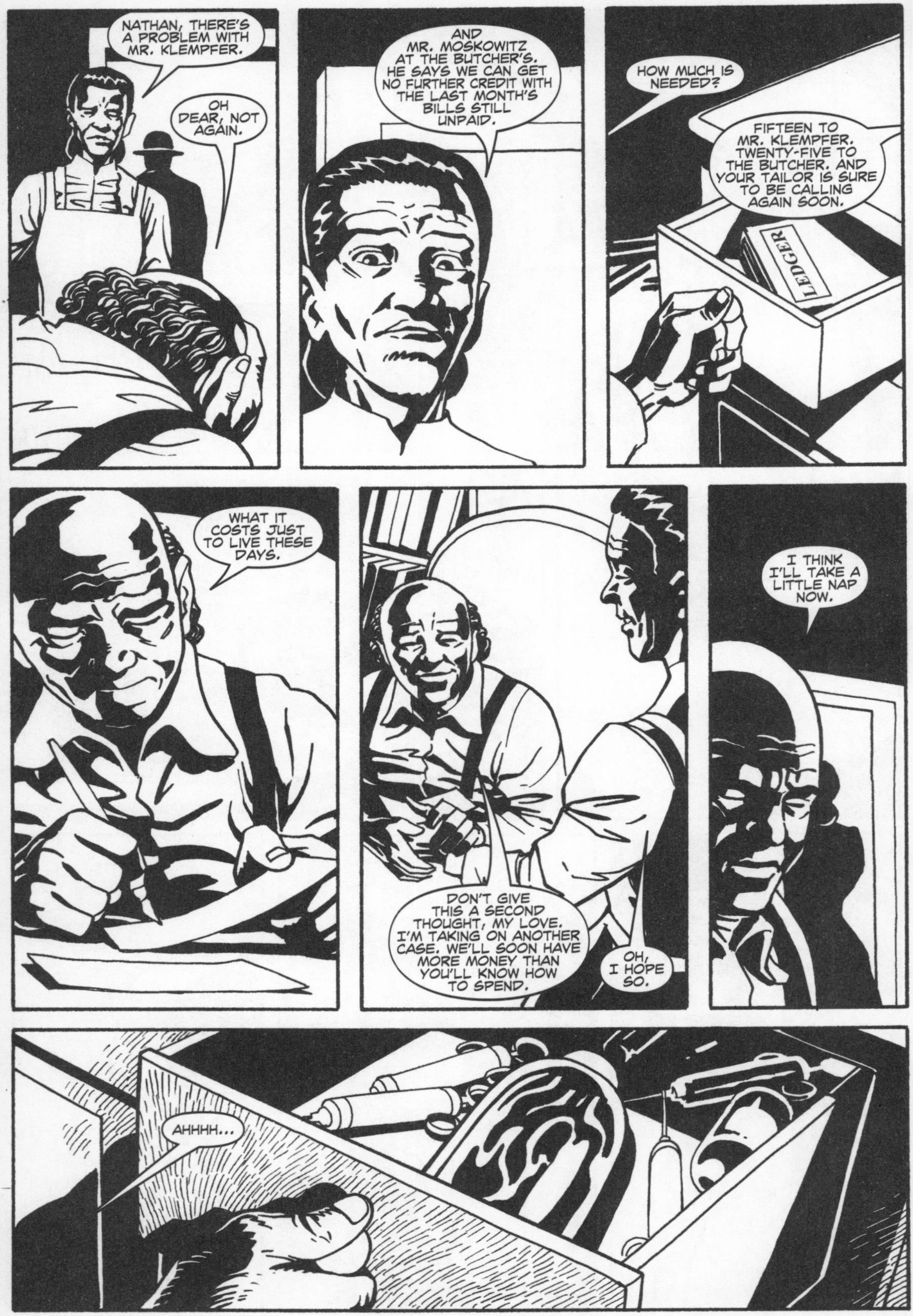
NATHAN, THERE'S A PROBLEM WITH MR. KLEMPFER.
OH DEAR, NOT AGAIN.
AND MR. MOSKOWITZ AT THE BUTCHER'S. HE SAYS WE CAN GET NO FURTHER CREDIT WITH THE LAST MONTH'S BILLS STILL UNPAID.
HOW MUCH IS NEEDED?
FIFTEEN TO MR. KLEMPFER. TWENTY-FIVE TO THE BUTCHER. AND YOUR TAILOR IS SURE TO BE CALLING AGAIN SOON.
LEDGER
WHAT IT COSTS JUST TO LIVE THESE DAYS.
DON'T GIVE THIS A SECOND THOUGHT, MY LOVE. I'M TAKING ON ANOTHER CASE. WE'LL SOON HAVE MORE MONEY THAN YOU'LL KNOW HOW TO SPEND.
OH, I HOPE SO.
I THINK I'LL TAKE A LITTLE NAP NOW.
AHHHH...

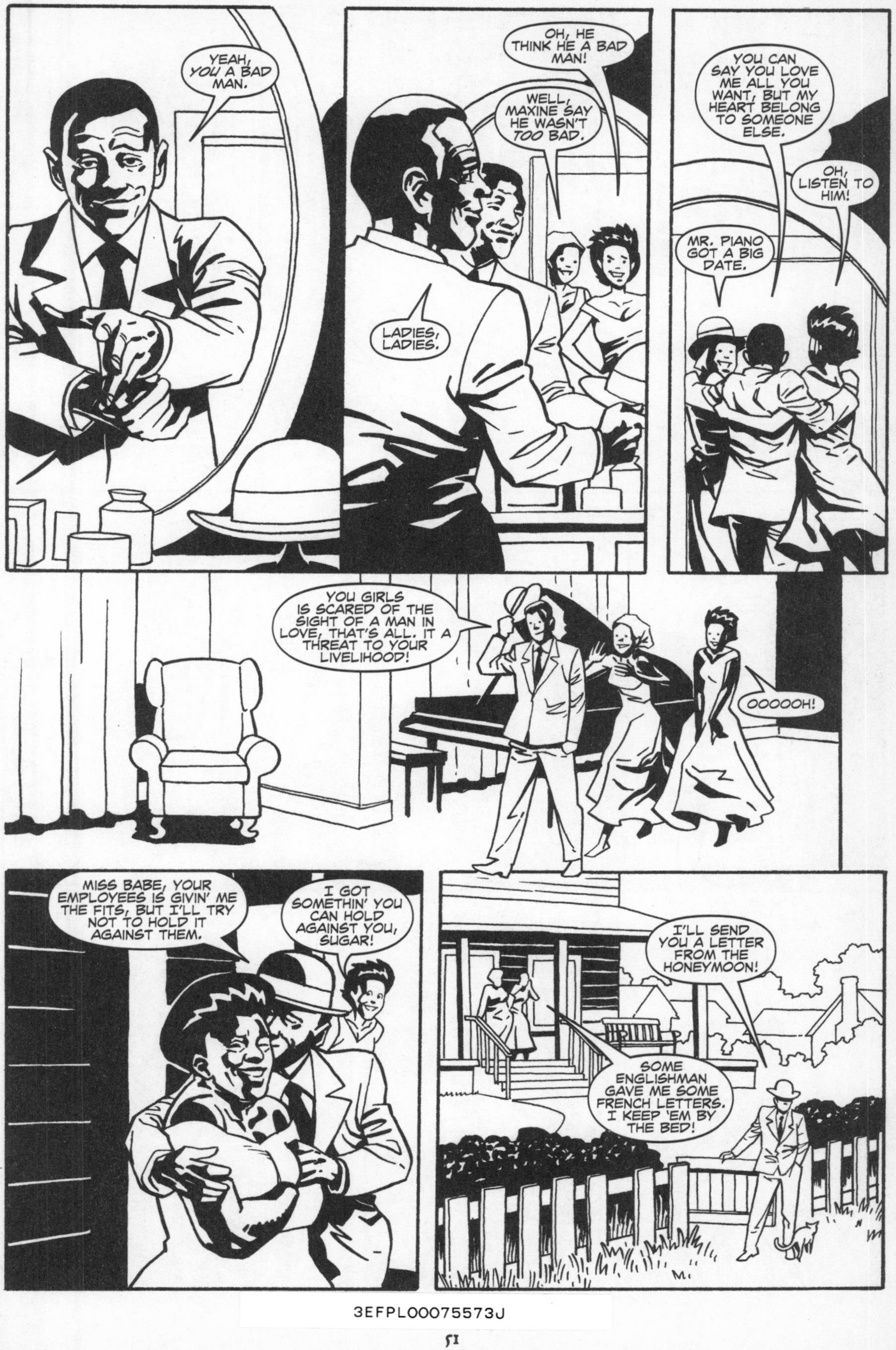
YEAH, YOU A BAD MAN.
OH, HE THINK HE A BAD MAN!
WELL, MAXINE SAY HE WASN'T TOO BAD.
LADIES, LADIES.
YOU CAN SAY YOU LOVE ME ALL YOU WANT, BUT MY HEART BELONG TO SOMEONE ELSE.
OH, LISTEN TO HIM!
MR. PIANO GOT A BIG DATE.
YOU GIRLS IS SCARED OF THE SIGHT OF A MAN IN LOVE, THAT'S ALL. IT A THREAT TO YOUR LIVELIHOOD!
OOOOOH!
MISS BABE, YOUR EMPLOYEES IS GIVIN' ME THE FITS, BUT I'LL TRY NOT TO HOLD IT AGAINST THEM.
I GOT SOMETHIN' YOU CAN HOLD AGAINST YOU, SUGAR!
I'LL SEND YOU A LETTER FROM THE HONEYMOON!
SOME ENGLISHMAN GAVE ME SOME FRENCH LETTERS. I KEEP 'EM BY THE BED!

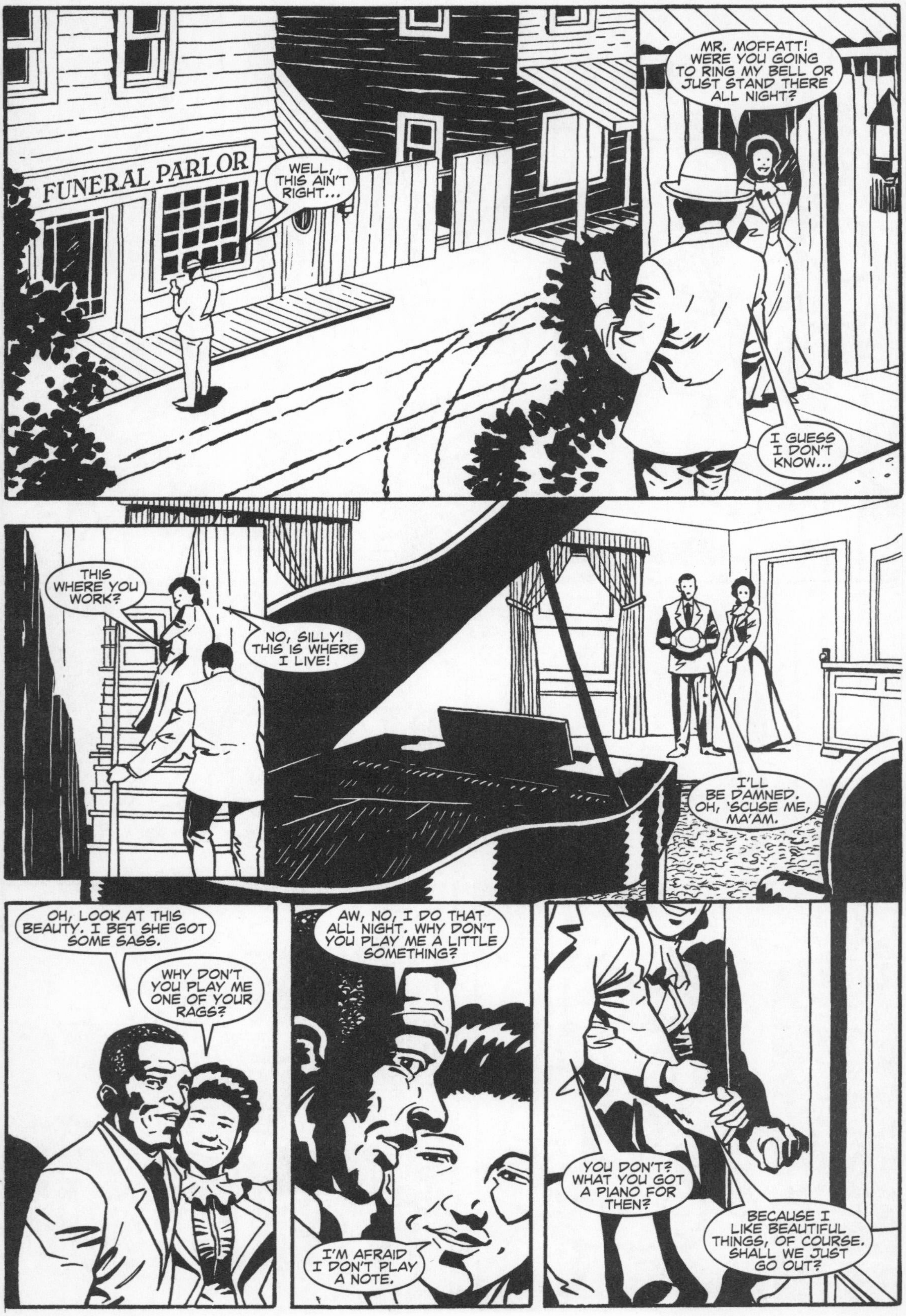
FUNERAL PARLOR
WELL, THIS AIN'T RIGHT...
MR. MOFFATT! WERE YOU GOING TO RING MY BELL OR JUST STAND THERE ALL NIGHT?
I GUESS I DON'T KNOW...
THIS WHERE YOU WORK?
NO, SILLY! THIS IS WHERE I LIVE!
I'LL BE DAMNED. OH, 'SCUSE ME, MA'AM.
OH, LOOK AT THIS BEAUTY. I BET SHE GOT SOME SASS.
WHY DON'T YOU PLAY ME ONE OF YOUR RAGS?
AW, NO, I DO THAT ALL NIGHT. WHY DON'T YOU PLAY ME A LITTLE SOMETHING?
I'M AFRAID I DON'T PLAY A NOTE.
YOU DON'T? WHAT YOU GOT A PIANO FOR THEN?
BECAUSE I LIKE BEAUTIFUL THINGS, OF COURSE. SHALL WE JUST GO OUT?

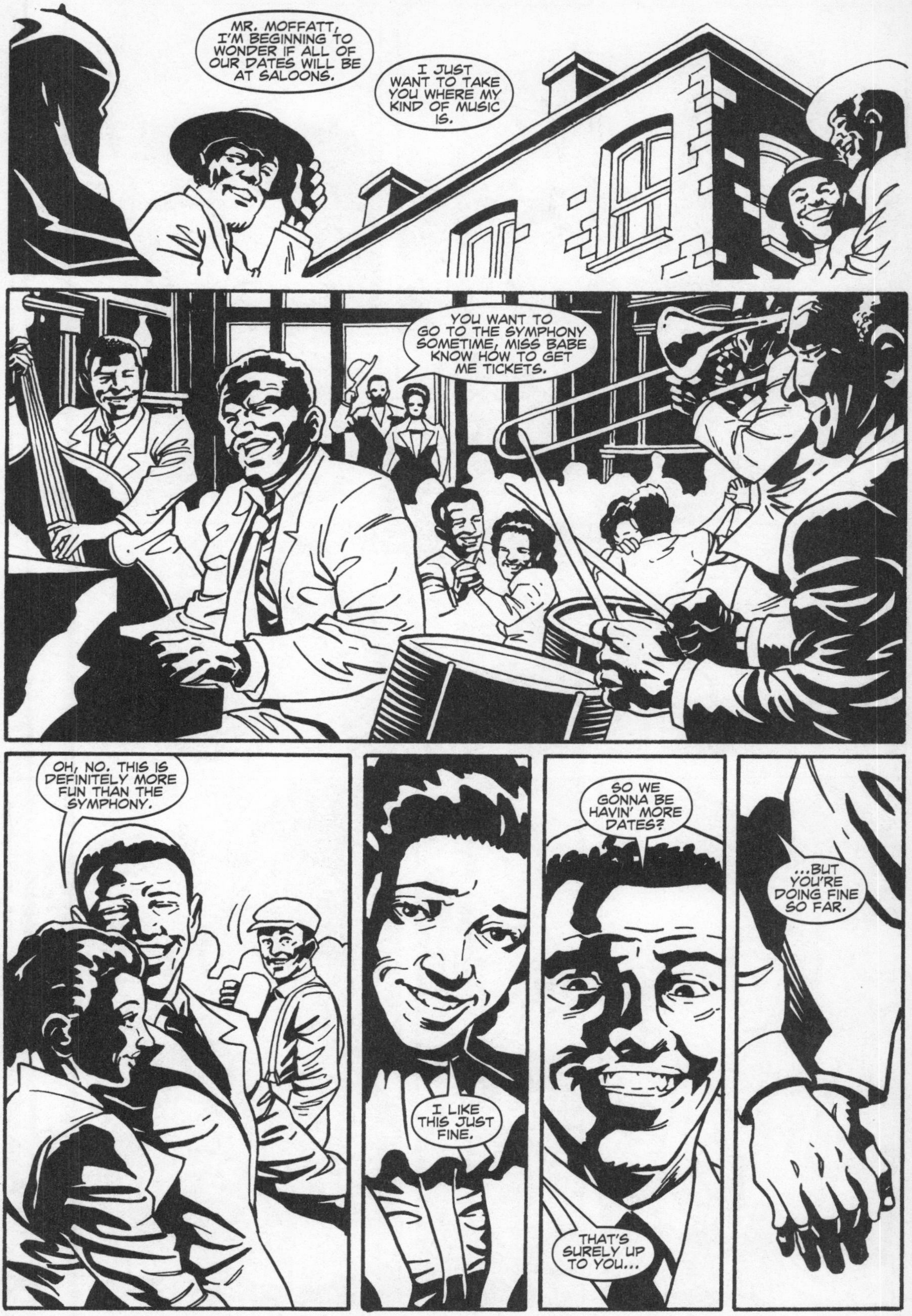
MR. MOFFATT, I'M BEGINNING TO WONDER IF ALL OF OUR DATES WILL BE AT SALOONS.
I JUST WANT TO TAKE YOU WHERE MY KIND OF MUSIC IS.
YOU WANT TO GO TO THE SYMPHONY SOMETIME, MISS BABE KNOW HOW TO GET ME TICKETS.
OH, NO. THIS IS DEFINITELY MORE FUN THAN THE SYMPHONY.
I LIKE THIS JUST FINE.
SO WE GONNA BE HAVIN' MORE DATES?
THAT'S SURELY UP TO YOU...
...BUT YOU'RE DOING FINE SO FAR.

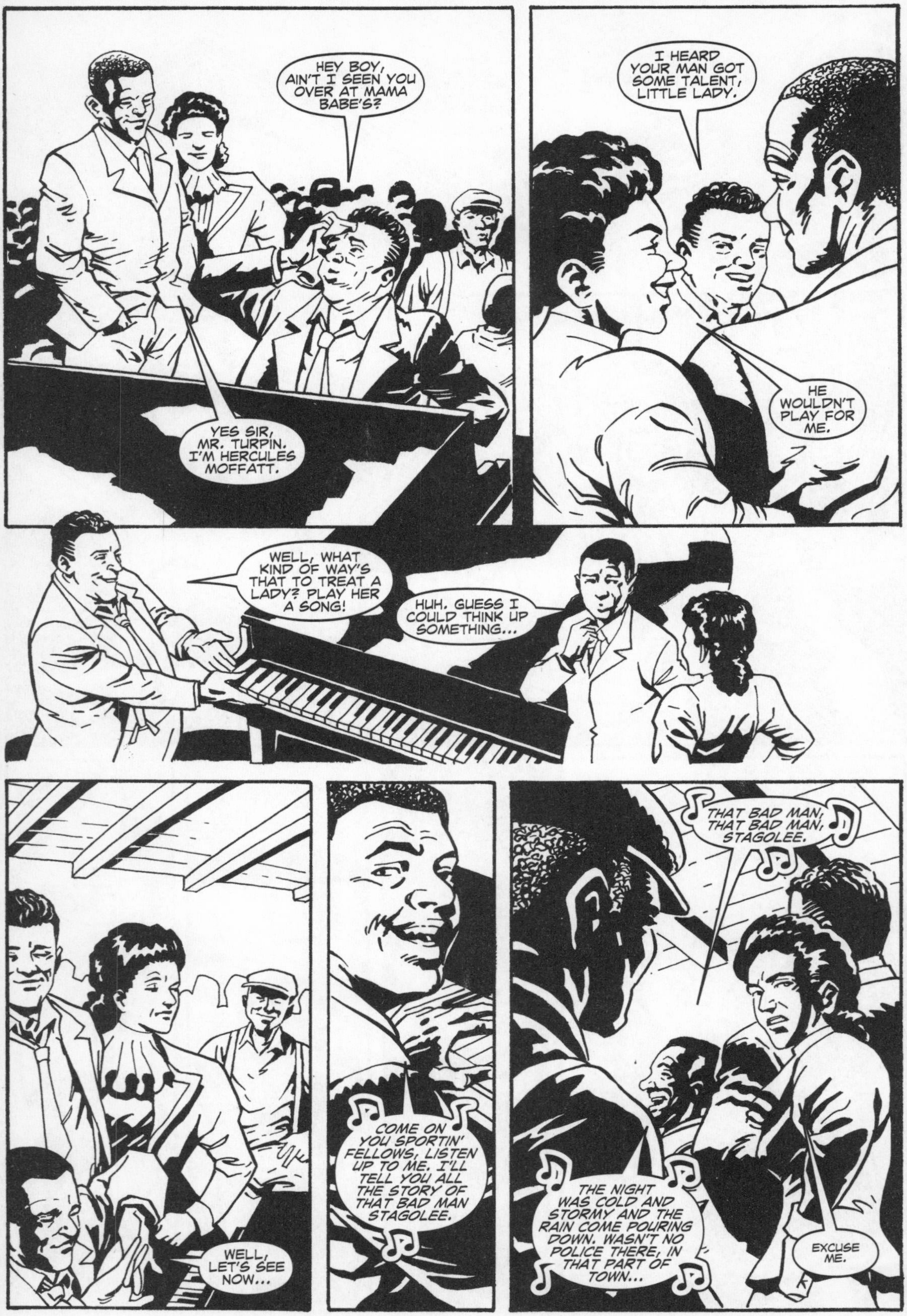
HEY BOY, AIN'T I SEEN YOU OVER AT MAMA BABE'S?
YES SIR, MR. TURPIN. I'M HERCULES MOFFATT.
I HEARD YOUR MAN GOT SOME TALENT, LITTLE LADY.
HE WOULDN'T PLAY FOR ME.
WELL, WHAT KIND OF WAY'S THAT TO TREAT A LADY? PLAY HER A SONG!
HUH. GUESS I COULD THINK UP SOMETHING...
WELL, LET'S SEE NOW...
COME ON YOU SPORTIN' FELLOWS, LISTEN UP TO ME. I'LL TELL YOU ALL THE STORY OF THAT BAD MAN STAGOLEE.
THAT BAD MAN, THAT BAD MAN, STAGOLEE.
THE NIGHT WAS COLD AND STORMY AND THE RAIN COME POURING DOWN. WASN'T NO POLICE THERE, IN THAT PART OF TOWN...
EXCUSE ME.

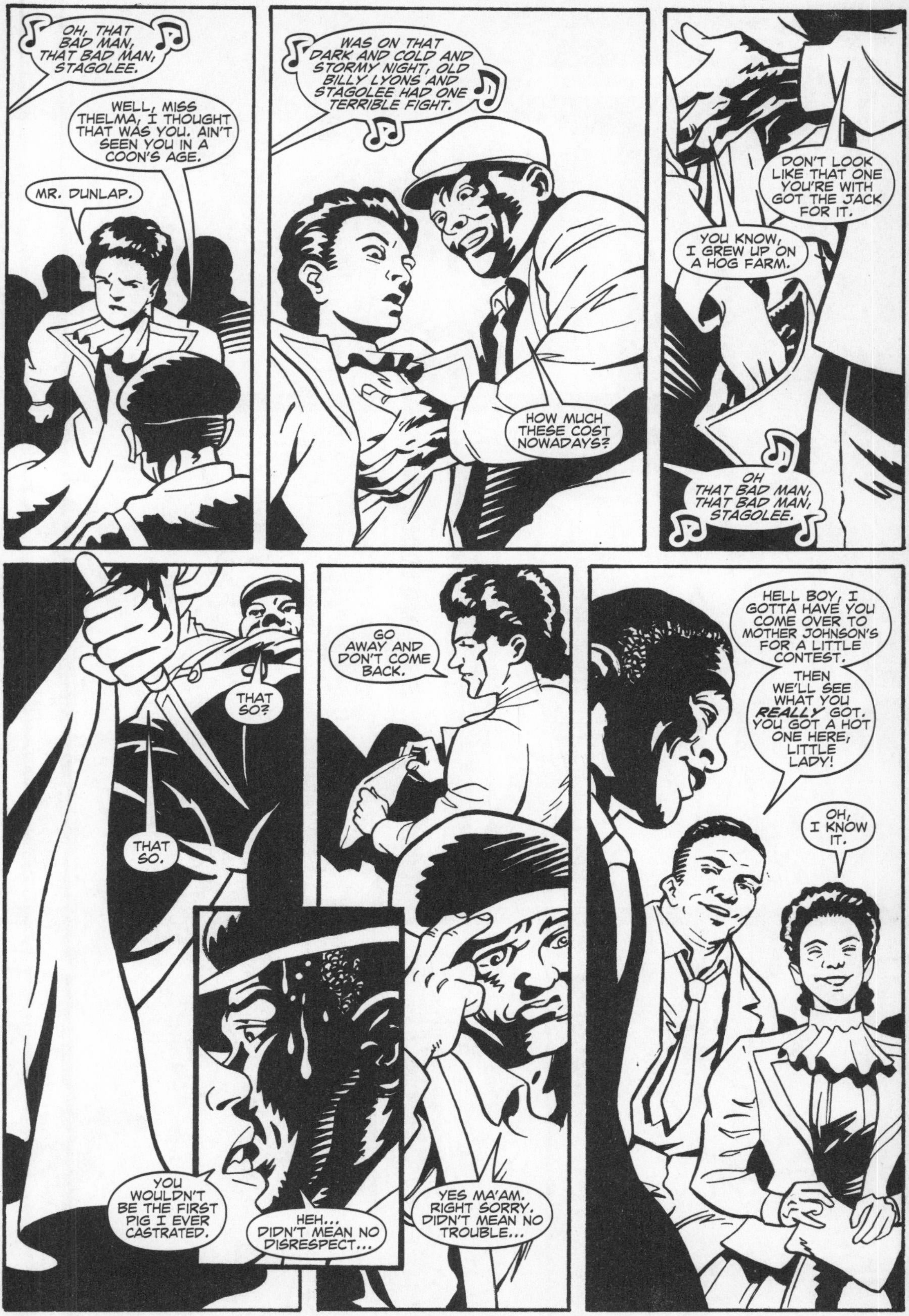
OH, THAT BAD MAN, THAT BAD MAN, STAGOLEE.
WELL, MISS THELMA, I THOUGHT THAT WAS YOU. AIN'T SEEN YOU IN A COON'S AGE.
MR. DUNLAP.
WAS ON THAT DARK AND COLD AND STORMY NIGHT, OLD BILLY LYONS AND STAGOLEE HAD ONE TERRIBLE FIGHT.
HOW MUCH THESE COST NOWADAYS?
DON'T LOOK LIKE THAT ONE YOU'RE WITH GOT THE JACK FOR IT.
YOU KNOW, I GREW UP ON A HOG FARM.
OH THAT BAD MAN, THAT BAD MAN, STAGOLEE.
THAT SO?
THAT SO.
YOU WOULDN'T BE THE FIRST PIG I EVER CASTRATED.
HEH... DIDN'T MEAN NO DISRESPECT...
GO AWAY AND DON'T COME BACK.
YES MA'AM. RIGHT SORRY. DIDN'T MEAN NO TROUBLE...
HELL BOY, I GOTTA HAVE YOU COME OVER TO MOTHER JOHNSON'S FOR A LITTLE CONTEST.
THEN WE'LL SEE WHAT YOU REALLY GOT. YOU GOT A HOT ONE HERE, LITTLE LADY!
OH, I KNOW IT.

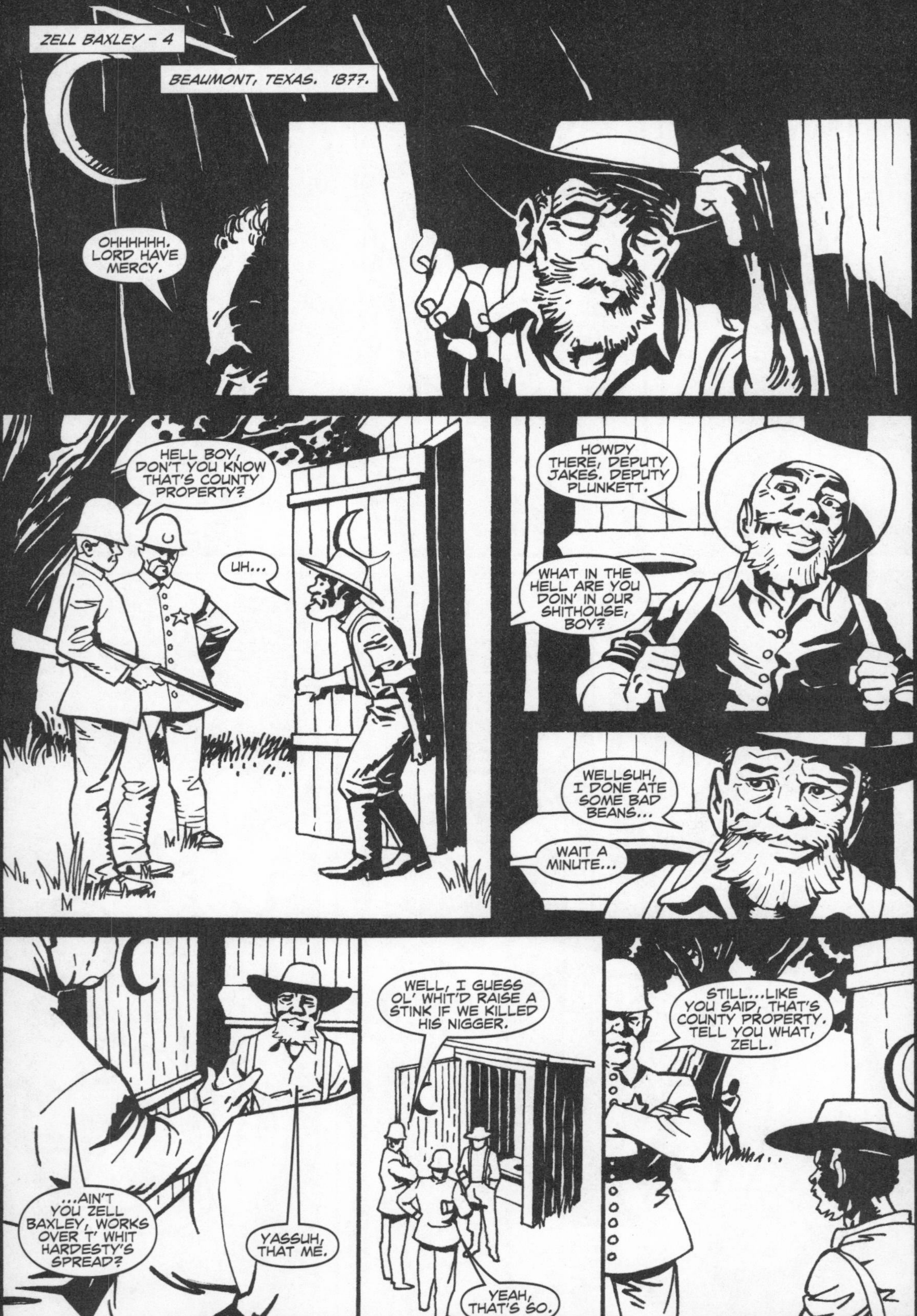
ZELL BAXLEY – 4
BEAUMONT, TEXAS. 1877.
OHHHHHH. LORD HAVE MERCY.
HELL BOY, DON'T YOU KNOW THAT'S COUNTY PROPERTY?
UH...
HOWDY THERE, DEPUTY JAKES. DEPUTY PLUNKETT.
WHAT IN THE HELL ARE YOU DOIN' IN OUR SHITHOUSE, BOY?
WELLSUH, I DONE ATE SOME BAD BEANS...
WAIT A MINUTE...
...AIN'T YOU ZELL BAXLEY, WORKS OVER T' WHIT HARDESTY'S SPREAD?
YASSUH, THAT ME.
WELL, I GUESS OL' WHIT'D RAISE A STINK IF WE KILLED HIS NIGGER.
YEAH, THAT'S SO.
STILL...LIKE YOU SAID, THAT'S COUNTY PROPERTY. TELL YOU WHAT, ZELL.

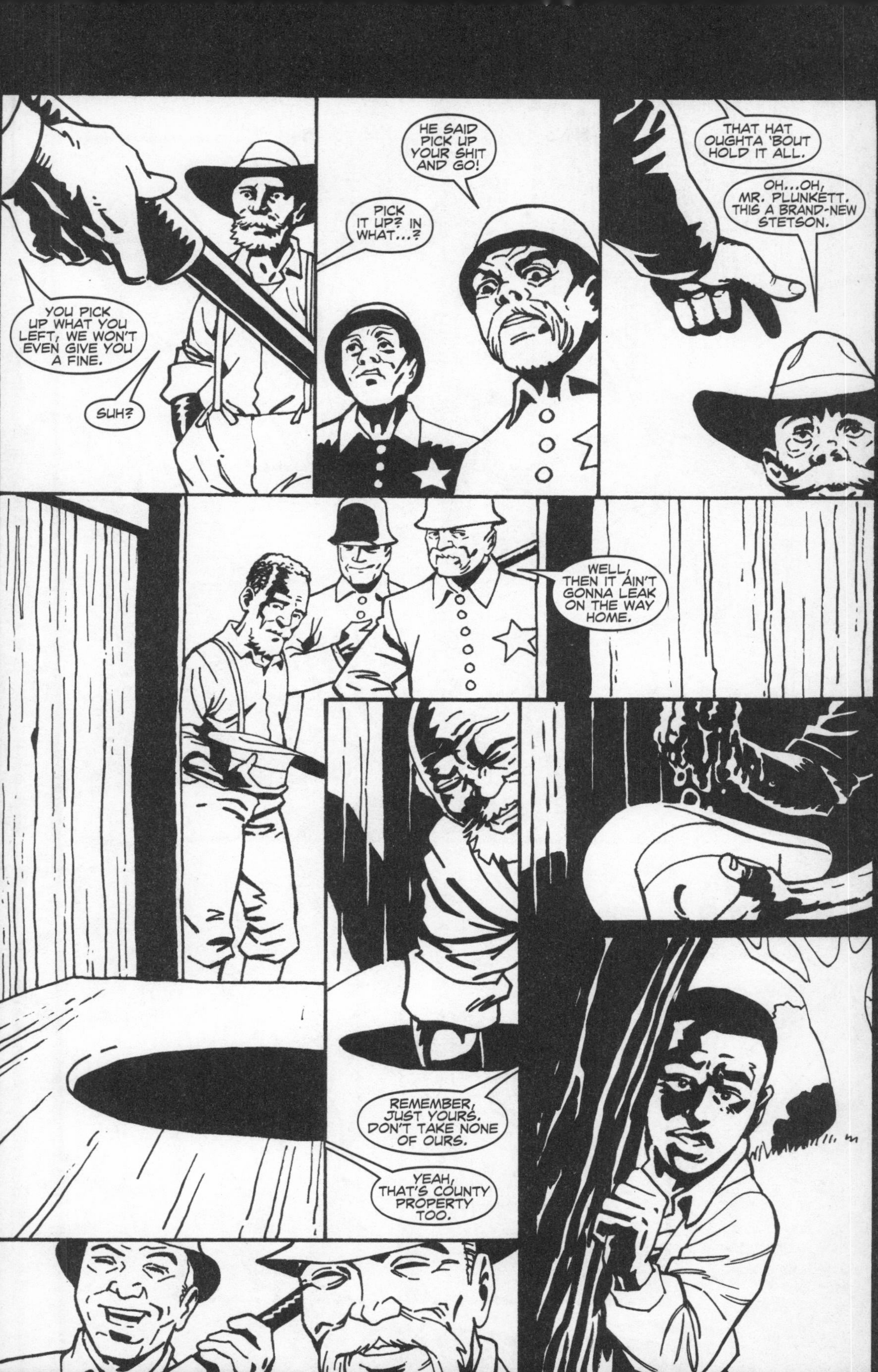
YOU PICK UP WHAT YOU LEFT, WE WON'T EVEN GIVE YOU A FINE.
SUH?
PICK IT UP? IN WHAT...?
HE SAID PICK UP YOUR SHIT AND GO!
THAT HAT OUGHTA 'BOUT HOLD IT ALL.
OH...OH, MR. PLUNKETT. THIS A BRAND-NEW STETSON.
WELL, THEN IT AIN'T GONNA LEAK ON THE WAY HOME.
REMEMBER, JUST YOURS. DON'T TAKE NONE OF OURS.
YEAH, THAT'S COUNTY PROPERTY TOO.

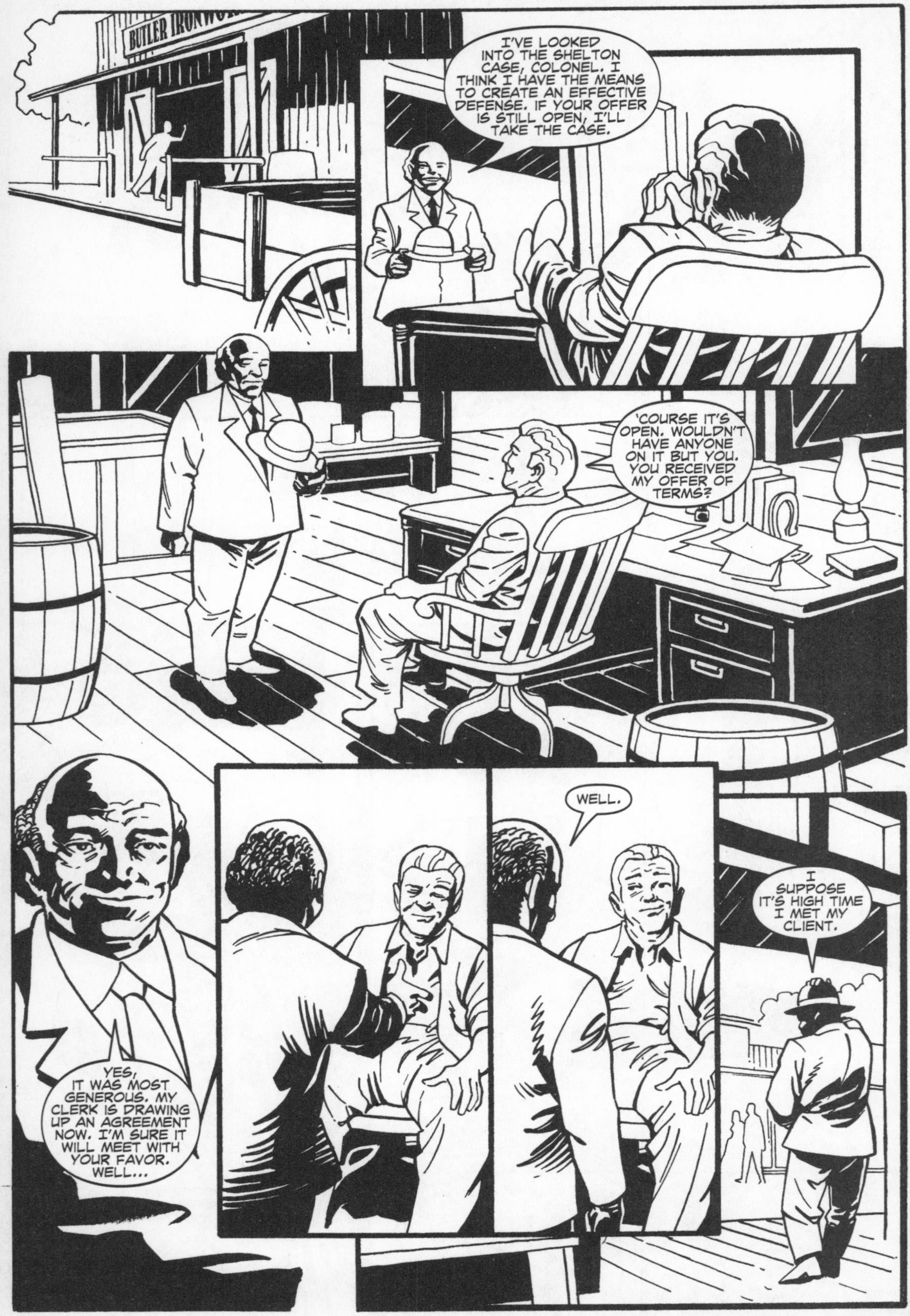
BUTLER IRONWO
I'VE LOOKED INTO THE SHELTON CASE, COLONEL. I THINK I HAVE THE MEANS TO CREATE AN EFFECTIVE DEFENSE. IF YOUR OFFER IS STILL OPEN, I'LL TAKE THE CASE.
'COURSE IT'S OPEN. WOULDN'T HAVE ANYONE ON IT BUT YOU. YOU RECEIVED MY OFFER OF TERMS?
YES, IT WAS MOST GENEROUS. MY CLERK IS DRAWING UP AN AGREEMENT NOW. I'M SURE IT WILL MEET WITH YOUR FAVOR. WELL...
WELL.
I SUPPOSE IT'S HIGH TIME I MET MY CLIENT.

PART TWO

,The GUN

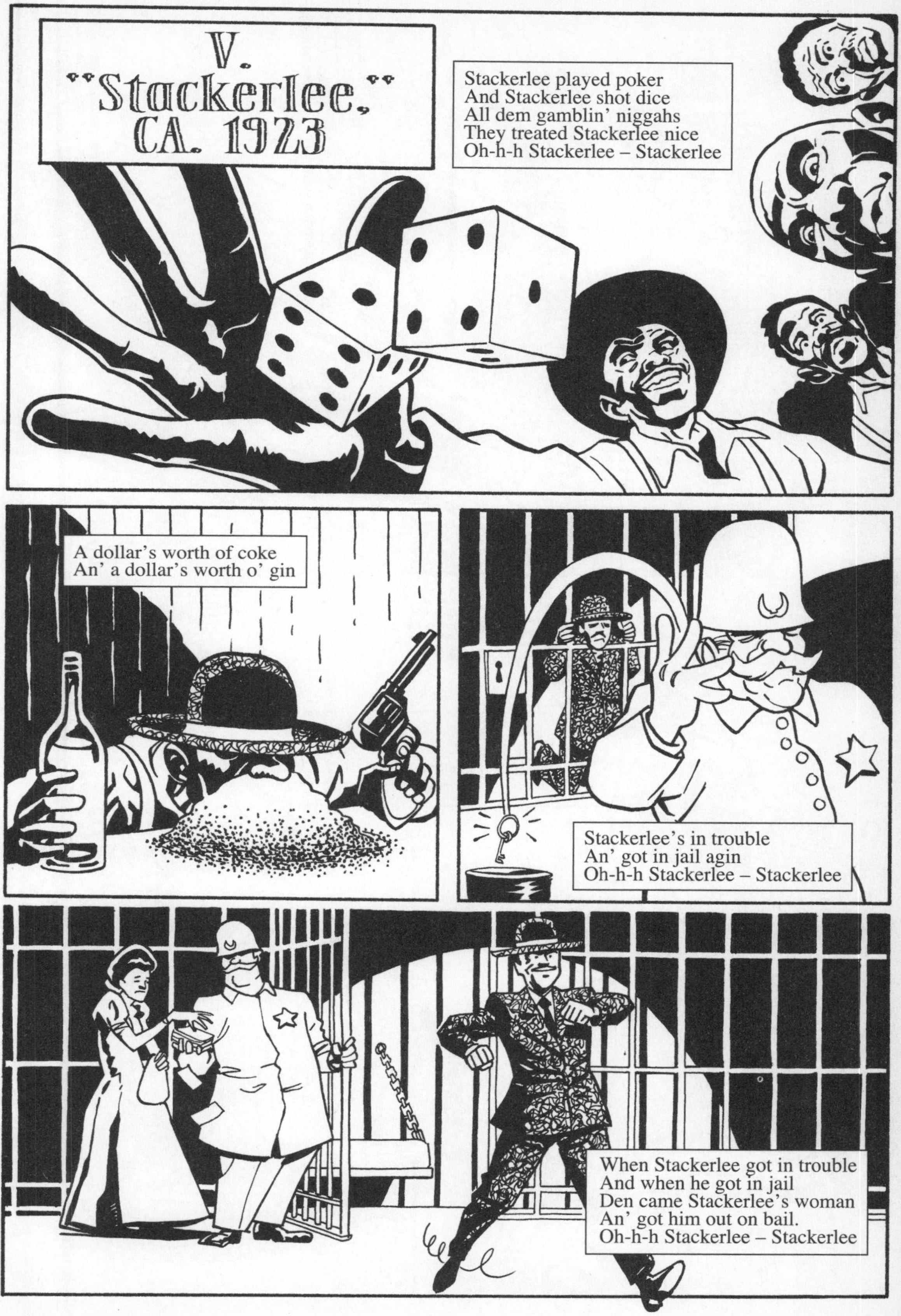
V.
"Stackerlee,"
CA. 1923
Stackerlee played poker
And Stackerlee shot dice
All dem gamblin' niggahs
They treated Stackerlee nice
Oh-h-h Stackerlee – Stackerlee
A dollar's worth of coke
An' a dollar's worth o' gin
Stackerlee's in trouble
An' got in jail agin
Oh-h-h Stackerlee – Stackerlee
When Stackerlee got in trouble
And when he got in jail
Den came Stackerlee's woman
An' got him out on bail.
Oh-h-h Stackerlee – Stackerlee

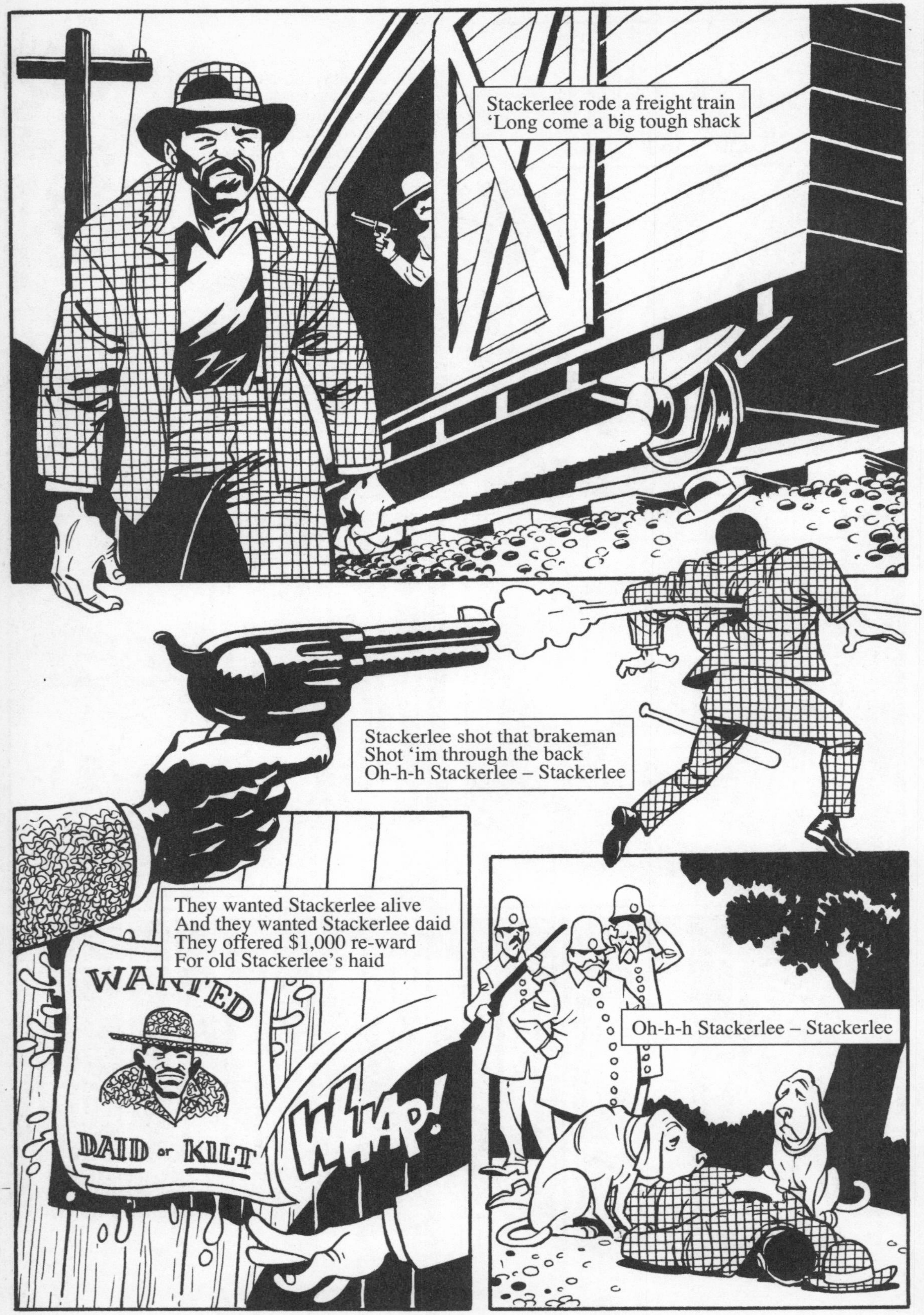

Stackerlee rode a freight train
'Long come a big tough shack
Stackerlee shot that brakeman
Shot 'im through the back
Oh-h-h Stackerlee – Stackerlee
They wanted Stackerlee alive
And they wanted Stackerlee daid
They offered $1,000 re-ward
For old Stackerlee's haid
WANTED
DAID or KILT
WHAP!
Oh-h-h Stackerlee – Stackerlee

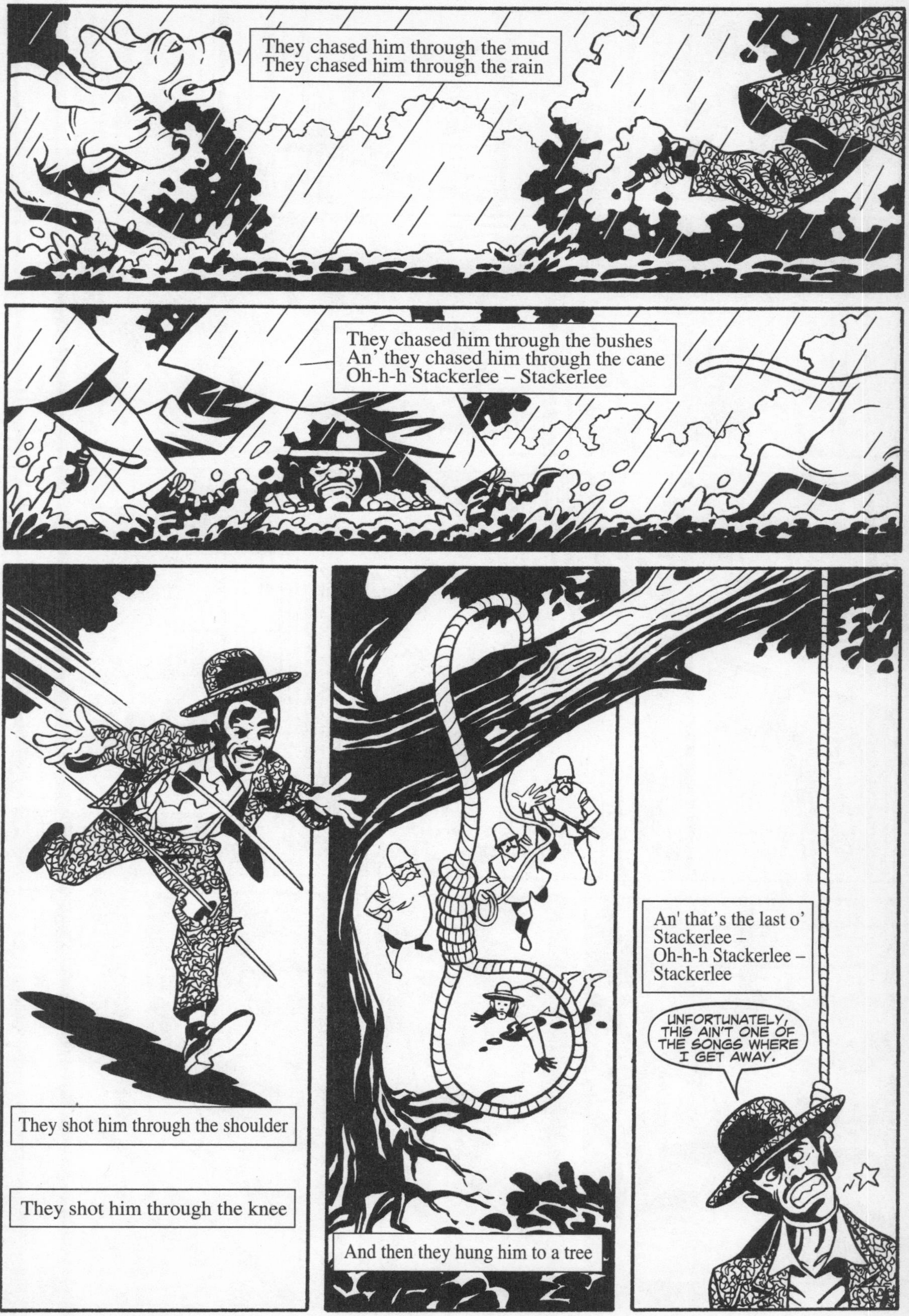
They chased him through the mud
They chased him through the rain
They chased him through the bushes
An' they chased him through the cane
Oh-h-h Stackerlee – Stackerlee
They shot him through the shoulder
They shot him through the knee
And then they hung him to a tree
An' that's the last o' Stackerlee –
Oh-h-h Stackerlee –
Stackerlee
UNFORTUNATELY, THIS AIN'T ONE OF THE SONGS WHERE I GET AWAY.

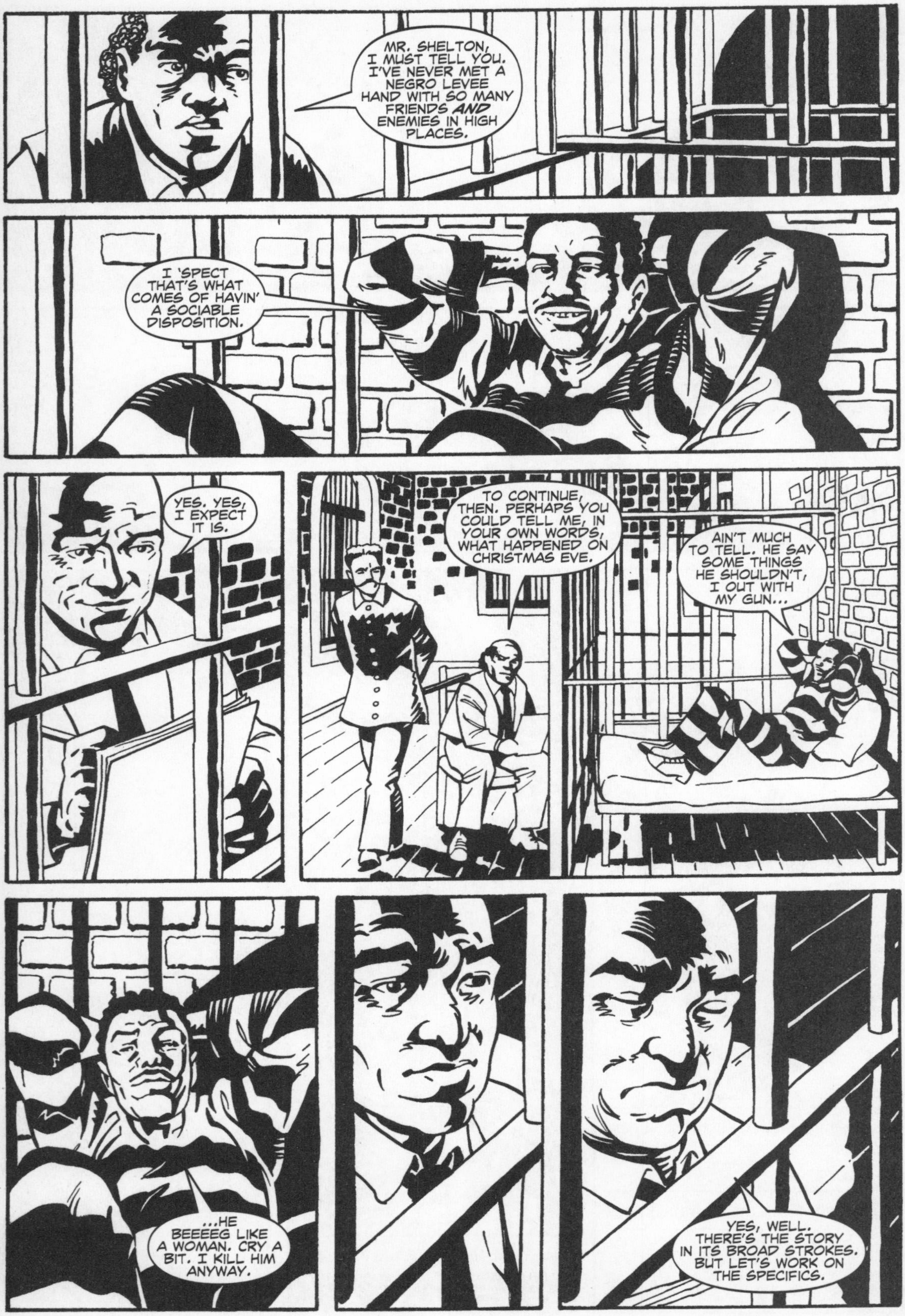
MR. SHELTON, I MUST TELL YOU. I'VE NEVER MET A NEGRO LEVEE HAND WITH SO MANY FRIENDS AND ENEMIES IN HIGH PLACES.
I 'SPECT THAT'S WHAT COMES OF HAVIN' A SOCIABLE DISPOSITION.
YES. YES, I EXPECT IT IS.
TO CONTINUE, THEN. PERHAPS YOU COULD TELL ME, IN YOUR OWN WORDS, WHAT HAPPENED ON CHRISTMAS EVE.
AIN'T MUCH TO TELL. HE SAY SOME THINGS HE SHOULDN'T, I OUT WITH MY GUN...
...HE BEEEEG LIKE A WOMAN. CRY A BIT. I KILL HIM ANYWAY.
YES, WELL. THERE'S THE STORY IN ITS BROAD STROKES. BUT LET'S WORK ON THE SPECIFICS.

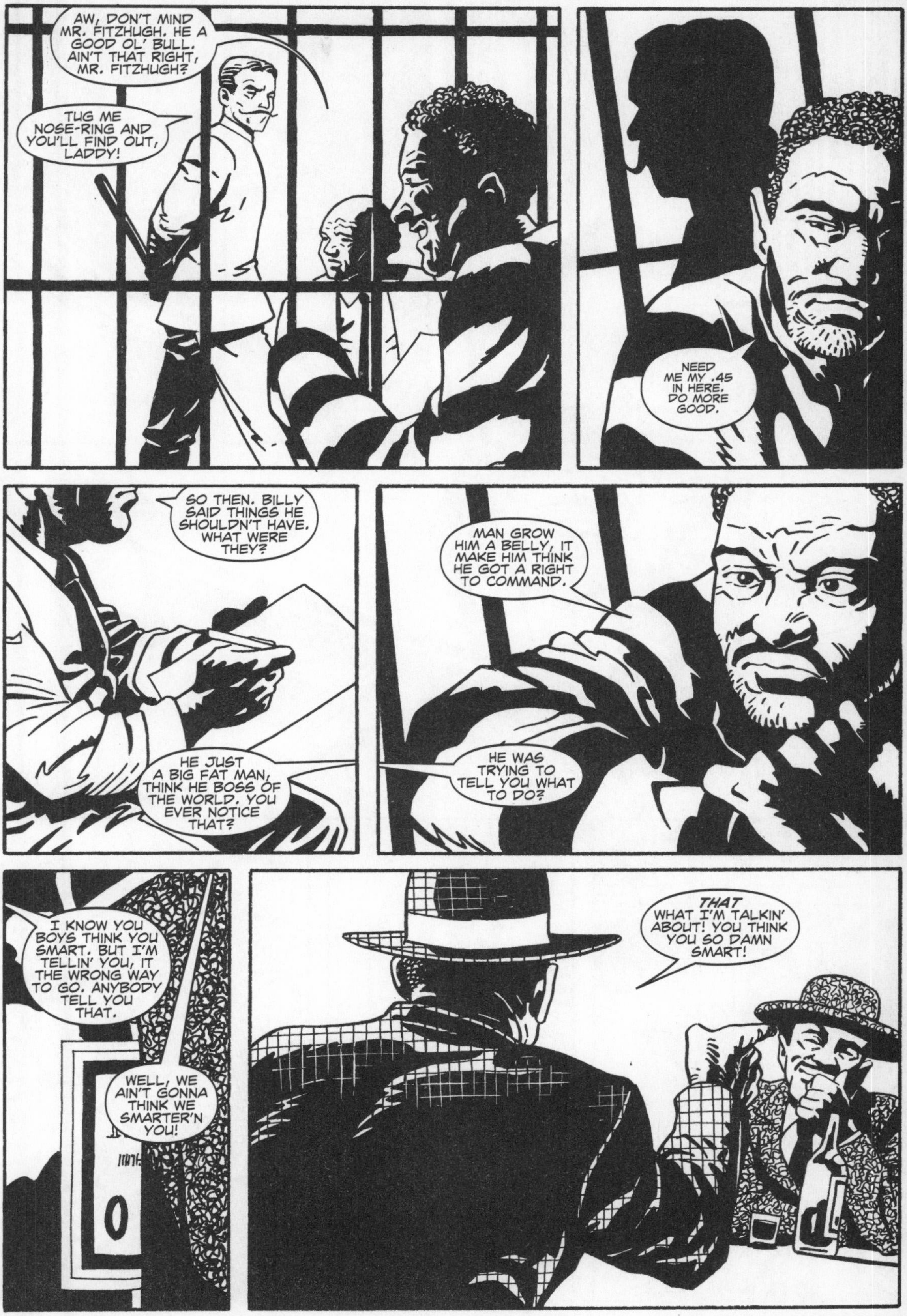
AW, DON'T MIND MR. FITZHUGH. HE A GOOD OL' BULL. AIN'T THAT RIGHT, MR. FITZHUGH?
TUG ME NOSE-RING AND YOU'LL FIND OUT, LADDY!
NEED ME MY .45 IN HERE. DO MORE GOOD.
SO THEN. BILLY SAID THINGS HE SHOULDN'T HAVE. WHAT WERE THEY?
MAN GROW HIM A BELLY, IT MAKE HIM THINK HE GOT A RIGHT TO COMMAND.
HE JUST A BIG FAT MAN, THINK HE BOSS OF THE WORLD. YOU EVER NOTICE THAT?
HE WAS TRYING TO TELL YOU WHAT TO DO?
I KNOW YOU BOYS THINK YOU SMART. BUT I'M TELLIN' YOU, IT THE WRONG WAY TO GO. ANYBODY TELL YOU THAT.
WELL, WE AIN'T GONNA THINK WE SMARTER'N YOU!
THAT WHAT I'M TALKIN' ABOUT! YOU THINK YOU SO DAMN SMART!

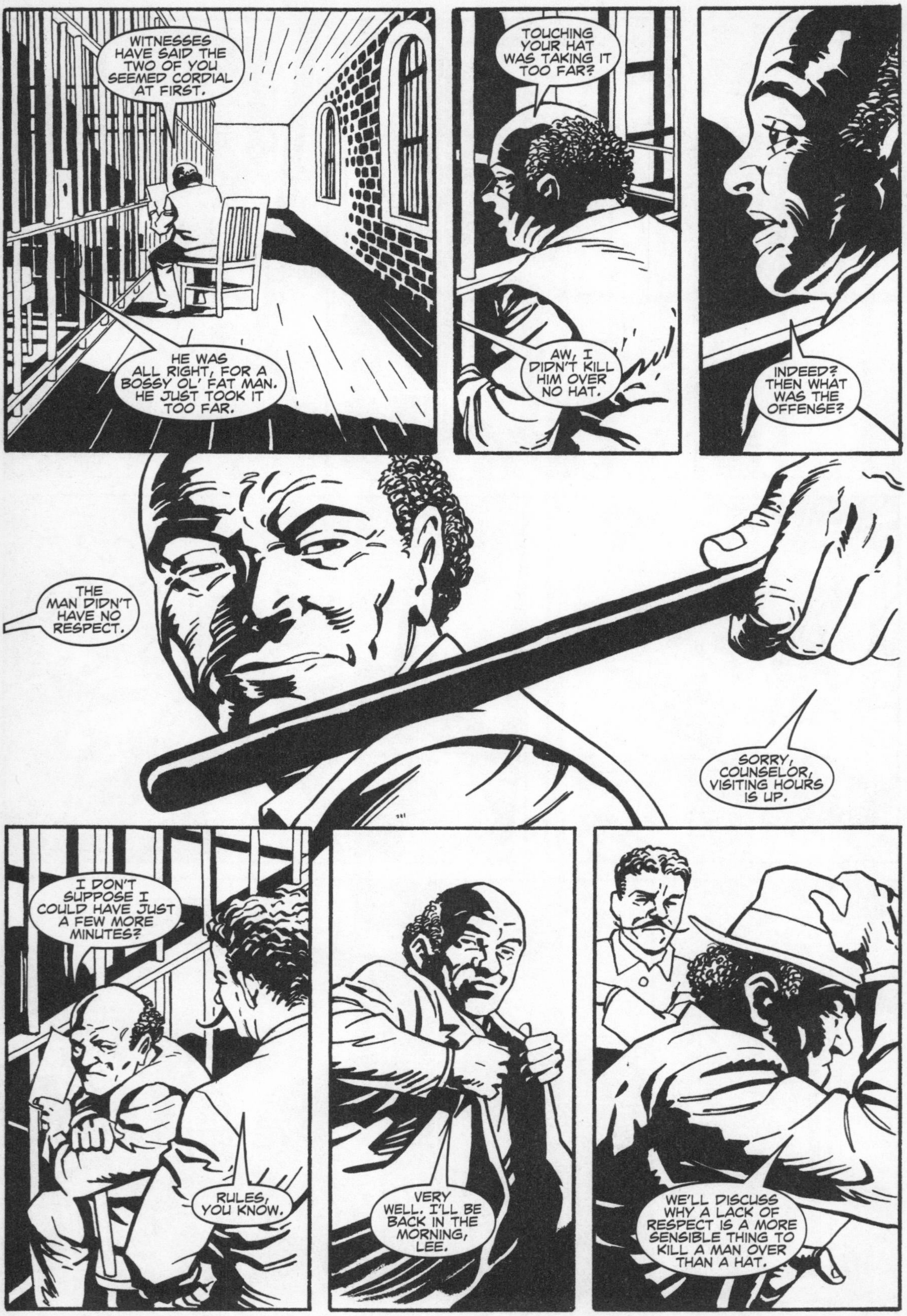
WITNESSES HAVE SAID THE TWO OF YOU SEEMED CORDIAL AT FIRST.
HE WAS ALL RIGHT, FOR A BOSSY OL' FAT MAN. HE JUST TOOK IT TOO FAR.
TOUCHING YOUR HAT WAS TAKING IT TOO FAR?
AW, I DIDN'T KILL HIM OVER NO HAT.
INDEED? THEN WHAT WAS THE OFFENSE?
THE MAN DIDN'T HAVE NO RESPECT.
SORRY, COUNSELOR, VISITING HOURS IS UP.
I DON'T SUPPOSE I COULD HAVE JUST A FEW MORE MINUTES?
RULES, YOU KNOW.
VERY WELL. I'LL BE BACK IN THE MORNING, LEE.
WE'LL DISCUSS WHY A LACK OF RESPECT IS A MORE SENSIBLE THING TO KILL A MAN OVER THAN A HAT.

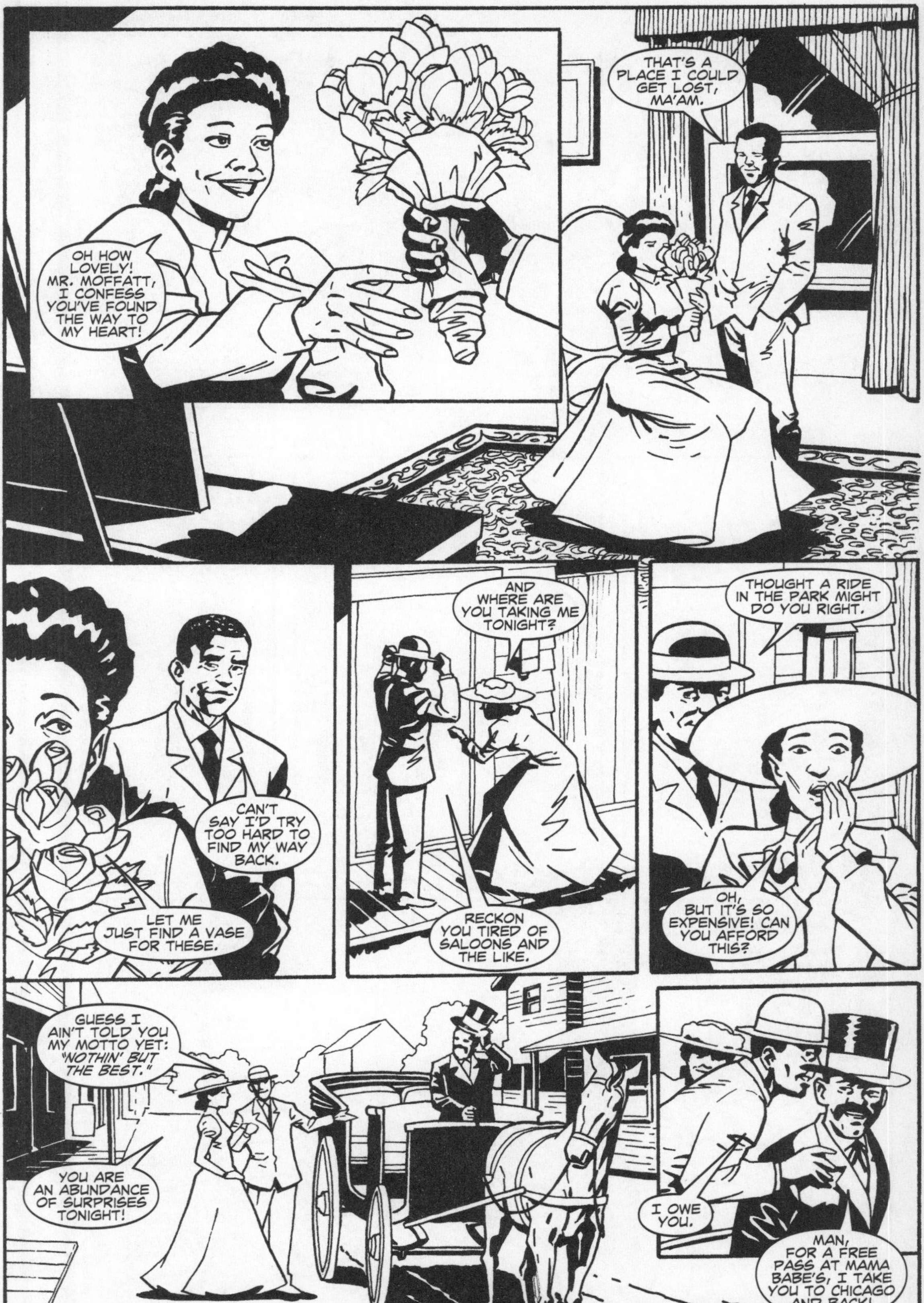
OH HOW LOVELY! MR. MOFFATT, I CONFESS YOU'VE FOUND THE WAY TO MY HEART!
THAT'S A PLACE I COULD GET LOST, MA'AM.
CAN'T SAY I'D TRY TOO HARD TO FIND MY WAY BACK.
LET ME JUST FIND A VASE FOR THESE.
AND WHERE ARE YOU TAKING ME TONIGHT?
RECKON YOU TIRED OF SALOONS AND THE LIKE.
THOUGHT A RIDE IN THE PARK MIGHT DO YOU RIGHT.
OH, BUT IT'S SO EXPENSIVE! CAN YOU AFFORD THIS?
GUESS I AIN'T TOLD YOU MY MOTTO YET: *"NOTHIN' BUT THE BEST."*
YOU ARE AN ABUNDANCE OF SURPRISES TONIGHT!
I OWE YOU.
MAN, FOR A FREE PASS AT MAMA BABE'S, I TAKE YOU TO CHICAGO AND BACK!

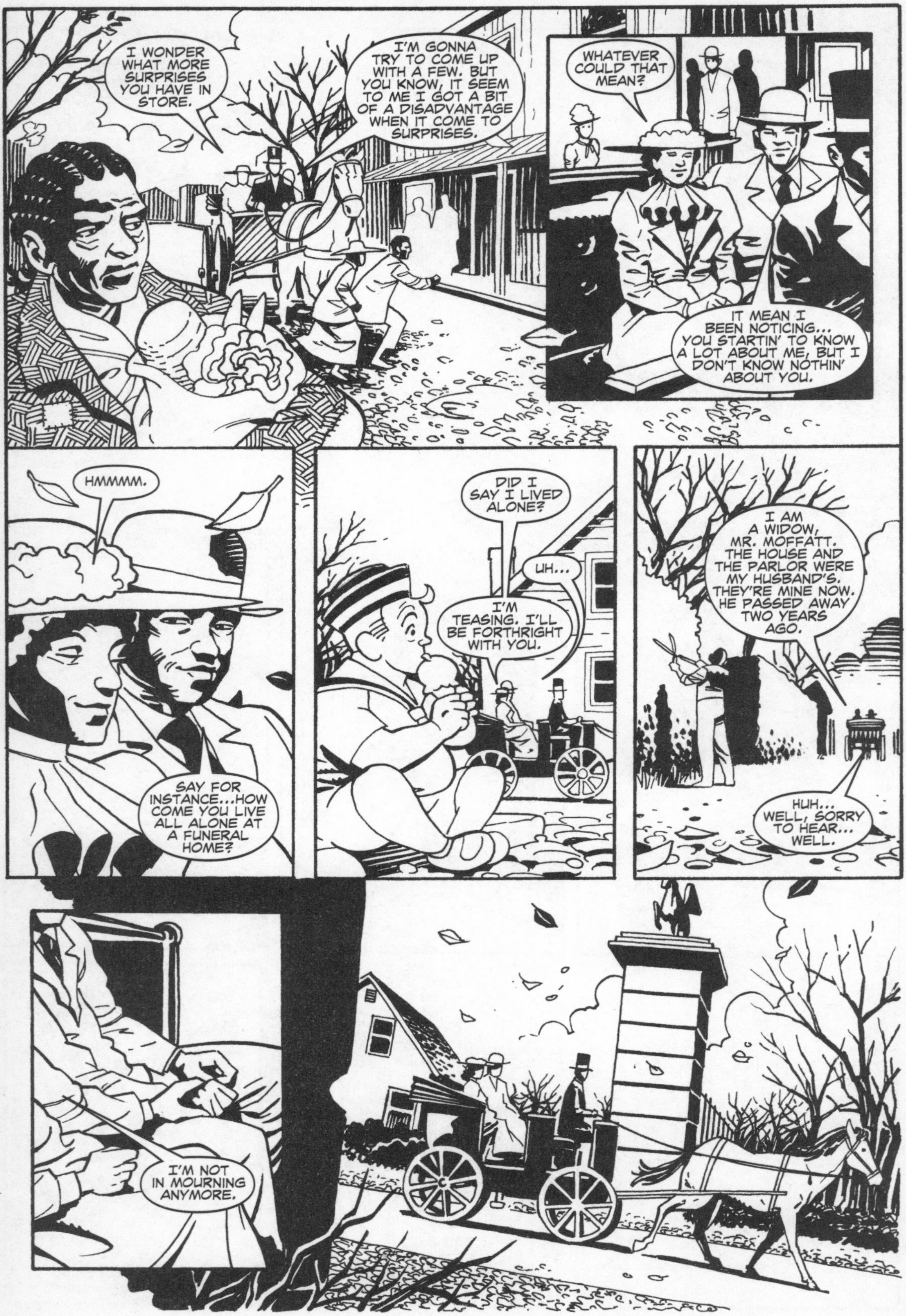
I WONDER WHAT MORE SURPRISES YOU HAVE IN STORE.
I'M GONNA TRY TO COME UP WITH A FEW. BUT YOU KNOW, IT SEEM TO ME I GOT A BIT OF A DISADVANTAGE WHEN IT COME TO SURPRISES.
WHATEVER COULD THAT MEAN?
IT MEAN I BEEN NOTICING... YOU STARTIN' TO KNOW A LOT ABOUT ME, BUT I DON'T KNOW NOTHIN' ABOUT YOU.
HMMMM.
SAY FOR INSTANCE...HOW COME YOU LIVE ALL ALONE AT A FUNERAL HOME?
DID I SAY I LIVED ALONE?
UH...
I'M TEASING. I'LL BE FORTHRIGHT WITH YOU.
I AM A WIDOW, MR. MOFFATT. THE HOUSE AND THE PARLOR WERE MY HUSBAND'S. THEY'RE MINE NOW. HE PASSED AWAY TWO YEARS AGO.
HUH... WELL, SORRY TO HEAR... WELL.
I'M NOT IN MOURNING ANYMORE.

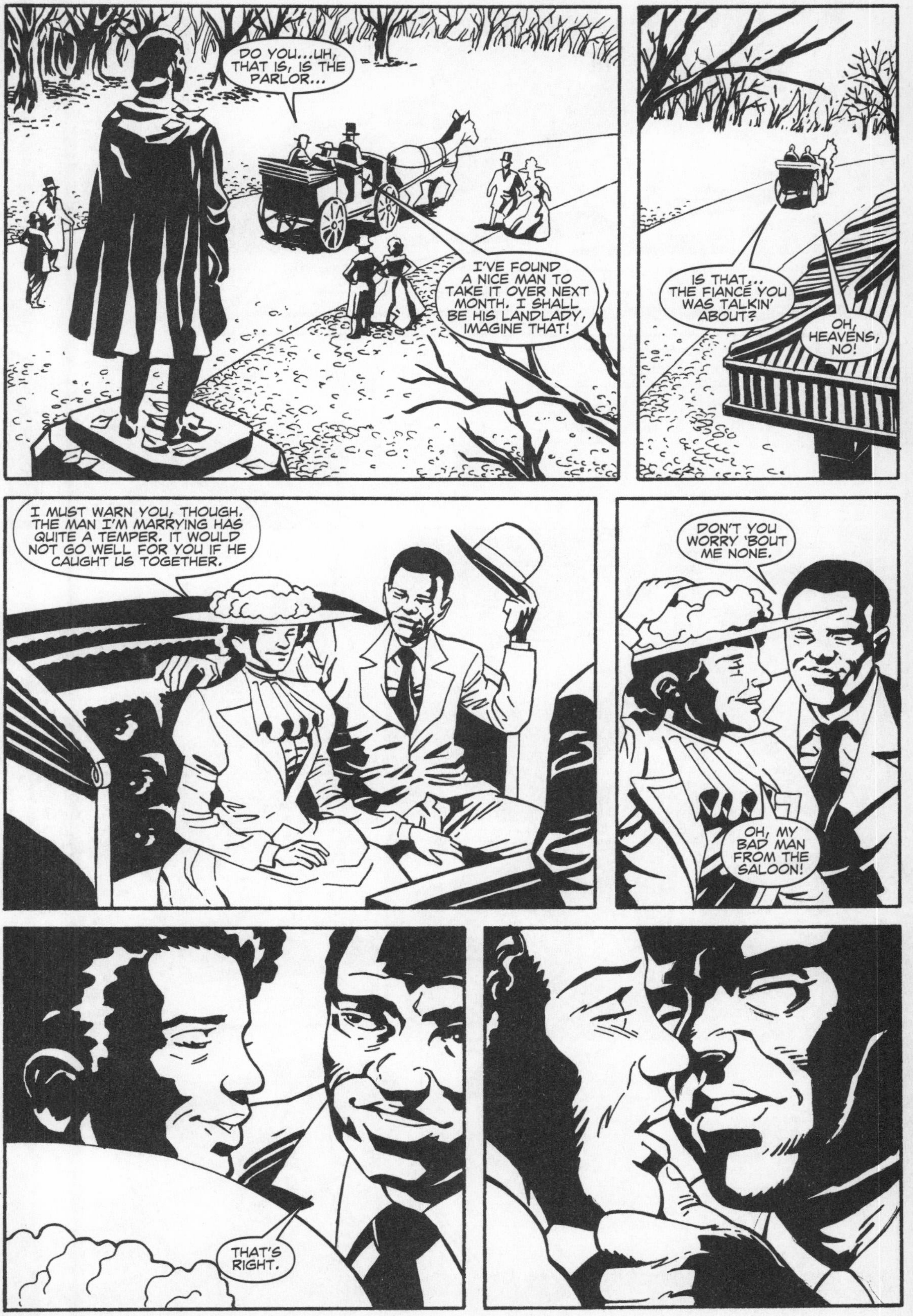
DO YOU...UH, THAT IS, IS THE PARLOR...
I'VE FOUND A NICE MAN TO TAKE IT OVER NEXT MONTH. I SHALL BE HIS LANDLADY, IMAGINE THAT!
IS THAT... THE FIANCÉ YOU WAS TALKIN' ABOUT?
OH, HEAVENS, NO!
I MUST WARN YOU, THOUGH. THE MAN I'M MARRYING HAS QUITE A TEMPER. IT WOULD NOT GO WELL FOR YOU IF HE CAUGHT US TOGETHER.
DON'T YOU WORRY 'BOUT ME NONE.
OH, MY BAD MAN FROM THE SALOON!
THAT'S RIGHT.

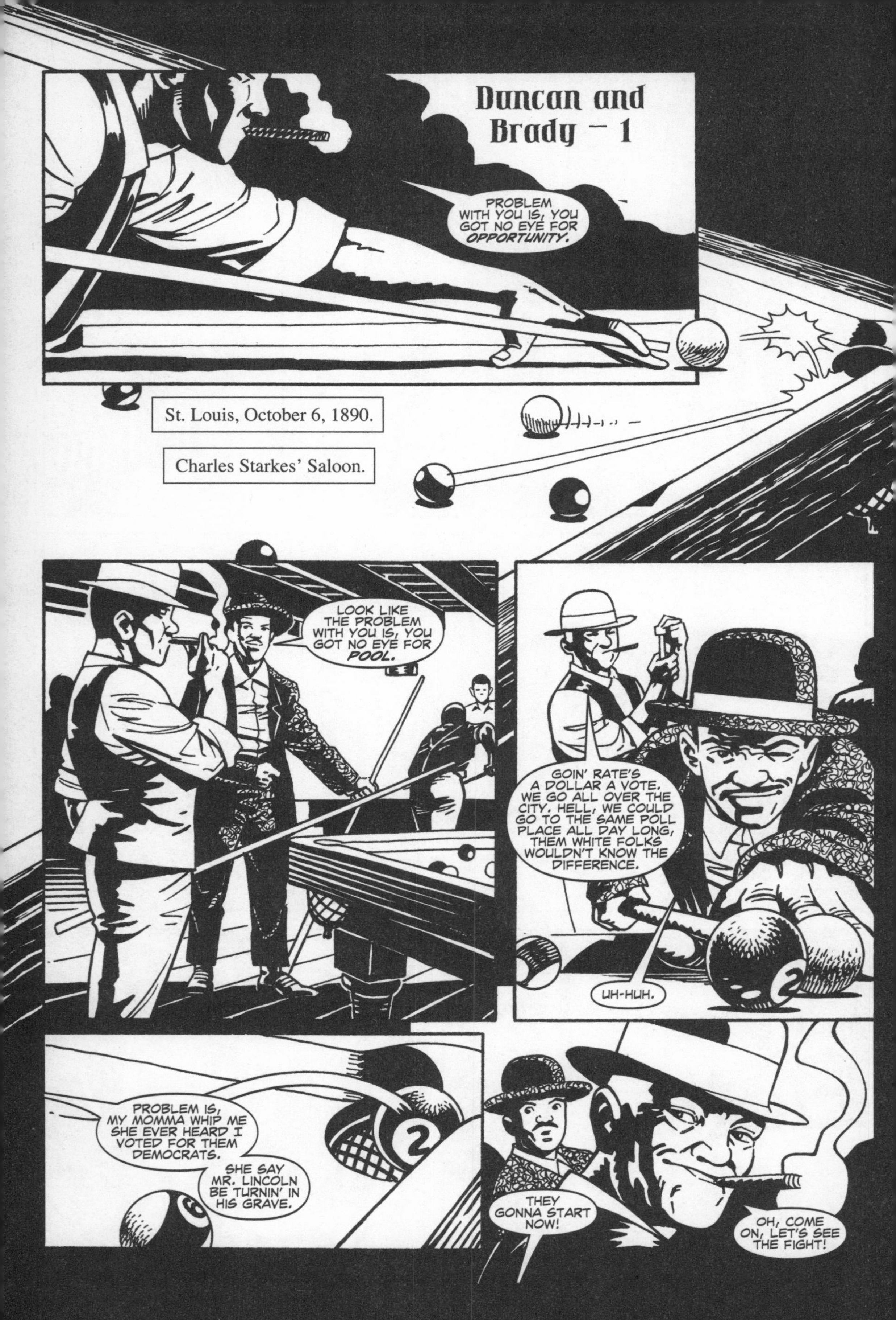
Duncan and Brady – 1
PROBLEM WITH YOU IS, YOU GOT NO EYE FOR OPPORTUNITY.
St. Louis, October 6, 1890.
Charles Starkes' Saloon.
LOOK LIKE THE PROBLEM WITH YOU IS, YOU GOT NO EYE FOR POOL.
GOIN' RATE'S A DOLLAR A VOTE. WE GO ALL OVER THE CITY. HELL, WE COULD GO TO THE SAME POLL PLACE ALL DAY LONG, THEM WHITE FOLKS WOULDN'T KNOW THE DIFFERENCE.
UH-HUH.
PROBLEM IS, MY MOMMA WHIP ME SHE EVER HEARD I VOTED FOR THEM DEMOCRATS.
SHE SAY MR. LINCOLN BE TURNIN' IN HIS GRAVE.
THEY GONNA START NOW!
OH, COME ON, LET'S SEE THE FIGHT!

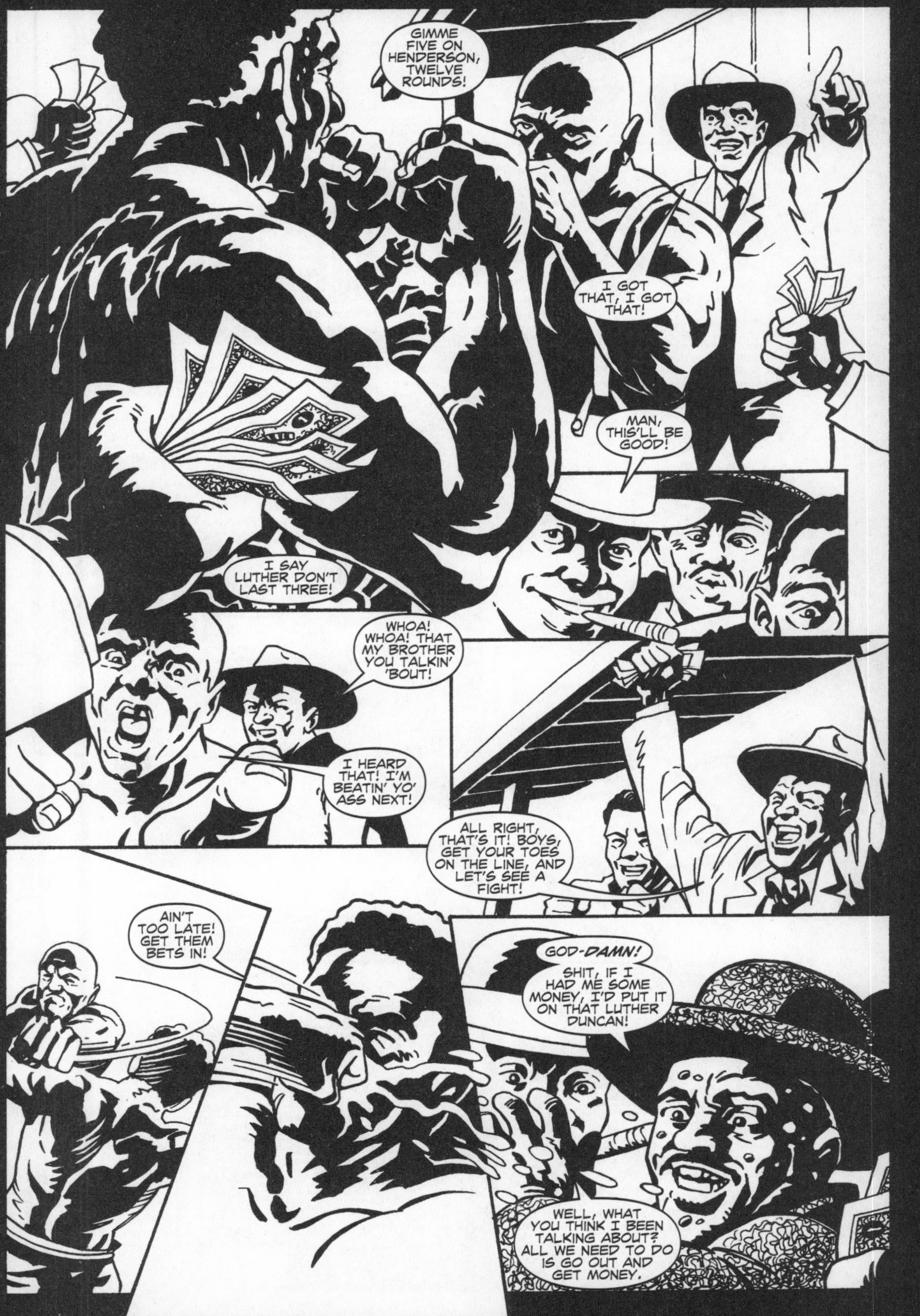
GIMME FIVE ON HENDERSON, TWELVE ROUNDS!
I GOT THAT, I GOT THAT!
MAN, THIS'LL BE GOOD!
I SAY LUTHER DON'T LAST THREE!
WHOA! WHOA! THAT MY BROTHER YOU TALKIN' 'BOUT!
I HEARD THAT! I'M BEATIN' YO' ASS NEXT!
ALL RIGHT, THAT'S IT! BOYS, GET YOUR TOES ON THE LINE, AND LET'S SEE A FIGHT!
AIN'T TOO LATE! GET THEM BETS IN!
GOD-*DAMN!*
SHIT, IF I HAD ME SOME MONEY, I'D PUT IT ON THAT LUTHER DUNCAN!
WELL, WHAT YOU THINK I BEEN TALKING ABOUT? ALL WE NEED TO DO IS GO OUT AND GET MONEY.

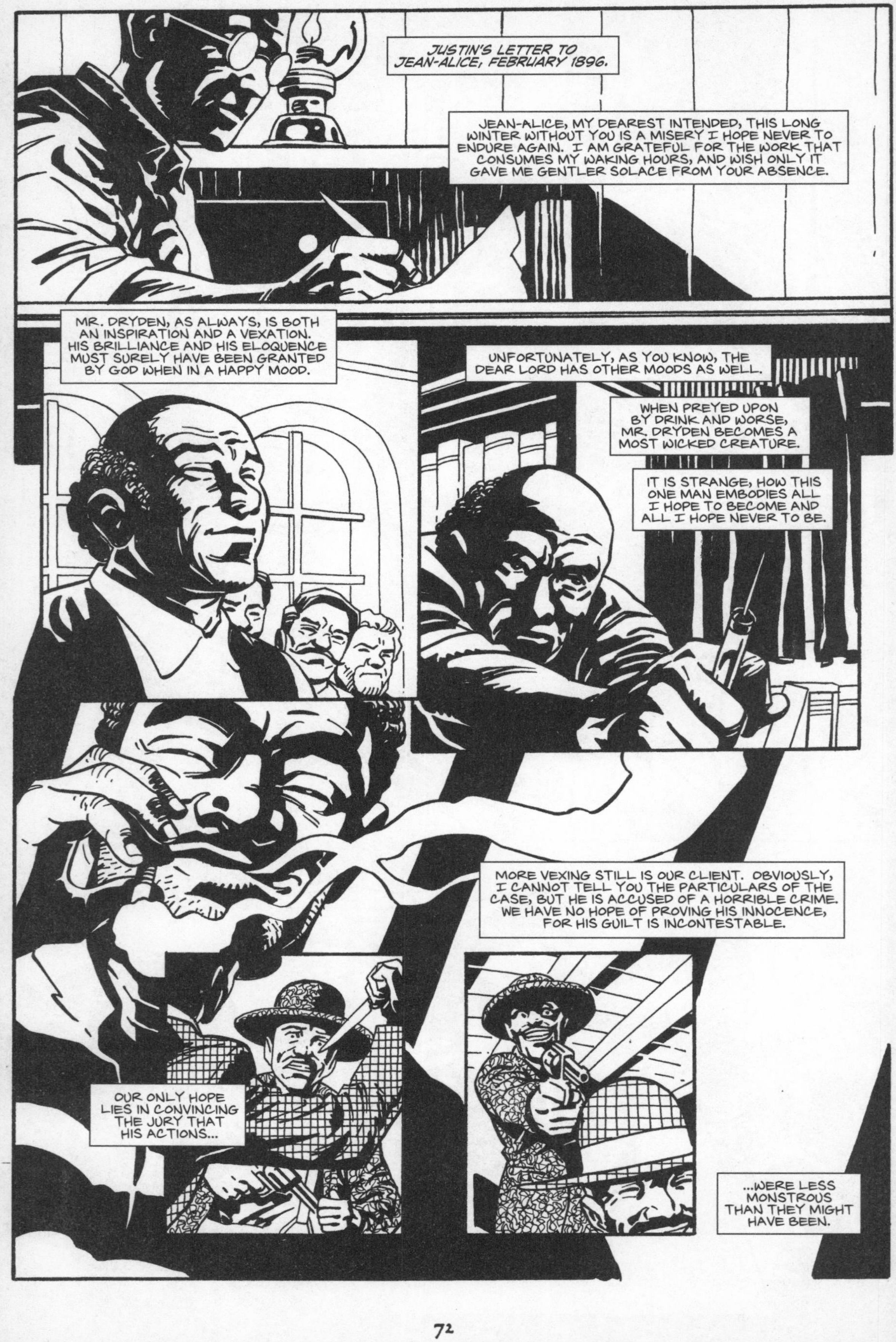
JUSTIN'S LETTER TO JEAN-ALICE, FEBRUARY 1896.
JEAN-ALICE, MY DEAREST INTENDED, THIS LONG WINTER WITHOUT YOU IS A MISERY I HOPE NEVER TO ENDURE AGAIN. I AM GRATEFUL FOR THE WORK THAT CONSUMES MY WAKING HOURS, AND WISH ONLY IT GAVE ME GENTLER SOLACE FROM YOUR ABSENCE.
MR. DRYDEN, AS ALWAYS, IS BOTH AN INSPIRATION AND A VEXATION. HIS BRILLIANCE AND HIS ELOQUENCE MUST SURELY HAVE BEEN GRANTED BY GOD WHEN IN A HAPPY MOOD.
UNFORTUNATELY, AS YOU KNOW, THE DEAR LORD HAS OTHER MOODS AS WELL.
WHEN PREYED UPON BY DRINK AND WORSE, MR. DRYDEN BECOMES A MOST WICKED CREATURE.
IT IS STRANGE, HOW THIS ONE MAN EMBODIES ALL I HOPE TO BECOME AND ALL I HOPE NEVER TO BE.
MORE VEXING STILL IS OUR CLIENT. OBVIOUSLY, I CANNOT TELL YOU THE PARTICULARS OF THE CASE, BUT HE IS ACCUSED OF A HORRIBLE CRIME. WE HAVE NO HOPE OF PROVING HIS INNOCENCE, FOR HIS GUILT IS INCONTESTABLE.
OUR ONLY HOPE LIES IN CONVINCING THE JURY THAT HIS ACTIONS...
...WERE LESS MONSTROUS THAN THEY MIGHT HAVE BEEN.

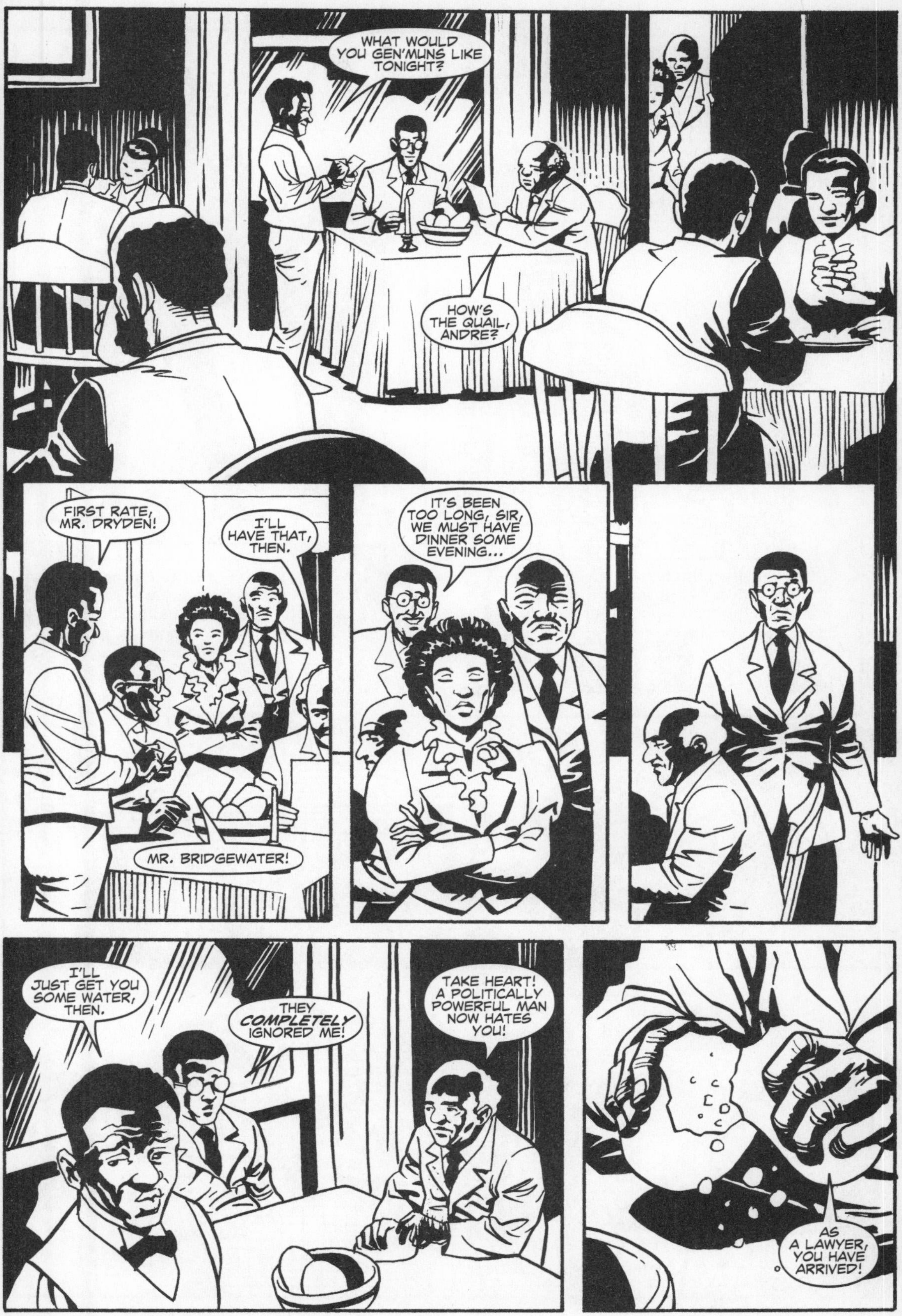
WHAT WOULD YOU GEN'MUNS LIKE TONIGHT?
HOW'S THE QUAIL, ANDRE?
FIRST RATE, MR. DRYDEN!
I'LL HAVE THAT, THEN.
MR. BRIDGEWATER!
IT'S BEEN TOO LONG, SIR, WE MUST HAVE DINNER SOME EVENING...
I'LL JUST GET YOU SOME WATER, THEN.
THEY *COMPLETELY* IGNORED ME!
TAKE HEART! A POLITICALLY POWERFUL MAN NOW HATES YOU!
AS A LAWYER, YOU HAVE ARRIVED!

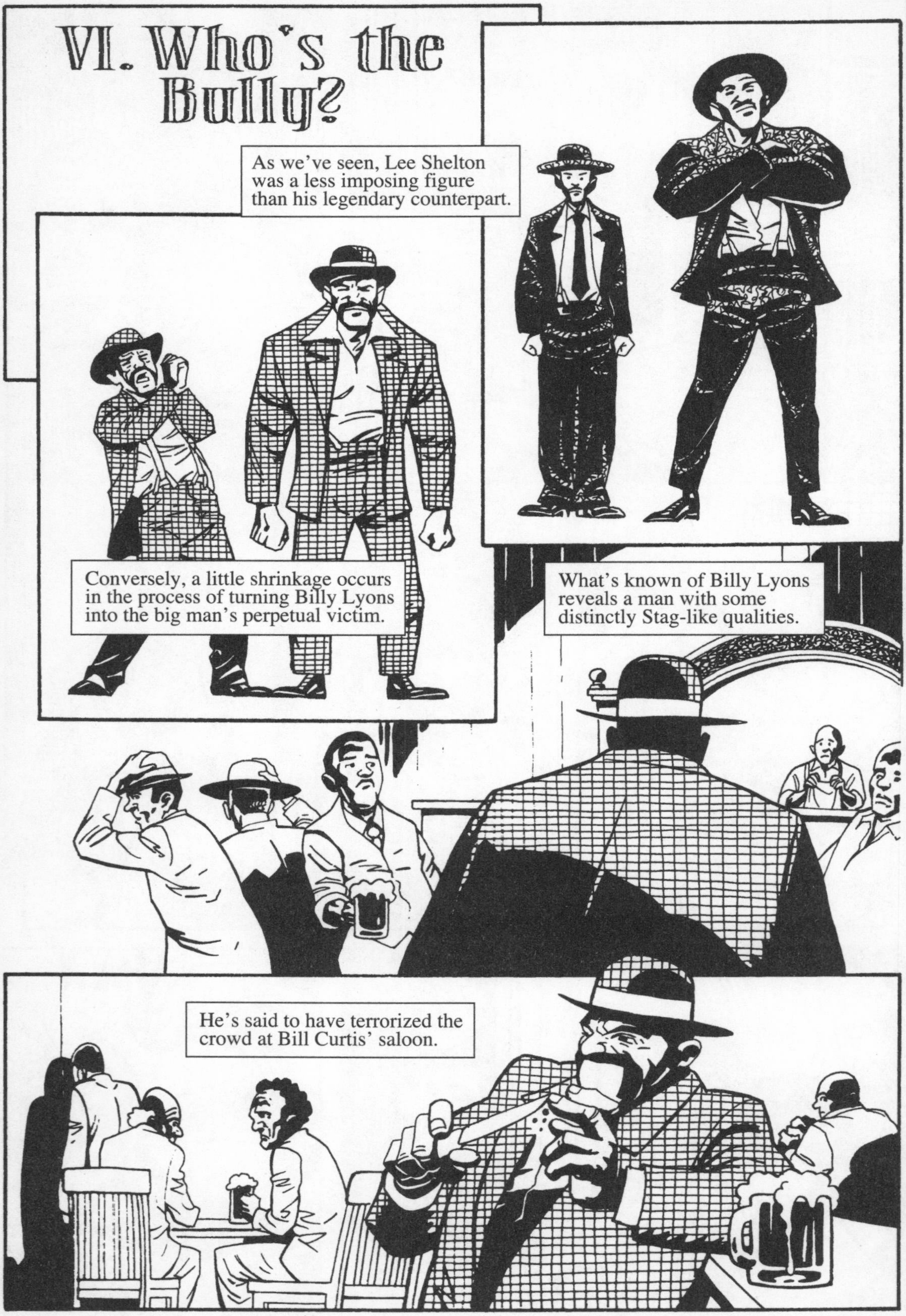
VI. Who's the Bully?
As we've seen, Lee Shelton was a less imposing figure than his legendary counterpart.
Conversely, a little shrinkage occurs in the process of turning Billy Lyons into the big man's perpetual victim.
What's known of Billy Lyons reveals a man with some distinctly Stag-like qualities.
He's said to have terrorized the crowd at Bill Curtis' saloon.

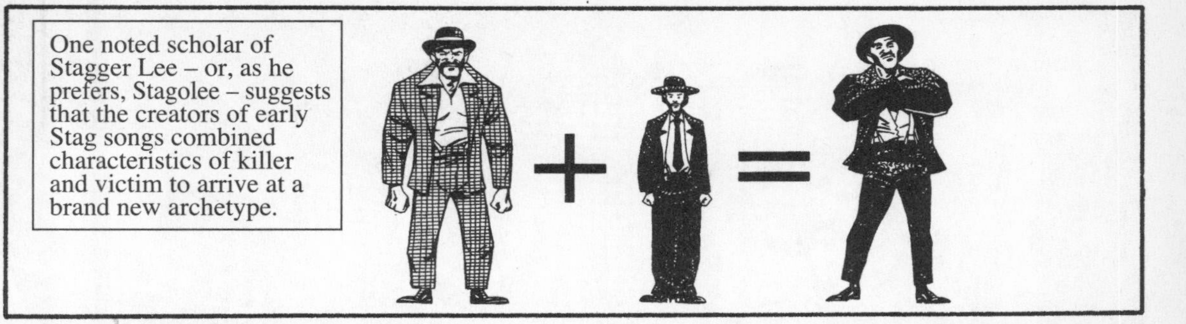
One noted scholar of Stagger Lee – or, as he prefers, Stagolee – suggests that the creators of early Stag songs combined characteristics of killer and victim to arrive at a brand new archetype.

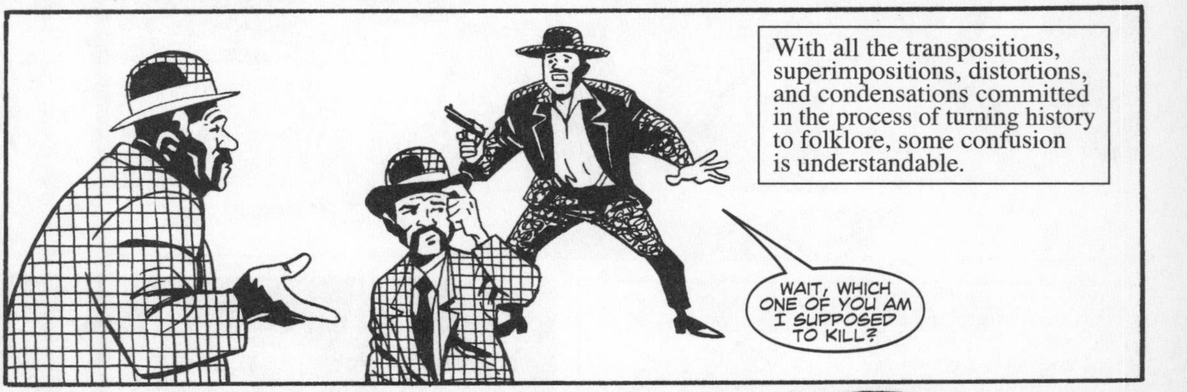
With all the transpositions, superimpositions, distortions, and condensations committed in the process of turning history to folklore, some confusion is understandable.
WAIT, WHICH ONE OF YOU AM I SUPPOSED TO KILL?

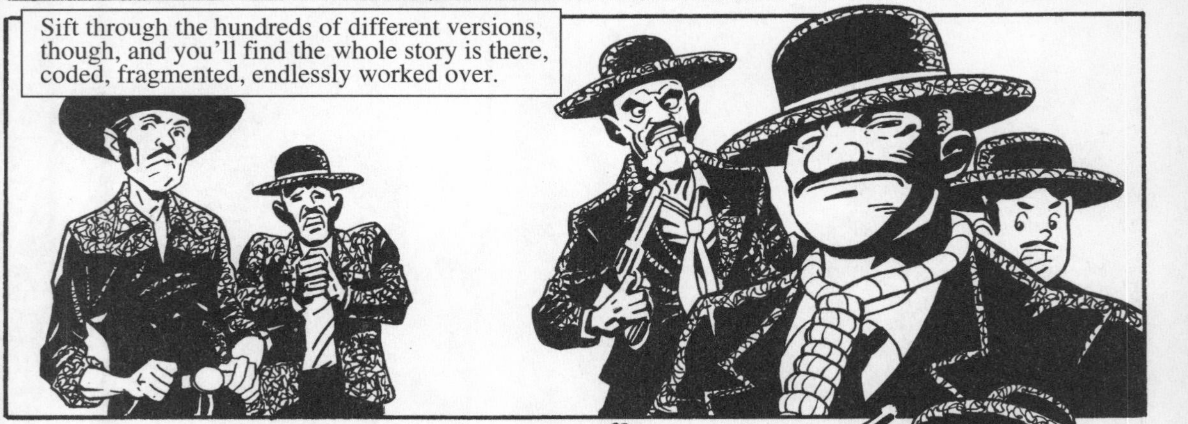
Sift through the hundreds of different versions, though, and you'll find the whole story is there, coded, fragmented, endlessly worked over.

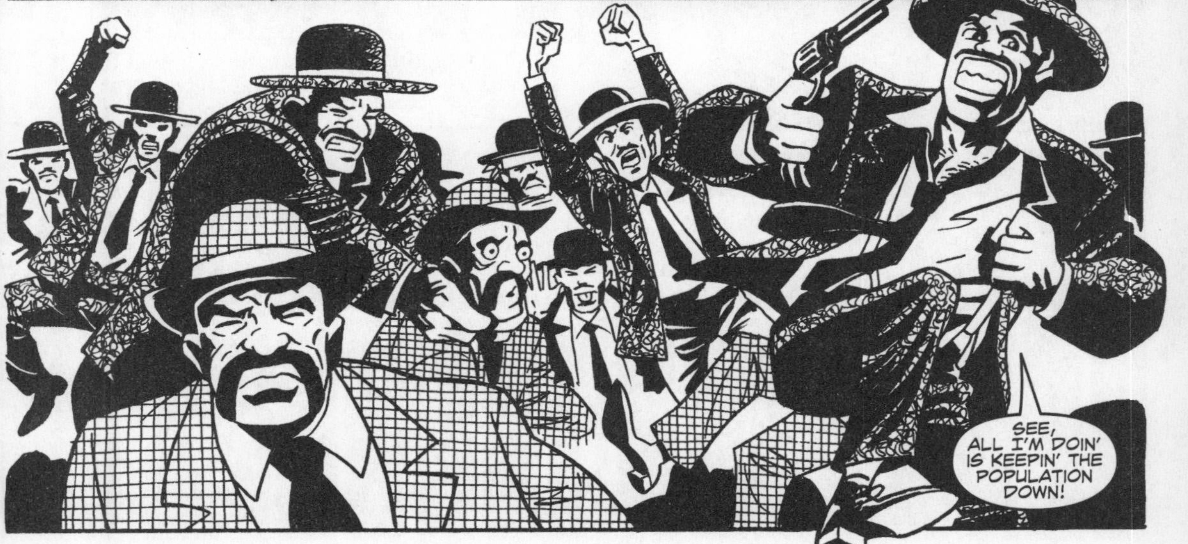
SEE, ALL I'M DOIN' IS KEEPIN' THE POPULATION DOWN!

For example, there's a stanza in a version from 1927...

Billy Lyons on the sidewalk
Dropped his razor from his hand,
In front of him a-shootin'
Old Stackalee did stand.
That bad, that bad man Stackalee.

No transcripts of Lee Shelton's murder trials survive, so it's not known what his defense was.

It's tempting to assume, though, that Billy's history with the knife might have come up.

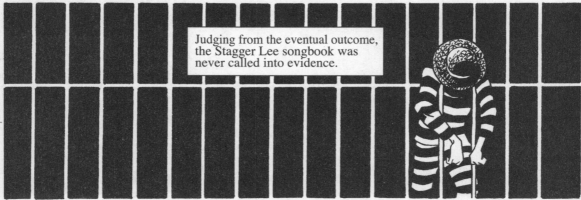

Judging from the eventual outcome, the Stagger Lee songbook was never called into evidence.

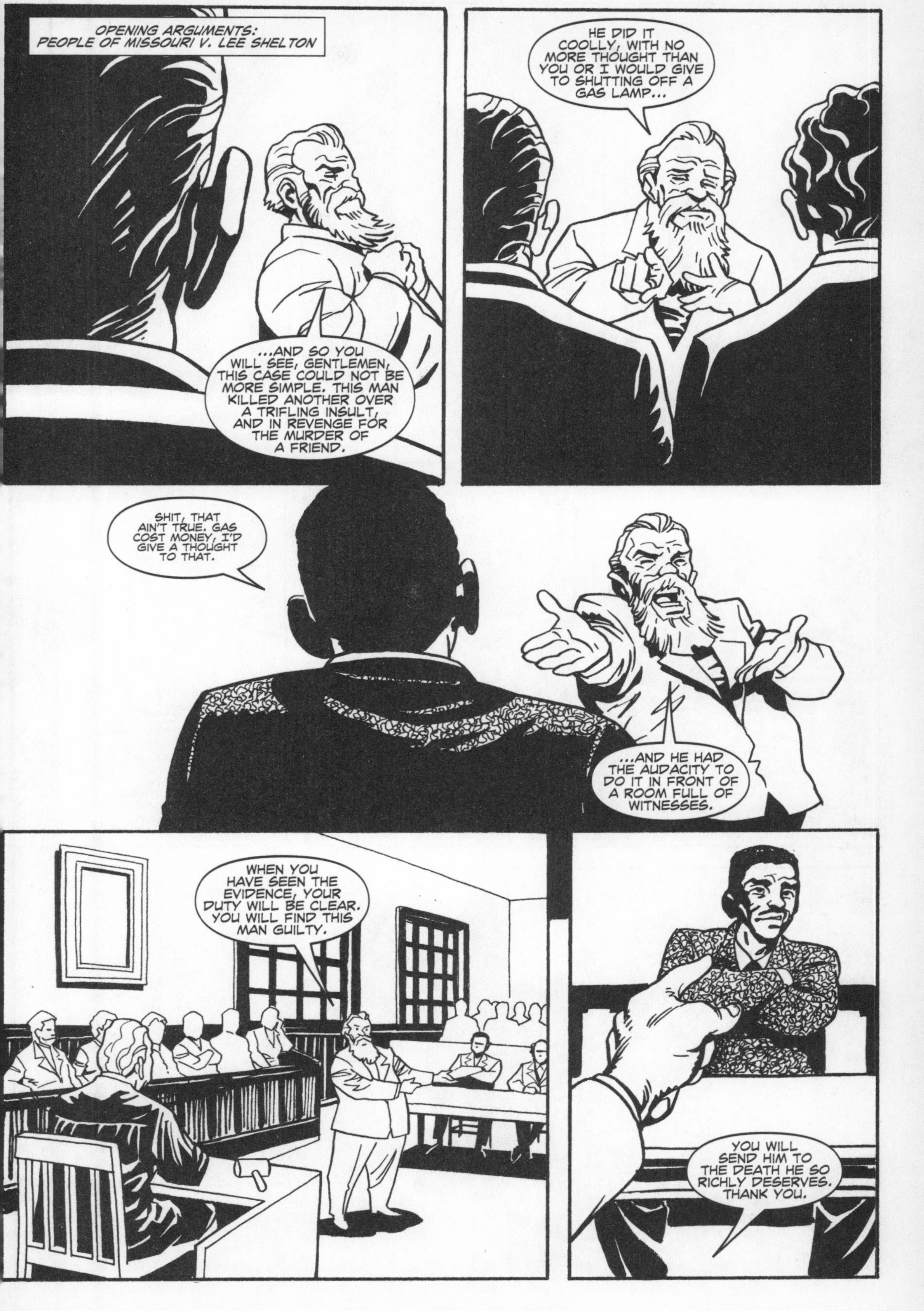
OPENING ARGUMENTS: PEOPLE OF MISSOURI V. LEE SHELTON
...AND SO YOU WILL SEE, GENTLEMEN, THIS CASE COULD NOT BE MORE SIMPLE. THIS MAN KILLED ANOTHER OVER A TRIFLING INSULT, AND IN REVENGE FOR THE MURDER OF A FRIEND.
HE DID IT COOLLY, WITH NO MORE THOUGHT THAN YOU OR I WOULD GIVE TO SHUTTING OFF A GAS LAMP...
SHIT, THAT AIN'T TRUE. GAS COST MONEY, I'D GIVE A THOUGHT TO THAT.
...AND HE HAD THE AUDACITY TO DO IT IN FRONT OF A ROOM FULL OF WITNESSES.
WHEN YOU HAVE SEEN THE EVIDENCE, YOUR DUTY WILL BE CLEAR. YOU WILL FIND THIS MAN GUILTY.
YOU WILL SEND HIM TO THE DEATH HE SO RICHLY DESERVES. THANK YOU.

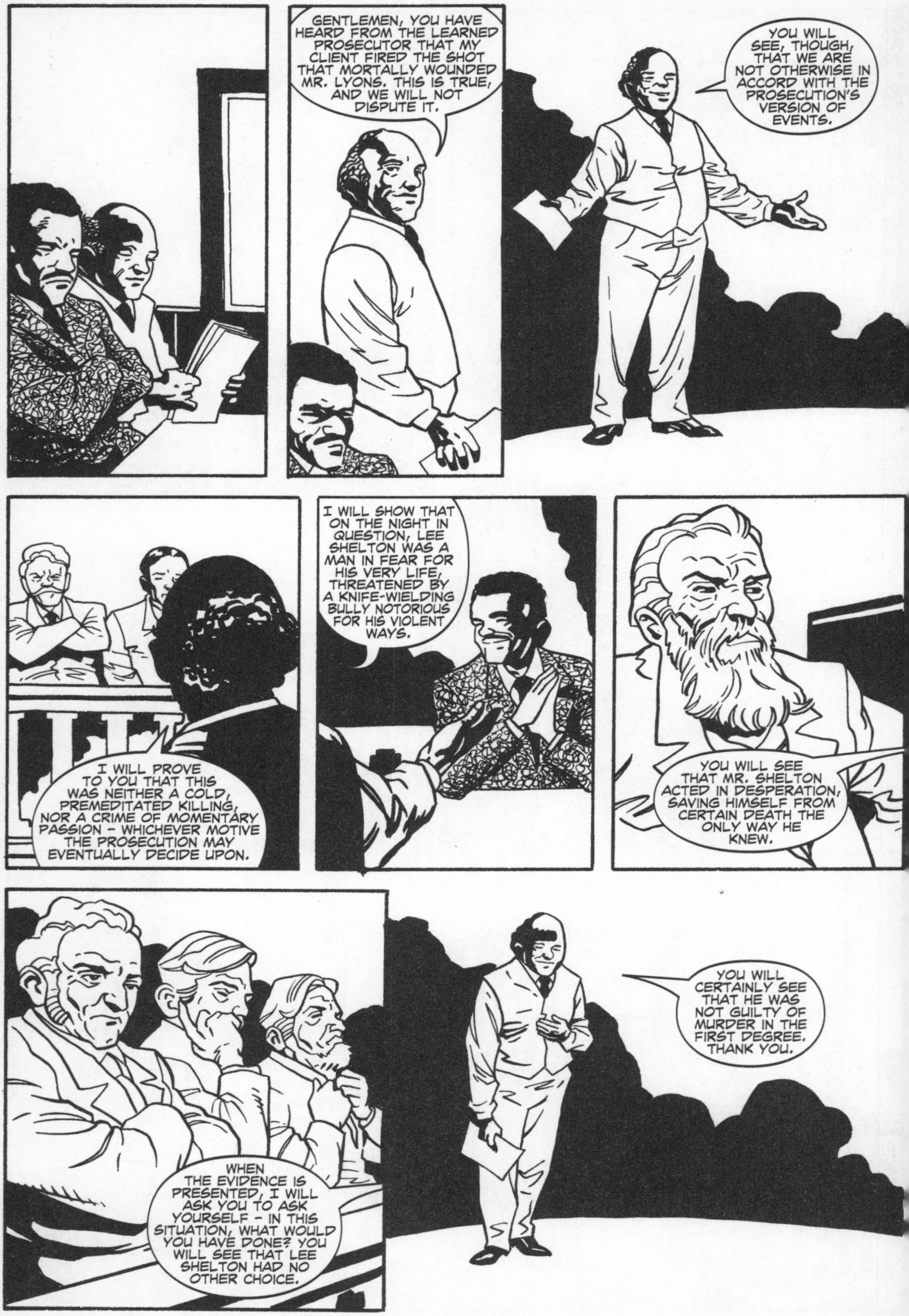
GENTLEMEN, YOU HAVE HEARD FROM THE LEARNED PROSECUTOR THAT MY CLIENT FIRED THE SHOT THAT MORTALLY WOUNDED MR. LYONS. THIS IS TRUE, AND WE WILL NOT DISPUTE IT.
YOU WILL SEE, THOUGH, THAT WE ARE NOT OTHERWISE IN ACCORD WITH THE PROSECUTION'S VERSION OF EVENTS.
I WILL PROVE TO YOU THAT THIS WAS NEITHER A COLD, PREMEDITATED KILLING, NOR A CRIME OF MOMENTARY PASSION - WHICHEVER MOTIVE THE PROSECUTION MAY EVENTUALLY DECIDE UPON.
I WILL SHOW THAT ON THE NIGHT IN QUESTION, LEE SHELTON WAS A MAN IN FEAR FOR HIS VERY LIFE, THREATENED BY A KNIFE-WIELDING BULLY NOTORIOUS FOR HIS VIOLENT WAYS.
YOU WILL SEE THAT MR. SHELTON ACTED IN DESPERATION, SAVING HIMSELF FROM CERTAIN DEATH THE ONLY WAY HE KNEW.
WHEN THE EVIDENCE IS PRESENTED, I WILL ASK YOU TO ASK YOURSELF - IN THIS SITUATION, WHAT WOULD YOU HAVE DONE? YOU WILL SEE THAT LEE SHELTON HAD NO OTHER CHOICE.
YOU WILL CERTAINLY SEE THAT HE WAS NOT GUILTY OF MURDER IN THE FIRST DEGREE. THANK YOU.

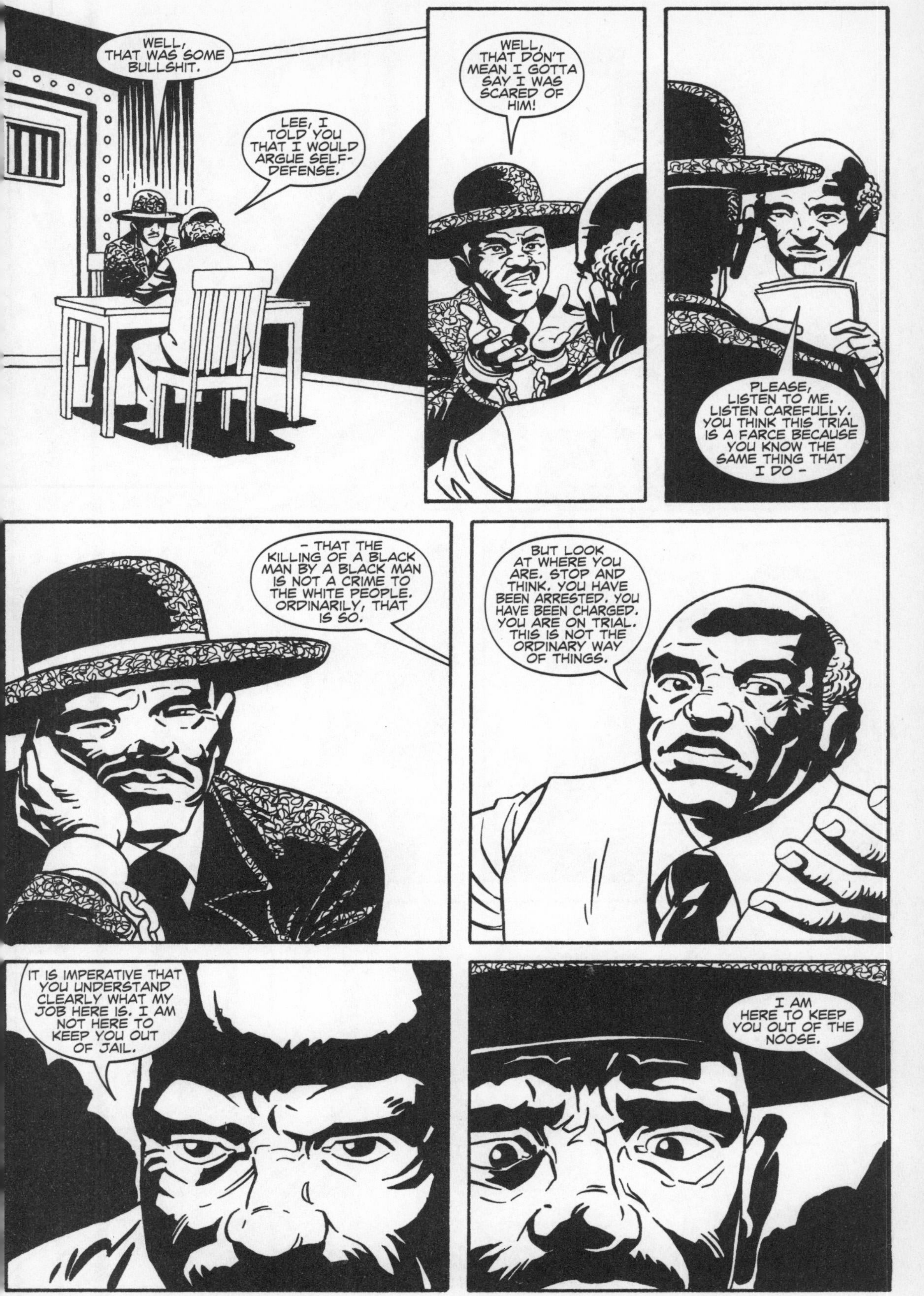
WELL, THAT WAS SOME BULLSHIT.
LEE, I TOLD YOU THAT I WOULD ARGUE SELF-DEFENSE.
WELL, THAT DON'T MEAN I GOTTA SAY I WAS SCARED OF HIM!
PLEASE, LISTEN TO ME. LISTEN CAREFULLY. YOU THINK THIS TRIAL IS A FARCE BECAUSE YOU KNOW THE SAME THING THAT I DO -
- THAT THE KILLING OF A BLACK MAN BY A BLACK MAN IS NOT A CRIME TO THE WHITE PEOPLE. ORDINARILY, THAT IS SO.
BUT LOOK AT WHERE YOU ARE. STOP AND THINK. YOU HAVE BEEN ARRESTED. YOU HAVE BEEN CHARGED. YOU ARE ON TRIAL. THIS IS NOT THE ORDINARY WAY OF THINGS.
IT IS IMPERATIVE THAT YOU UNDERSTAND CLEARLY WHAT MY JOB HERE IS. I AM NOT HERE TO KEEP YOU OUT OF JAIL.
I AM HERE TO KEEP YOU OUT OF THE NOOSE.

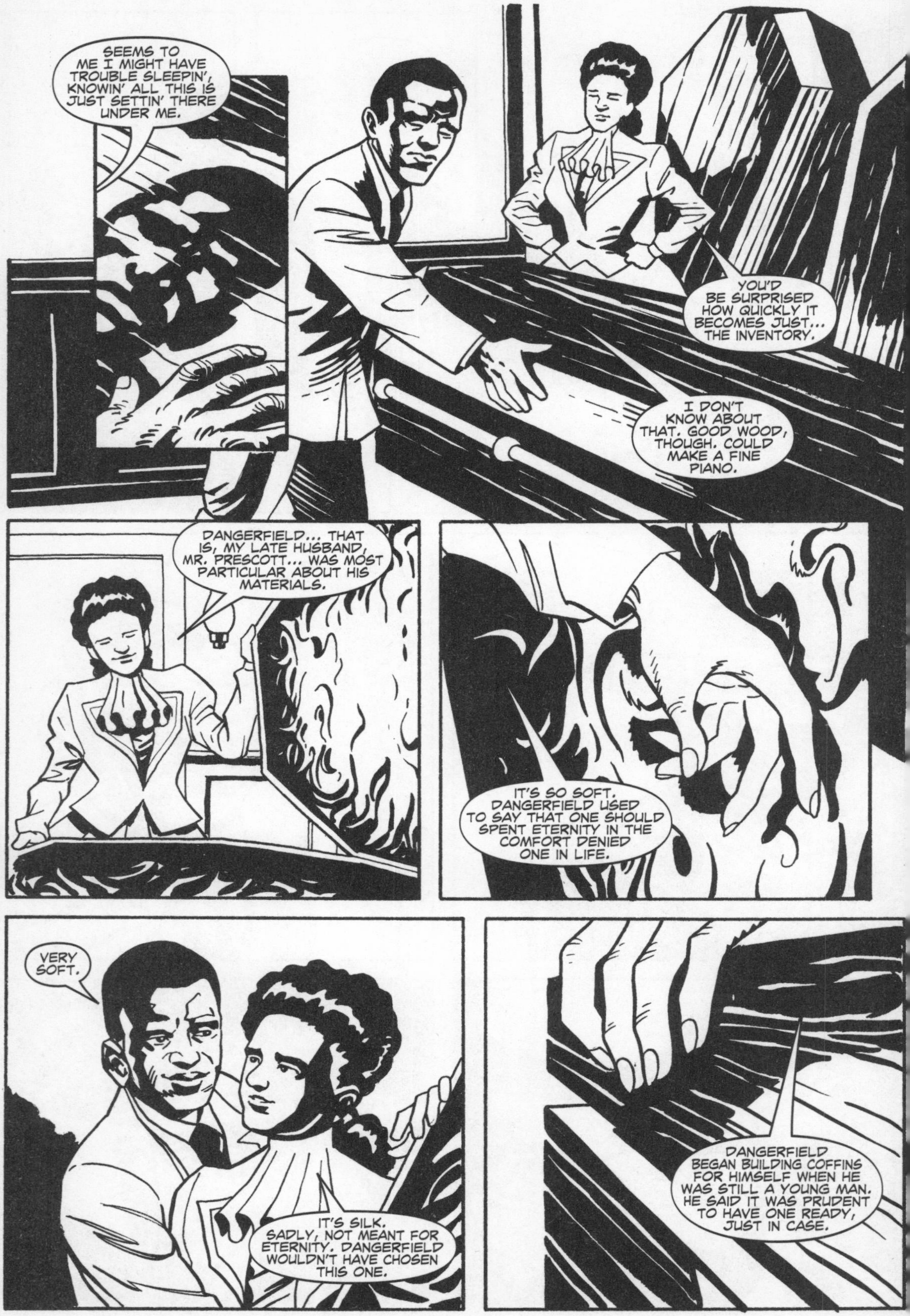
SEEMS TO ME I MIGHT HAVE TROUBLE SLEEPIN', KNOWIN' ALL THIS IS JUST SETTIN' THERE UNDER ME.
YOU'D BE SURPRISED HOW QUICKLY IT BECOMES JUST... THE INVENTORY.
I DON'T KNOW ABOUT THAT. GOOD WOOD, THOUGH. COULD MAKE A FINE PIANO.
DANGERFIELD... THAT IS, MY LATE HUSBAND, MR. PRESCOTT... WAS MOST PARTICULAR ABOUT HIS MATERIALS.
IT'S SO SOFT. DANGERFIELD USED TO SAY THAT ONE SHOULD SPENT ETERNITY IN THE COMFORT DENIED ONE IN LIFE.
VERY SOFT.
IT'S SILK. SADLY, NOT MEANT FOR ETERNITY. DANGERFIELD WOULDN'T HAVE CHOSEN THIS ONE.
DANGERFIELD BEGAN BUILDING COFFINS FOR HIMSELF WHEN HE WAS STILL A YOUNG MAN. HE SAID IT WAS PRUDENT TO HAVE ONE READY, JUST IN CASE.

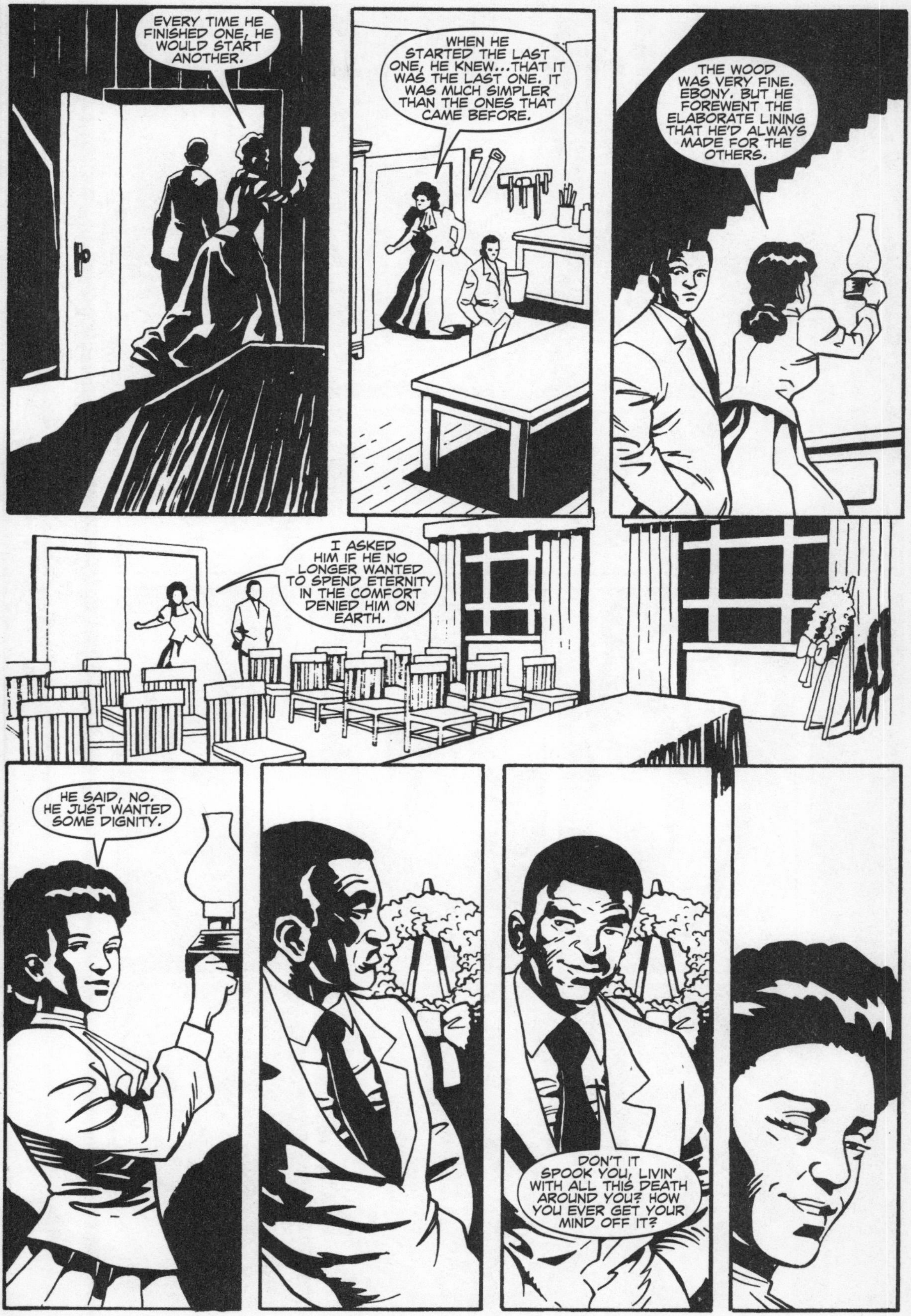

EVERY TIME HE FINISHED ONE, HE WOULD START ANOTHER.
WHEN HE STARTED THE LAST ONE, HE KNEW...THAT IT WAS THE LAST ONE. IT WAS MUCH SIMPLER THAN THE ONES THAT CAME BEFORE.
THE WOOD WAS VERY FINE. EBONY. BUT HE FOREWENT THE ELABORATE LINING THAT HE'D ALWAYS MADE FOR THE OTHERS.
I ASKED HIM IF HE NO LONGER WANTED TO SPEND ETERNITY IN THE COMFORT DENIED HIM ON EARTH.
HE SAID, NO. HE JUST WANTED SOME DIGNITY.
DON'T IT SPOOK YOU, LIVIN' WITH ALL THIS DEATH AROUND YOU? HOW YOU EVER GET YOUR MIND OFF IT?

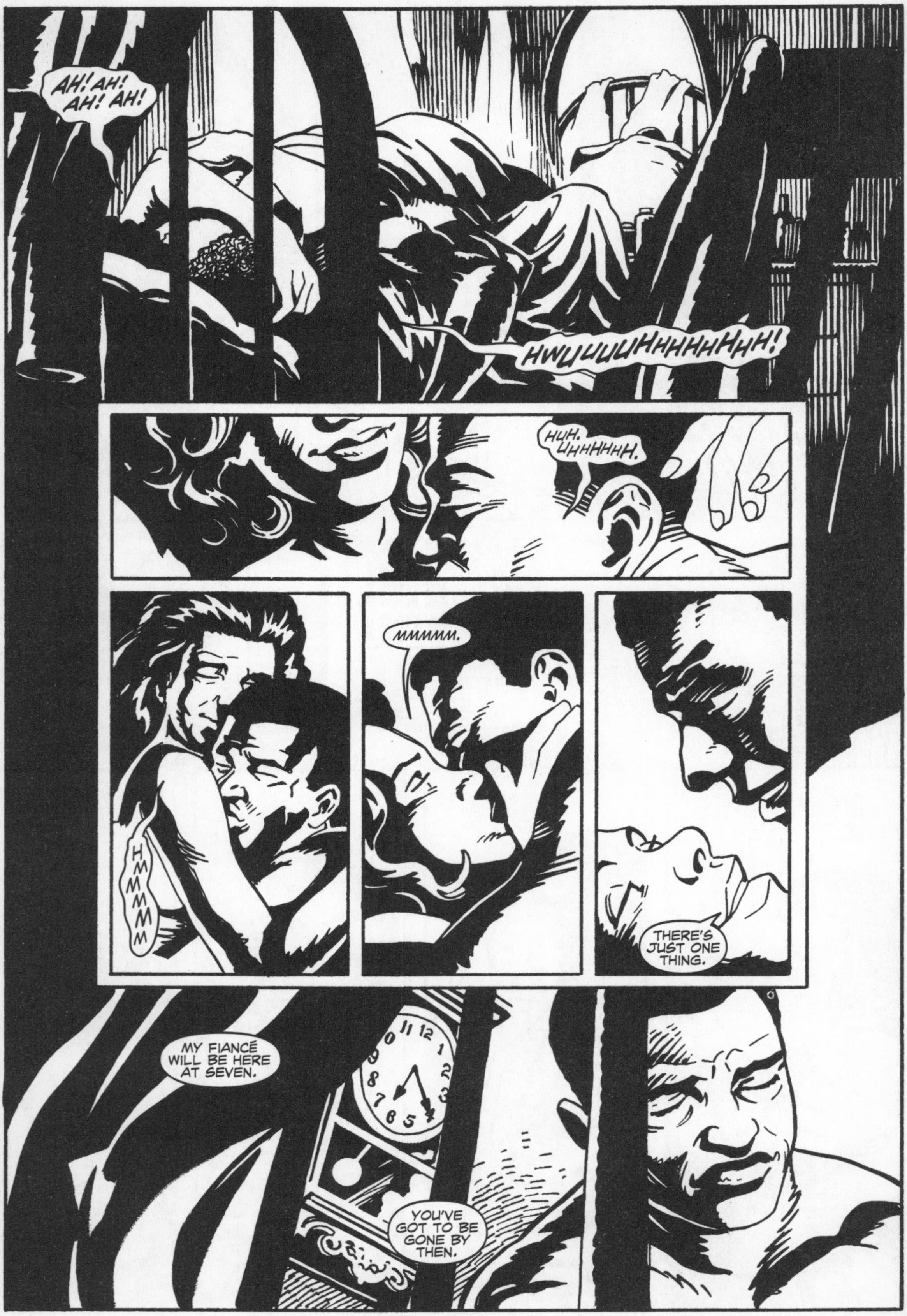
AH! AH! AH! AH!
HWUUUUHHHHHHH!
HUH. UHHHHHH.
HMMMMM
MMMMM.
THERE'S JUST ONE THING.
MY FIANCÉ WILL BE HERE AT SEVEN.
YOU'VE GOT TO BE GONE BY THEN.

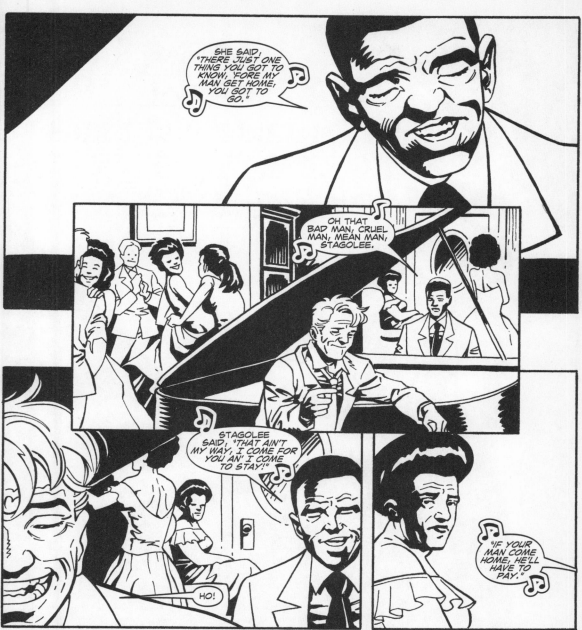

SHE SAID, "THERE JUST ONE THING YOU GOT TO KNOW, 'FORE MY MAN GET HOME, YOU GOT TO GO."

OH THAT BAD MAN, CRUEL MAN, MEAN MAN, STAGOLEE.

STAGOLEE SAID, "THAT AIN'T MY WAY, I COME FOR YOU AN' I COME TO STAY!"

HO!

"IF YOUR MAN COME HOME, HE'LL HAVE TO PAY."

OH THAT BAD MAN, CRUEL MAN, MEAN MAN, STAGOLEE.

LET'S STORM THE CASTLE!

WHO STOLE THE LOCK OFF THE GOD-DAMNED DOOR AND LET YOU PECKERWOODS IN?

WELCOME TO THE CASTLE, BOYS! LET'S FIND YOU SOME MAIDENS!

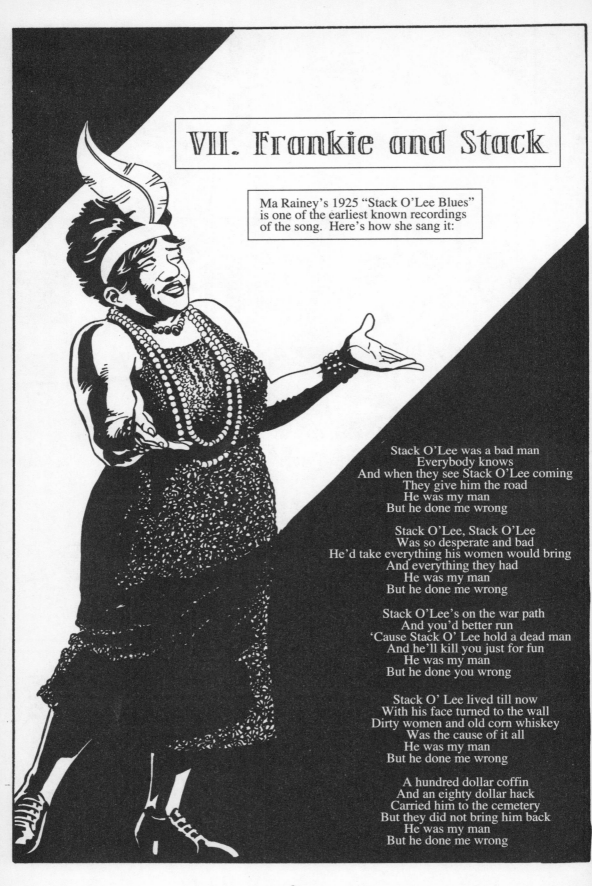

VII. Frankie and Stack

Ma Rainey's 1925 "Stack O'Lee Blues" is one of the earliest known recordings of the song. Here's how she sang it:

Stack O'Lee was a bad man
Everybody knows
And when they see Stack O'Lee coming
They give him the road
He was my man
But he done me wrong

Stack O'Lee, Stack O'Lee
Was so desperate and bad
He'd take everything his women would bring
And everything they had
He was my man
But he done me wrong

Stack O'Lee's on the war path
And you'd better run
'Cause Stack O' Lee hold a dead man
And he'll kill you just for fun
He was my man
But he done you wrong

Stack O' Lee lived till now
With his face turned to the wall
Dirty women and old corn whiskey
Was the cause of it all
He was my man
But he done me wrong

A hundred dollar coffin
And an eighty dollar hack
Carried him to the cemetery
But they did not bring him back
He was my man
But he done me wrong

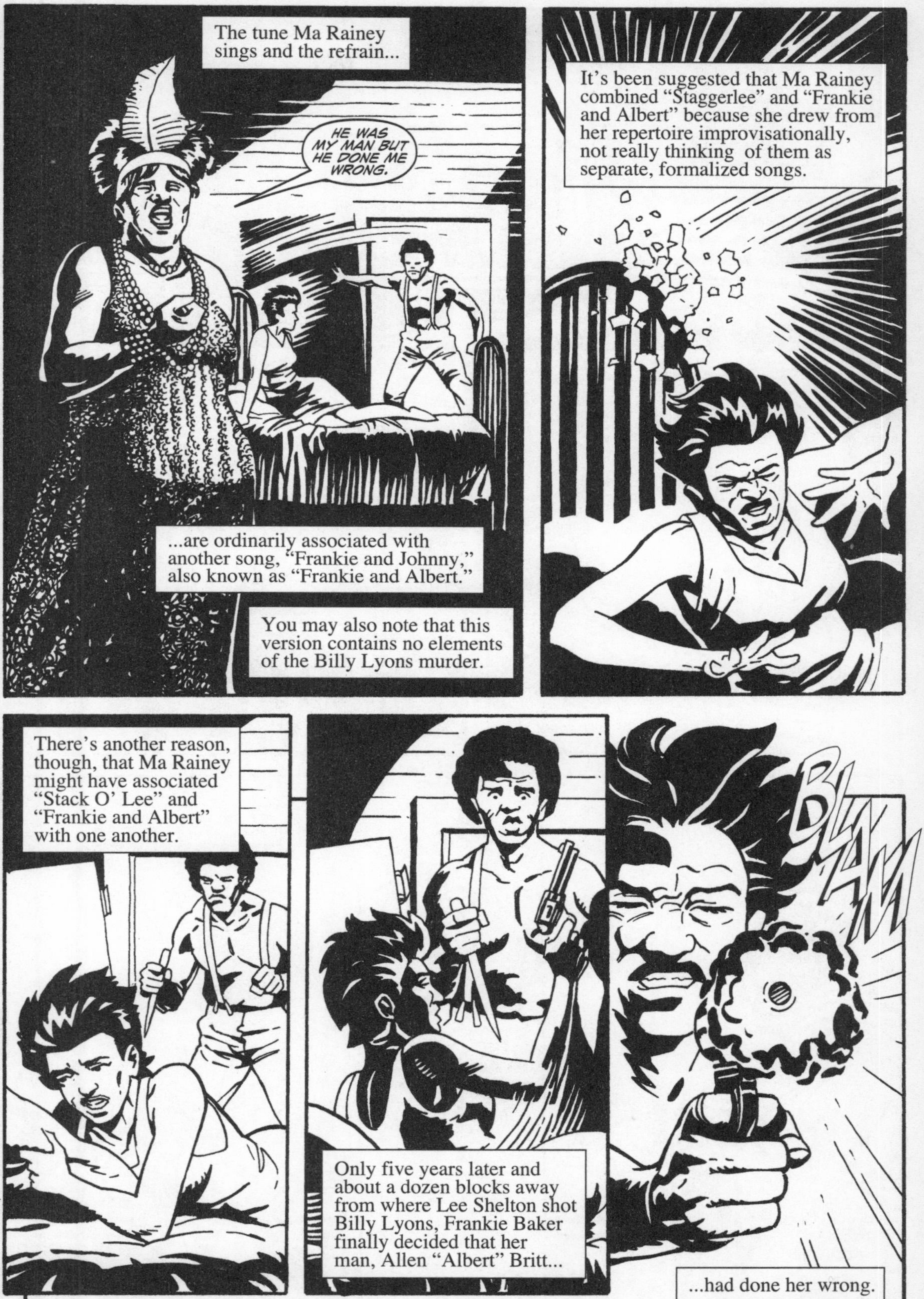
The tune Ma Rainey sings and the refrain...
HE WAS MY MAN BUT HE DONE ME WRONG.
...are ordinarily associated with another song, "Frankie and Johnny," also known as "Frankie and Albert."
You may also note that this version contains no elements of the Billy Lyons murder.
It's been suggested that Ma Rainey combined "Staggerlee" and "Frankie and Albert" because she drew from her repertoire improvisationally, not really thinking of them as separate, formalized songs.
There's another reason, though, that Ma Rainey might have associated "Stack O' Lee" and "Frankie and Albert" with one another.
Only five years later and about a dozen blocks away from where Lee Shelton shot Billy Lyons, Frankie Baker finally decided that her man, Allen "Albert" Britt...
BLAM
...had done her wrong.

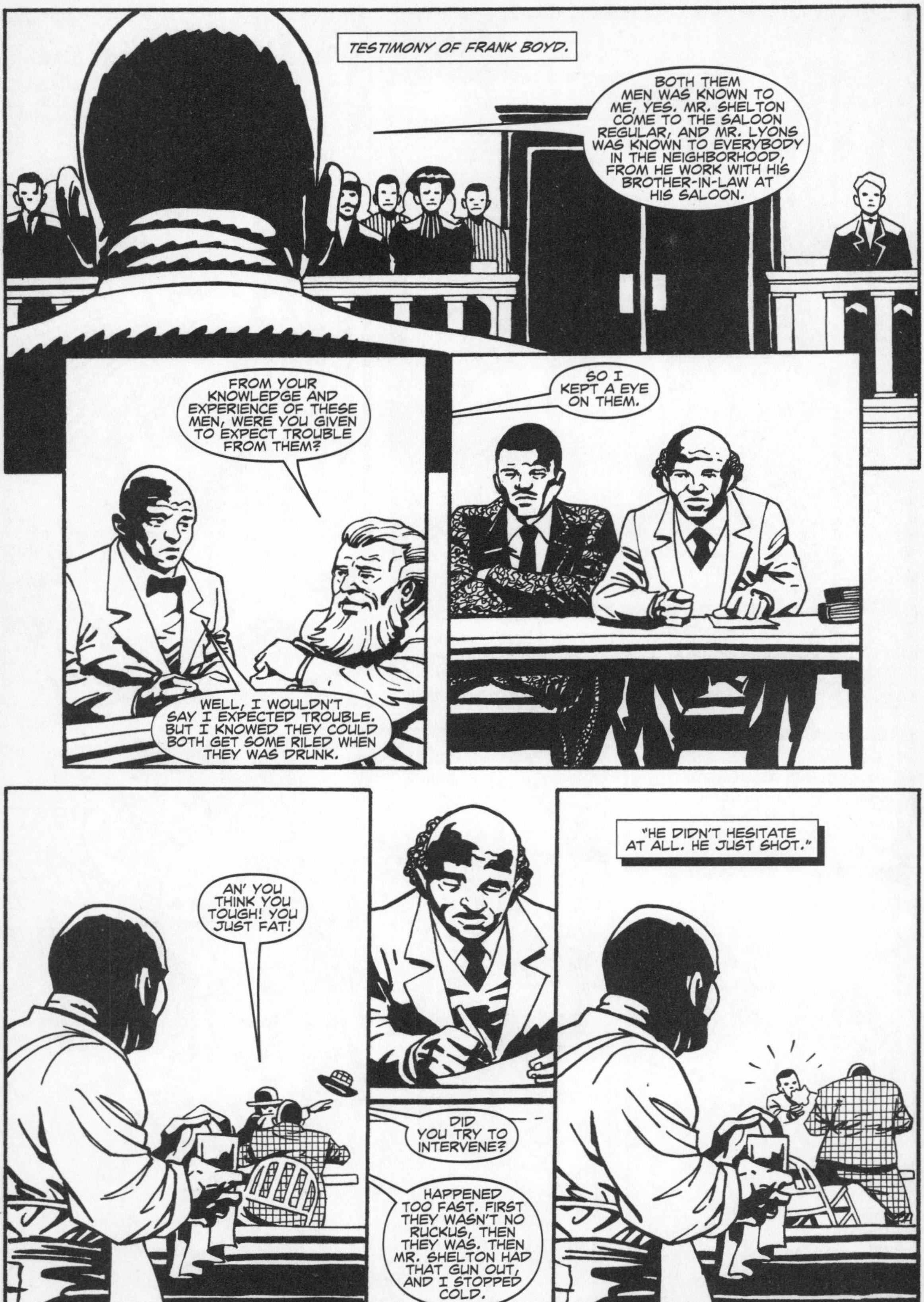
TESTIMONY OF FRANK BOYD.
BOTH THEM MEN WAS KNOWN TO ME, YES. MR. SHELTON COME TO THE SALOON REGULAR, AND MR. LYONS WAS KNOWN TO EVERYBODY IN THE NEIGHBORHOOD, FROM HE WORK WITH HIS BROTHER-IN-LAW AT HIS SALOON.
FROM YOUR KNOWLEDGE AND EXPERIENCE OF THESE MEN, WERE YOU GIVEN TO EXPECT TROUBLE FROM THEM?
WELL, I WOULDN'T SAY I EXPECTED TROUBLE. BUT I KNOWED THEY COULD BOTH GET SOME RILED WHEN THEY WAS DRUNK.
SO I KEPT A EYE ON THEM.
AN' YOU THINK YOU TOUGH! YOU JUST FAT!
DID YOU TRY TO INTERVENE?
HAPPENED TOO FAST. FIRST THEY WASN'T NO RUCKUS, THEN THEY WAS. THEN MR. SHELTON HAD THAT GUN OUT, AND I STOPPED COLD.
"HE DIDN'T HESITATE AT ALL. HE JUST SHOT."

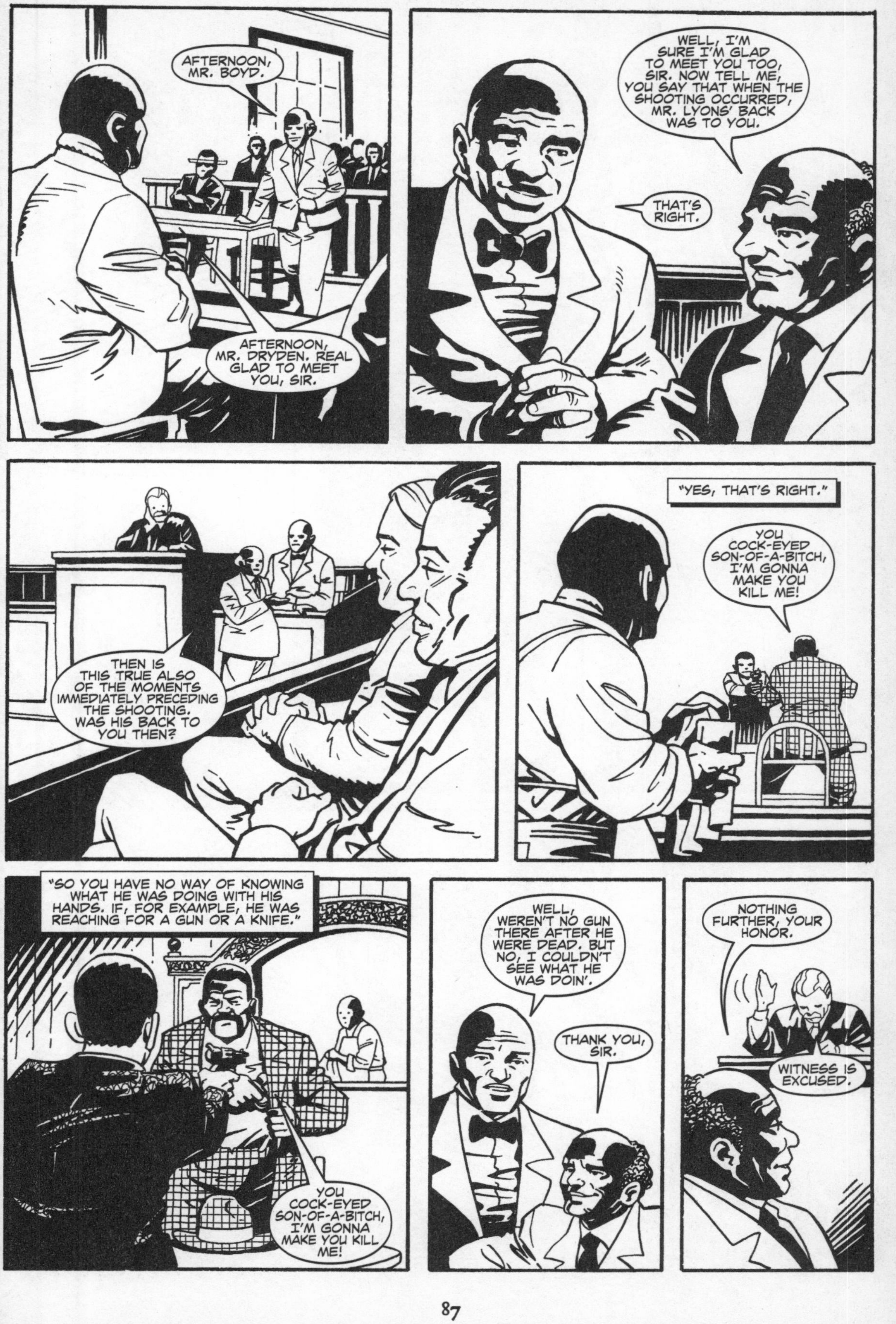
AFTERNOON, MR. BOYD.
AFTERNOON, MR. DRYDEN. REAL GLAD TO MEET YOU, SIR.
WELL, I'M SURE I'M GLAD TO MEET YOU TOO, SIR. NOW TELL ME, YOU SAY THAT WHEN THE SHOOTING OCCURRED, MR. LYONS' BACK WAS TO YOU.
THAT'S RIGHT.
THEN IS THIS TRUE ALSO OF THE MOMENTS IMMEDIATELY PRECEDING THE SHOOTING. WAS HIS BACK TO YOU THEN?
"YES, THAT'S RIGHT."
YOU COCK-EYED SON-OF-A-BITCH, I'M GONNA MAKE YOU KILL ME!
"SO YOU HAVE NO WAY OF KNOWING WHAT HE WAS DOING WITH HIS HANDS. IF, FOR EXAMPLE, HE WAS REACHING FOR A GUN OR A KNIFE."
YOU COCK-EYED SON-OF-A-BITCH, I'M GONNA MAKE YOU KILL ME!
WELL, WEREN'T NO GUN THERE AFTER HE WERE DEAD. BUT NO, I COULDN'T SEE WHAT HE WAS DOIN'.
THANK YOU, SIR.
NOTHING FURTHER, YOUR HONOR.
WITNESS IS EXCUSED.

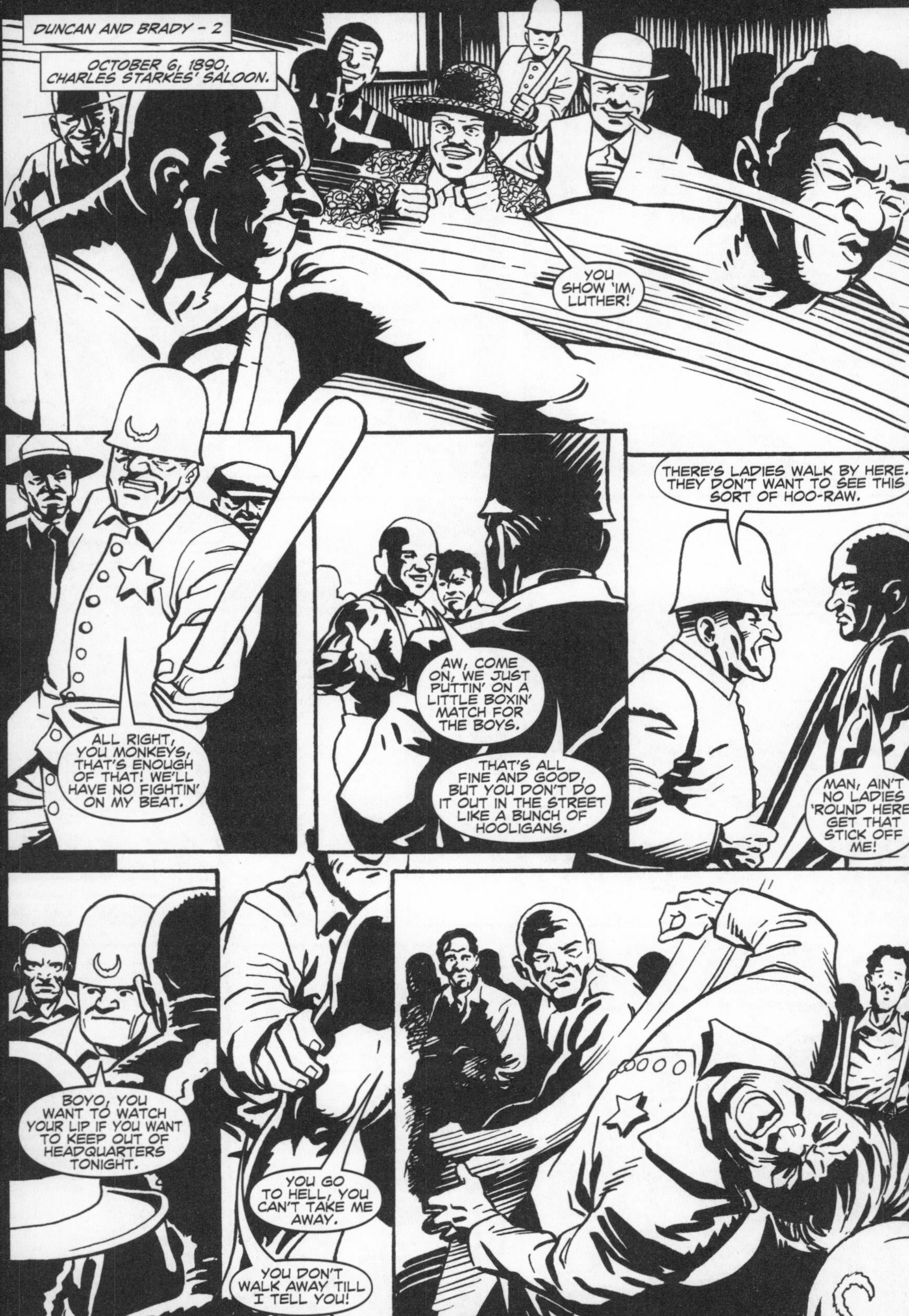
DUNCAN AND BRADY - 2
OCTOBER 6, 1890, CHARLES STARKES' SALOON.
YOU SHOW 'IM, LUTHER!
ALL RIGHT, YOU MONKEYS, THAT'S ENOUGH OF THAT! WE'LL HAVE NO FIGHTIN' ON MY BEAT.
AW, COME ON, WE JUST PUTTIN' ON A LITTLE BOXIN' MATCH FOR THE BOYS.
THAT'S ALL FINE AND GOOD, BUT YOU DON'T DO IT OUT IN THE STREET LIKE A BUNCH OF HOOLIGANS.
THERE'S LADIES WALK BY HERE. THEY DON'T WANT TO SEE THIS SORT OF HOO-RAW.
MAN, AIN'T NO LADIES 'ROUND HERE! GET THAT STICK OFF ME!
BOYO, YOU WANT TO WATCH YOUR LIP IF YOU WANT TO KEEP OUT OF HEADQUARTERS TONIGHT.
YOU GO TO HELL, YOU CAN'T TAKE ME AWAY.
YOU DON'T WALK AWAY TILL I TELL YOU!

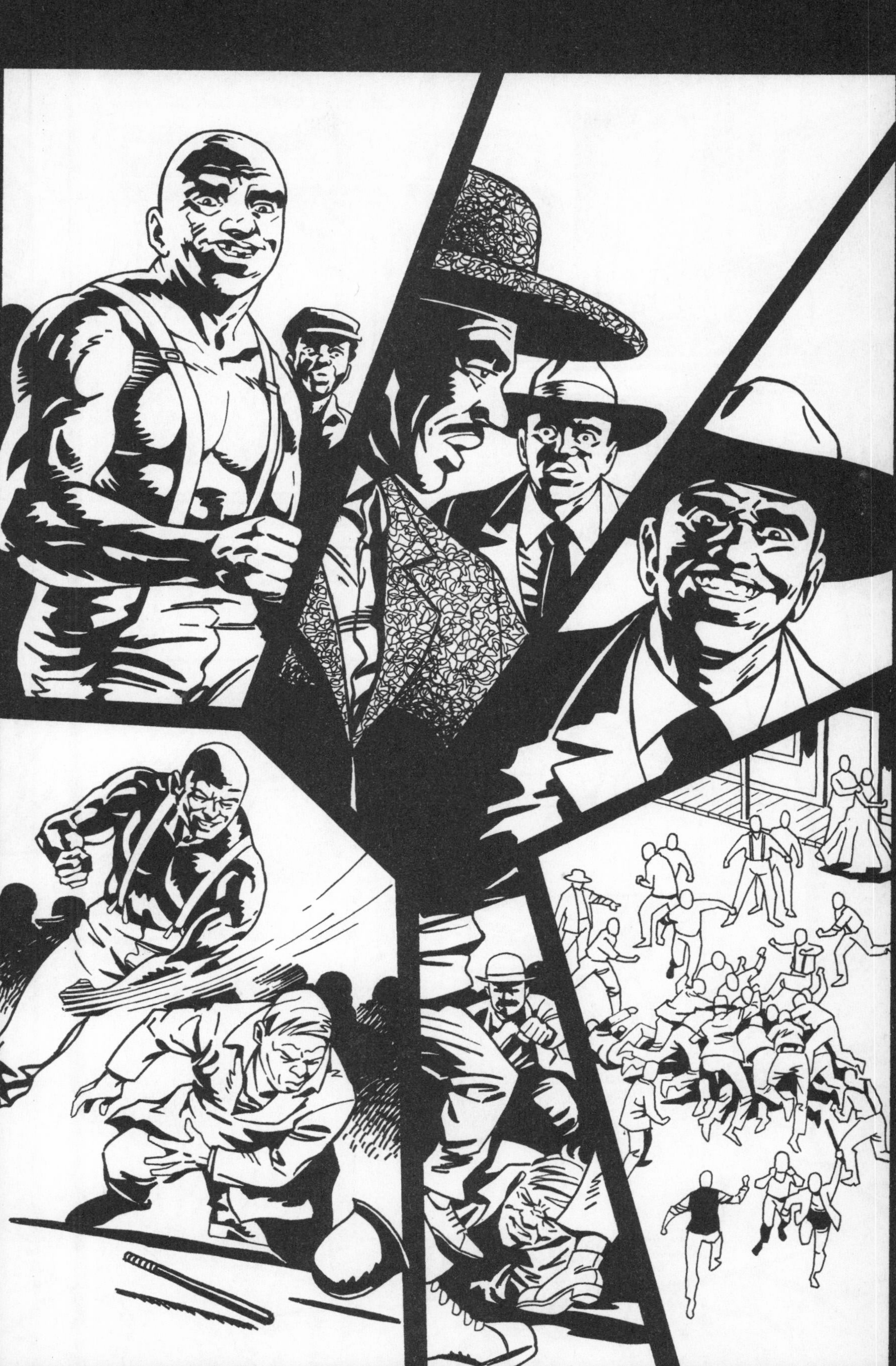

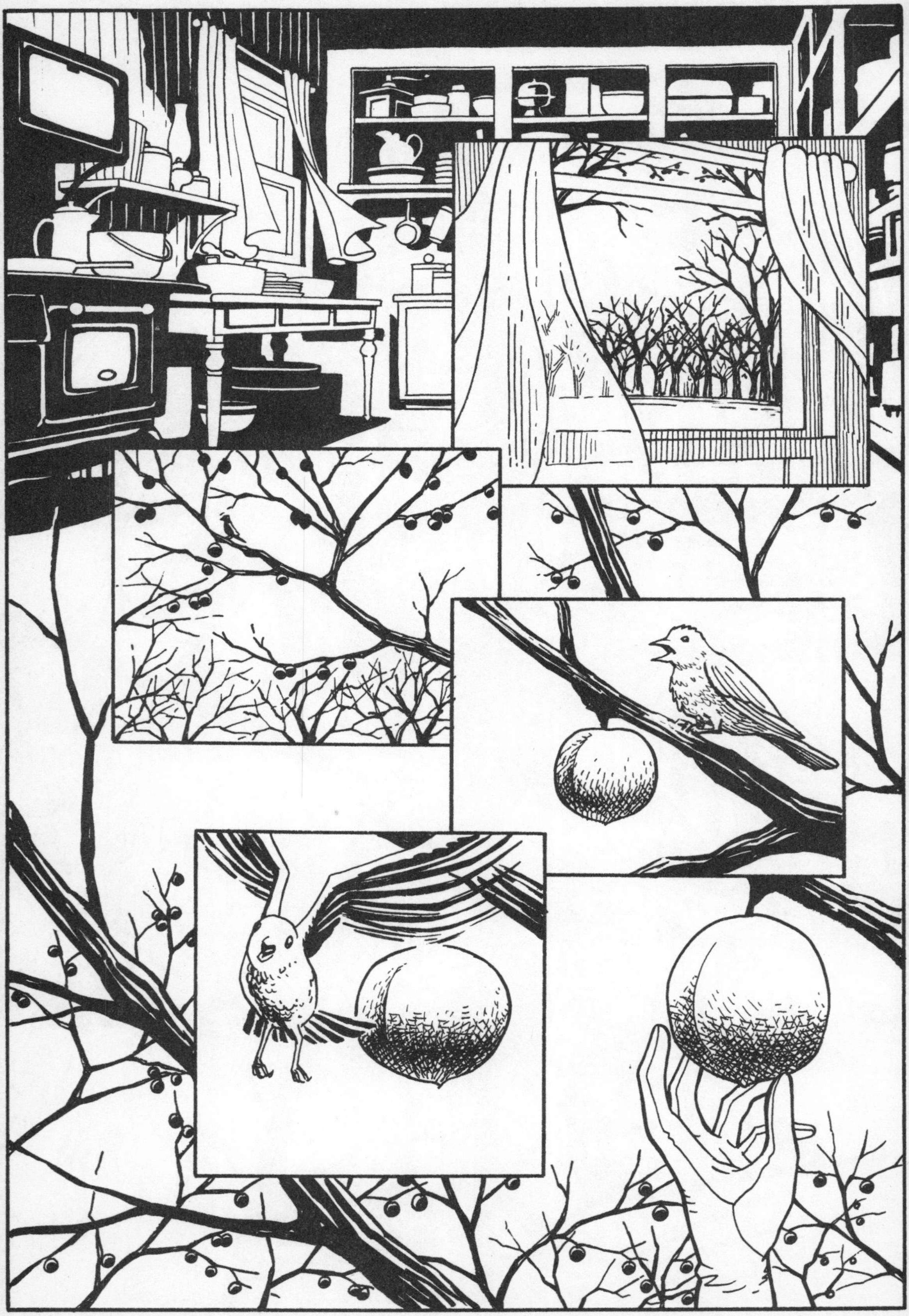

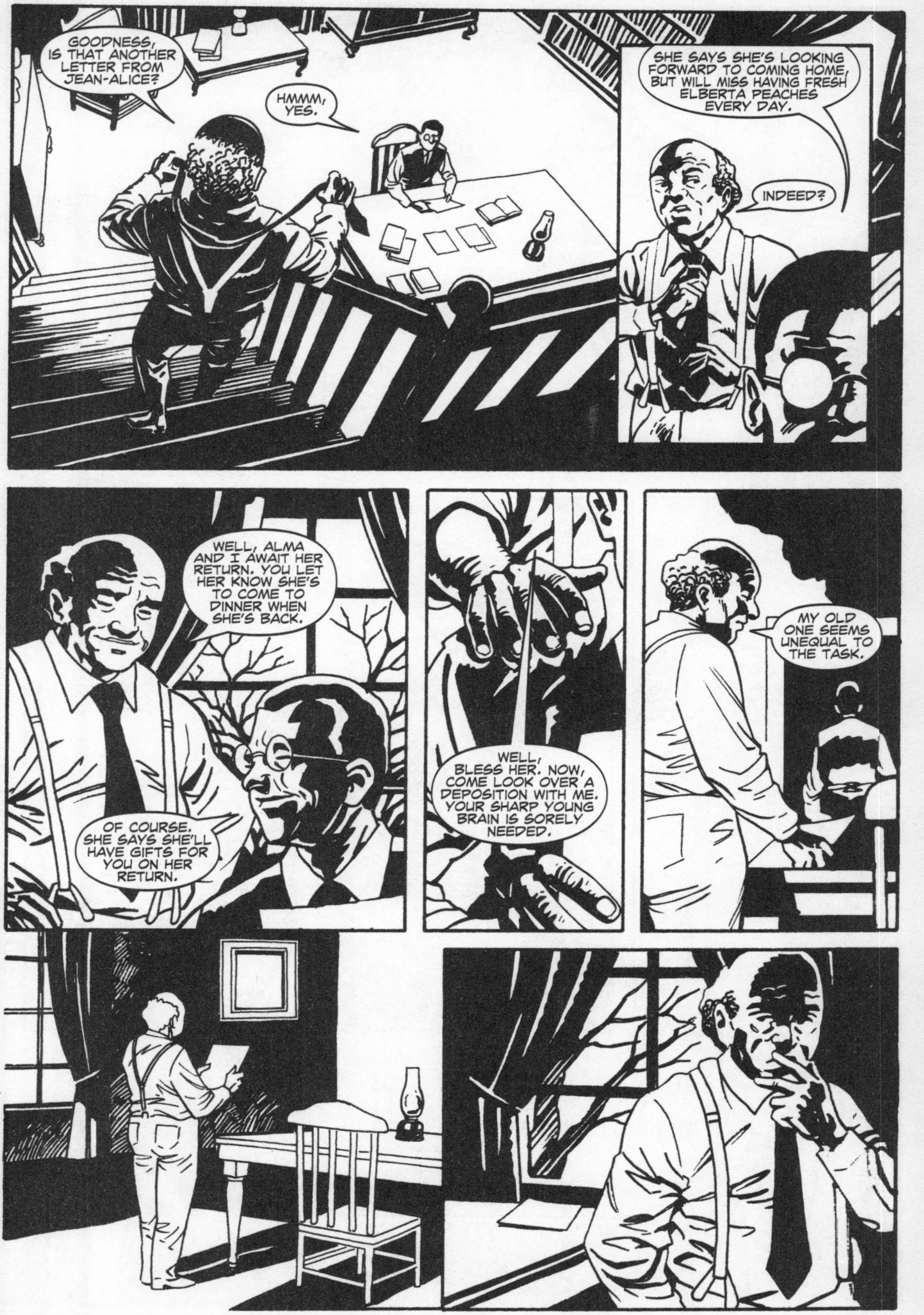
GOODNESS, IS THAT ANOTHER LETTER FROM JEAN-ALICE?
HMMM, YES.
SHE SAYS SHE'S LOOKING FORWARD TO COMING HOME, BUT WILL MISS HAVING FRESH ELBERTA PEACHES EVERY DAY.
INDEED?
WELL, ALMA AND I AWAIT HER RETURN. YOU LET HER KNOW SHE'S TO COME TO DINNER WHEN SHE'S BACK.
OF COURSE. SHE SAYS SHE'LL HAVE GIFTS FOR YOU ON HER RETURN.
WELL, BLESS HER. NOW, COME LOOK OVER A DEPOSITION WITH ME. YOUR SHARP YOUNG BRAIN IS SORELY NEEDED.
MY OLD ONE SEEMS UNEQUAL TO THE TASK.

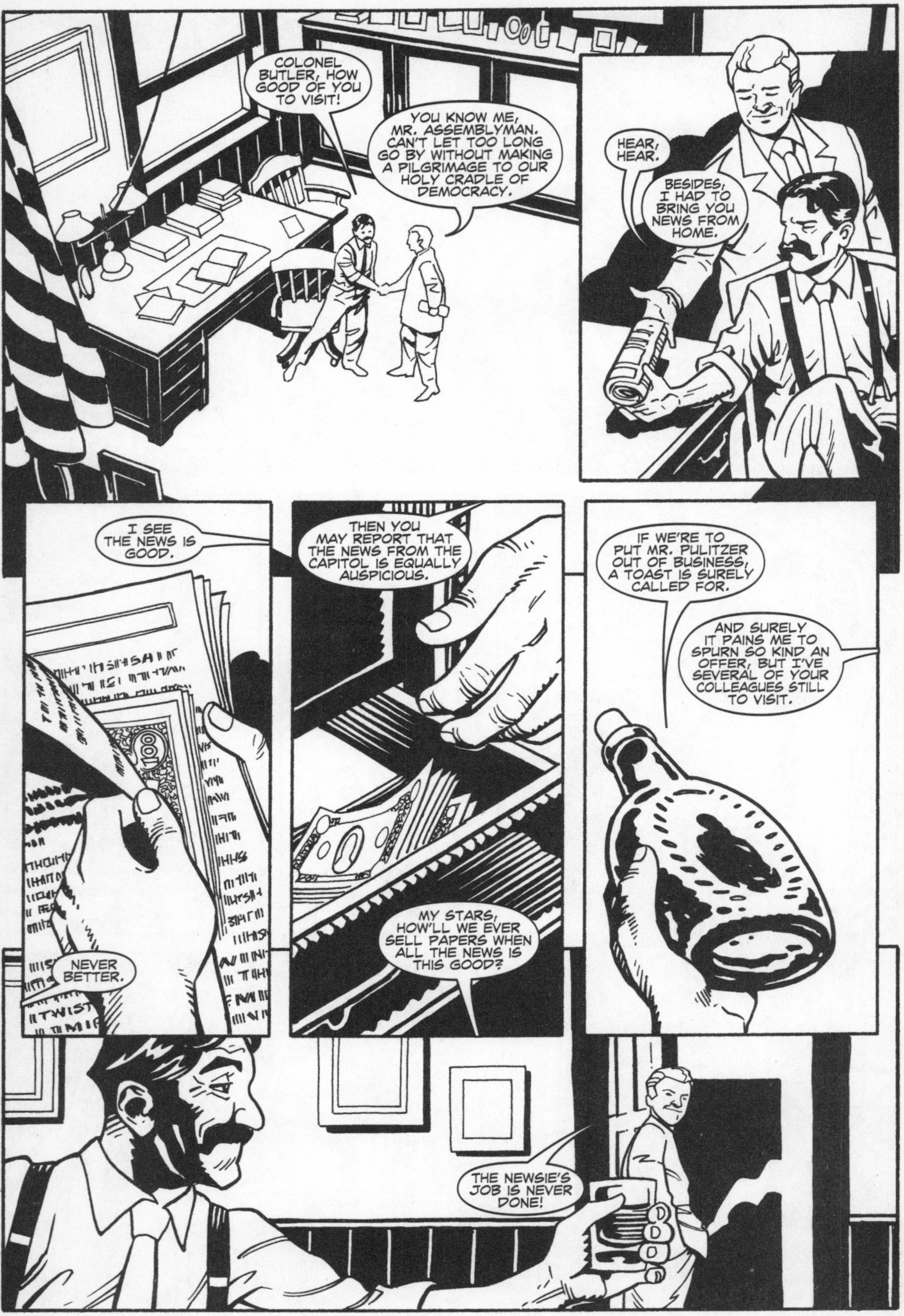
COLONEL BUTLER, HOW GOOD OF YOU TO VISIT!
YOU KNOW ME, MR. ASSEMBLYMAN. CAN'T LET TOO LONG GO BY WITHOUT MAKING A PILGRIMAGE TO OUR HOLY CRADLE OF DEMOCRACY.
HEAR, HEAR.
BESIDES, I HAD TO BRING YOU NEWS FROM HOME.
I SEE THE NEWS IS GOOD.
NEVER BETTER.
THEN YOU MAY REPORT THAT THE NEWS FROM THE CAPITOL IS EQUALLY AUSPICIOUS.
MY STARS, HOW'LL WE EVER SELL PAPERS WHEN ALL THE NEWS IS THIS GOOD?
IF WE'RE TO PUT MR. PULITZER OUT OF BUSINESS, A TOAST IS SURELY CALLED FOR.
AND SURELY IT PAINS ME TO SPURN SO KIND AN OFFER, BUT I'VE SEVERAL OF YOUR COLLEAGUES STILL TO VISIT.
THE NEWSIE'S JOB IS NEVER DONE!

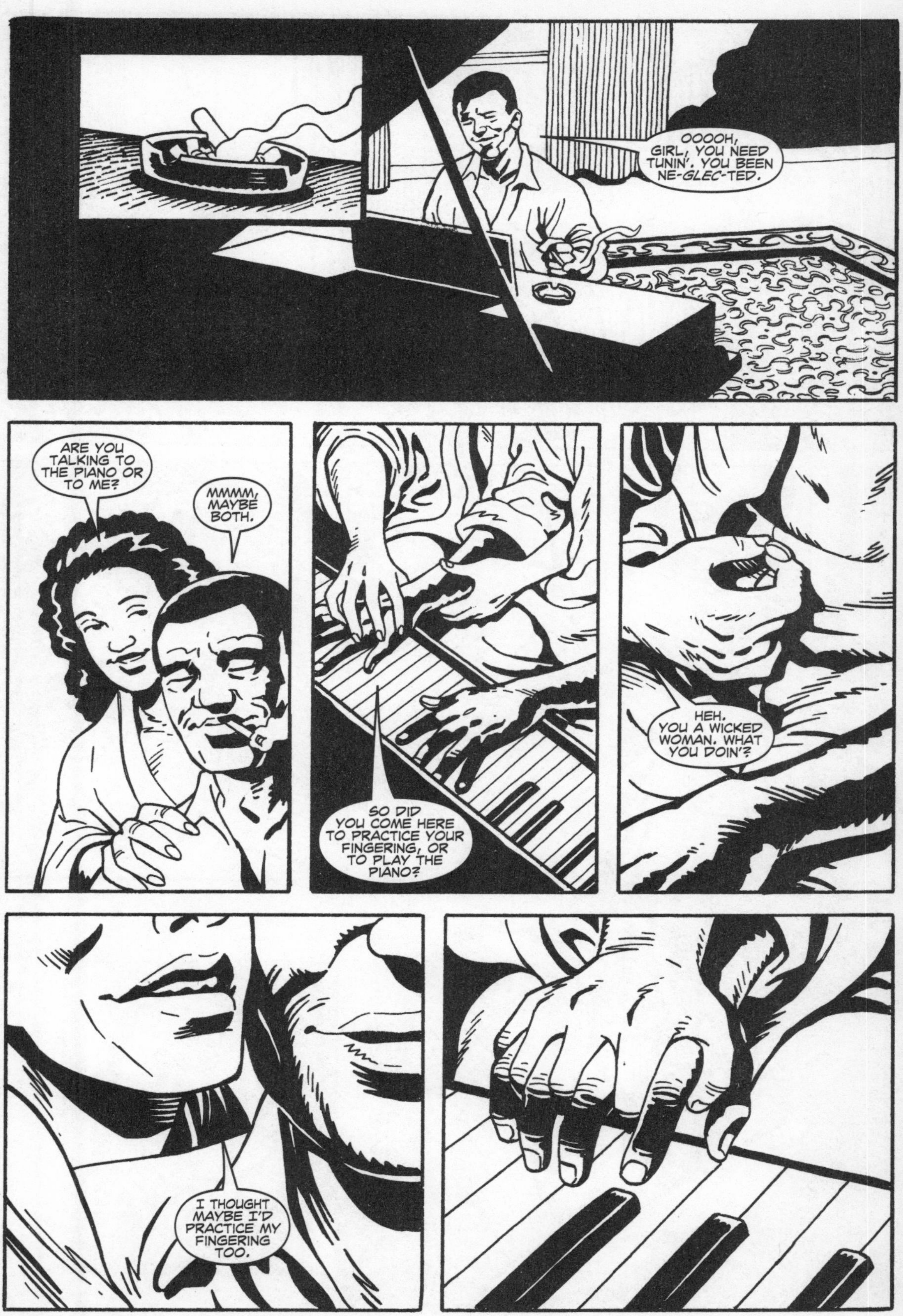
OOOOH, GIRL, YOU NEED TUNIN'. YOU BEEN NE-GLEC-TED.
ARE YOU TALKING TO THE PIANO OR TO ME?
MMMM, MAYBE BOTH.
SO DID YOU COME HERE TO PRACTICE YOUR FINGERING, OR TO PLAY THE PIANO?
HEH. YOU A WICKED WOMAN. WHAT YOU DOIN'?
I THOUGHT MAYBE I'D PRACTICE MY FINGERING TOO.

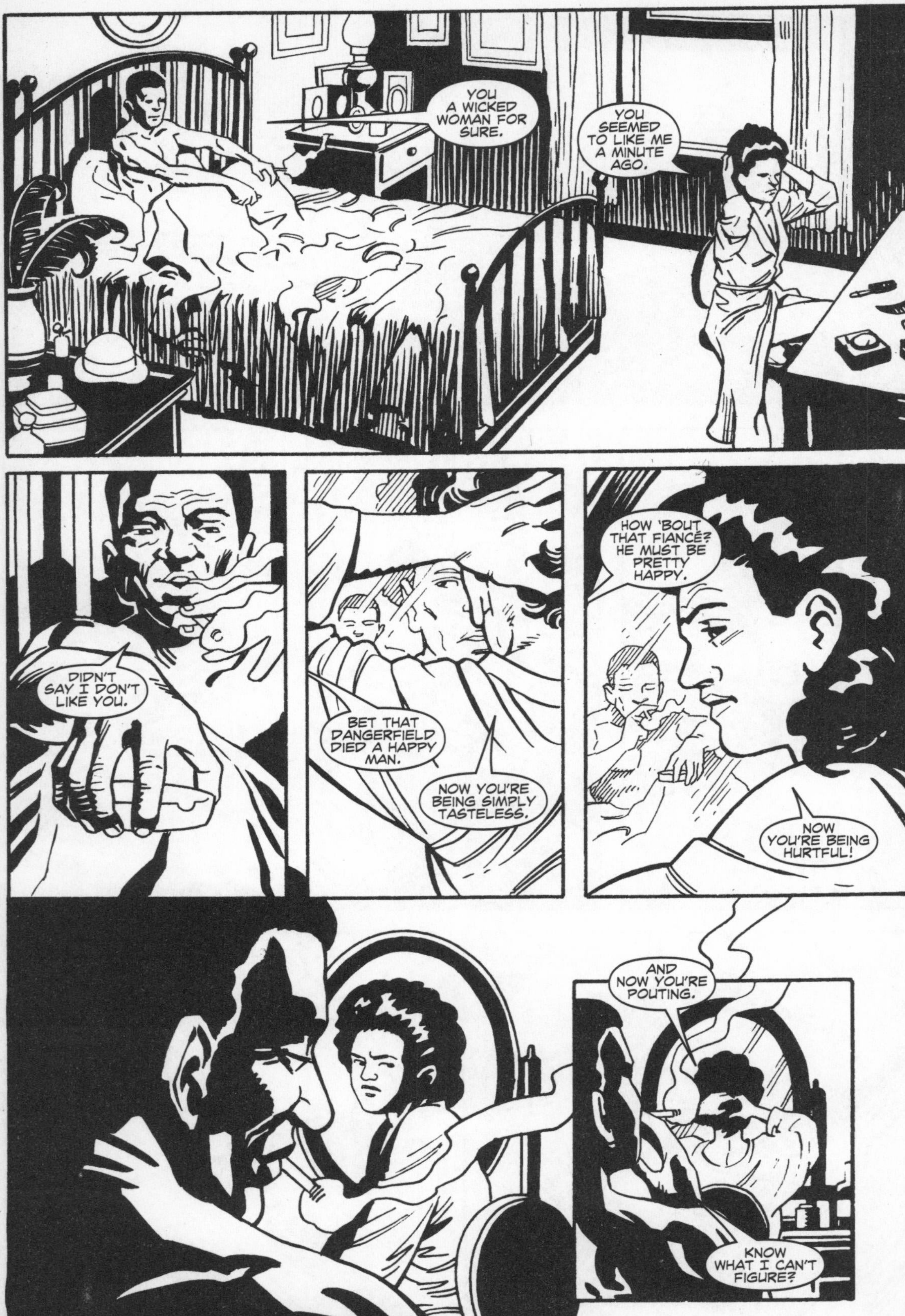
YOU A WICKED WOMAN FOR SURE.
YOU SEEMED TO LIKE ME A MINUTE AGO.
DIDN'T SAY I DON'T LIKE YOU.
BET THAT DANGERFIELD DIED A HAPPY MAN.
NOW YOU'RE BEING SIMPLY TASTELESS.
HOW 'BOUT THAT FIANCÉ? HE MUST BE PRETTY HAPPY.
NOW YOU'RE BEING HURTFUL!
AND NOW YOU'RE POUTING.
KNOW WHAT I CAN'T FIGURE?

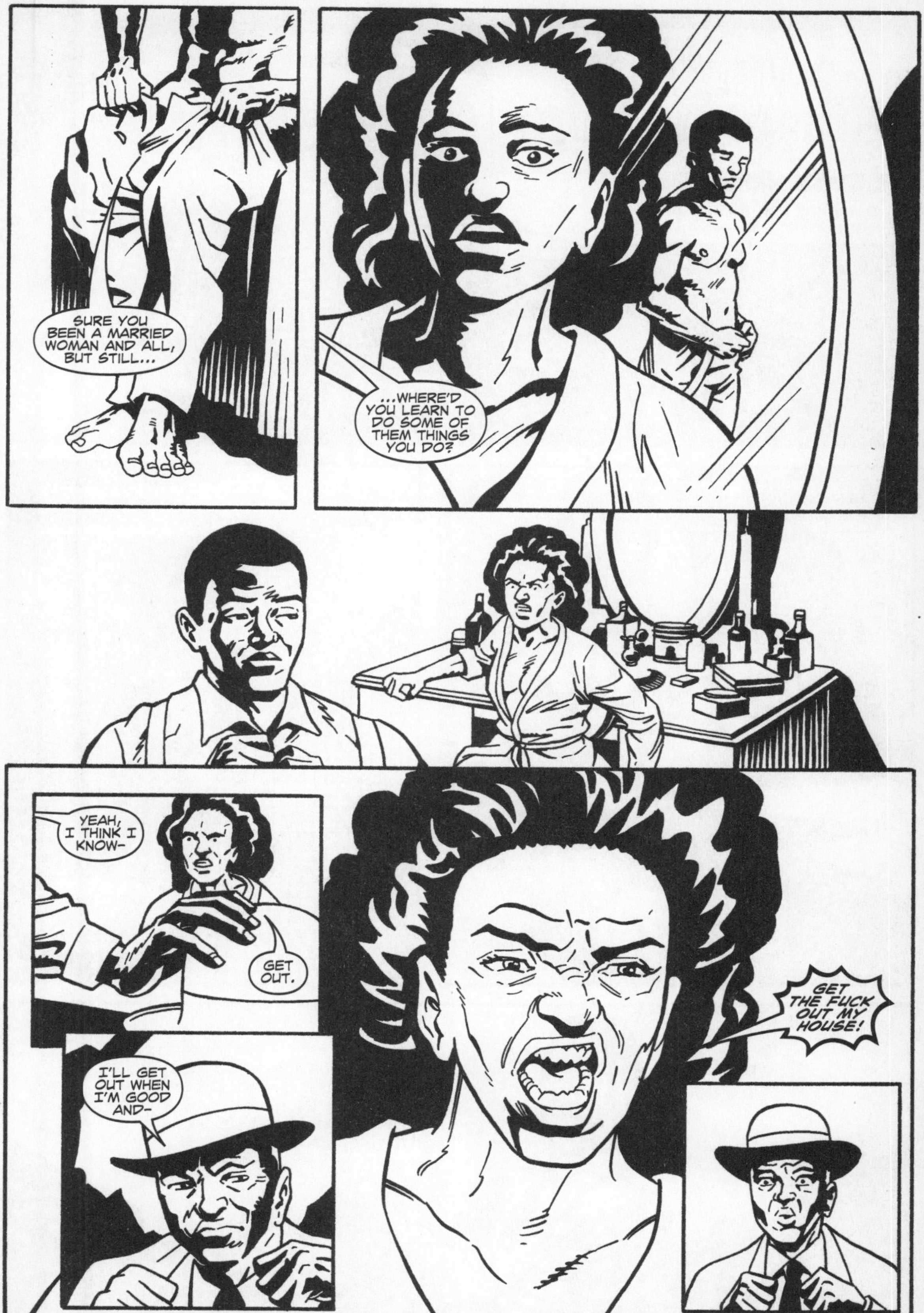
SURE YOU BEEN A MARRIED WOMAN AND ALL, BUT STILL...
...WHERE'D YOU LEARN TO DO SOME OF THEM THINGS YOU DO?
YEAH, I THINK I KNOW-
GET OUT.
I'LL GET OUT WHEN I'M GOOD AND-
GET THE FUCK OUT MY HOUSE!

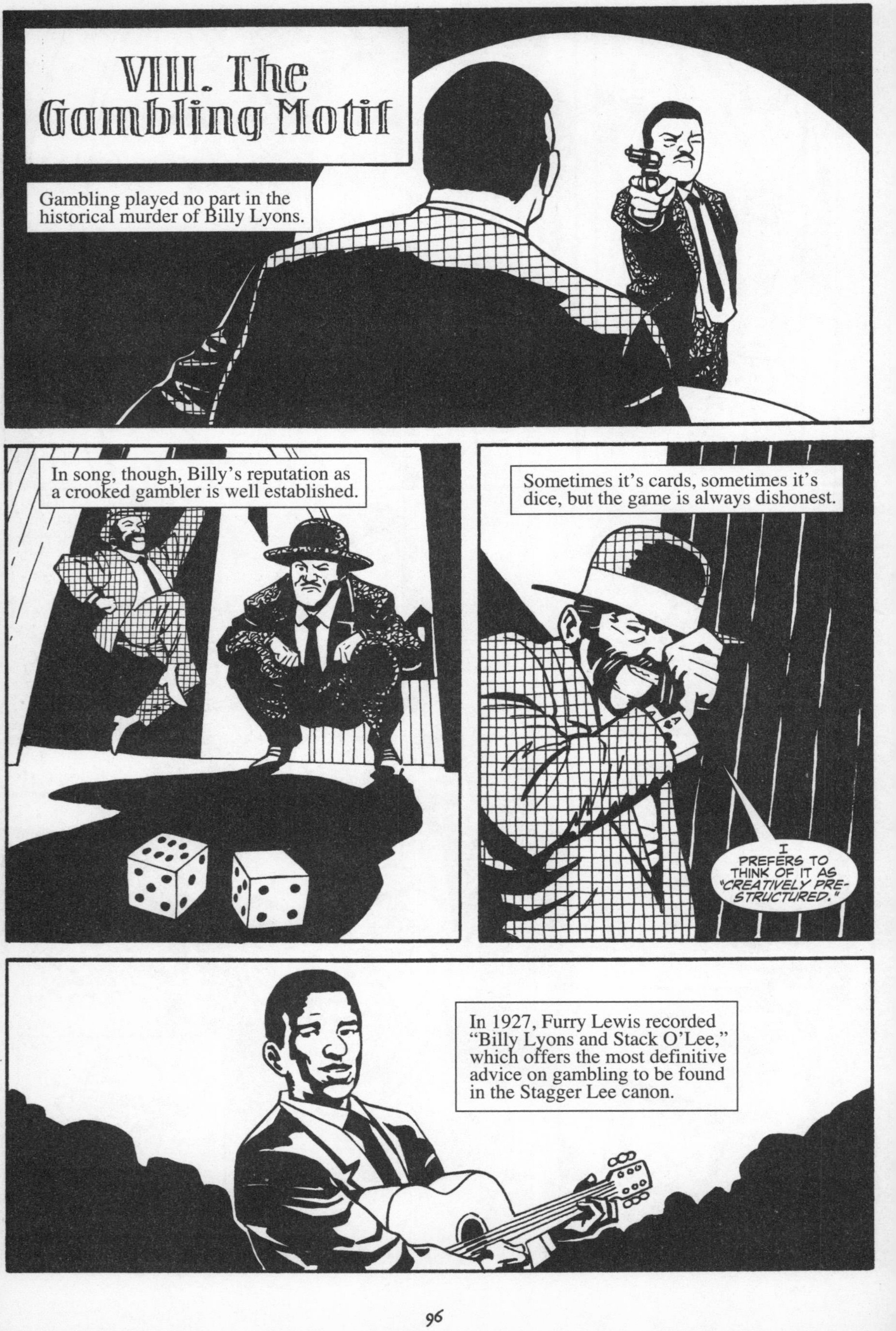
VIII. The Gambling Motif
Gambling played no part in the historical murder of Billy Lyons.
In song, though, Billy's reputation as a crooked gambler is well established.
Sometimes it's cards, sometimes it's dice, but the game is always dishonest.
I PREFERS TO THINK OF IT AS "CREATIVELY PRE-STRUCTURED."
In 1927, Furry Lewis recorded "Billy Lyons and Stack O'Lee," which offers the most definitive advice on gambling to be found in the Stagger Lee canon.

I remember one September on one Friday night,
Stack O'Lee an' Billy Lyons had a great fight.
Cryin', when you lose your money,
learn to lose.

Billy Lyons shot six bits,
Stack O'Lee bet he pass,
Stack O'Lee out with his forty-five,
said you done shot your last
When you lose your money, learn to lose.

Lord, a woman come a-runnin',
fell down on her knees,
Cryin' "Oh Mr. Stack O'Lee
don't shoot my brother, please."
When you lose your money...

I ain't talkin' 'bout some gamblers,
oughta see Richard Lee,
Shot one thousand dollars,
an' come out on a three.
Cryin', when you lose your money,
learn to lose.

Lord, the judge told the sheriff,
"We want him dead or alive,
How in the world can we bring him in,
when he totes a forty-five?"
When you lose your money, learn to lose.

"Lord," the woman told the judge,
"my husband's name Jack, Sheriff,
"Wanna arrest po' Stack O'Lee,
better go somewheres else."
When you lose your money, learn to lose.

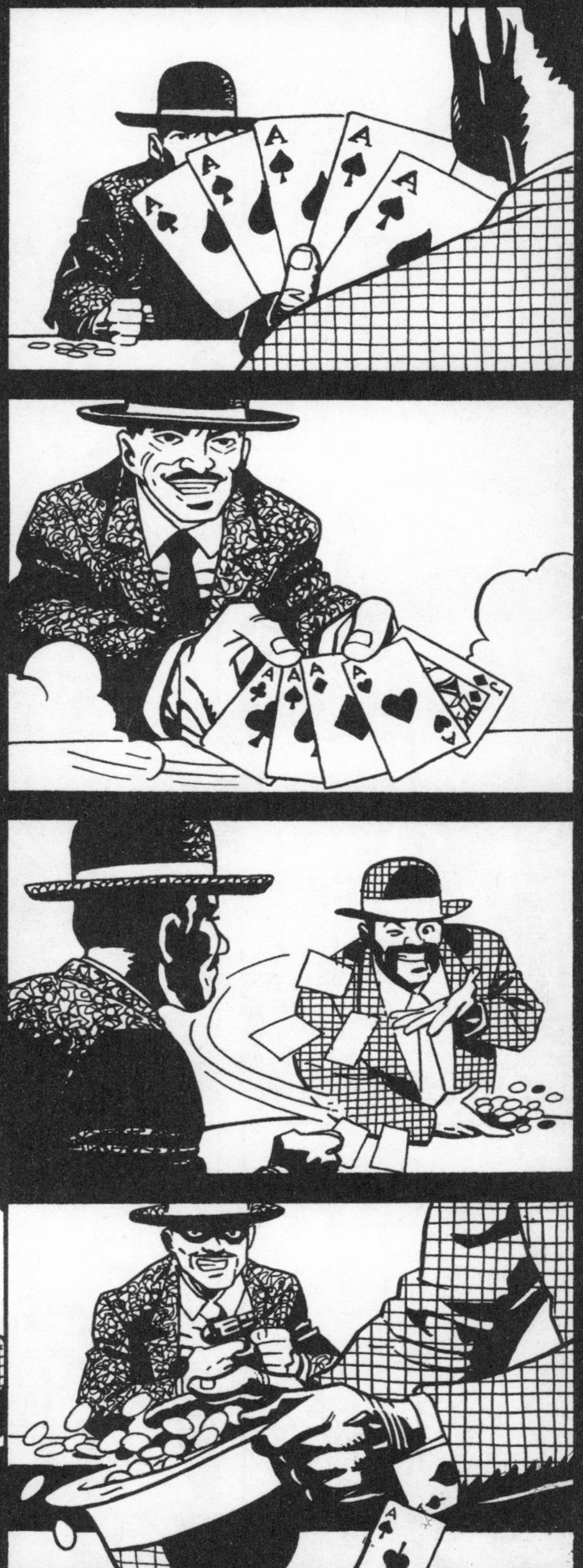

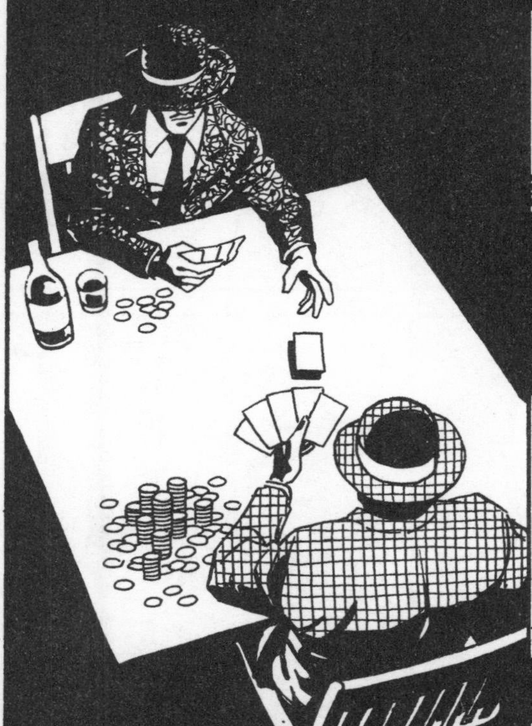

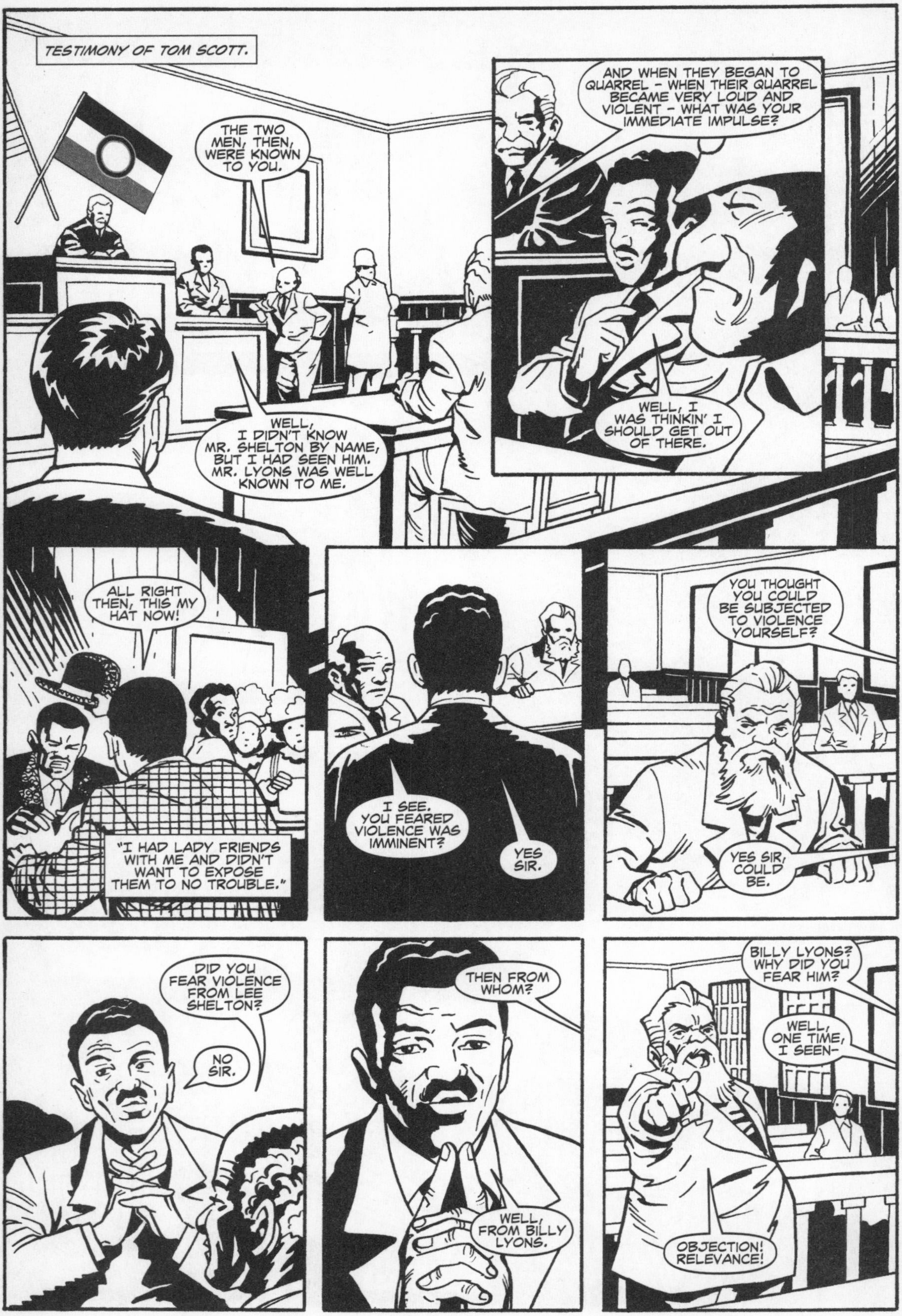
TESTIMONY OF TOM SCOTT.
THE TWO MEN, THEN, WERE KNOWN TO YOU.
WELL, I DIDN'T KNOW MR. SHELTON BY NAME, BUT I HAD SEEN HIM. MR. LYONS WAS WELL KNOWN TO ME.
AND WHEN THEY BEGAN TO QUARREL - WHEN THEIR QUARREL BECAME VERY LOUD AND VIOLENT - WHAT WAS YOUR IMMEDIATE IMPULSE?
WELL, I WAS THINKIN' I SHOULD GET OUT OF THERE.
ALL RIGHT THEN, THIS MY HAT NOW!
"I HAD LADY FRIENDS WITH ME AND DIDN'T WANT TO EXPOSE THEM TO NO TROUBLE."
I SEE. YOU FEARED VIOLENCE WAS IMMINENT?
YES SIR.
YOU THOUGHT YOU COULD BE SUBJECTED TO VIOLENCE YOURSELF?
YES SIR, COULD BE.
DID YOU FEAR VIOLENCE FROM LEE SHELTON?
NO SIR.
THEN FROM WHOM?
WELL, FROM BILLY LYONS.
BILLY LYONS? WHY DID YOU FEAR HIM?
WELL, ONE TIME, I SEEN–
OBJECTION! RELEVANCE!

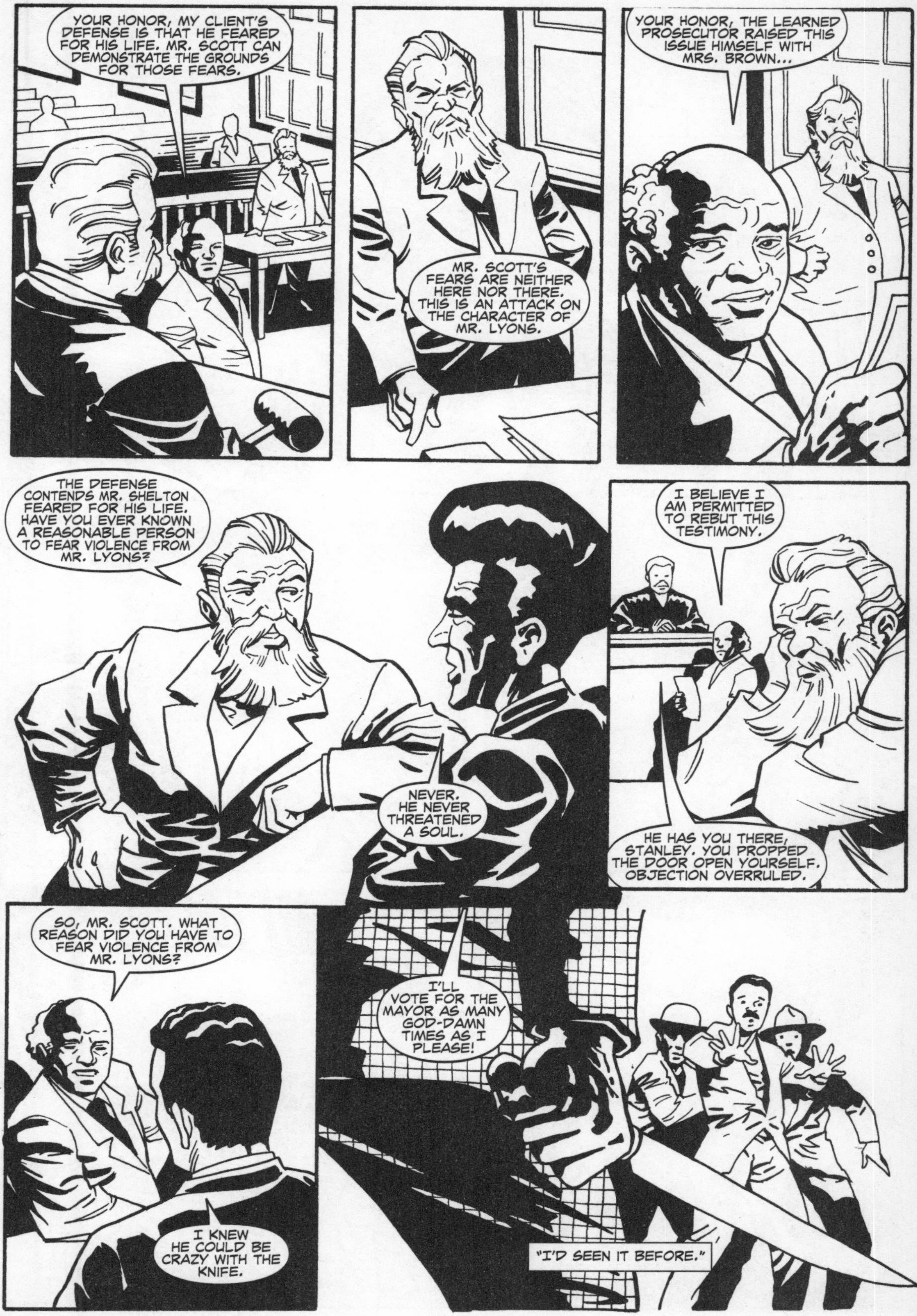
YOUR HONOR, MY CLIENT'S DEFENSE IS THAT HE FEARED FOR HIS LIFE. MR. SCOTT CAN DEMONSTRATE THE GROUNDS FOR THOSE FEARS.
MR. SCOTT'S FEARS ARE NEITHER HERE NOR THERE. THIS IS AN ATTACK ON THE CHARACTER OF MR. LYONS.
YOUR HONOR, THE LEARNED PROSECUTOR RAISED THIS ISSUE HIMSELF WITH MRS. BROWN...
THE DEFENSE CONTENDS MR. SHELTON FEARED FOR HIS LIFE. HAVE YOU EVER KNOWN A REASONABLE PERSON TO FEAR VIOLENCE FROM MR. LYONS?
NEVER. HE NEVER THREATENED A SOUL.
I BELIEVE I AM PERMITTED TO REBUT THIS TESTIMONY.
HE HAS YOU THERE, STANLEY. YOU PROPPED THE DOOR OPEN YOURSELF. OBJECTION OVERRULED.
SO, MR. SCOTT. WHAT REASON DID YOU HAVE TO FEAR VIOLENCE FROM MR. LYONS?
I KNEW HE COULD BE CRAZY WITH THE KNIFE.
I'LL VOTE FOR THE MAYOR AS MANY GOD-DAMN TIMES AS I PLEASE!
"I'D SEEN IT BEFORE."

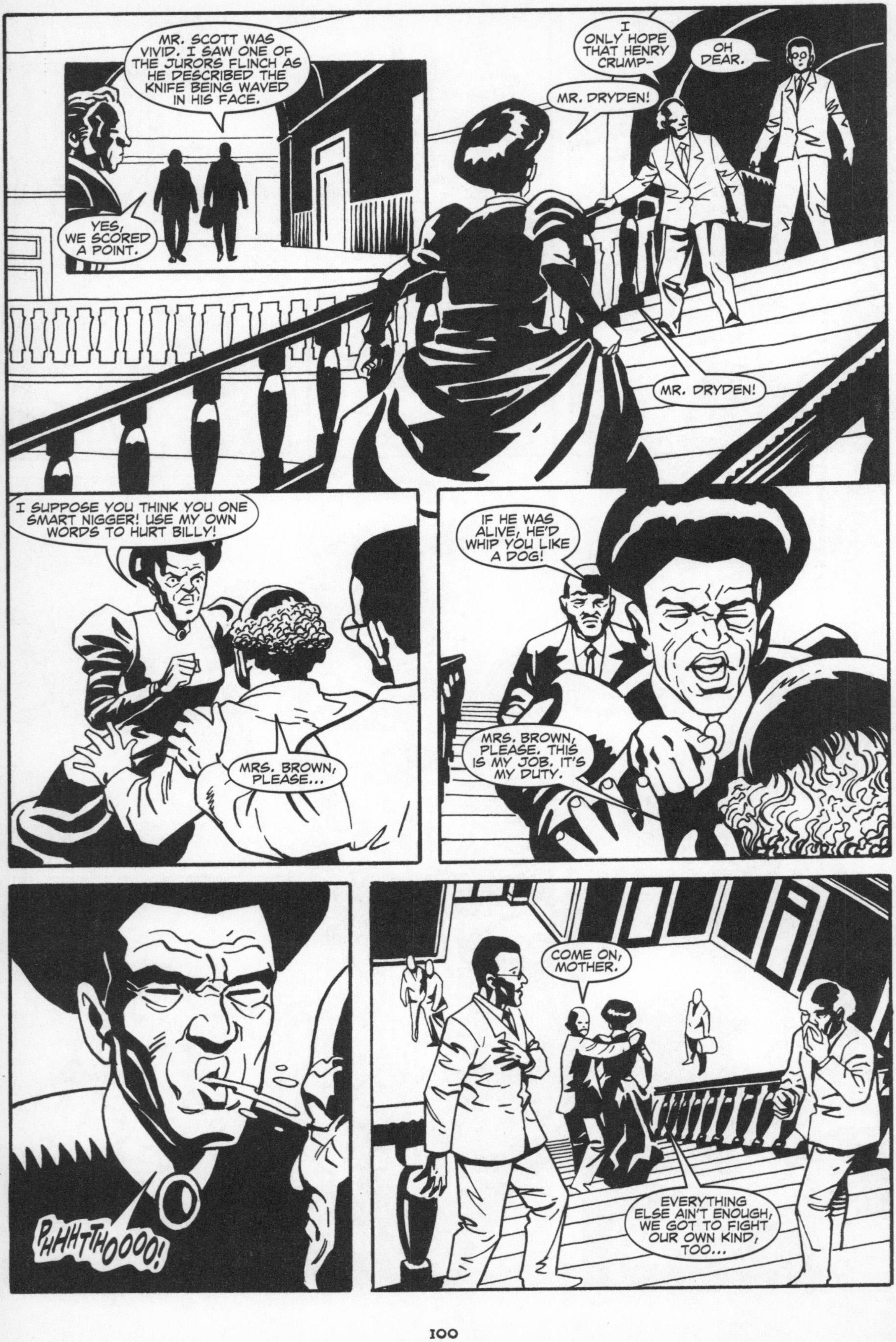
MR. SCOTT WAS VIVID. I SAW ONE OF THE JURORS FLINCH AS HE DESCRIBED THE KNIFE BEING WAVED IN HIS FACE.
YES, WE SCORED A POINT.
I ONLY HOPE THAT HENRY CRUMP-
OH DEAR.
MR. DRYDEN!
MR. DRYDEN!
I SUPPOSE YOU THINK YOU ONE SMART NIGGER! USE MY OWN WORDS TO HURT BILLY!
MRS. BROWN, PLEASE...
IF HE WAS ALIVE, HE'D WHIP YOU LIKE A DOG!
MRS. BROWN, PLEASE. THIS IS MY JOB. IT'S MY DUTY.
PHHHTTHOOOO!
COME ON, MOTHER.
EVERYTHING ELSE AIN'T ENOUGH, WE GOT TO FIGHT OUR OWN KIND, TOO...

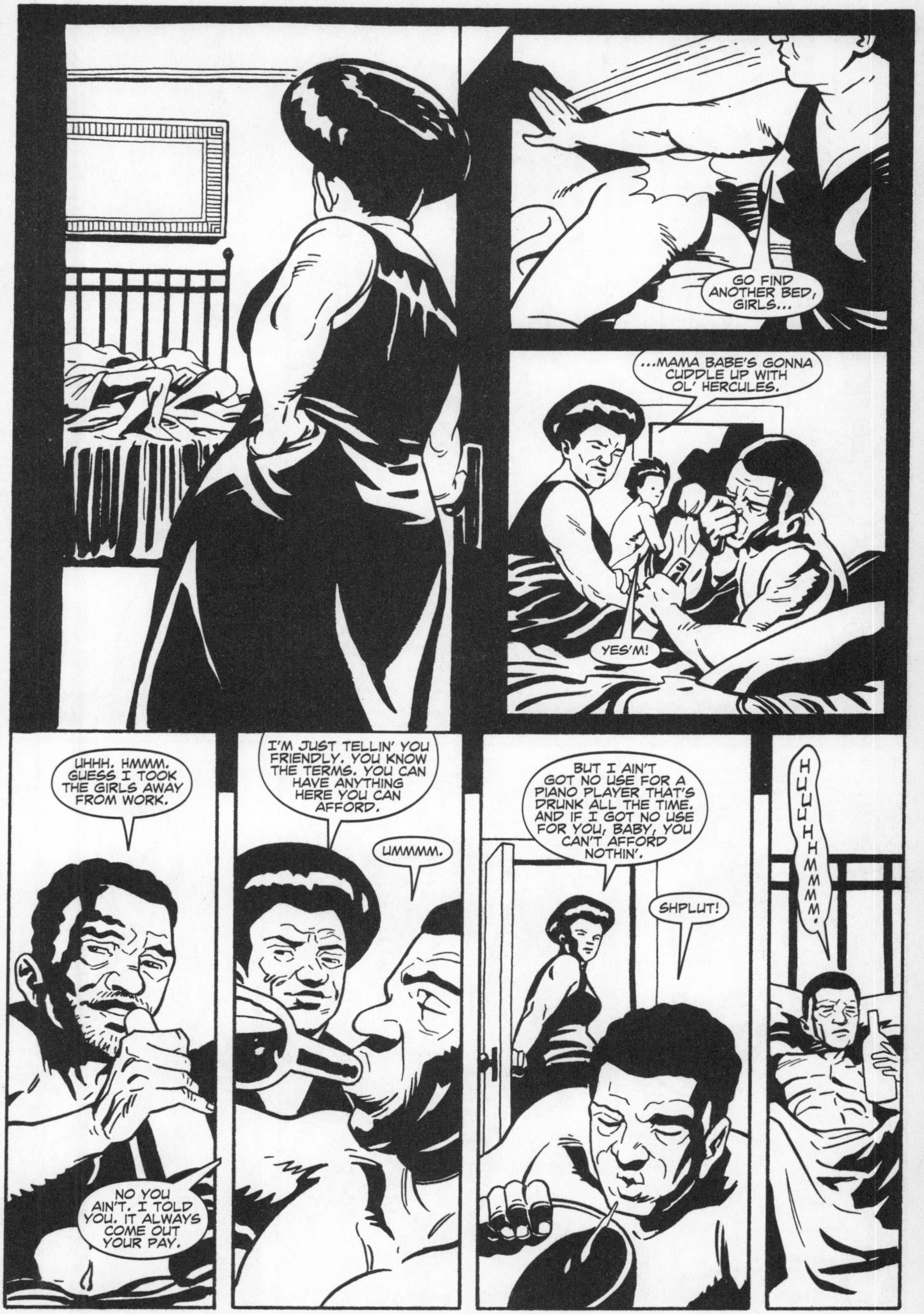
GO FIND ANOTHER BED, GIRLS...
...MAMA BABE'S GONNA CUDDLE UP WITH OL' HERCULES.
YES'M!
UHHH. HMMM. GUESS I TOOK THE GIRLS AWAY FROM WORK.
NO YOU AIN'T. I TOLD YOU. IT ALWAYS COME OUT YOUR PAY.
I'M JUST TELLIN' YOU FRIENDLY. YOU KNOW THE TERMS. YOU CAN HAVE ANYTHING HERE YOU CAN AFFORD.
UMMMM.
BUT I AIN'T GOT NO USE FOR A PIANO PLAYER THAT'S DRUNK ALL THE TIME. AND IF I GOT NO USE FOR YOU, BABY, YOU CAN'T AFFORD NOTHIN'.
SHPLUT!
HUUUHHMMMM.

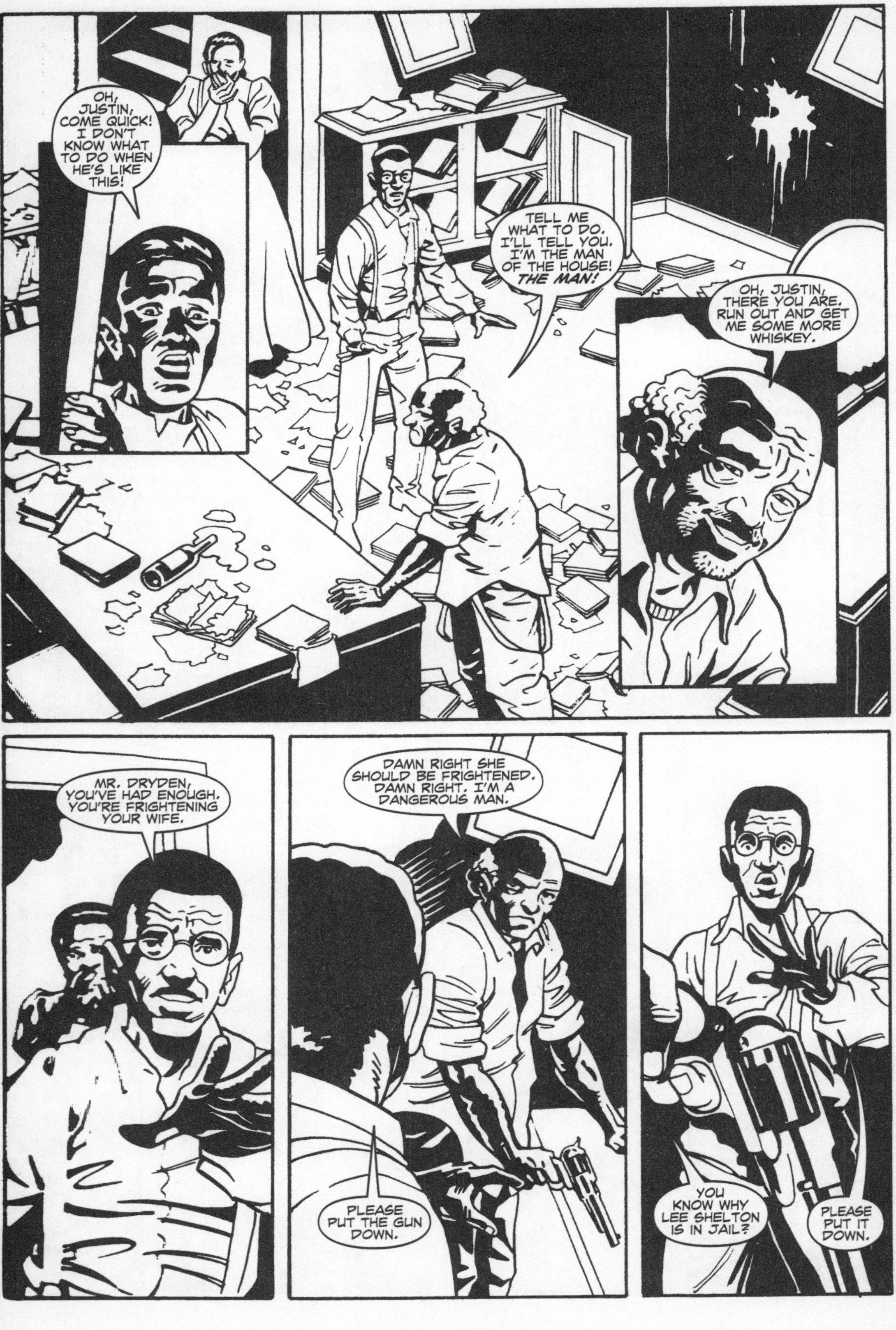
OH, JUSTIN, COME QUICK! I DON'T KNOW WHAT TO DO WHEN HE'S LIKE THIS!
TELL ME WHAT TO DO. I'LL TELL YOU. I'M THE MAN OF THE HOUSE! THE MAN!
OH, JUSTIN, THERE YOU ARE. RUN OUT AND GET ME SOME MORE WHISKEY.
MR. DRYDEN, YOU'VE HAD ENOUGH. YOU'RE FRIGHTENING YOUR WIFE.
DAMN RIGHT SHE SHOULD BE FRIGHTENED. DAMN RIGHT. I'M A DANGEROUS MAN.
PLEASE PUT THE GUN DOWN.
YOU KNOW WHY LEE SHELTON IS IN JAIL?
PLEASE PUT IT DOWN.

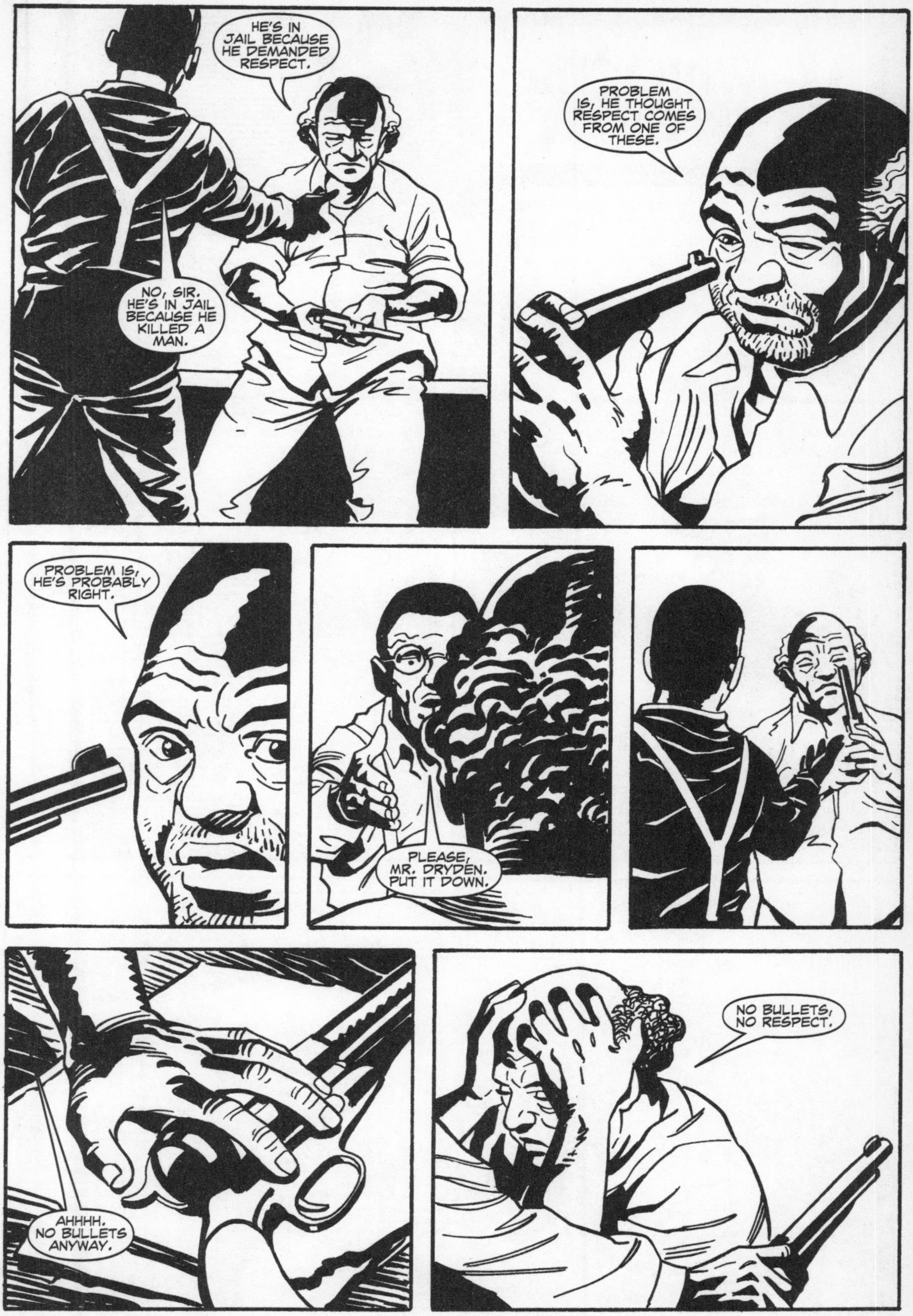
HE'S IN JAIL BECAUSE HE DEMANDED RESPECT.
NO, SIR. HE'S IN JAIL BECAUSE HE KILLED A MAN.
PROBLEM IS, HE THOUGHT RESPECT COMES FROM ONE OF THESE.
PROBLEM IS, HE'S PROBABLY RIGHT.
PLEASE, MR. DRYDEN. PUT IT DOWN.
AHHHH. NO BULLETS ANYWAY.
NO BULLETS, NO RESPECT.

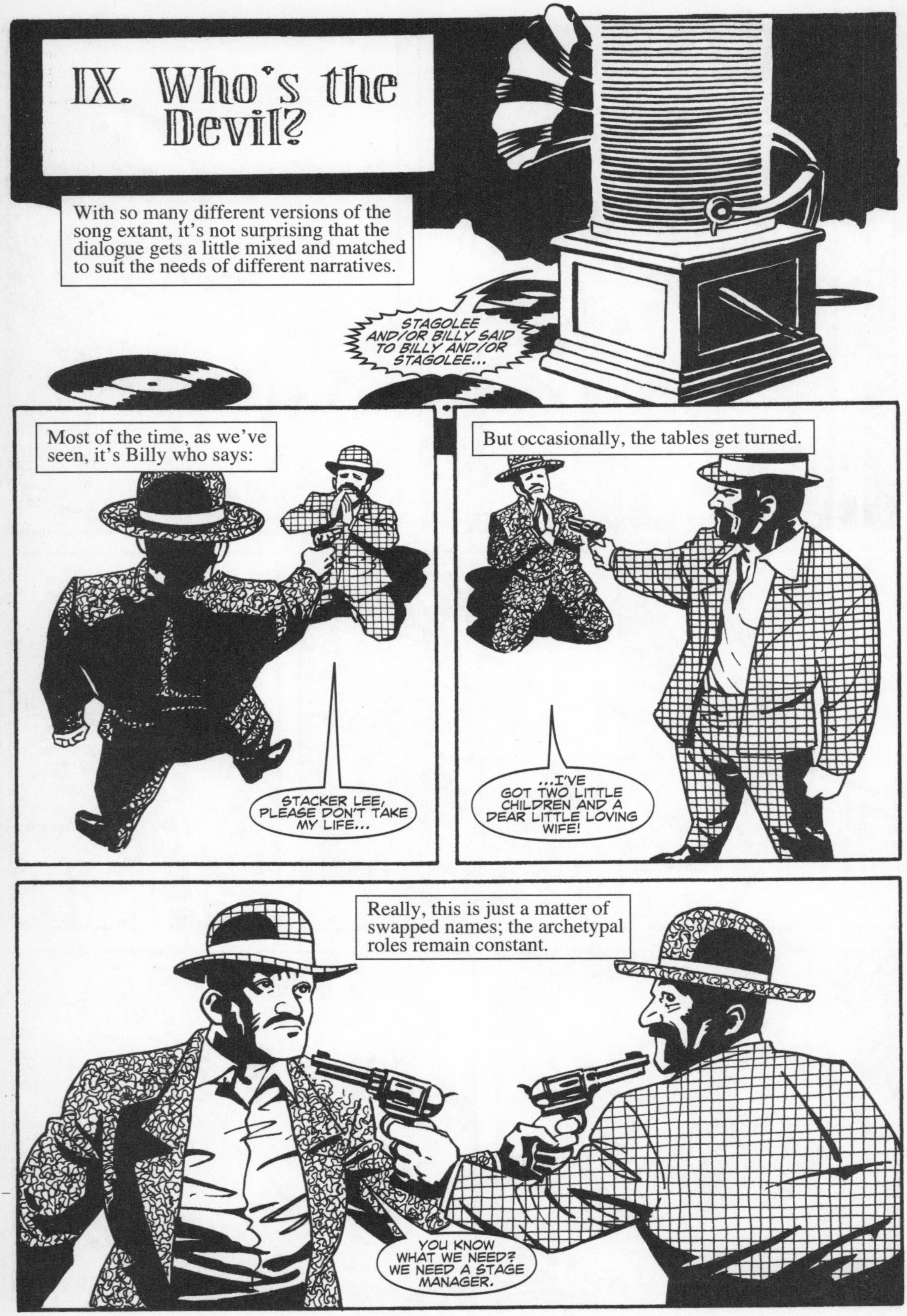
IX. Who's the Devil?
With so many different versions of the song extant, it's not surprising that the dialogue gets a little mixed and matched to suit the needs of different narratives.
STAGOLEE AND/OR BILLY SAID TO BILLY AND/OR STAGOLEE...
Most of the time, as we've seen, it's Billy who says:
STACKER LEE, PLEASE DON'T TAKE MY LIFE...
But occasionally, the tables get turned.
...I'VE GOT TWO LITTLE CHILDREN AND A DEAR LITTLE LOVING WIFE!
Really, this is just a matter of swapped names; the archetypal roles remain constant.
YOU KNOW WHAT WE NEED? WE NEED A STAGE MANAGER.

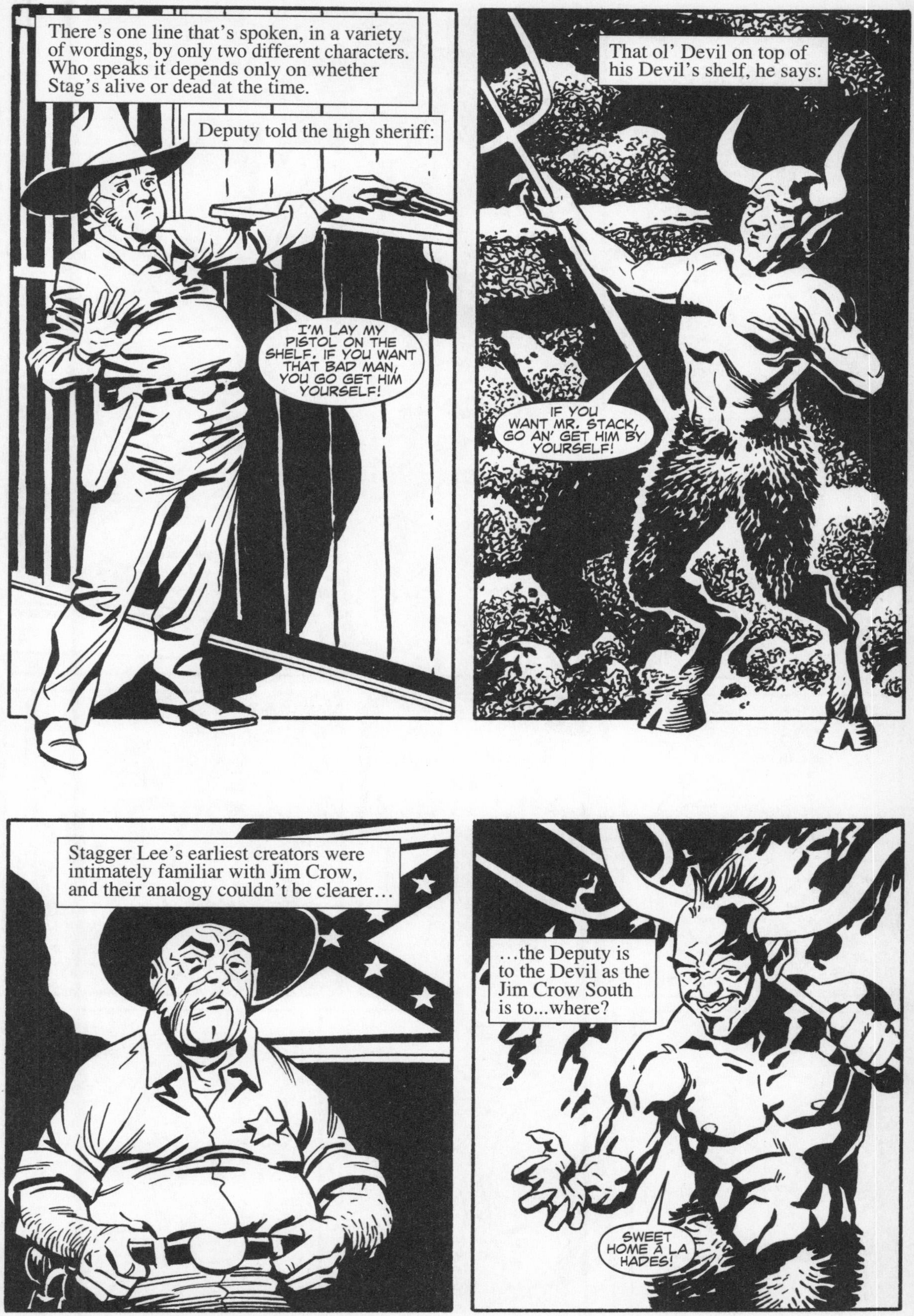
There's one line that's spoken, in a variety of wordings, by only two different characters. Who speaks it depends only on whether Stag's alive or dead at the time.
Deputy told the high sheriff:
I'M LAY MY PISTOL ON THE SHELF. IF YOU WANT THAT BAD MAN, YOU GO GET HIM YOURSELF!
That ol' Devil on top of his Devil's shelf, he says:
IF YOU WANT MR. STACK, GO AN' GET HIM BY YOURSELF!
Stagger Lee's earliest creators were intimately familiar with Jim Crow, and their analogy couldn't be clearer...
...the Deputy is to the Devil as the Jim Crow South is to...where?
SWEET HOME À LA HADES!

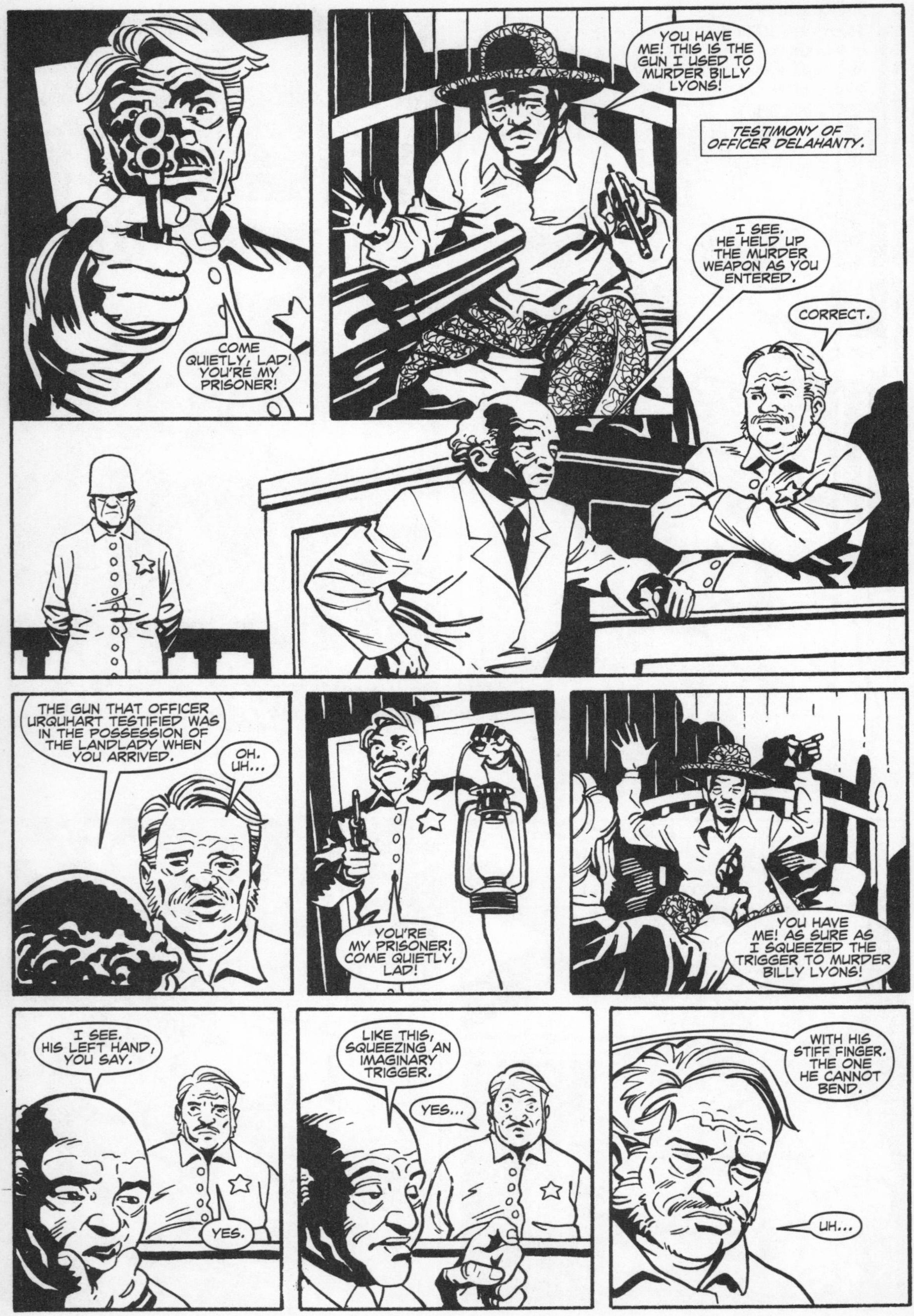
COME QUIETLY, LAD! YOU'RE MY PRISONER!
YOU HAVE ME! THIS IS THE GUN I USED TO MURDER BILLY LYONS!
TESTIMONY OF OFFICER DELAHANTY.
I SEE. HE HELD UP THE MURDER WEAPON AS YOU ENTERED.
CORRECT.
THE GUN THAT OFFICER URQUHART TESTIFIED WAS IN THE POSSESSION OF THE LANDLADY WHEN YOU ARRIVED.
OH. UH...
YOU'RE MY PRISONER! COME QUIETLY, LAD!
YOU HAVE ME! AS SURE AS I SQUEEZED THE TRIGGER TO MURDER BILLY LYONS!
I SEE. HIS LEFT HAND, YOU SAY.
YES.
LIKE THIS, SQUEEZING AN IMAGINARY TRIGGER.
YES...
WITH HIS STIFF FINGER. THE ONE HE CANNOT BEND.
UH...

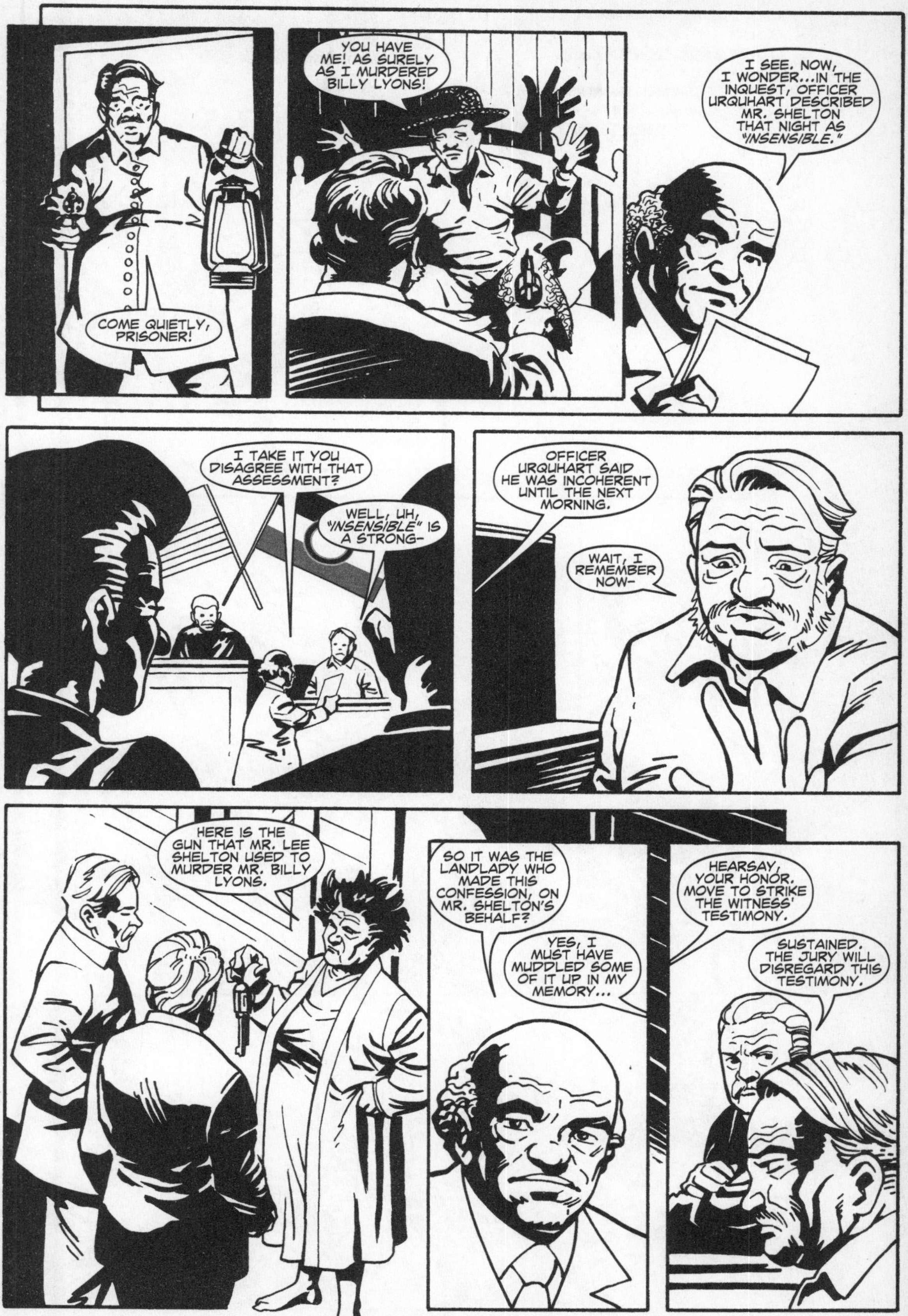
COME QUIETLY, PRISONER!
YOU HAVE ME! AS SURELY AS I MURDERED BILLY LYONS!
I SEE. NOW, I WONDER...IN THE INQUEST, OFFICER URQUHART DESCRIBED MR. SHELTON THAT NIGHT AS "INSENSIBLE."
I TAKE IT YOU DISAGREE WITH THAT ASSESSMENT?
WELL, UH, "INSENSIBLE" IS A STRONG-
OFFICER URQUHART SAID HE WAS INCOHERENT UNTIL THE NEXT MORNING.
WAIT, I REMEMBER NOW-
HERE IS THE GUN THAT MR. LEE SHELTON USED TO MURDER MR. BILLY LYONS.
SO IT WAS THE LANDLADY WHO MADE THIS CONFESSION, ON MR. SHELTON'S BEHALF?
YES, I MUST HAVE MUDDLED SOME OF IT UP IN MY MEMORY...
HEARSAY, YOUR HONOR. MOVE TO STRIKE THE WITNESS' TESTIMONY.
SUSTAINED. THE JURY WILL DISREGARD THIS TESTIMONY.

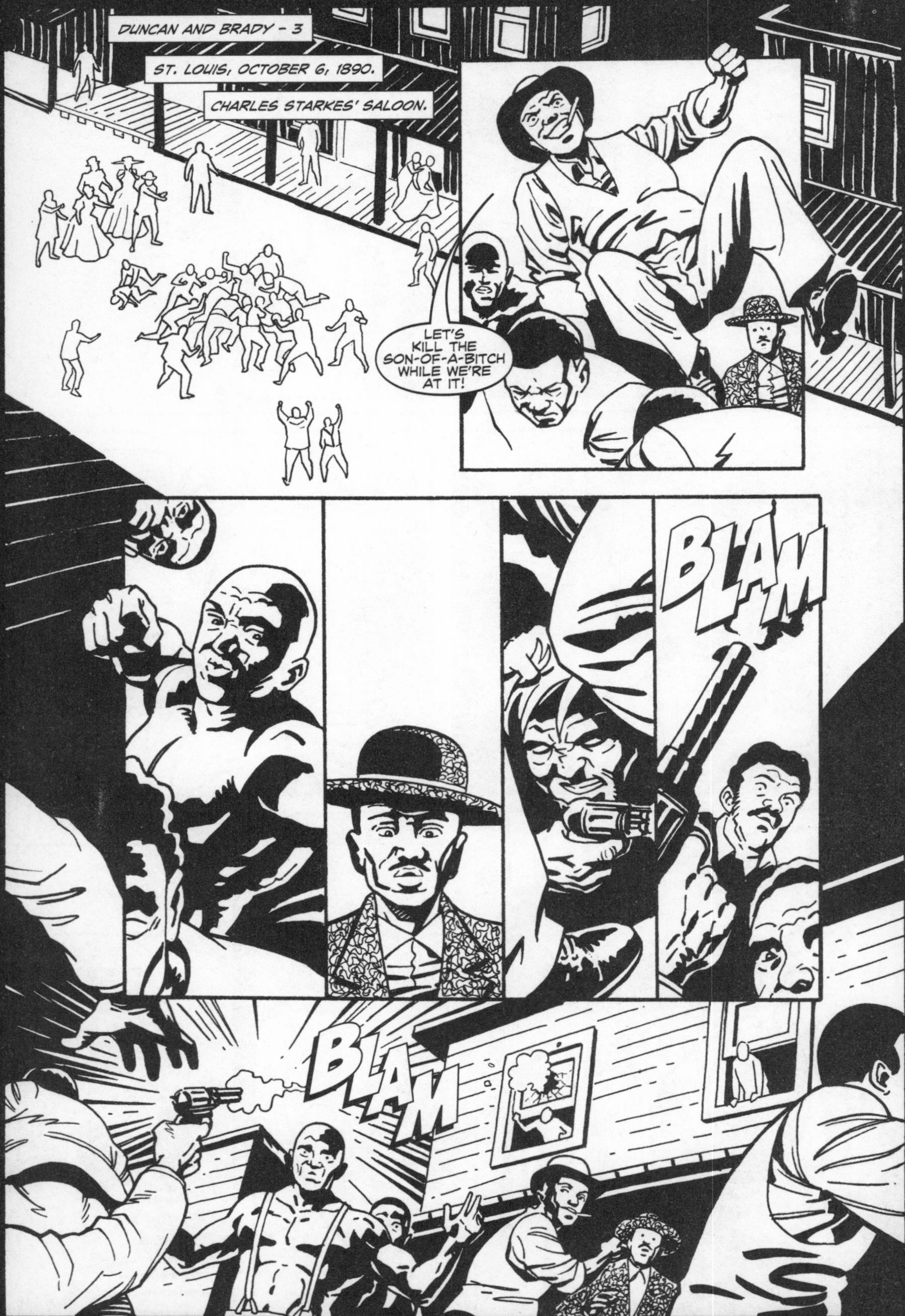
DUNCAN AND BRADY - 3
ST. LOUIS, OCTOBER 6, 1890.
CHARLES STARKES' SALOON.
LET'S KILL THE SON-OF-A-BITCH WHILE WE'RE AT IT!
BLAM
BLAM

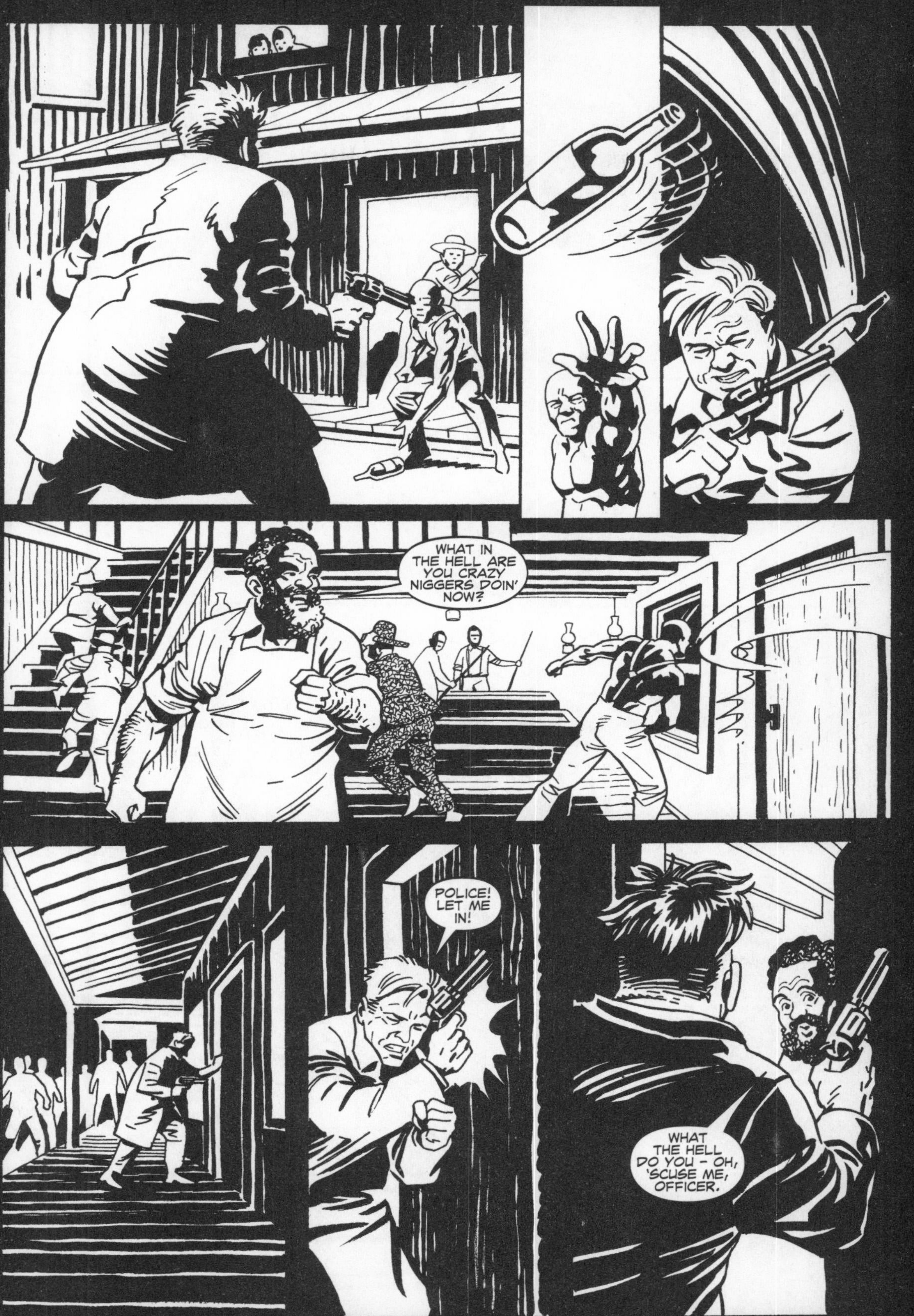

WHAT IN THE HELL ARE YOU CRAZY NIGGERS DOIN' NOW?
POLICE! LET ME IN!
WHAT THE HELL DO YOU - OH, 'SCUSE ME, OFFICER.

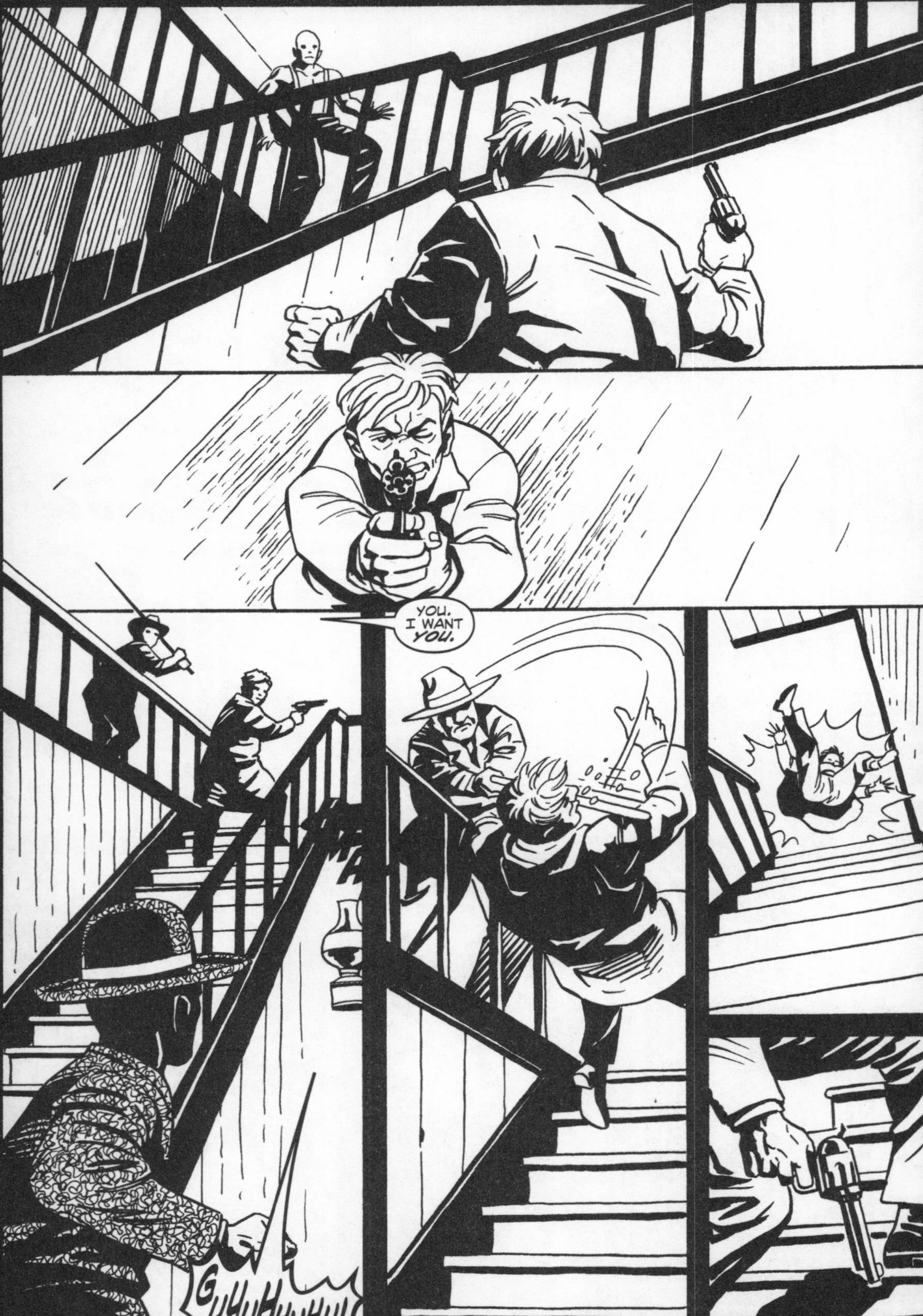
YOU. I WANT YOU.
GUUUHHHHH!

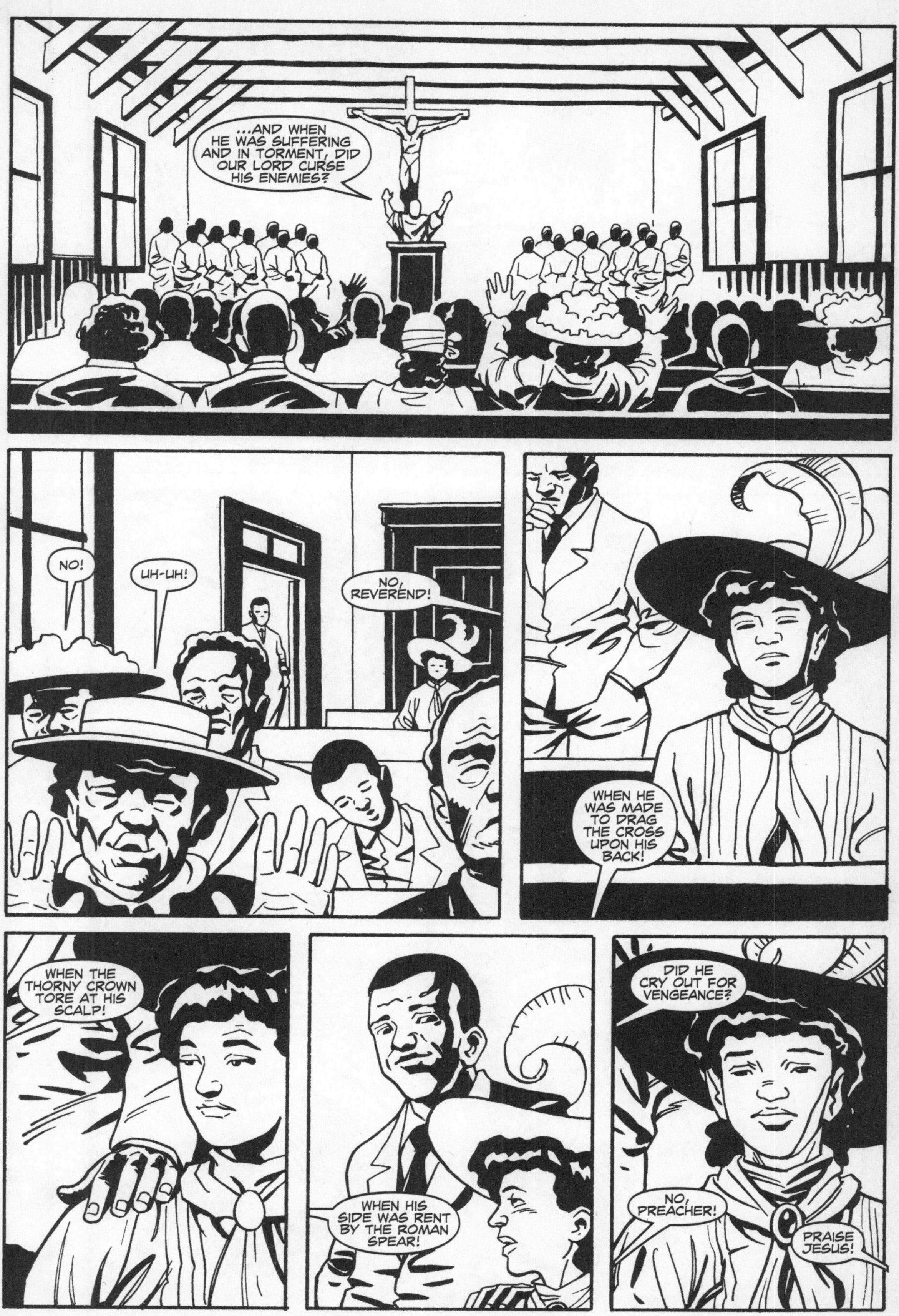
...AND WHEN HE WAS SUFFERING AND IN TORMENT, DID OUR LORD CURSE HIS ENEMIES?
NO!
UH-UH!
NO, REVEREND!
WHEN HE WAS MADE TO DRAG THE CROSS UPON HIS BACK!
WHEN THE THORNY CROWN TORE AT HIS SCALP!
WHEN HIS SIDE WAS RENT BY THE ROMAN SPEAR!
DID HE CRY OUT FOR VENGEANCE?
NO, PREACHER!
PRAISE JESUS!

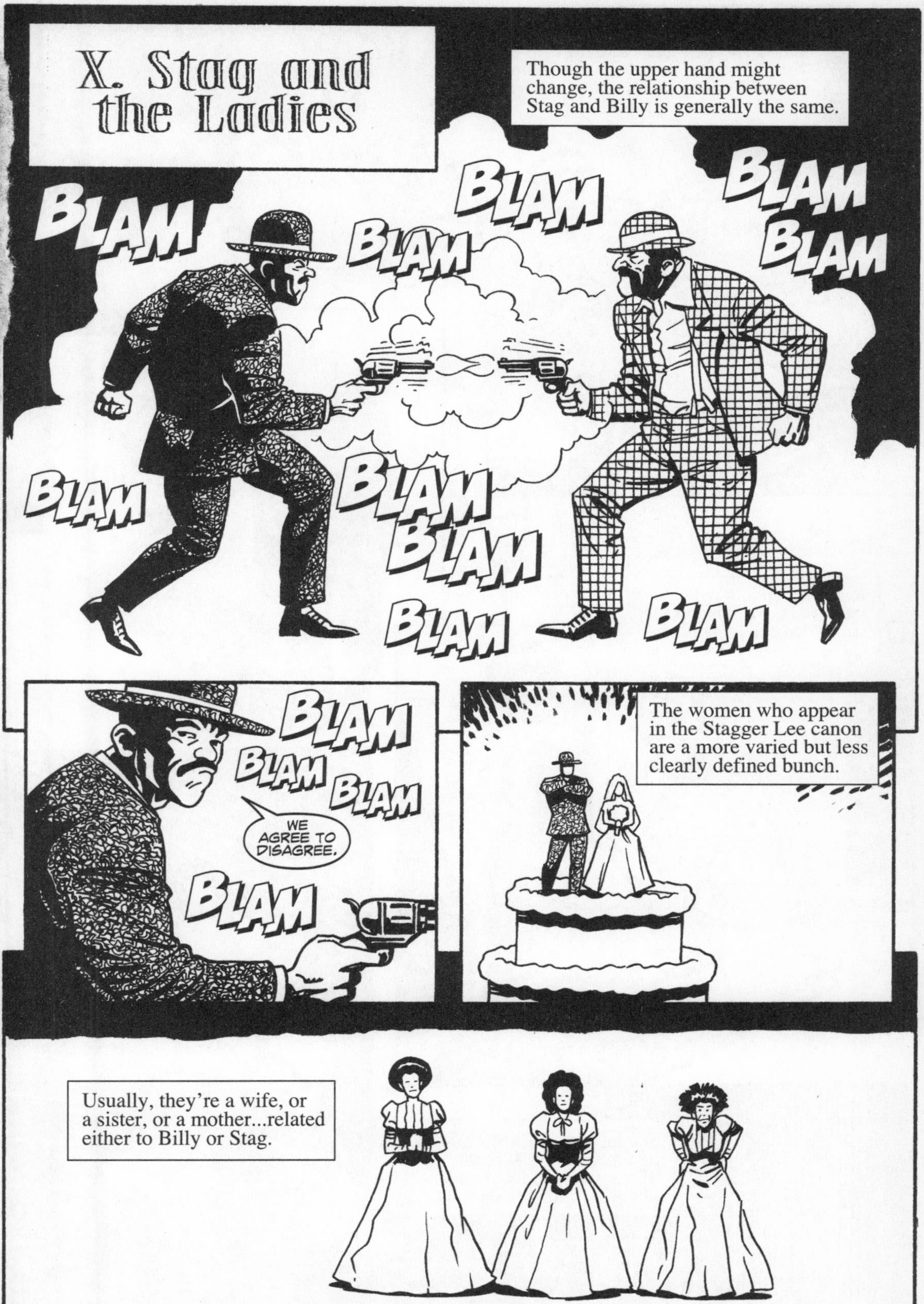
X. Stag and the Ladies
Though the upper hand might change, the relationship between Stag and Billy is generally the same.
BLAM
BLAM
BLAM
BLAM
BLAM
BLAM
BLAM
BLAM
BLAM
BLAM
BLAM
BLAM
BLAM
BLAM
WE AGREE TO DISAGREE.
BLAM
The women who appear in the Stagger Lee canon are a more varied but less clearly defined bunch.
Usually, they're a wife, or a sister, or a mother...related either to Billy or Stag.

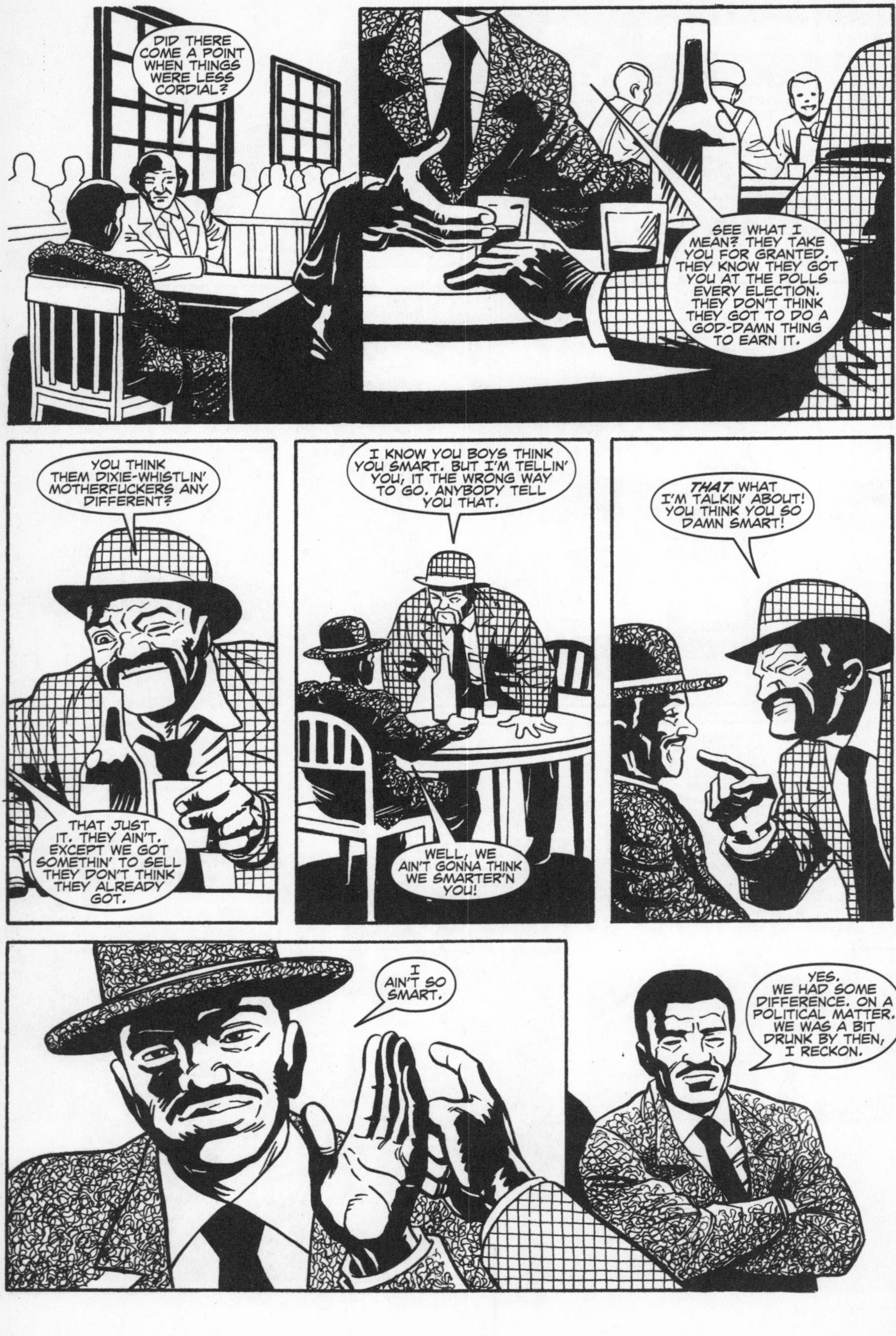
DID THERE COME A POINT WHEN THINGS WERE LESS CORDIAL?
SEE WHAT I MEAN? THEY TAKE YOU FOR GRANTED. THEY KNOW THEY GOT YOU AT THE POLLS EVERY ELECTION. THEY DON'T THINK THEY GOT TO DO A GOD-DAMN THING TO EARN IT.
YOU THINK THEM DIXIE-WHISTLIN' MOTHERFUCKERS ANY DIFFERENT?
THAT JUST IT. THEY AIN'T. EXCEPT WE GOT SOMETHIN' TO SELL THEY DON'T THINK THEY ALREADY GOT.
I KNOW YOU BOYS THINK YOU SMART. BUT I'M TELLIN' YOU, IT THE WRONG WAY TO GO. ANYBODY TELL YOU THAT.
WELL, WE AIN'T GONNA THINK WE SMARTER'N YOU!
THAT WHAT I'M TALKIN' ABOUT! YOU THINK YOU SO DAMN SMART!
I AIN'T SO SMART.
YES. WE HAD SOME DIFFERENCE. ON A POLITICAL MATTER. WE WAS A BIT DRUNK BY THEN, I RECKON.

133

111

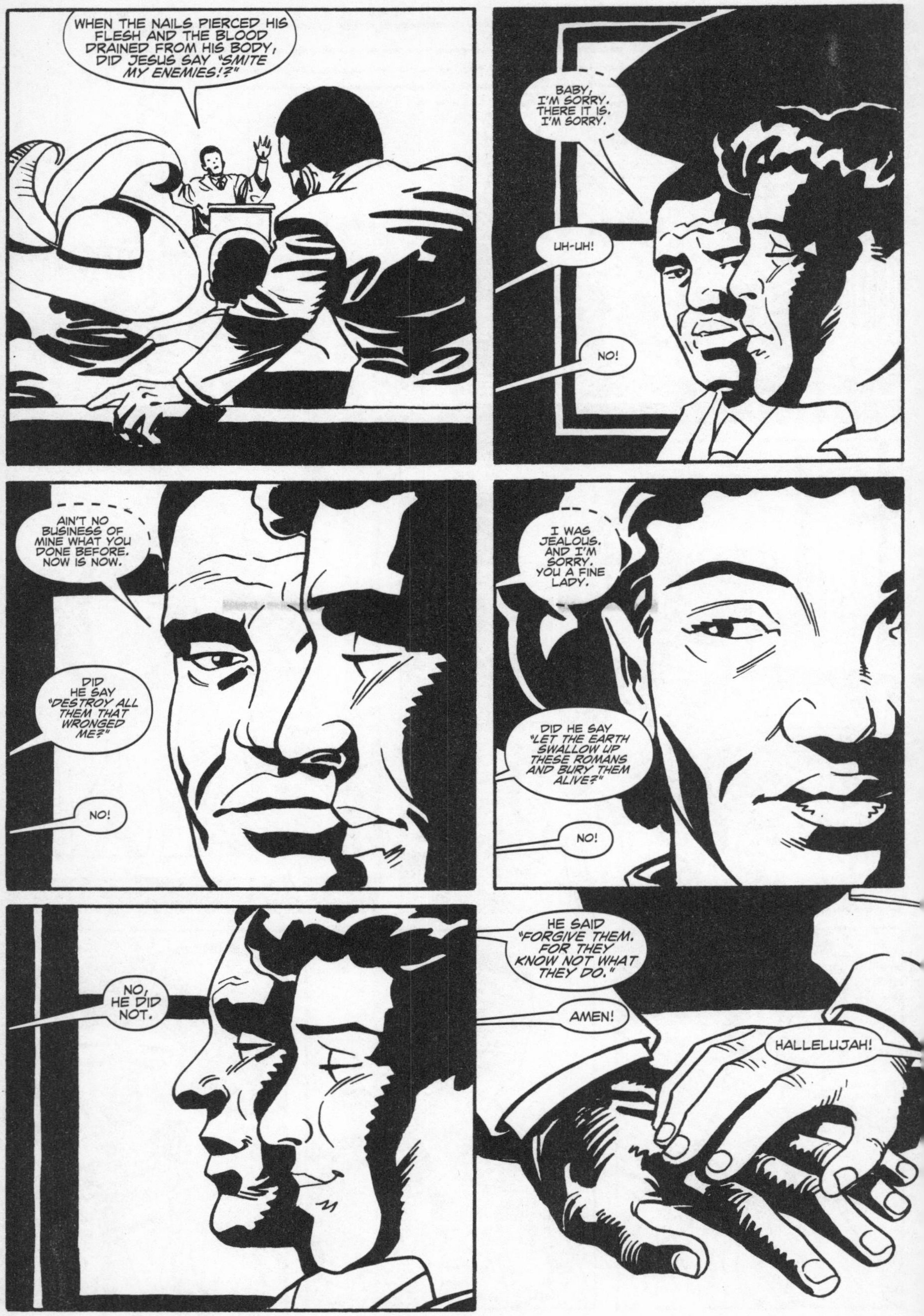
WHEN THE NAILS PIERCED HIS FLESH AND THE BLOOD DRAINED FROM HIS BODY, DID JESUS SAY "SMITE MY ENEMIES!?"
BABY, I'M SORRY. THERE IT IS. I'M SORRY.
UH-UH!
NO!
AIN'T NO BUSINESS OF MINE WHAT YOU DONE BEFORE. NOW IS NOW.
DID HE SAY "DESTROY ALL THEM THAT WRONGED ME?"
NO!
I WAS JEALOUS. AND I'M SORRY. YOU A FINE LADY.
DID HE SAY "LET THE EARTH SWALLOW UP THESE ROMANS AND BURY THEM ALIVE?"
NO!
NO, HE DID NOT.
HE SAID "FORGIVE THEM. FOR THEY KNOW NOT WHAT THEY DO."
AMEN!
HALLELUJAH!

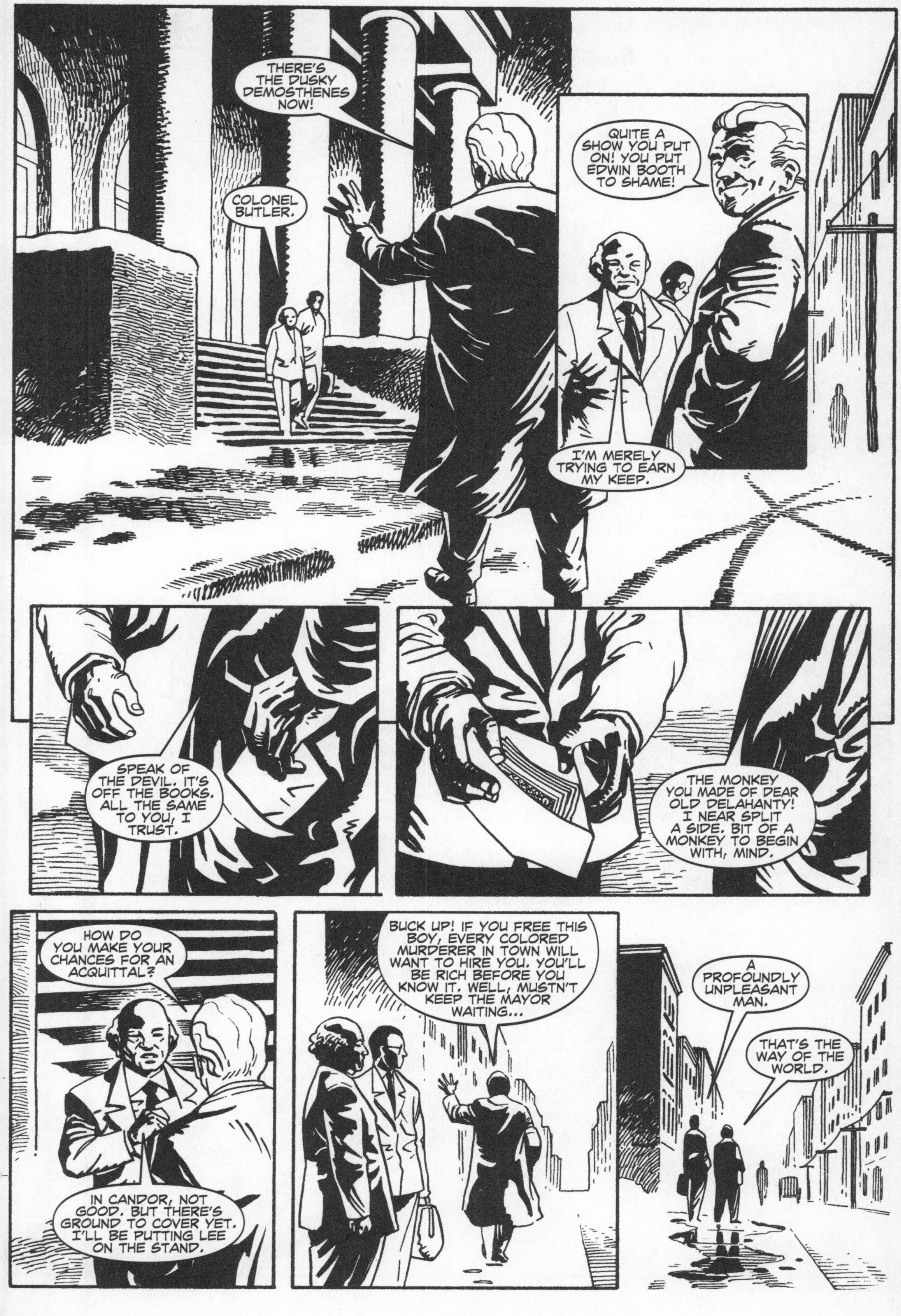
THERE'S THE DUSKY DEMOSTHENES NOW!
COLONEL BUTLER.
QUITE A SHOW YOU PUT ON! YOU PUT EDWIN BOOTH TO SHAME!
I'M MERELY TRYING TO EARN MY KEEP.
SPEAK OF THE DEVIL. IT'S OFF THE BOOKS. ALL THE SAME TO YOU, I TRUST.
THE MONKEY YOU MADE OF DEAR OLD DELAHANTY! I NEAR SPLIT A SIDE. BIT OF A MONKEY TO BEGIN WITH, MIND.
HOW DO YOU MAKE YOUR CHANCES FOR AN ACQUITTAL?
IN CANDOR, NOT GOOD. BUT THERE'S GROUND TO COVER YET. I'LL BE PUTTING LEE ON THE STAND.
BUCK UP! IF YOU FREE THIS BOY, EVERY COLORED MURDERER IN TOWN WILL WANT TO HIRE YOU. YOU'LL BE RICH BEFORE YOU KNOW IT. WELL, MUSTN'T KEEP THE MAYOR WAITING...
A PROFOUNDLY UNPLEASANT MAN.
THAT'S THE WAY OF THE WORLD.

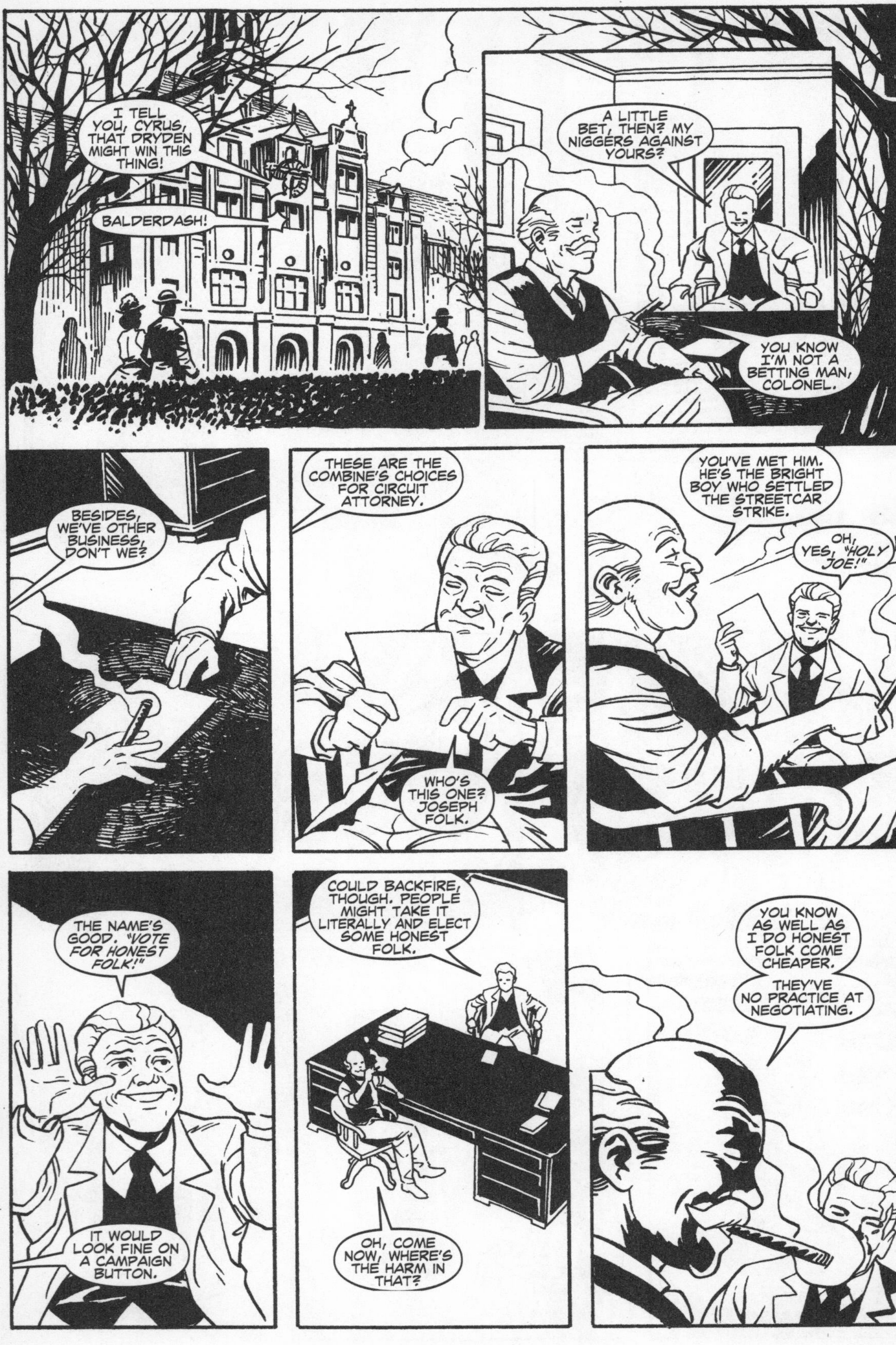
I TELL YOU, CYRUS, THAT DRYDEN MIGHT WIN THIS THING!
BALDERDASH!
A LITTLE BET, THEN? MY NIGGERS AGAINST YOURS?
YOU KNOW I'M NOT A BETTING MAN, COLONEL.
BESIDES, WE'VE OTHER BUSINESS, DON'T WE?
THESE ARE THE COMBINE'S CHOICES FOR CIRCUIT ATTORNEY.
WHO'S THIS ONE? JOSEPH FOLK.
YOU'VE MET HIM. HE'S THE BRIGHT BOY WHO SETTLED THE STREETCAR STRIKE.
OH, YES, "HOLY JOE!"
THE NAME'S GOOD. "VOTE FOR HONEST FOLK!"
IT WOULD LOOK FINE ON A CAMPAIGN BUTTON.
COULD BACKFIRE, THOUGH. PEOPLE MIGHT TAKE IT LITERALLY AND ELECT SOME HONEST FOLK.
OH, COME NOW, WHERE'S THE HARM IN THAT?
YOU KNOW AS WELL AS I DO HONEST FOLK COME CHEAPER.
THEY'VE NO PRACTICE AT NEGOTIATING.

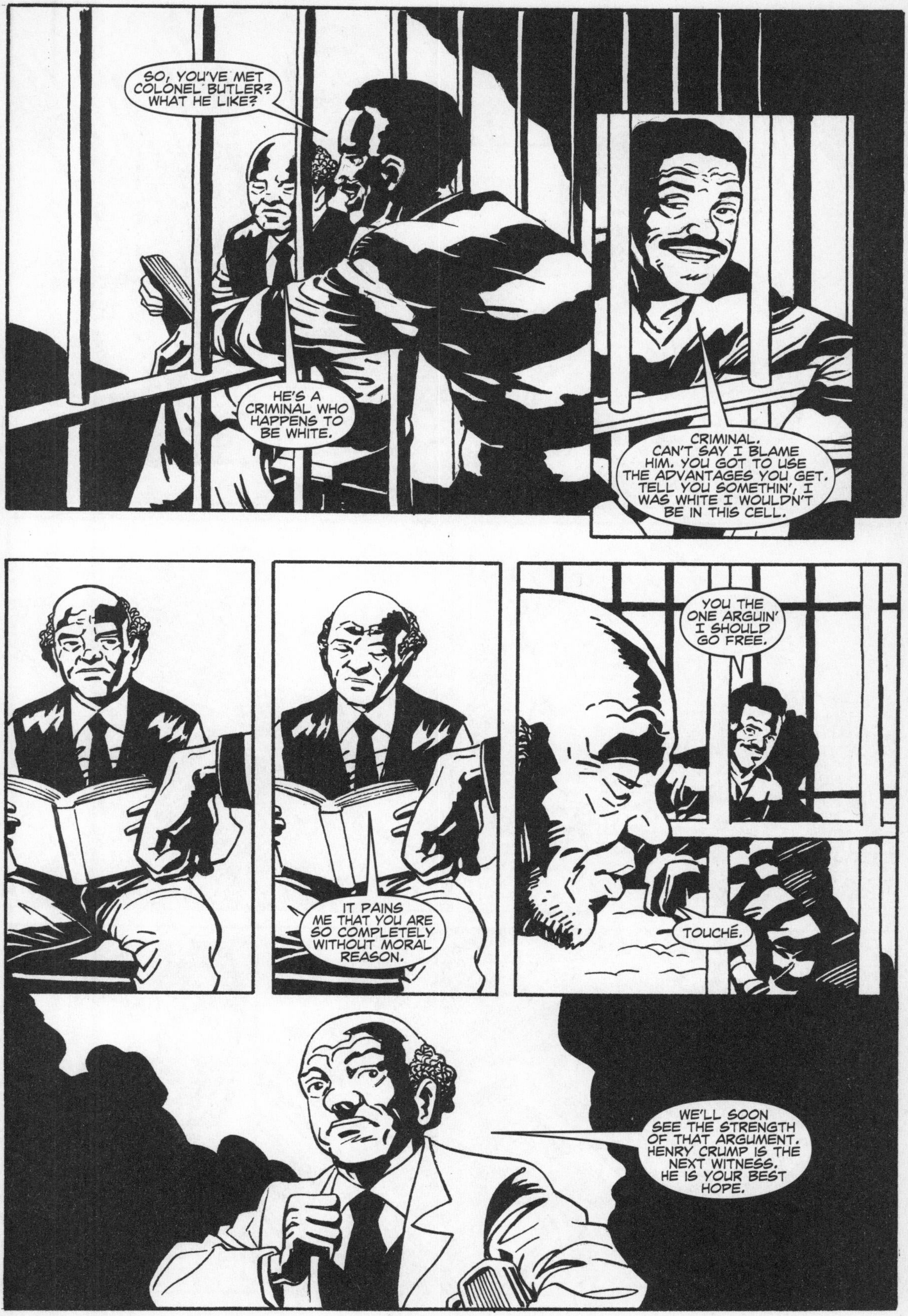
SO, YOU'VE MET COLONEL BUTLER? WHAT HE LIKE?
HE'S A CRIMINAL WHO HAPPENS TO BE WHITE.
CRIMINAL. CAN'T SAY I BLAME HIM. YOU GOT TO USE THE ADVANTAGES YOU GET. TELL YOU SOMETHIN', I WAS WHITE I WOULDN'T BE IN THIS CELL.
IT PAINS ME THAT YOU ARE SO COMPLETELY WITHOUT MORAL REASON.
YOU THE ONE ARGUIN' I SHOULD GO FREE.
TOUCHÉ.
WE'LL SOON SEE THE STRENGTH OF THAT ARGUMENT. HENRY CRUMP IS THE NEXT WITNESS. HE IS YOUR BEST HOPE.

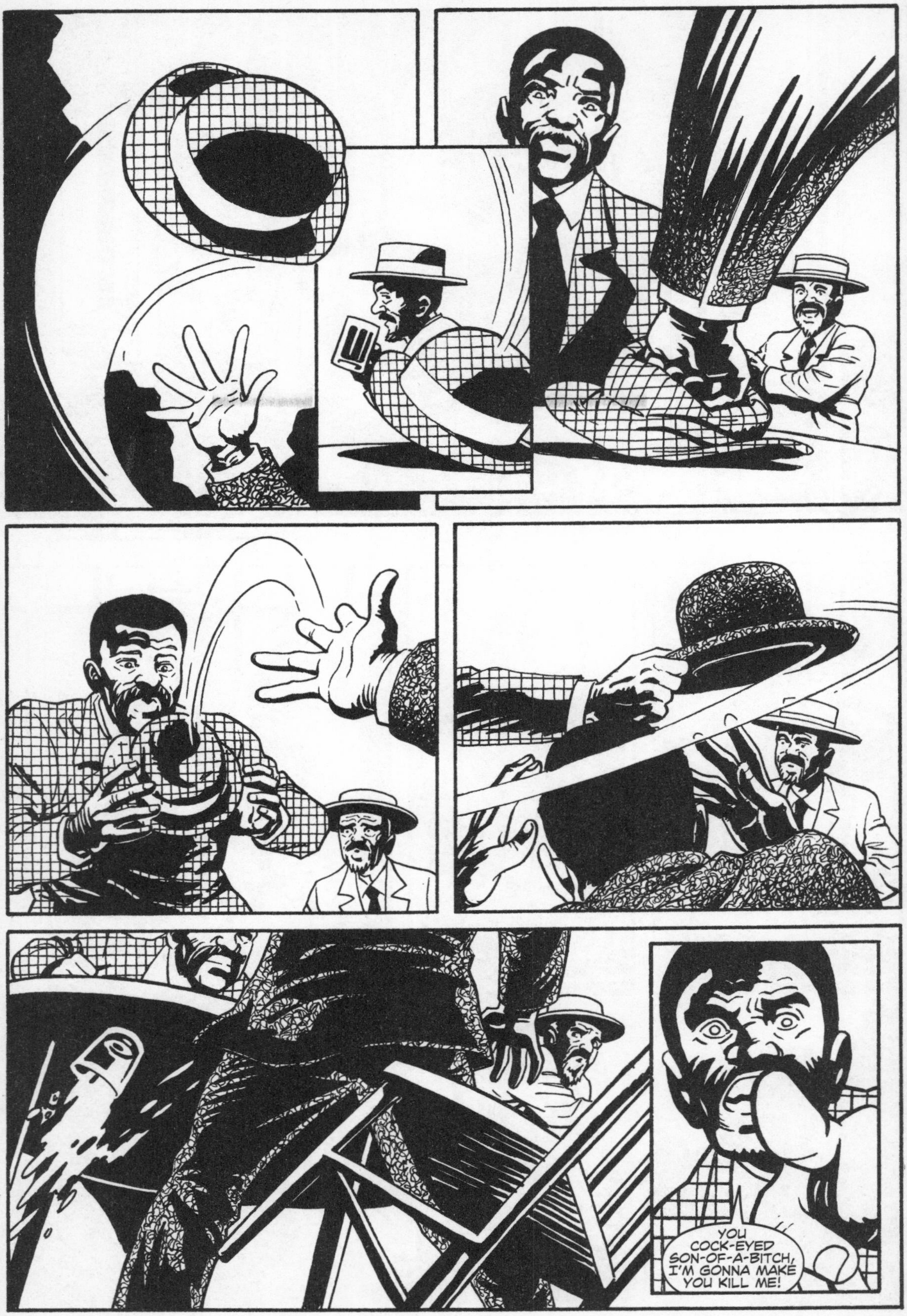
YOU COCK-EYED SON-OF-A-BITCH, I'M GONNA MAKE YOU KILL ME!

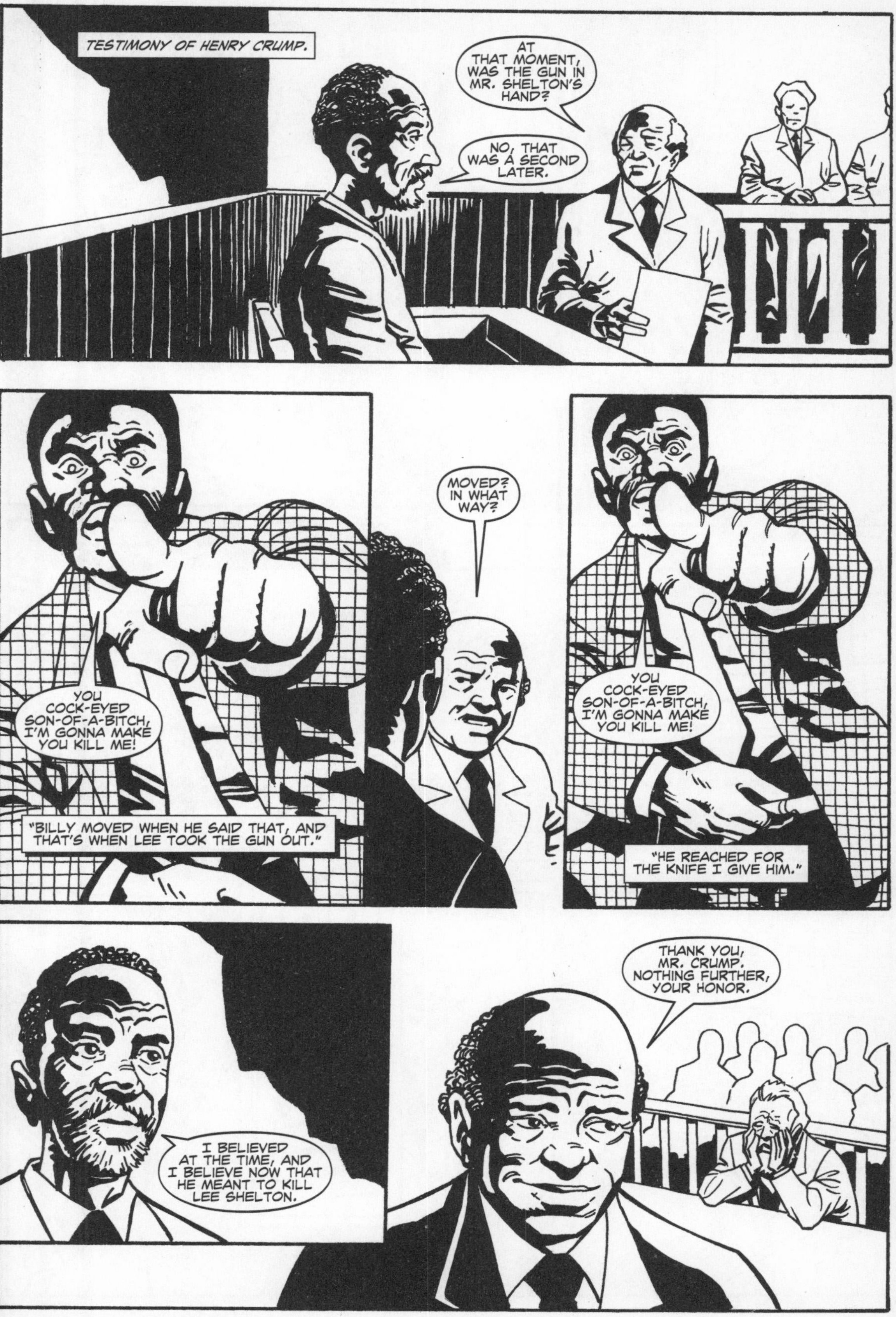
TESTIMONY OF HENRY CRUMP.
AT THAT MOMENT, WAS THE GUN IN MR. SHELTON'S HAND?
NO, THAT WAS A SECOND LATER.
YOU COCK-EYED SON-OF-A-BITCH, I'M GONNA MAKE YOU KILL ME!
"BILLY MOVED WHEN HE SAID THAT, AND THAT'S WHEN LEE TOOK THE GUN OUT."
MOVED? IN WHAT WAY?
YOU COCK-EYED SON-OF-A-BITCH, I'M GONNA MAKE YOU KILL ME!
"HE REACHED FOR THE KNIFE I GIVE HIM."
I BELIEVED AT THE TIME, AND I BELIEVE NOW THAT HE MEANT TO KILL LEE SHELTON.
THANK YOU, MR. CRUMP. NOTHING FURTHER, YOUR HONOR.

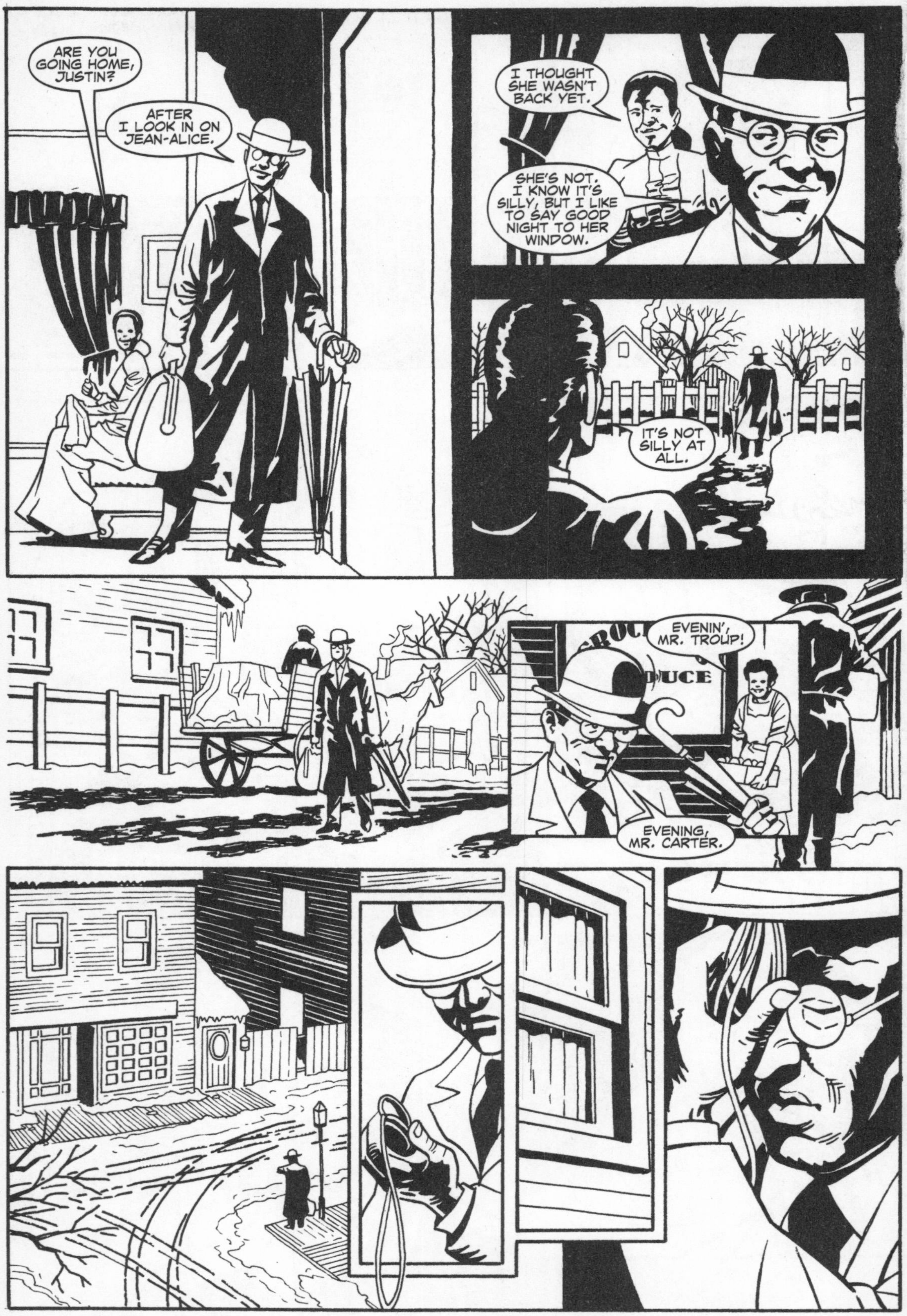

ARE YOU GOING HOME, JUSTIN?
AFTER I LOOK IN ON JEAN-ALICE.
I THOUGHT SHE WASN'T BACK YET.
SHE'S NOT. I KNOW IT'S SILLY, BUT I LIKE TO SAY GOOD NIGHT TO HER WINDOW.
IT'S NOT SILLY AT ALL.
EVENIN', MR. TROUP!
EVENING, MR. CARTER.

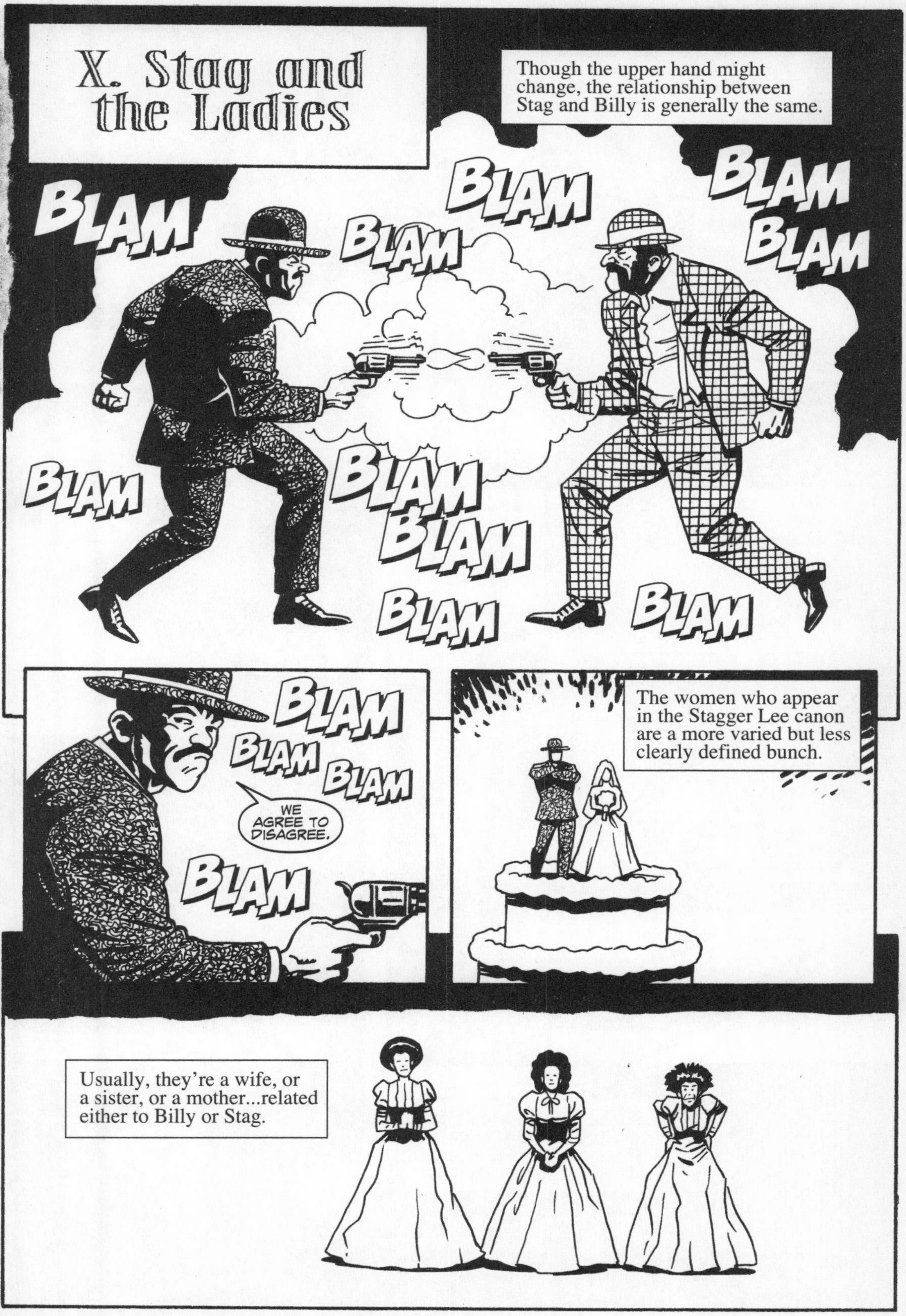
X. Stag and the Ladies
Though the upper hand might change, the relationship between Stag and Billy is generally the same.
BLAM
BLAM
BLAM
BLAM
BLAM
BLAM
BLAM
BLAM
BLAM
BLAM
BLAM
BLAM
BLAM
BLAM
WE AGREE TO DISAGREE.
BLAM
The women who appear in the Stagger Lee canon are a more varied but less clearly defined bunch.
Usually, they're a wife, or a sister, or a mother...related either to Billy or Stag.

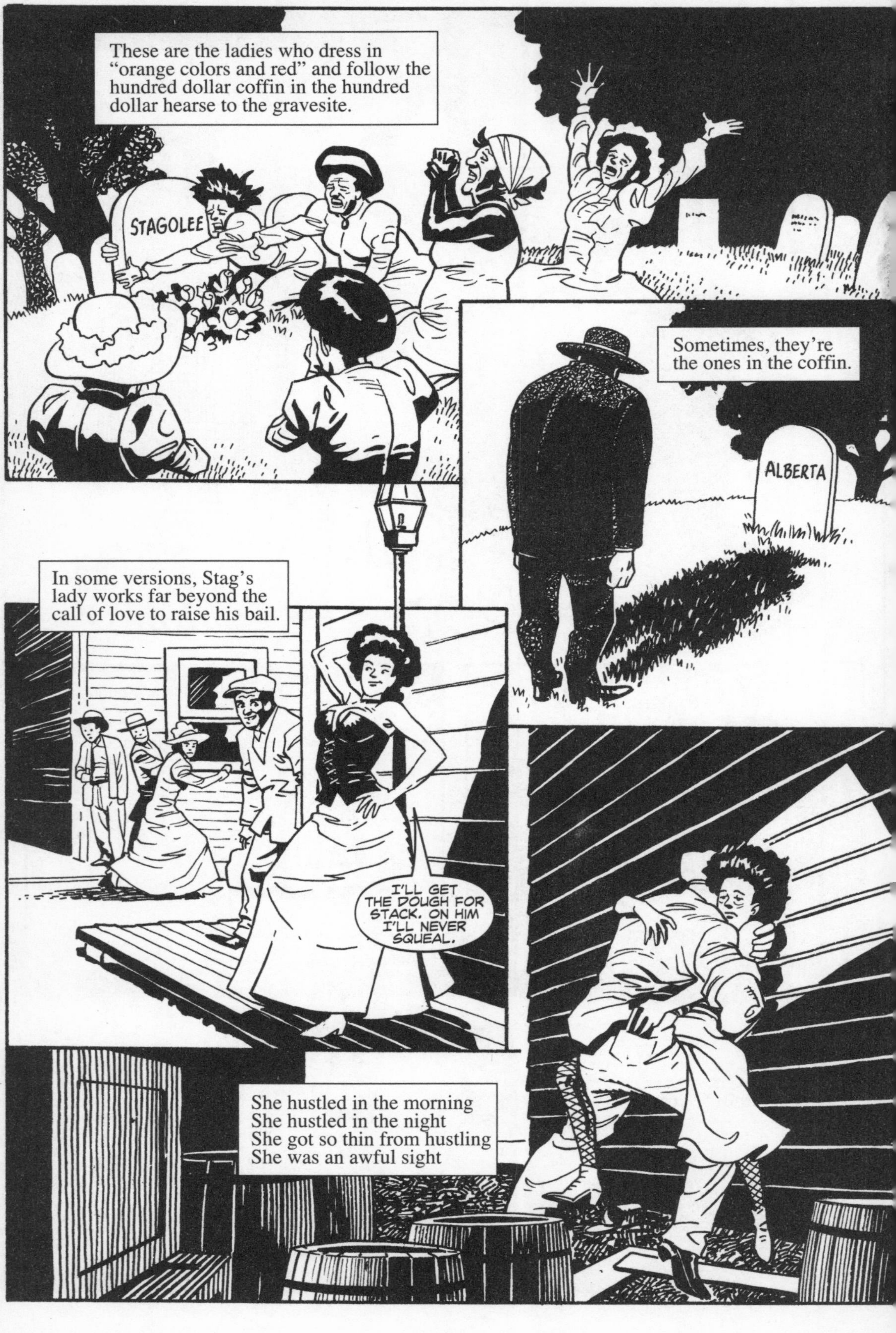

These are the ladies who dress in "orange colors and red" and follow the hundred dollar coffin in the hundred dollar hearse to the gravesite.
STAGOLEE
Sometimes, they're the ones in the coffin.
ALBERTA
In some versions, Stag's lady works far beyond the call of love to raise his bail.
I'LL GET THE DOUGH FOR STACK. ON HIM I'LL NEVER SQUEAL.
She hustled in the morning
She hustled in the night
She got so thin from hustling
She was an awful sight

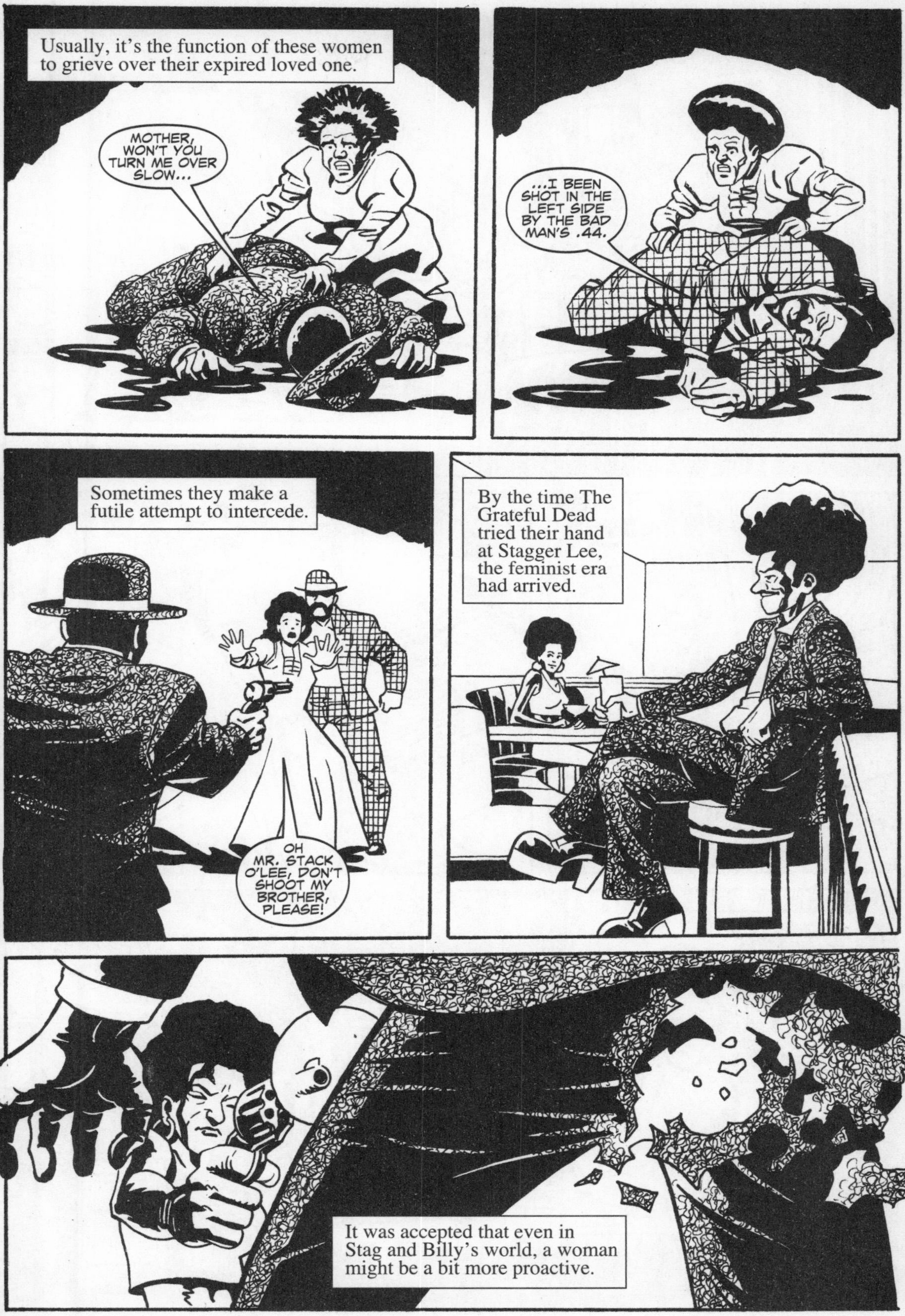
Usually, it's the function of these women to grieve over their expired loved one.
MOTHER, WON'T YOU TURN ME OVER SLOW...
...I BEEN SHOT IN THE LEFT SIDE BY THE BAD MAN'S .44.
Sometimes they make a futile attempt to intercede.
OH MR. STACK O'LEE, DON'T SHOOT MY BROTHER, PLEASE!
By the time The Grateful Dead tried their hand at Stagger Lee, the feminist era had arrived.
It was accepted that even in Stag and Billy's world, a woman might be a bit more proactive.

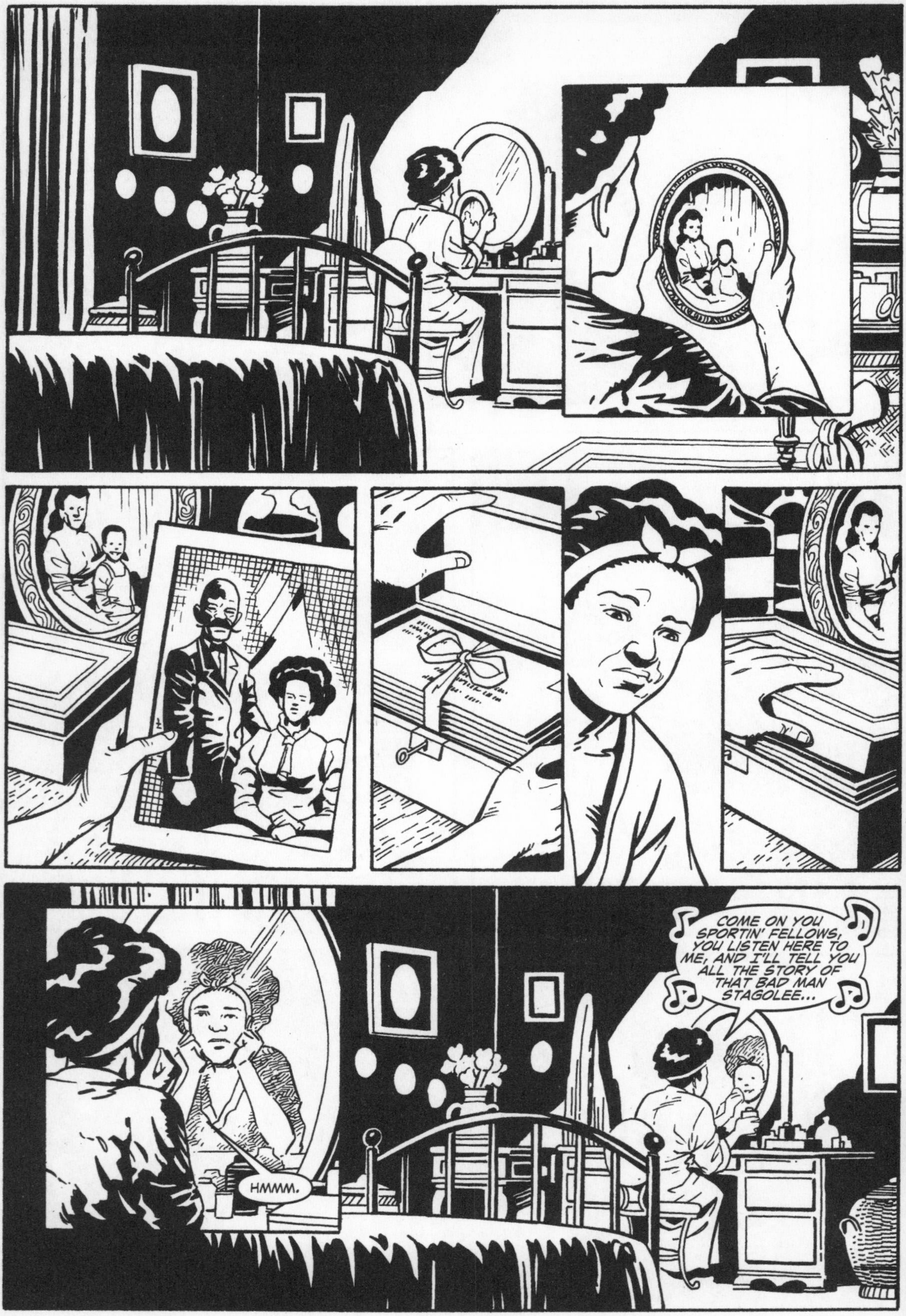
HMMM.
COME ON YOU SPORTIN' FELLOWS, YOU LISTEN HERE TO ME, AND I'LL TELL YOU ALL THE STORY OF THAT BAD MAN STAGOLEE...

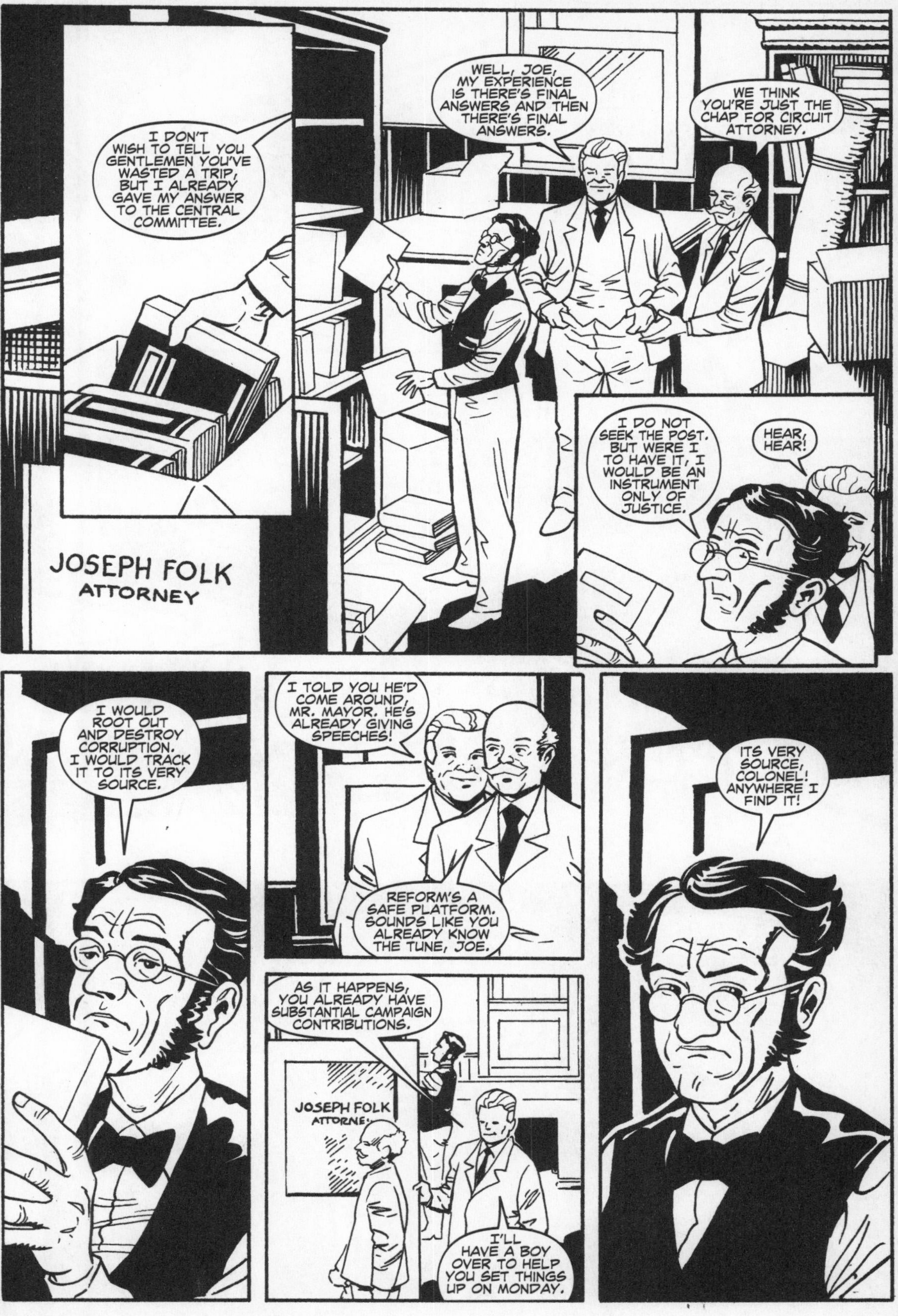
I DON'T WISH TO TELL YOU GENTLEMEN YOU'VE WASTED A TRIP, BUT I ALREADY GAVE MY ANSWER TO THE CENTRAL COMMITTEE.
JOSEPH FOLK ATTORNEY
WELL, JOE, MY EXPERIENCE IS THERE'S FINAL ANSWERS AND THEN THERE'S FINAL ANSWERS.
WE THINK YOU'RE JUST THE CHAP FOR CIRCUIT ATTORNEY.
I DO NOT SEEK THE POST. BUT WERE I TO HAVE IT, I WOULD BE AN INSTRUMENT ONLY OF JUSTICE.
HEAR, HEAR!
I WOULD ROOT OUT AND DESTROY CORRUPTION. I WOULD TRACK IT TO ITS VERY SOURCE.
I TOLD YOU HE'D COME AROUND, MR. MAYOR. HE'S ALREADY GIVING SPEECHES!
REFORM'S A SAFE PLATFORM. SOUNDS LIKE YOU ALREADY KNOW THE TUNE, JOE.
AS IT HAPPENS, YOU ALREADY HAVE SUBSTANTIAL CAMPAIGN CONTRIBUTIONS.
JOSEPH FOLK ATTORNE
I'LL HAVE A BOY OVER TO HELP YOU SET THINGS UP ON MONDAY.
ITS VERY SOURCE, COLONEL! ANYWHERE I FIND IT!

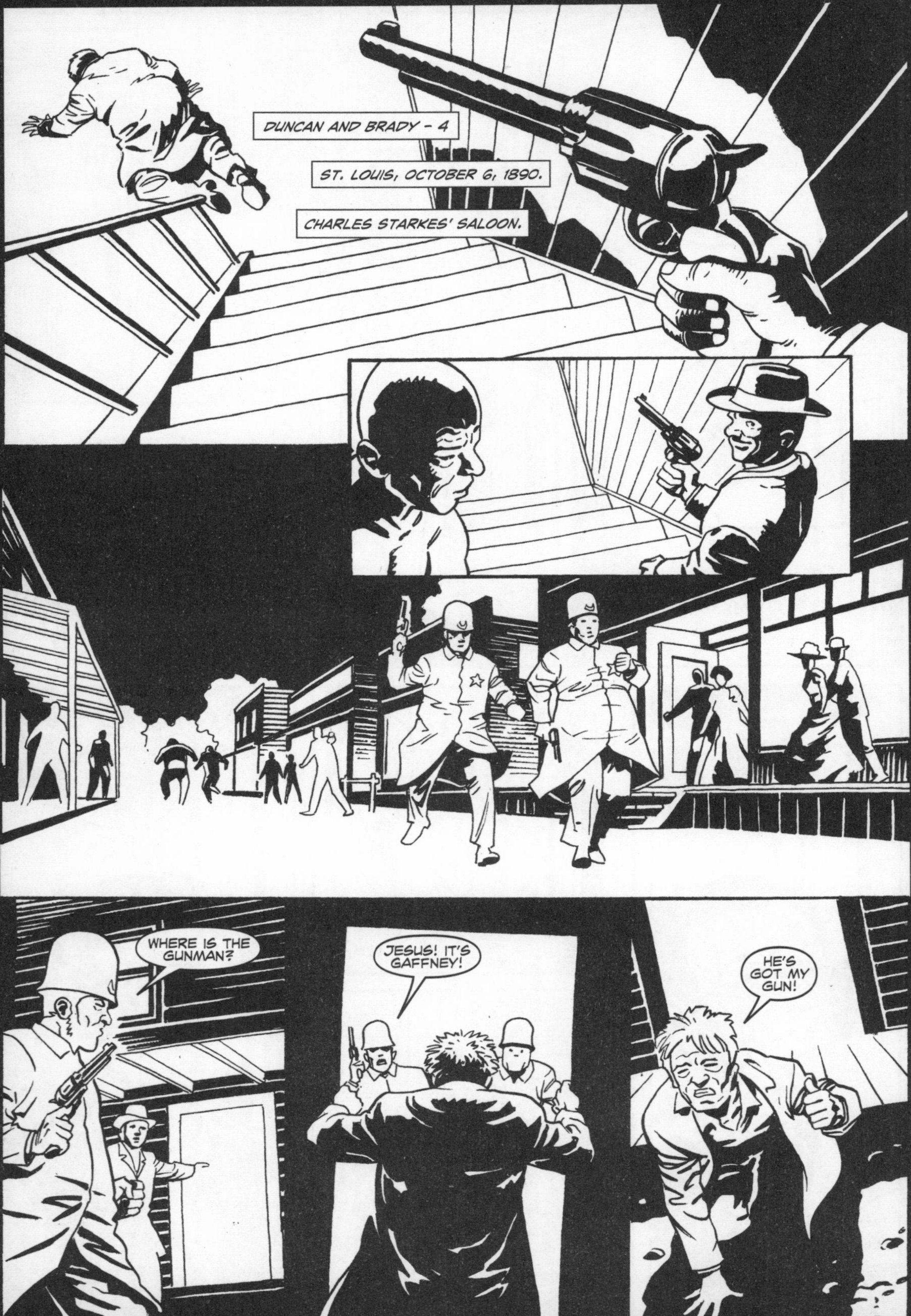
DUNCAN AND BRADY - 4
ST. LOUIS, OCTOBER 6, 1890.
CHARLES STARKES' SALOON.
WHERE IS THE GUNMAN?
JESUS! IT'S GAFFNEY!
HE'S GOT MY GUN!

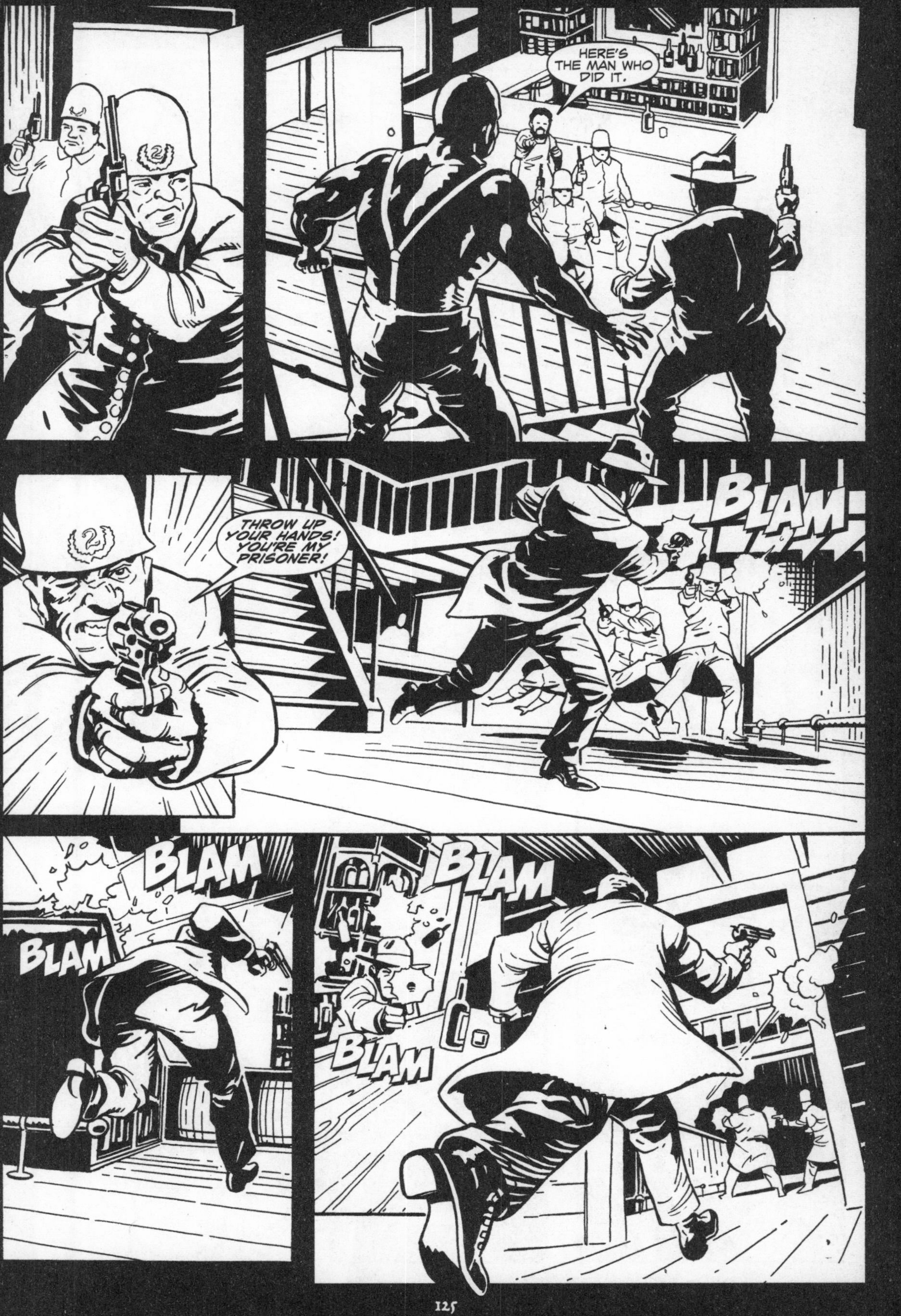
HERE'S THE MAN WHO DID IT.
THROW UP YOUR HANDS! YOU'RE MY PRISONER!
BLAM
BLAM
BLAM
BLAM
BLAM

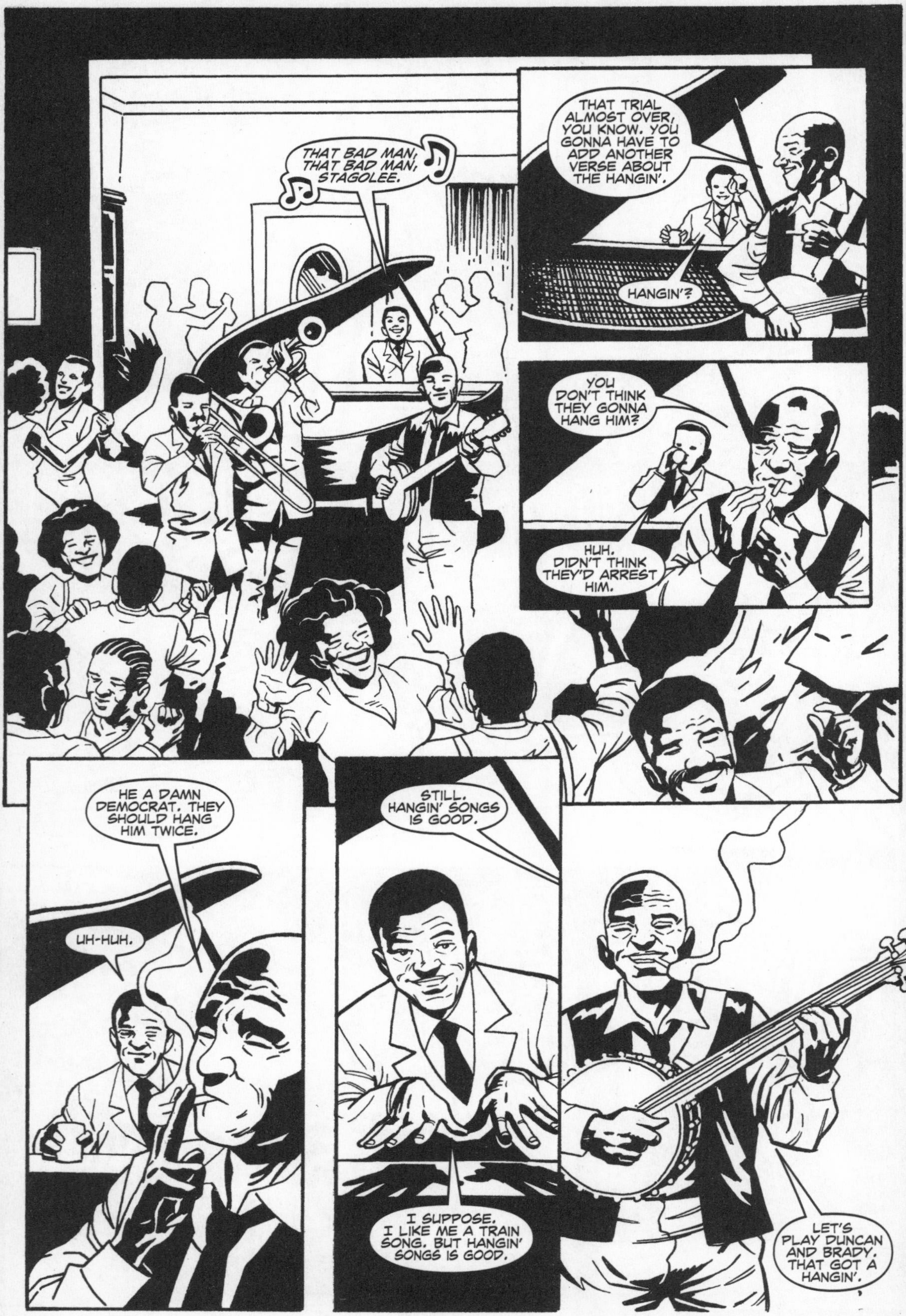
THAT BAD MAN, THAT BAD MAN, STAGOLEE.
THAT TRIAL ALMOST OVER, YOU KNOW. YOU GONNA HAVE TO ADD ANOTHER VERSE ABOUT THE HANGIN'.
HANGIN'?
YOU DON'T THINK THEY GONNA HANG HIM?
HUH. DIDN'T THINK THEY'D ARREST HIM.
HE A DAMN DEMOCRAT. THEY SHOULD HANG HIM TWICE.
UH-HUH.
STILL. HANGIN' SONGS IS GOOD.
I SUPPOSE. I LIKE ME A TRAIN SONG. BUT HANGIN' SONGS IS GOOD.
LET'S PLAY DUNCAN AND BRADY. THAT GOT A HANGIN'.

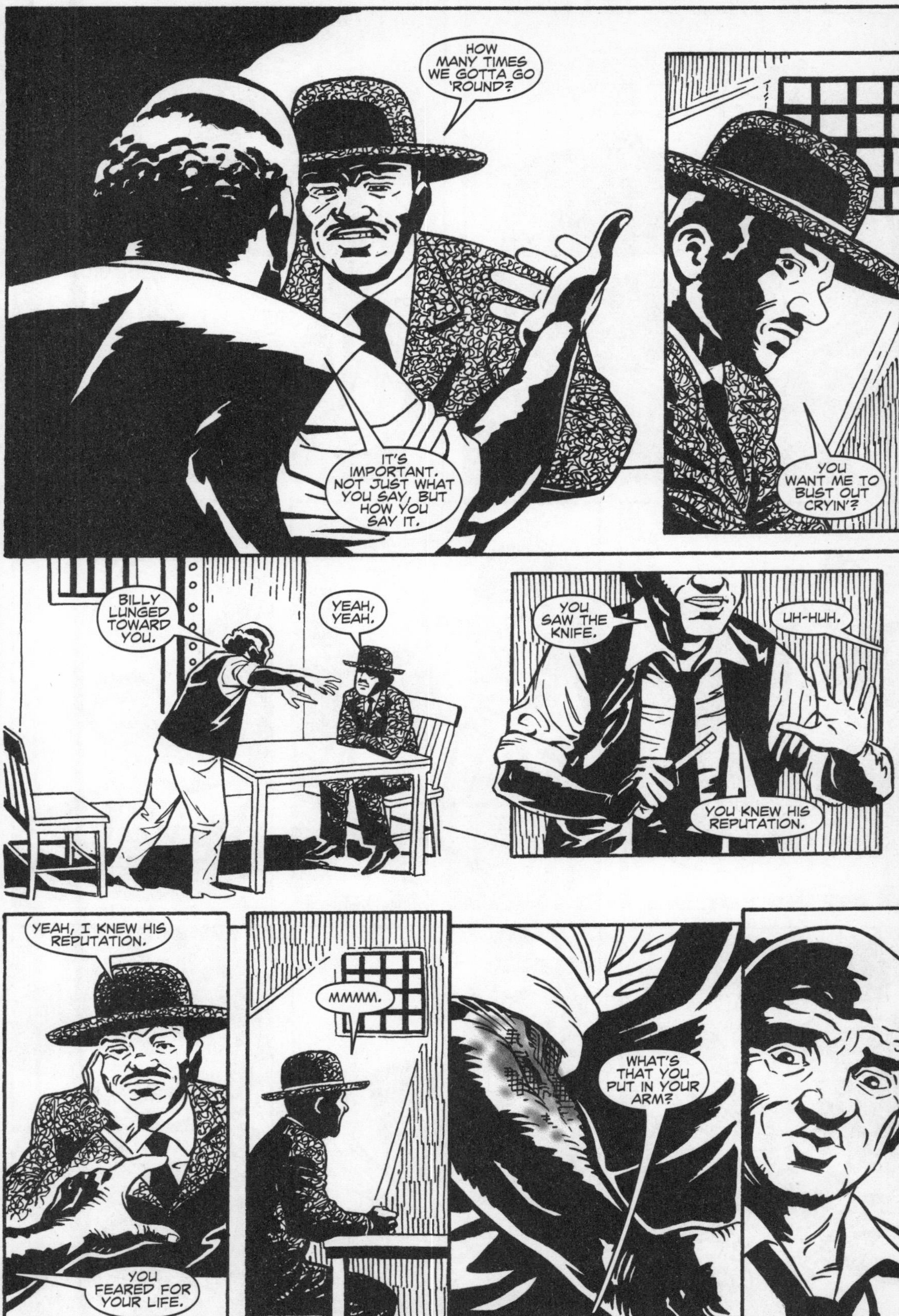
HOW MANY TIMES WE GOTTA GO 'ROUND?
IT'S IMPORTANT. NOT JUST WHAT YOU SAY, BUT HOW YOU SAY IT.
YOU WANT ME TO BUST OUT CRYIN'?
BILLY LUNGED TOWARD YOU.
YEAH, YEAH.
YOU SAW THE KNIFE.
UH-HUH.
YOU KNEW HIS REPUTATION.
YEAH, I KNEW HIS REPUTATION.
YOU FEARED FOR YOUR LIFE.
MMMM.
WHAT'S THAT YOU PUT IN YOUR ARM?

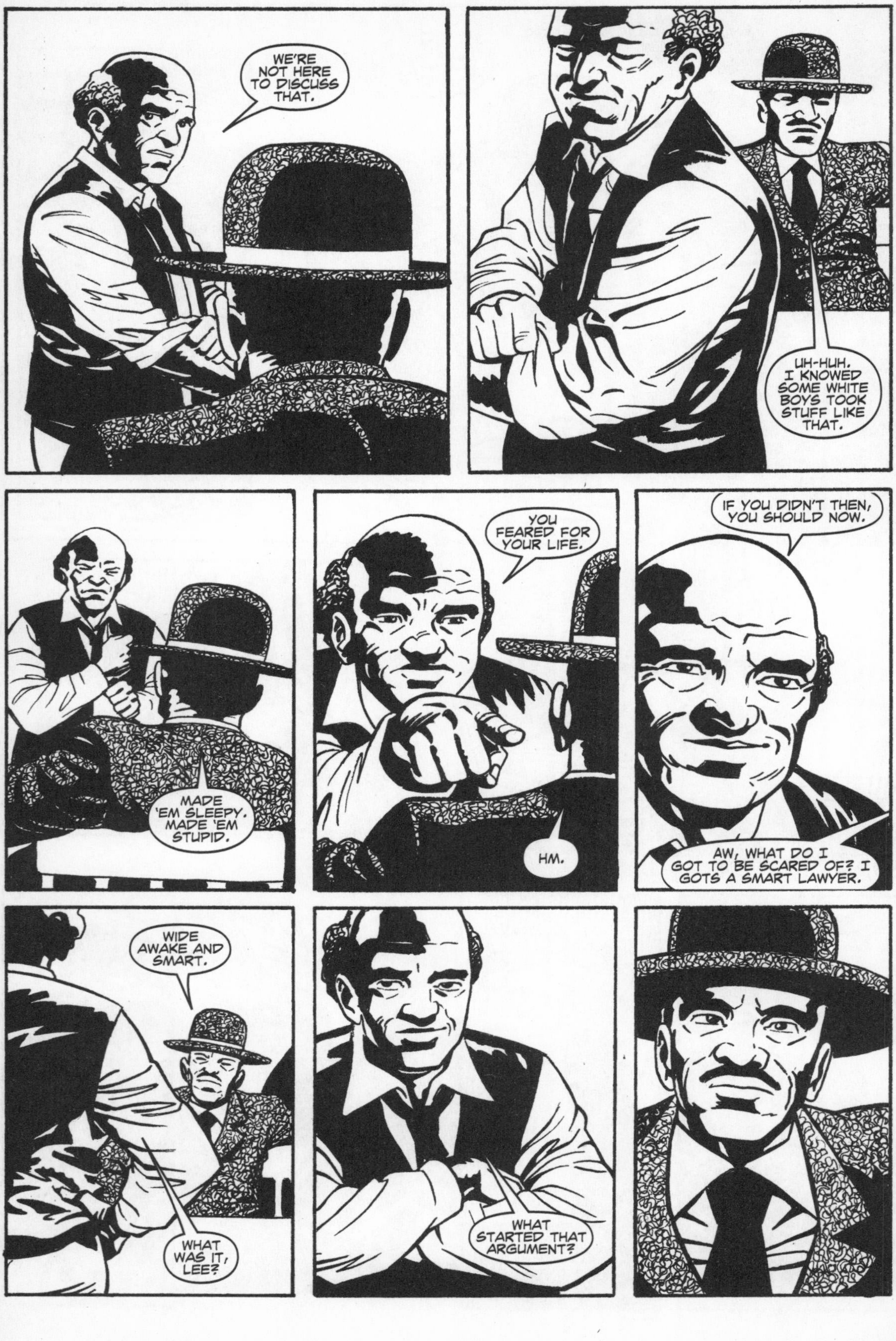
WE'RE NOT HERE TO DISCUSS THAT.
UH-HUH. I KNOWED SOME WHITE BOYS TOOK STUFF LIKE THAT.
MADE 'EM SLEEPY. MADE 'EM STUPID.
YOU FEARED FOR YOUR LIFE.
HM.
IF YOU DIDN'T THEN, YOU SHOULD NOW.
AW, WHAT DO I GOT TO BE SCARED OF? I GOTS A SMART LAWYER.
WIDE AWAKE AND SMART.
WHAT WAS IT, LEE?
WHAT STARTED THAT ARGUMENT?

XI. What Started that Argument?

Some versions of the Stagger Lee tale say that Stag and Billy were best of friends. So what brought them to the sorry pass of murder?

The Stetson hat, sure.

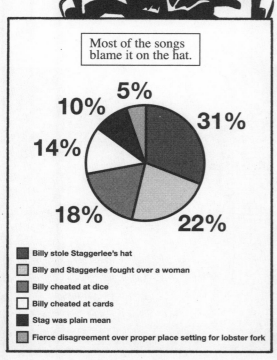

Most of the songs blame it on the hat.

5%
10%
14%
31%
18%
22%

- Billy stole Staggerlee's hat
- Billy and Staggerlee fought over a woman
- Billy cheated at dice
- Billy cheated at cards
- Stag was plain mean
- Fierce disagreement over proper place setting for lobster fork

In one "Wild West" version, Billy even spits in the hat.

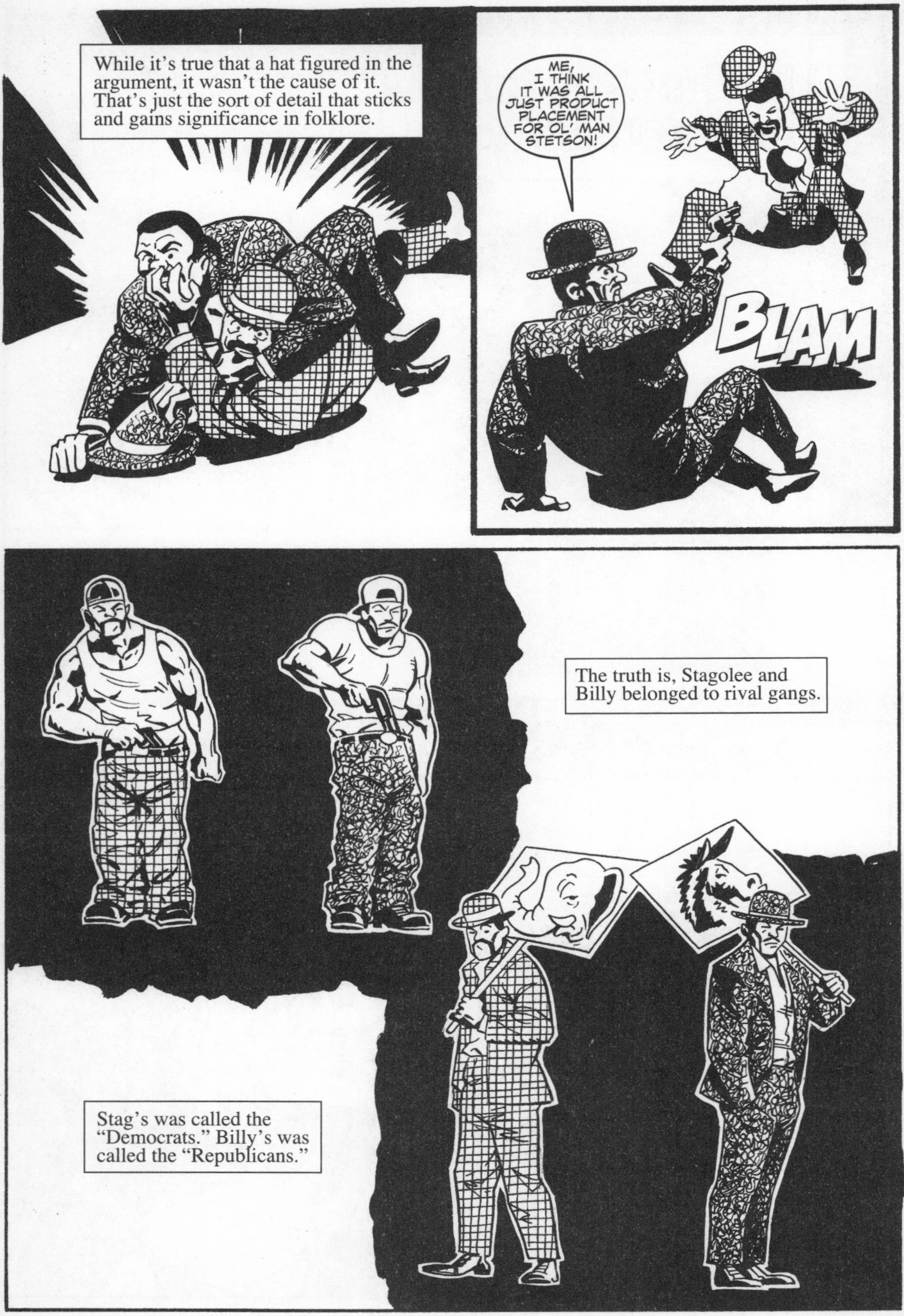
While it's true that a hat figured in the argument, it wasn't the cause of it. That's just the sort of detail that sticks and gains significance in folklore.
ME, I THINK IT WAS ALL JUST PRODUCT PLACEMENT FOR OL' MAN STETSON!
BLAM
The truth is, Stagolee and Billy belonged to rival gangs.
Stag's was called the "Democrats." Billy's was called the "Republicans."

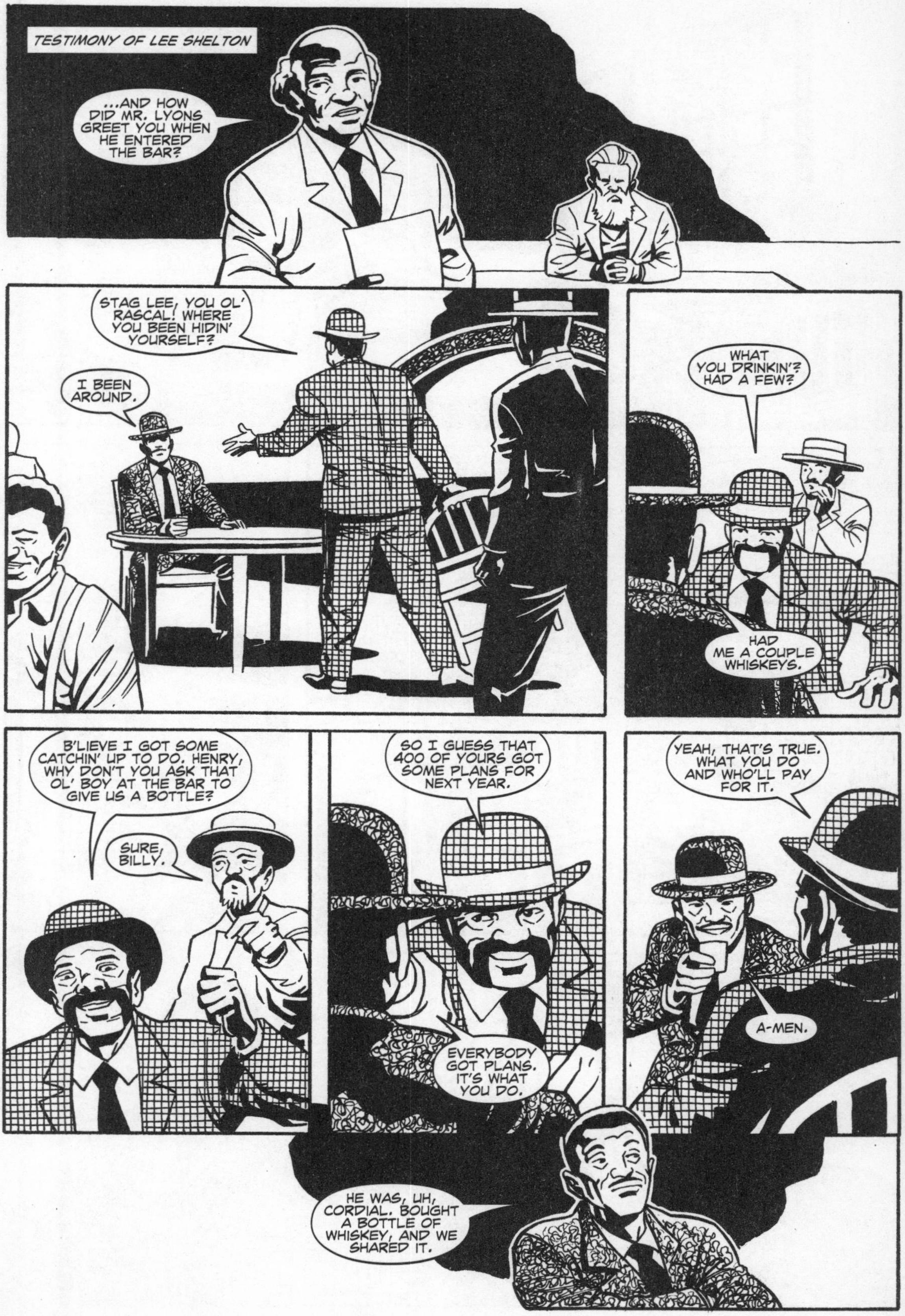
TESTIMONY OF LEE SHELTON
...AND HOW DID MR. LYONS GREET YOU WHEN HE ENTERED THE BAR?
STAG LEE, YOU OL' RASCAL! WHERE YOU BEEN HIDIN' YOURSELF?
I BEEN AROUND.
WHAT YOU DRINKIN'? HAD A FEW?
HAD ME A COUPLE WHISKEYS.
B'LIEVE I GOT SOME CATCHIN' UP TO DO. HENRY, WHY DON'T YOU ASK THAT OL' BOY AT THE BAR TO GIVE US A BOTTLE?
SURE, BILLY.
SO I GUESS THAT 400 OF YOURS GOT SOME PLANS FOR NEXT YEAR.
EVERYBODY GOT PLANS. IT'S WHAT YOU DO.
YEAH, THAT'S TRUE. WHAT YOU DO AND WHO'LL PAY FOR IT.
A-MEN.
HE WAS, UH, CORDIAL. BOUGHT A BOTTLE OF WHISKEY, AND WE SHARED IT.

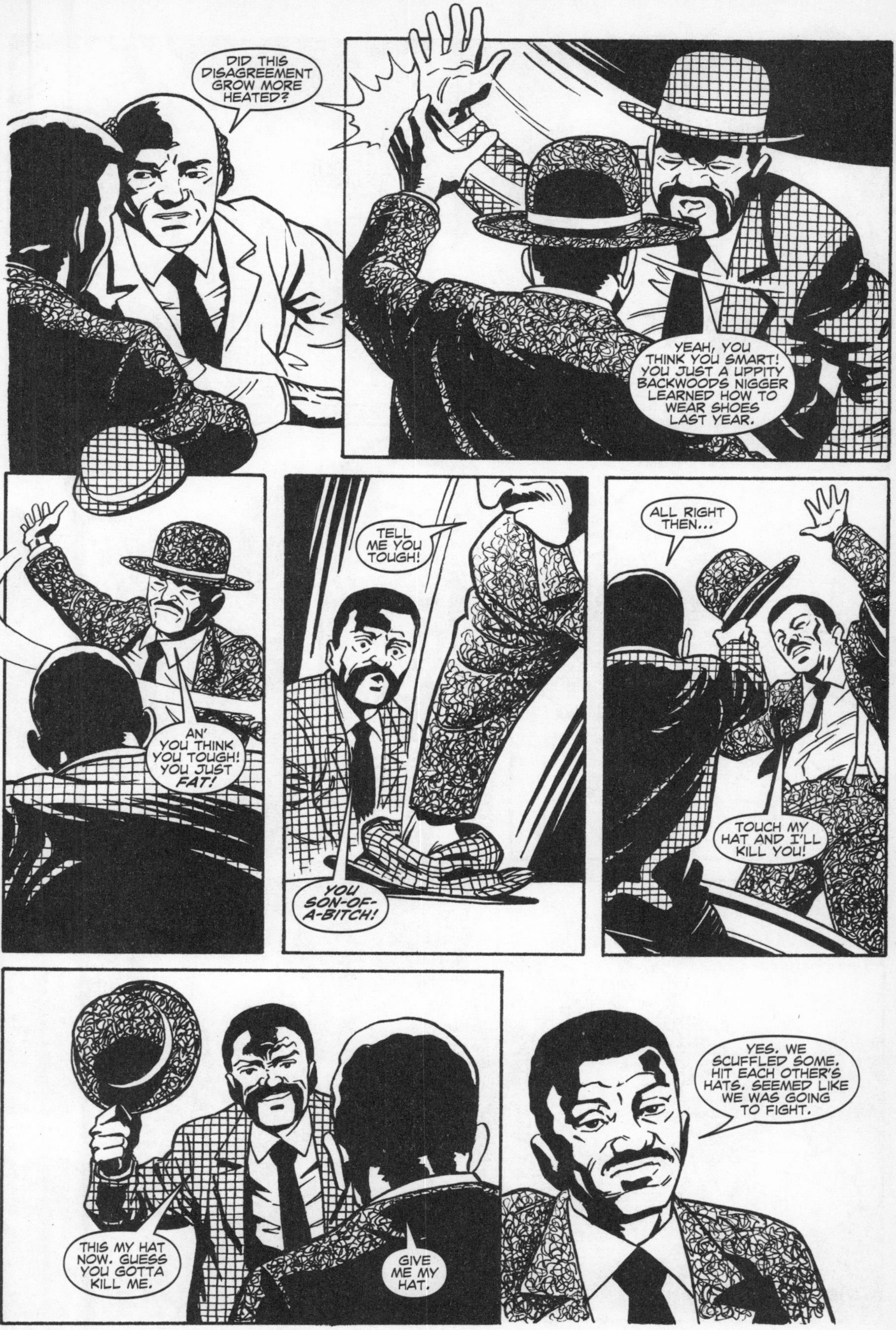

DID THIS DISAGREEMENT GROW MORE HEATED?
YEAH, YOU THINK YOU SMART! YOU JUST A UPPITY BACKWOODS NIGGER LEARNED HOW TO WEAR SHOES LAST YEAR.
AN' YOU THINK YOU TOUGH! YOU JUST *FAT!*
TELL ME YOU TOUGH!
YOU SON-OF-A-BITCH!
ALL RIGHT THEN...
TOUCH MY HAT AND I'LL KILL YOU!
THIS MY HAT NOW. GUESS YOU GOTTA KILL ME.
GIVE ME MY HAT.
YES. WE SCUFFLED SOME. HIT EACH OTHER'S HATS. SEEMED LIKE WE WAS GOING TO FIGHT.

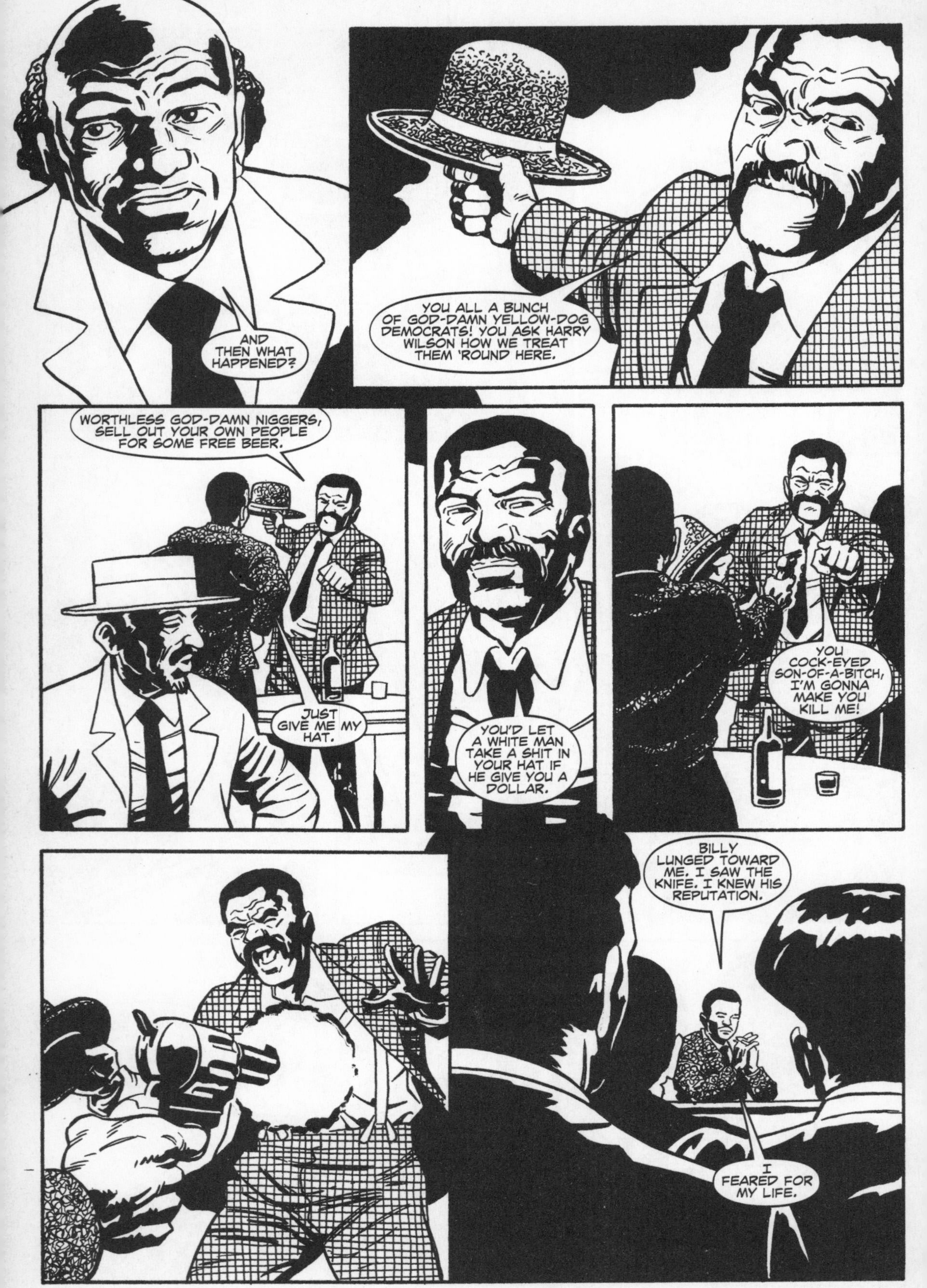
AND THEN WHAT HAPPENED?
YOU ALL A BUNCH OF GOD-DAMN YELLOW-DOG DEMOCRATS! YOU ASK HARRY WILSON HOW WE TREAT THEM 'ROUND HERE.
WORTHLESS GOD-DAMN NIGGERS, SELL OUT YOUR OWN PEOPLE FOR SOME FREE BEER.
JUST GIVE ME MY HAT.
YOU'D LET A WHITE MAN TAKE A SHIT IN YOUR HAT IF HE GIVE YOU A DOLLAR.
YOU COCK-EYED SON-OF-A-BITCH, I'M GONNA MAKE YOU KILL ME!
BILLY LUNGED TOWARD ME. I SAW THE KNIFE. I KNEW HIS REPUTATION.
I FEARED FOR MY LIFE.

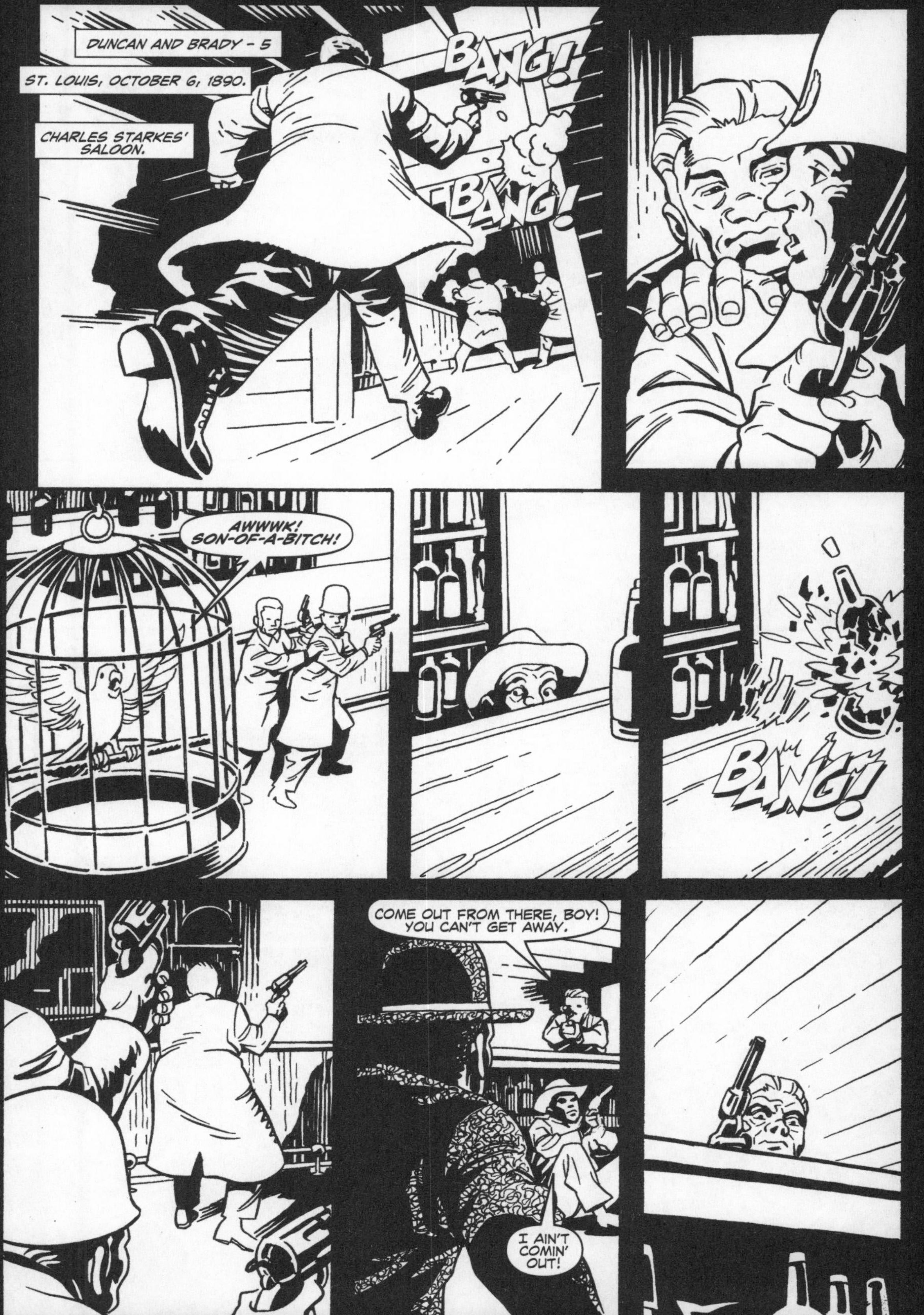
DUNCAN AND BRADY - 5
ST. LOUIS, OCTOBER 6, 1890.
CHARLES STARKES' SALOON.
BANG!
BANG!
AWWWK! SON-OF-A-BITCH!
BANG!
COME OUT FROM THERE, BOY! YOU CAN'T GET AWAY.
I AIN'T COMIN' OUT!

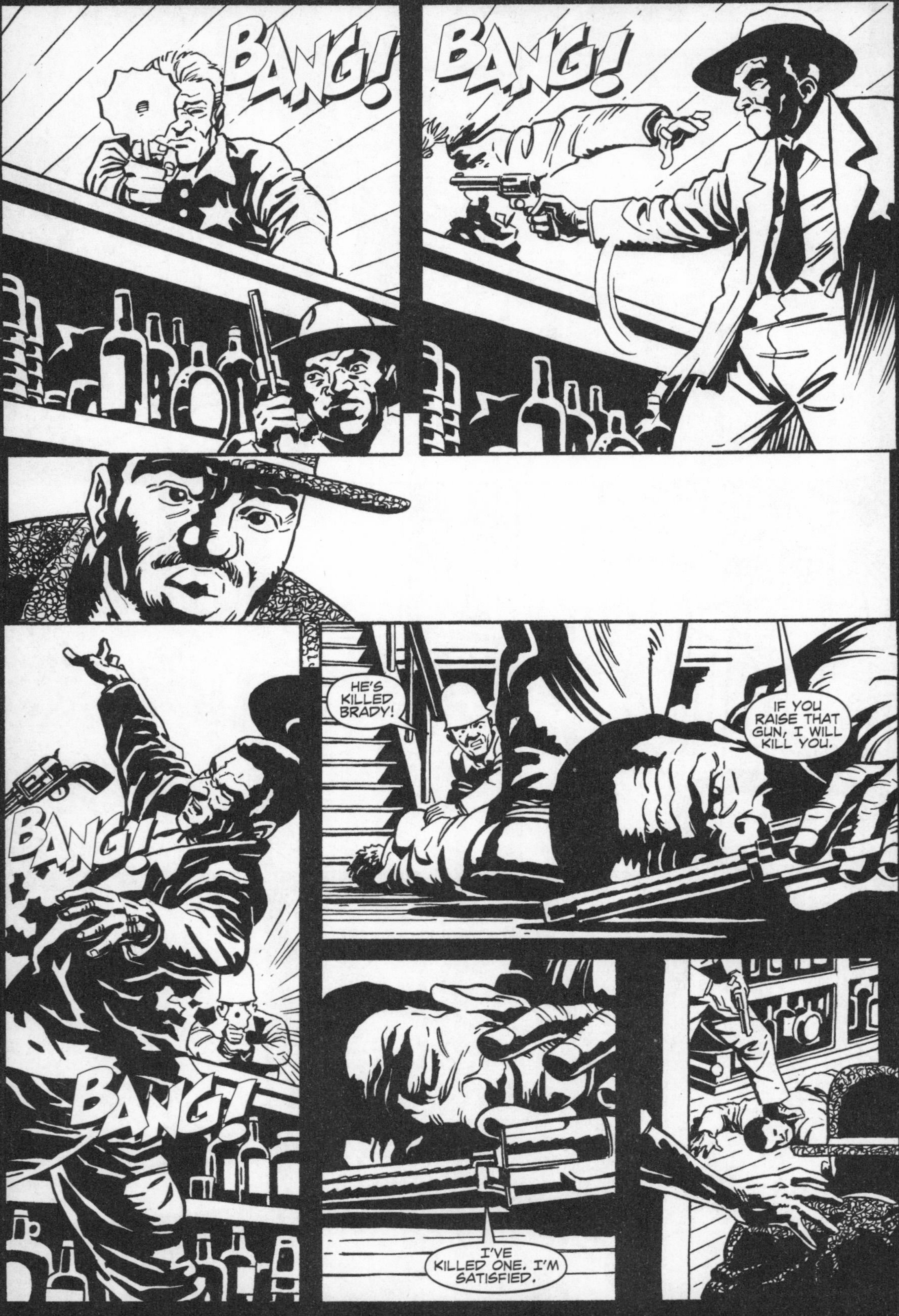
BANG!
BANG!
BANG!
BANG!
HE'S KILLED BRADY!
IF YOU RAISE THAT GUN, I WILL KILL YOU.
I'VE KILLED ONE. I'M SATISFIED.

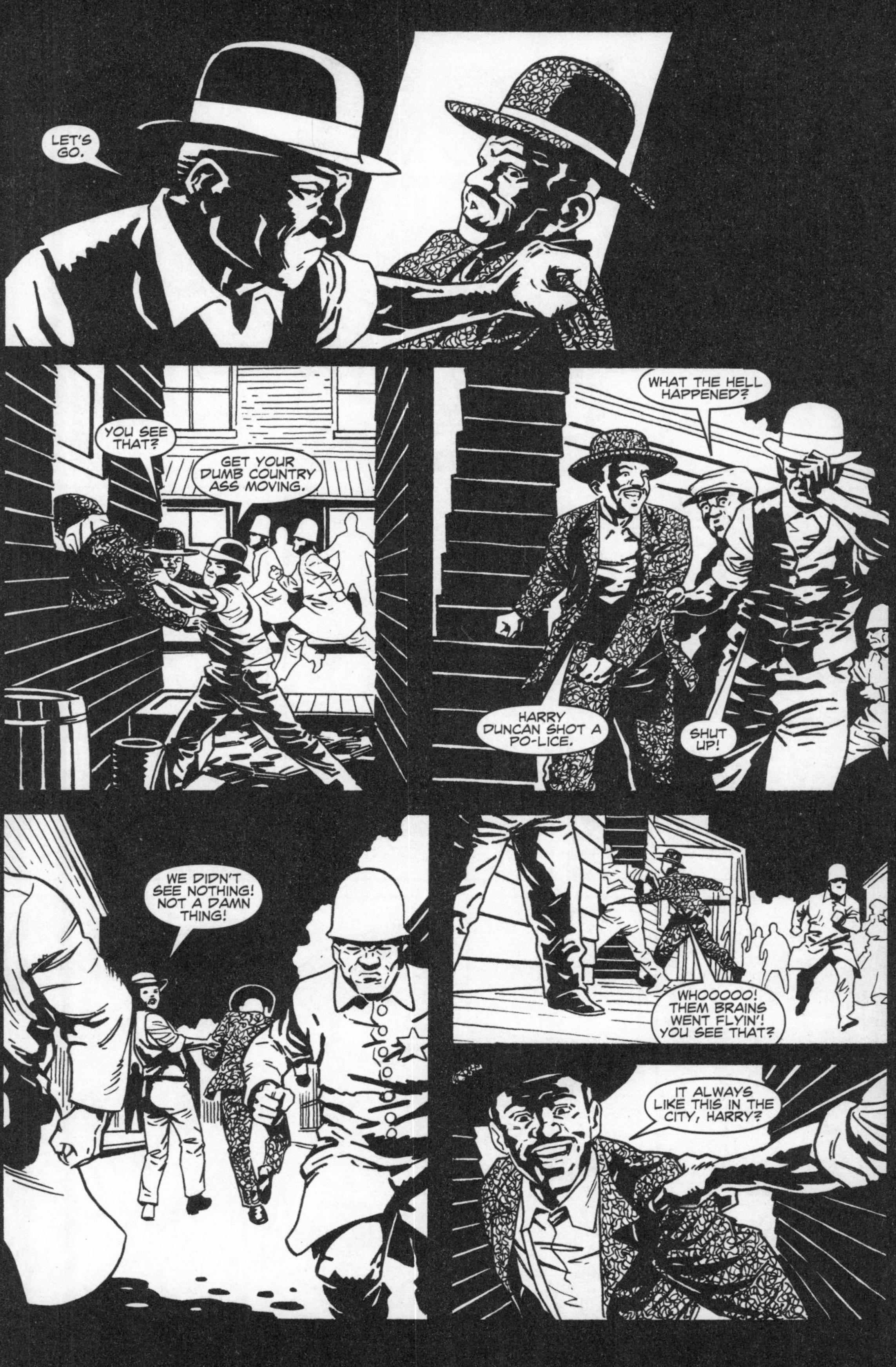
LET'S GO.
YOU SEE THAT?
GET YOUR DUMB COUNTRY ASS MOVING.
WHAT THE HELL HAPPENED?
HARRY DUNCAN SHOT A PO-LICE.
SHUT UP!
WE DIDN'T SEE NOTHING! NOT A DAMN THING!
WHOOOOO! THEM BRAINS WENT FLYIN'! YOU SEE THAT?
IT ALWAYS LIKE THIS IN THE CITY, HARRY?

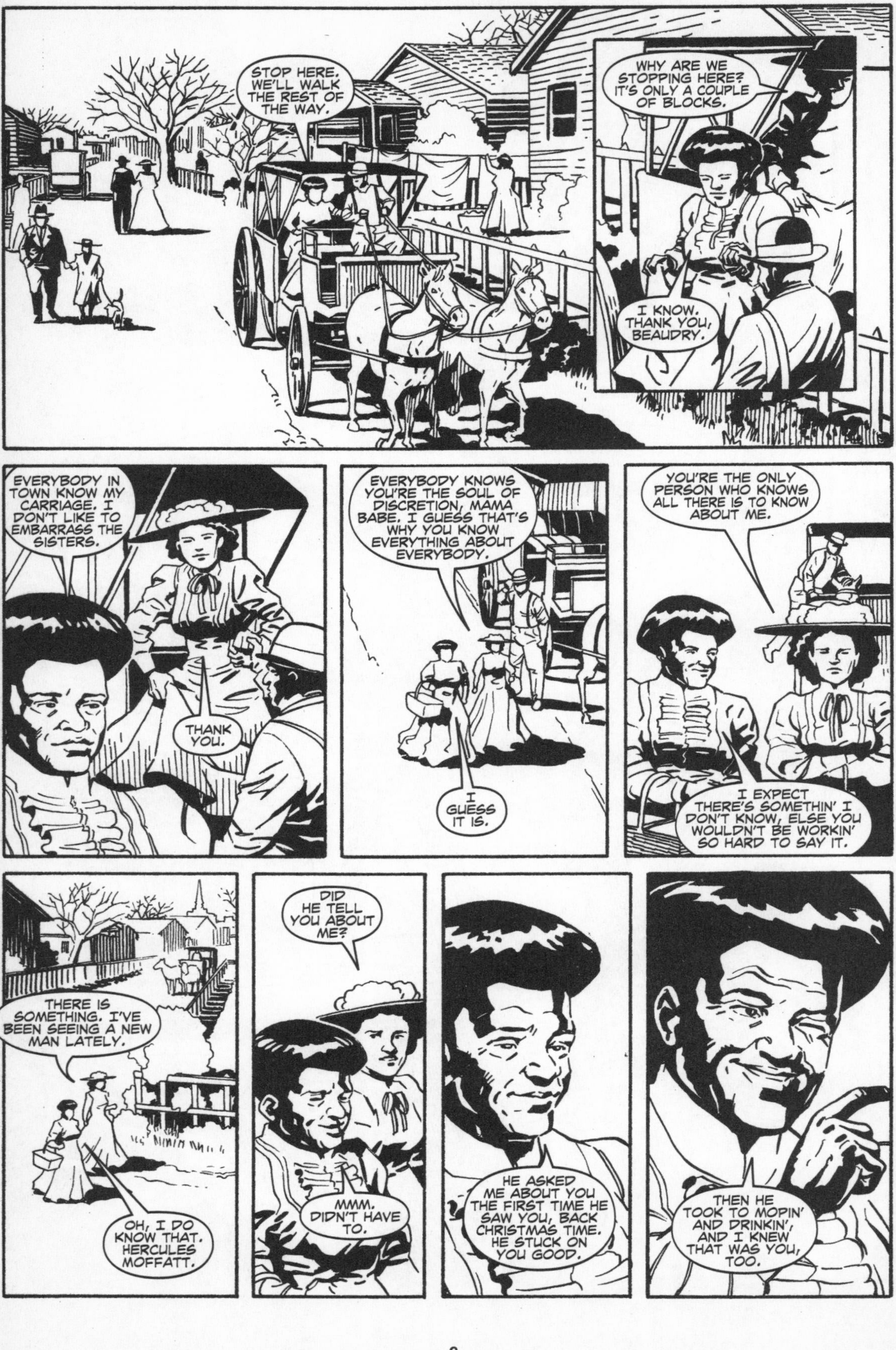
STOP HERE. WE'LL WALK THE REST OF THE WAY.
WHY ARE WE STOPPING HERE? IT'S ONLY A COUPLE OF BLOCKS.
I KNOW. THANK YOU, BEAUDRY.
EVERYBODY IN TOWN KNOW MY CARRIAGE. I DON'T LIKE TO EMBARRASS THE SISTERS.
THANK YOU.
EVERYBODY KNOWS YOU'RE THE SOUL OF DISCRETION, MAMA BABE. I GUESS THAT'S WHY YOU KNOW EVERYTHING ABOUT EVERYBODY.
I GUESS IT IS.
YOU'RE THE ONLY PERSON WHO KNOWS ALL THERE IS TO KNOW ABOUT ME.
I EXPECT THERE'S SOMETHIN' I DON'T KNOW, ELSE YOU WOULDN'T BE WORKIN' SO HARD TO SAY IT.
THERE IS SOMETHING. I'VE BEEN SEEING A NEW MAN LATELY.
OH, I DO KNOW THAT. HERCULES MOFFATT.
DID HE TELL YOU ABOUT ME?
MMM. DIDN'T HAVE TO.
HE ASKED ME ABOUT YOU THE FIRST TIME HE SAW YOU, BACK CHRISTMAS TIME. HE STUCK ON YOU GOOD.
THEN HE TOOK TO MOPIN' AND DRINKIN', AND I KNEW THAT WAS YOU, TOO.

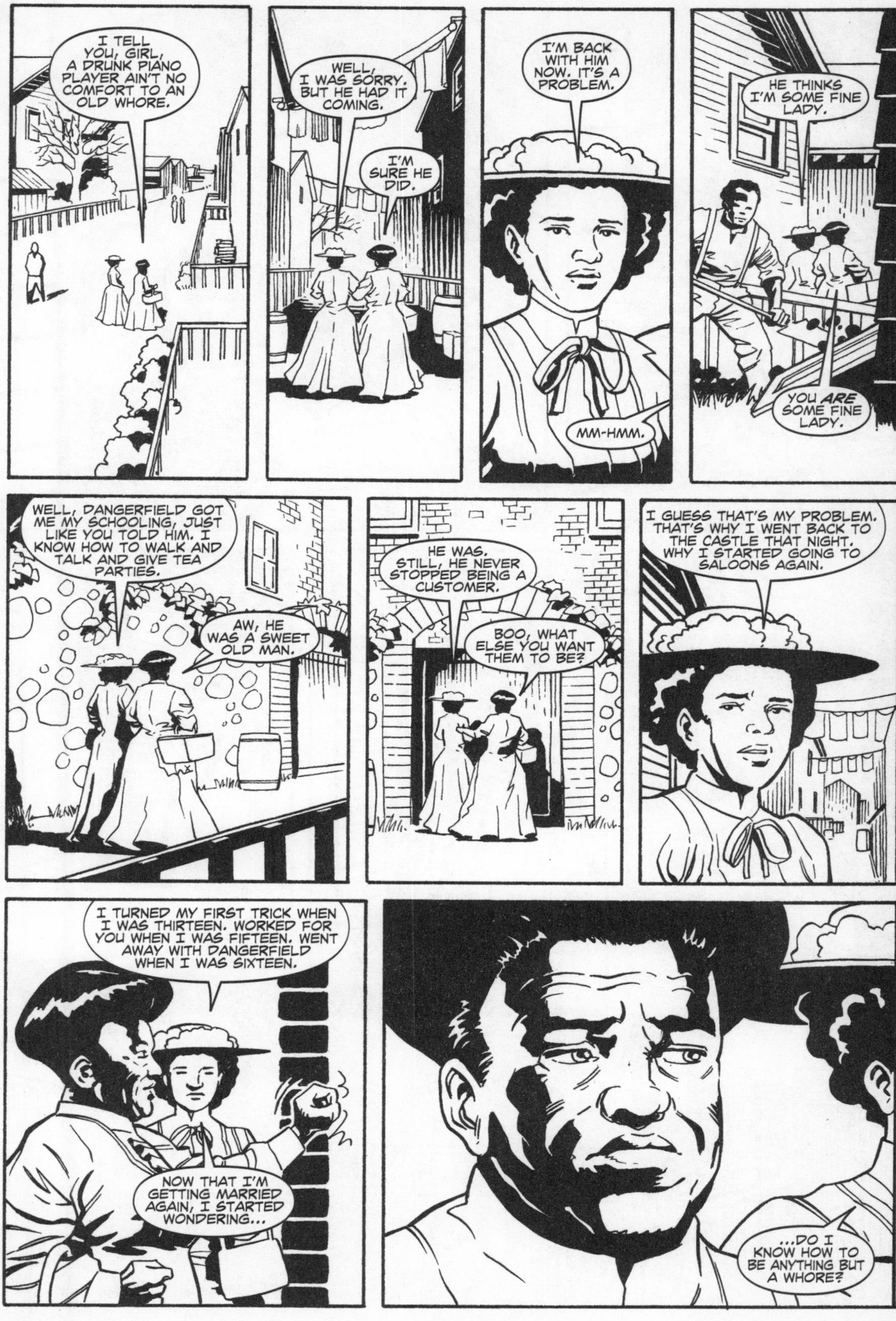
I TELL YOU, GIRL, A DRUNK PIANO PLAYER AIN'T NO COMFORT TO AN OLD WHORE.
WELL, I WAS SORRY. BUT HE HAD IT COMING.
I'M SURE HE DID.
I'M BACK WITH HIM NOW. IT'S A PROBLEM.
MM-HMM.
HE THINKS I'M SOME FINE LADY.
YOU ARE SOME FINE LADY.
WELL, DANGERFIELD GOT ME MY SCHOOLING, JUST LIKE YOU TOLD HIM. I KNOW HOW TO WALK AND TALK AND GIVE TEA PARTIES.
AW, HE WAS A SWEET OLD MAN.
HE WAS. STILL, HE NEVER STOPPED BEING A CUSTOMER.
BOO, WHAT ELSE YOU WANT THEM TO BE?
I GUESS THAT'S MY PROBLEM. THAT'S WHY I WENT BACK TO THE CASTLE THAT NIGHT. WHY I STARTED GOING TO SALOONS AGAIN.
I TURNED MY FIRST TRICK WHEN I WAS THIRTEEN. WORKED FOR YOU WHEN I WAS FIFTEEN. WENT AWAY WITH DANGERFIELD WHEN I WAS SIXTEEN.
NOW THAT I'M GETTING MARRIED AGAIN, I STARTED WONDERING...
...DO I KNOW HOW TO BE ANYTHING BUT A WHORE?

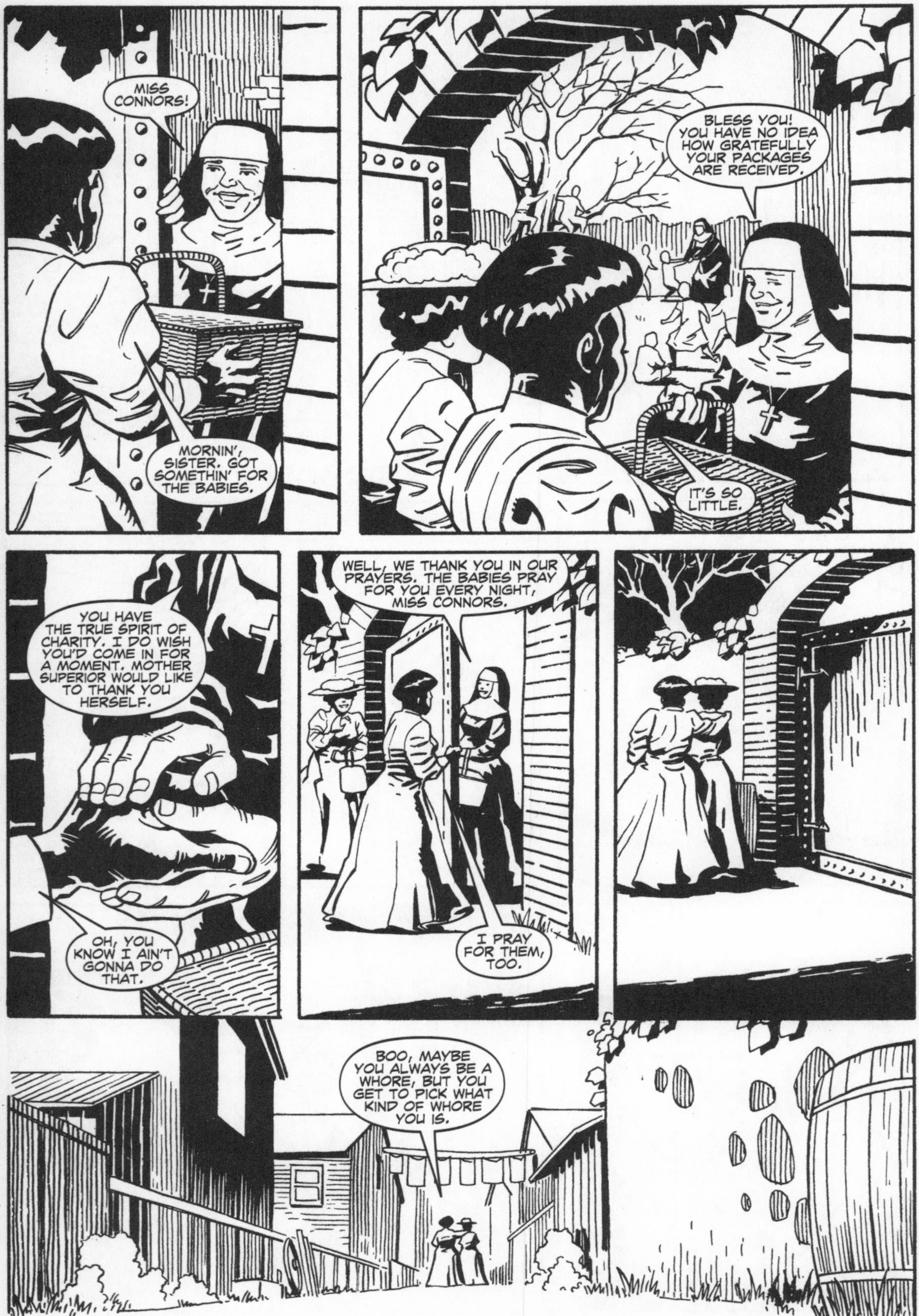
MISS CONNORS!
MORNIN', SISTER. GOT SOMETHIN' FOR THE BABIES.
BLESS YOU! YOU HAVE NO IDEA HOW GRATEFULLY YOUR PACKAGES ARE RECEIVED.
IT'S SO LITTLE.
YOU HAVE THE TRUE SPIRIT OF CHARITY. I DO WISH YOU'D COME IN FOR A MOMENT. MOTHER SUPERIOR WOULD LIKE TO THANK YOU HERSELF.
OH, YOU KNOW I AIN'T GONNA DO THAT.
WELL, WE THANK YOU IN OUR PRAYERS. THE BABIES PRAY FOR YOU EVERY NIGHT, MISS CONNORS.
I PRAY FOR THEM, TOO.
BOO, MAYBE YOU ALWAYS BE A WHORE, BUT YOU GET TO PICK WHAT KIND OF WHORE YOU IS.

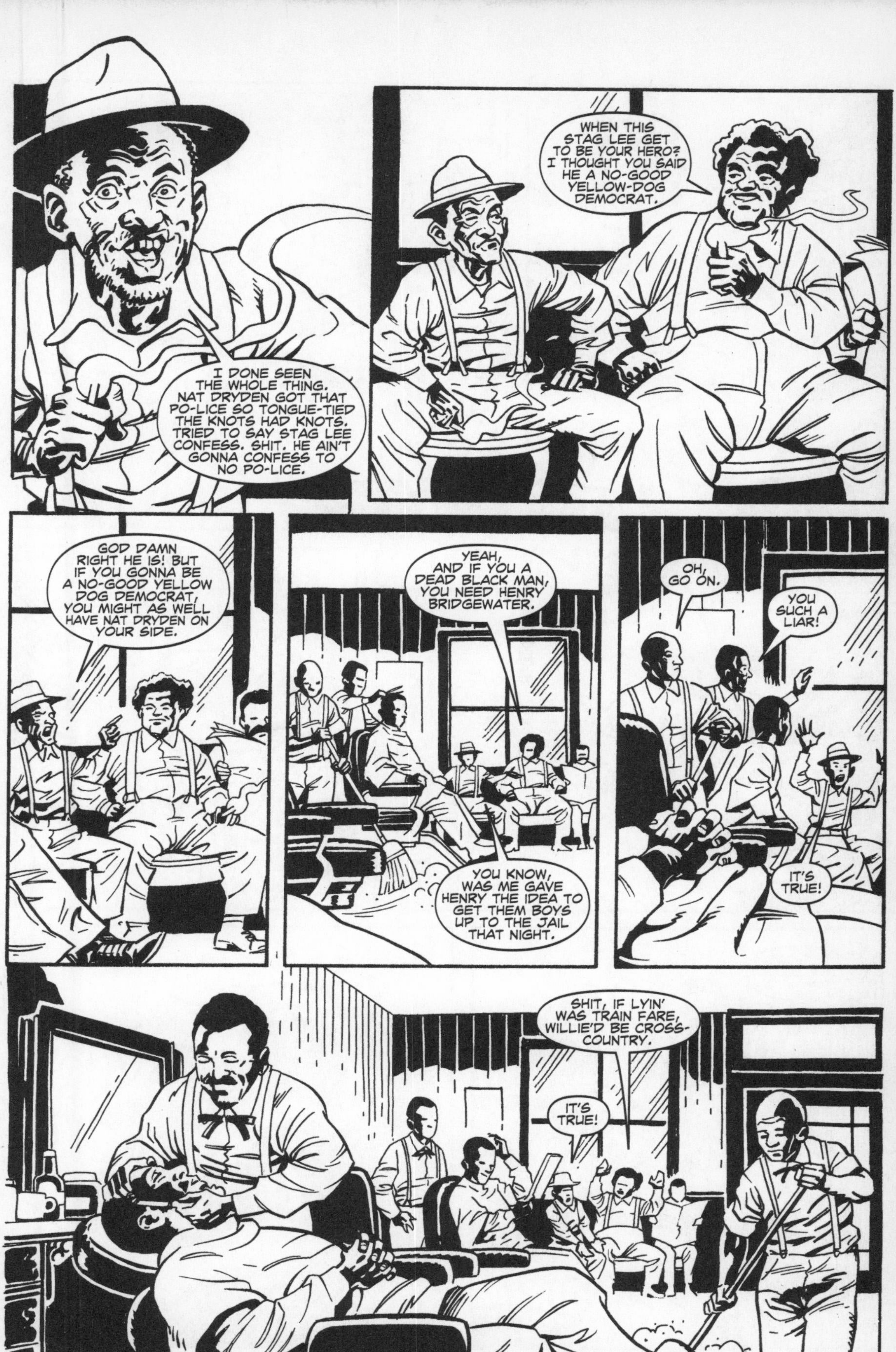
I DONE SEEN THE WHOLE THING. NAT DRYDEN GOT THAT PO-LICE SO TONGUE-TIED THE KNOTS HAD KNOTS. TRIED TO SAY STAG LEE CONFESS. SHIT. HE AIN'T GONNA CONFESS TO NO PO-LICE.
WHEN THIS STAG LEE GET TO BE YOUR HERO? I THOUGHT YOU SAID HE A NO-GOOD YELLOW-DOG DEMOCRAT.
GOD DAMN RIGHT HE IS! BUT IF YOU GONNA BE A NO-GOOD YELLOW DOG DEMOCRAT, YOU MIGHT AS WELL HAVE NAT DRYDEN ON YOUR SIDE.
YEAH, AND IF YOU A DEAD BLACK MAN, YOU NEED HENRY BRIDGEWATER.
YOU KNOW, WAS ME GAVE HENRY THE IDEA TO GET THEM BOYS UP TO THE JAIL THAT NIGHT.
OH, GO ON.
YOU SUCH A LIAR!
IT'S TRUE!
SHIT, IF LYIN' WAS TRAIN FARE, WILLIE'D BE CROSS-COUNTRY.
IT'S TRUE!

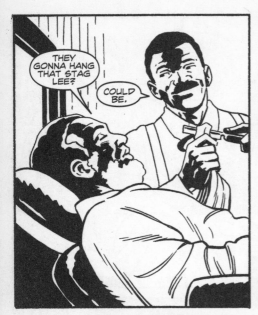

THEY GONNA HANG THAT STAG LEE?

COULD BE.

NOT WITH NAT DRYDEN. I GIVE HIM SOME GOOD IDEAS FOR THE DEFENSE. MOTIONS AND SUCH.

SORRY YOU GOT TO HEAR SUCH ALL-FIRED BULLSHIT, SIR.

IT'S TRUE!

YOU CROSS-COUNTRY AND BACK!

YOU CAN'T EVEN MAKE UP YOUR MIND WHICH SIDE YOU WANT TO TELL LIES ABOUT.

I AIN'T LYIN'!

I THINK THEY GONNA HANG HIM.

WHY'S THAT?

'CAUSE THAT'S THE WAY YOU END A SONG.

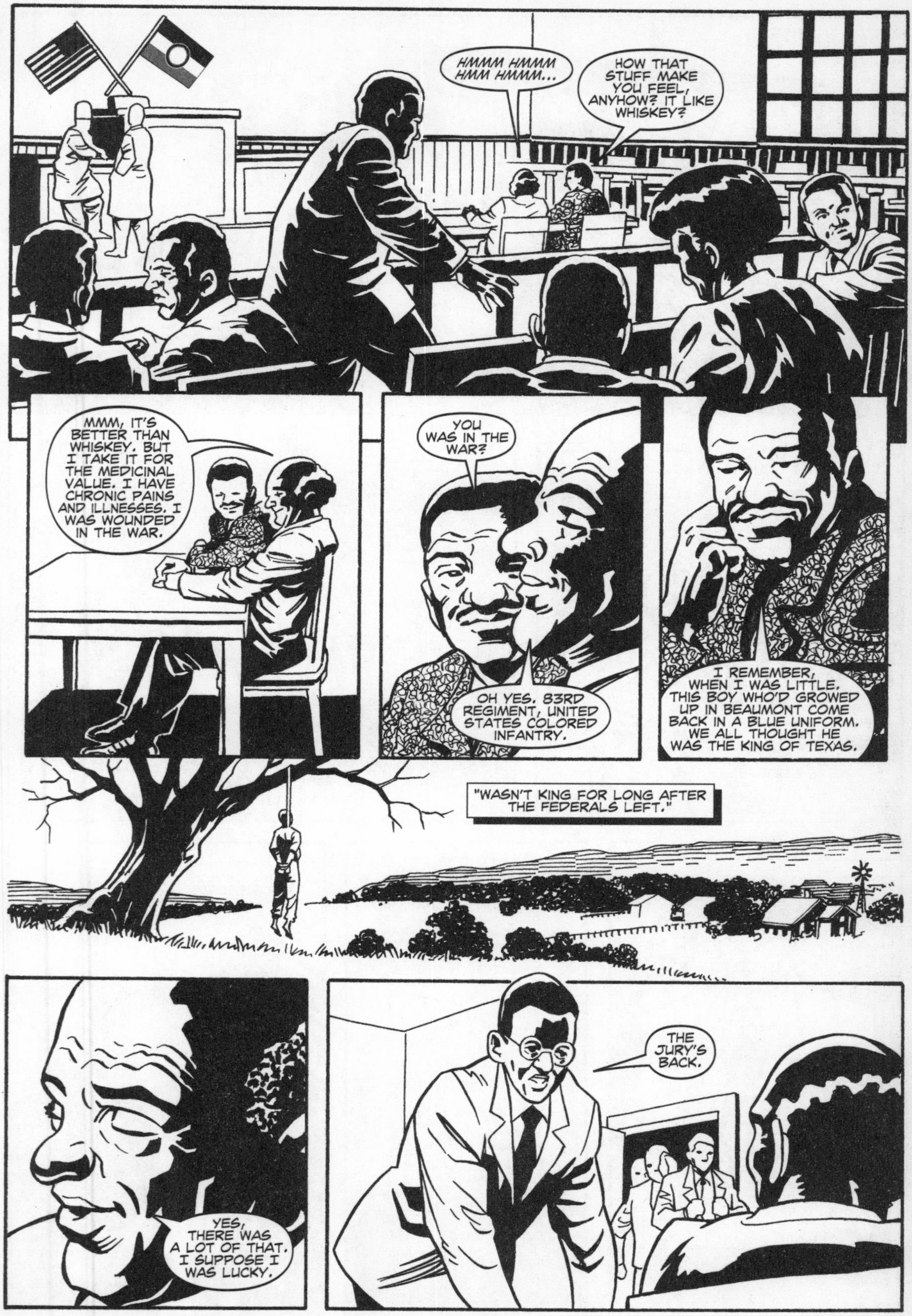
HMMM HMMM HMM HMMM...
HOW THAT STUFF MAKE YOU FEEL, ANYHOW? IT LIKE WHISKEY?
MMM, IT'S BETTER THAN WHISKEY. BUT I TAKE IT FOR THE MEDICINAL VALUE. I HAVE CHRONIC PAINS AND ILLNESSES. I WAS WOUNDED IN THE WAR.
YOU WAS IN THE WAR?
OH YES. 83RD REGIMENT, UNITED STATES COLORED INFANTRY.
I REMEMBER, WHEN I WAS LITTLE. THIS BOY WHO'D GROWED UP IN BEAUMONT COME BACK IN A BLUE UNIFORM. WE ALL THOUGHT HE WAS THE KING OF TEXAS.
"WASN'T KING FOR LONG AFTER THE FEDERALS LEFT."
YES, THERE WAS A LOT OF THAT. I SUPPOSE I WAS LUCKY.
THE JURY'S BACK.

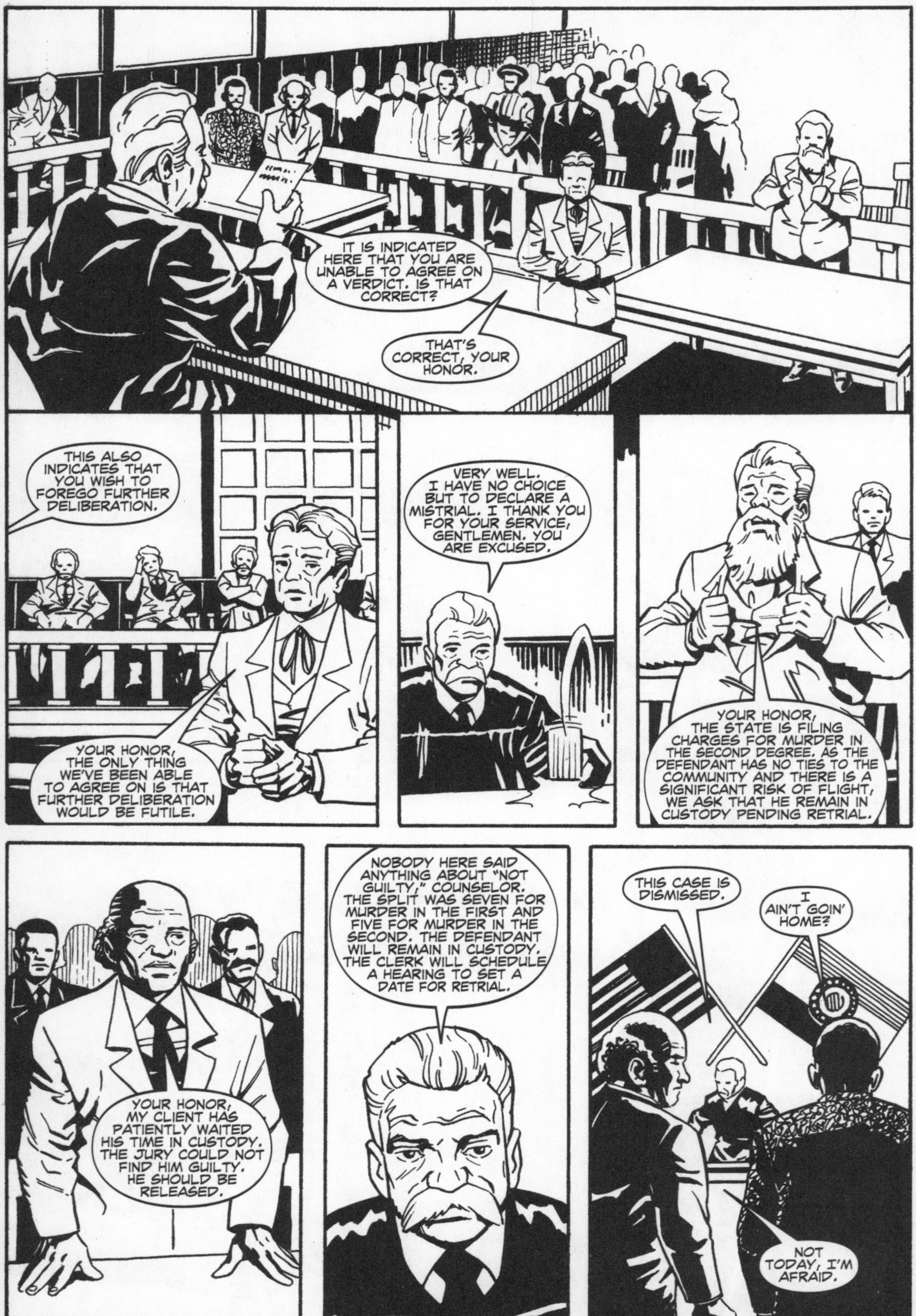
IT IS INDICATED HERE THAT YOU ARE UNABLE TO AGREE ON A VERDICT. IS THAT CORRECT?
THAT'S CORRECT, YOUR HONOR.
THIS ALSO INDICATES THAT YOU WISH TO FOREGO FURTHER DELIBERATION.
YOUR HONOR, THE ONLY THING WE'VE BEEN ABLE TO AGREE ON IS THAT FURTHER DELIBERATION WOULD BE FUTILE.
VERY WELL. I HAVE NO CHOICE BUT TO DECLARE A MISTRIAL. I THANK YOU FOR YOUR SERVICE, GENTLEMEN. YOU ARE EXCUSED.
YOUR HONOR, THE STATE IS FILING CHARGES FOR MURDER IN THE SECOND DEGREE. AS THE DEFENDANT HAS NO TIES TO THE COMMUNITY AND THERE IS A SIGNIFICANT RISK OF FLIGHT, WE ASK THAT HE REMAIN IN CUSTODY PENDING RETRIAL.
YOUR HONOR, MY CLIENT HAS PATIENTLY WAITED HIS TIME IN CUSTODY. THE JURY COULD NOT FIND HIM GUILTY. HE SHOULD BE RELEASED.
NOBODY HERE SAID ANYTHING ABOUT "NOT GUILTY," COUNSELOR. THE SPLIT WAS SEVEN FOR MURDER IN THE FIRST AND FIVE FOR MURDER IN THE SECOND. THE DEFENDANT WILL REMAIN IN CUSTODY. THE CLERK WILL SCHEDULE A HEARING TO SET A DATE FOR RETRIAL.
THIS CASE IS DISMISSED.
I AIN'T GOIN' HOME?
NOT TODAY, I'M AFRAID.

PART THREE

The GHOST

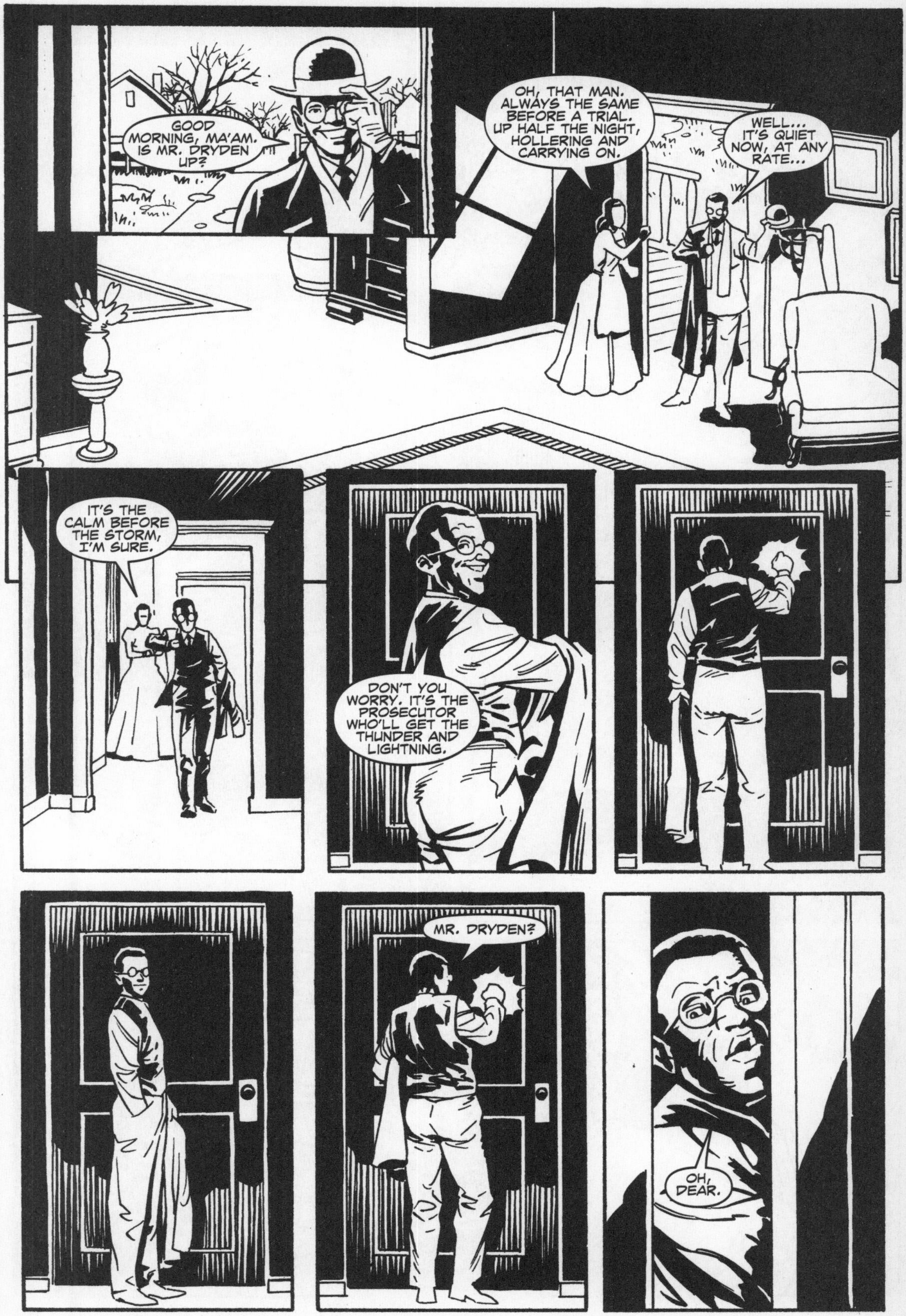
GOOD MORNING, MA'AM. IS MR. DRYDEN UP?
OH, THAT MAN. ALWAYS THE SAME BEFORE A TRIAL. UP HALF THE NIGHT, HOLLERING AND CARRYING ON.
WELL... IT'S QUIET NOW, AT ANY RATE...
IT'S THE CALM BEFORE THE STORM, I'M SURE.
DON'T YOU WORRY. IT'S THE PROSECUTOR WHO'LL GET THE THUNDER AND LIGHTNING.
MR. DRYDEN?
OH, DEAR.

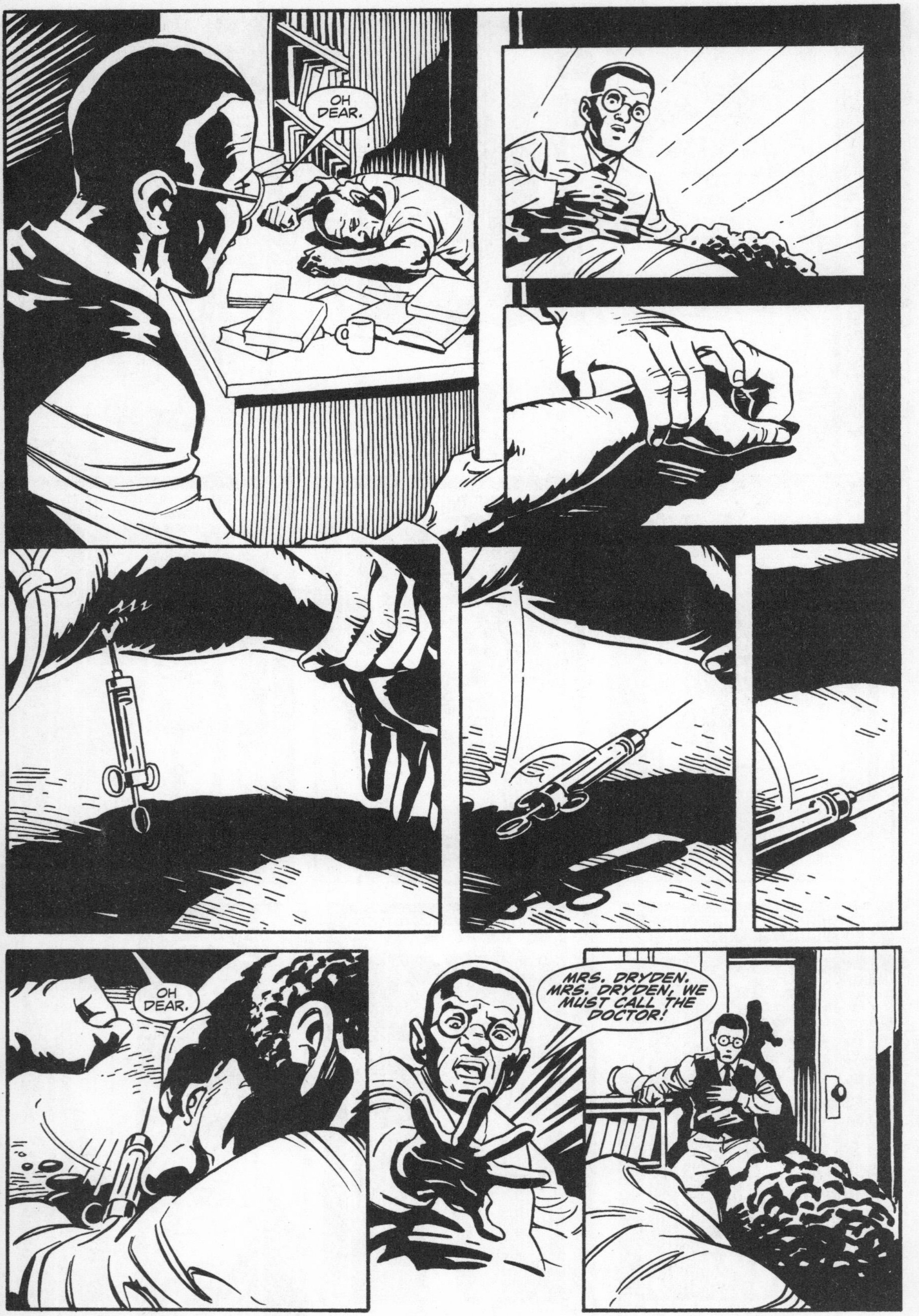
OH DEAR.
OH DEAR.
MRS. DRYDEN. MRS. DRYDEN, WE MUST CALL THE DOCTOR!

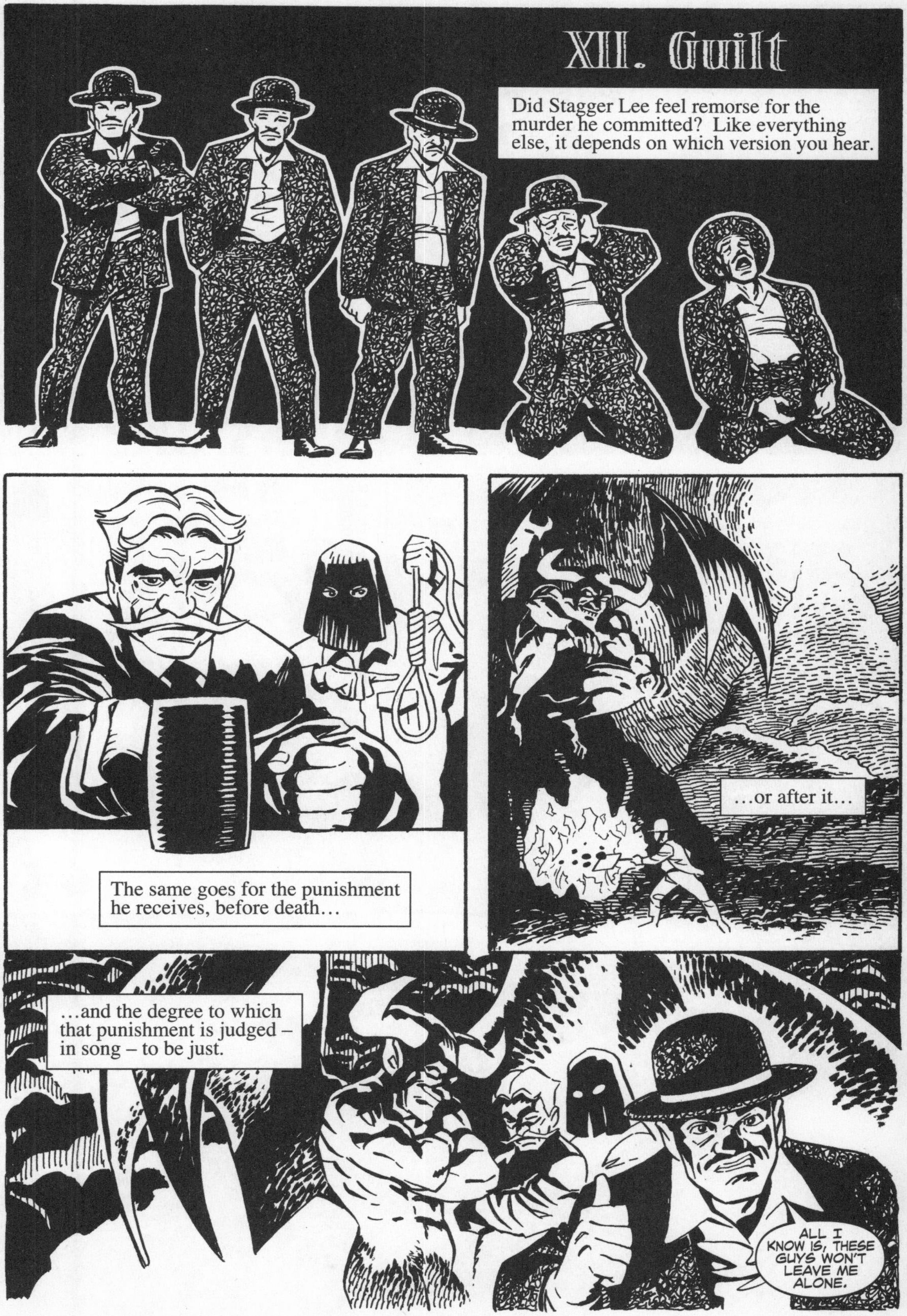
XII. Guilt
Did Stagger Lee feel remorse for the murder he committed? Like everything else, it depends on which version you hear.
The same goes for the punishment he receives, before death…
…or after it…
…and the degree to which that punishment is judged – in song – to be just.
ALL I KNOW IS, THESE GUYS WON'T LEAVE ME ALONE.

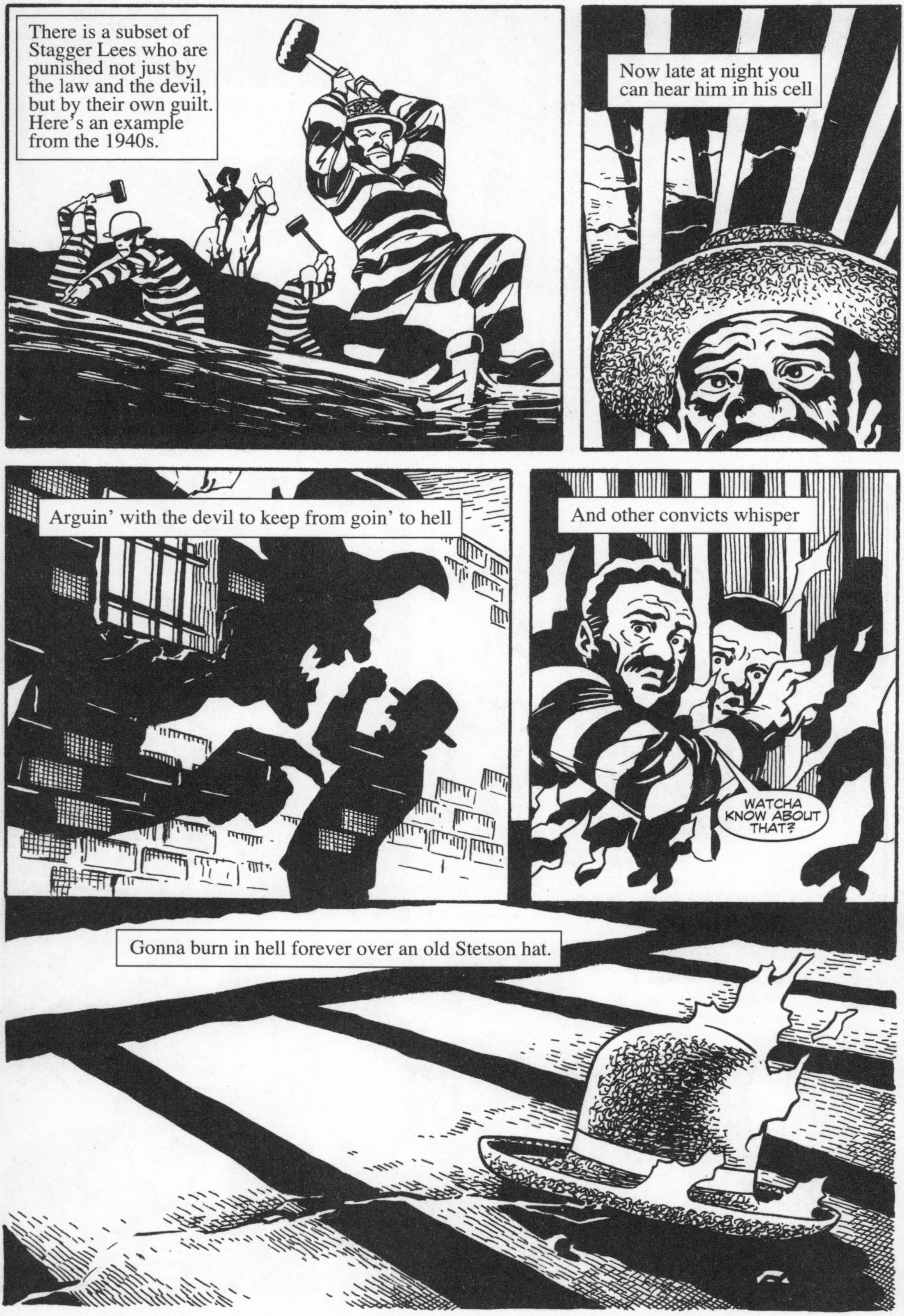
There is a subset of Stagger Lees who are punished not just by the law and the devil, but by their own guilt. Here's an example from the 1940s.
Now late at night you can hear him in his cell
Arguin' with the devil to keep from goin' to hell
And other convicts whisper
WATCHA KNOW ABOUT THAT?
Gonna burn in hell forever over an old Stetson hat.

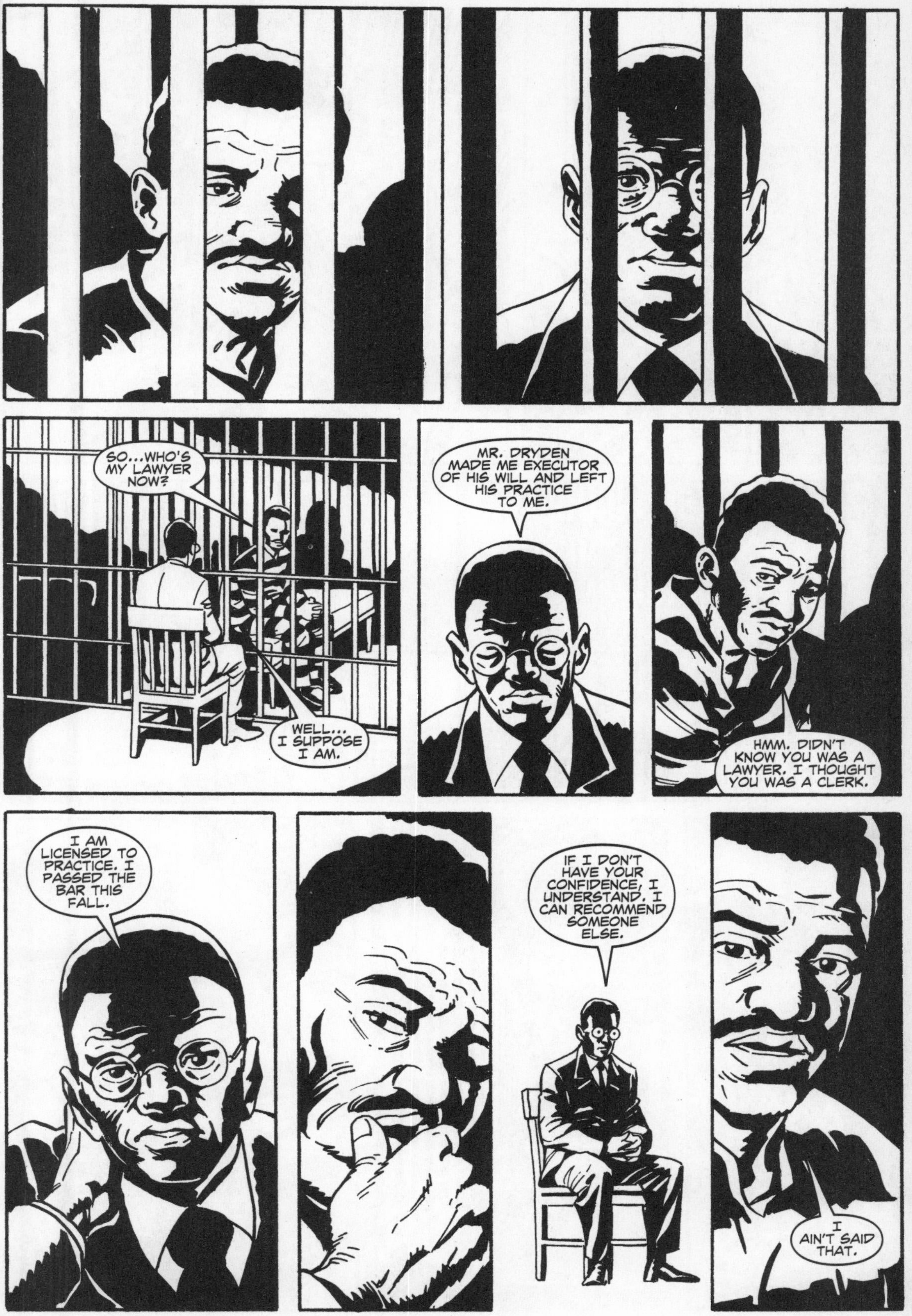
SO...WHO'S MY LAWYER NOW?
WELL... I SUPPOSE I AM.
MR. DRYDEN MADE ME EXECUTOR OF HIS WILL AND LEFT HIS PRACTICE TO ME.
HMM. DIDN'T KNOW YOU WAS A LAWYER. I THOUGHT YOU WAS A CLERK.
I AM LICENSED TO PRACTICE. I PASSED THE BAR THIS FALL.
IF I DON'T HAVE YOUR CONFIDENCE, I UNDERSTAND. I CAN RECOMMEND SOMEONE ELSE.
I AIN'T SAID THAT.

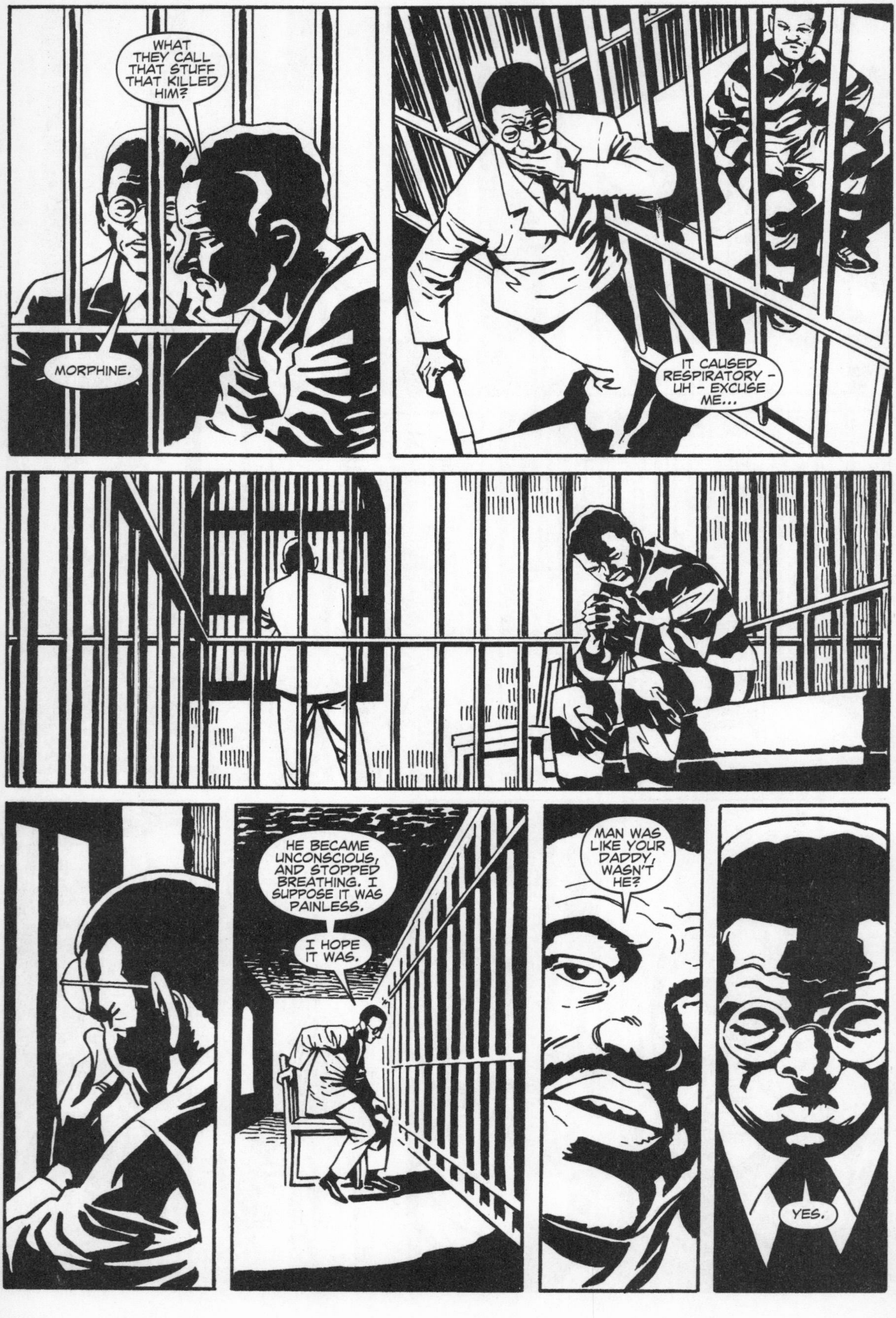
WHAT THEY CALL THAT STUFF THAT KILLED HIM?
MORPHINE.
IT CAUSED RESPIRATORY - UH - EXCUSE ME...
HE BECAME UNCONSCIOUS, AND STOPPED BREATHING. I SUPPOSE IT WAS PAINLESS.
I HOPE IT WAS.
MAN WAS LIKE YOUR DADDY, WASN'T HE?
YES.

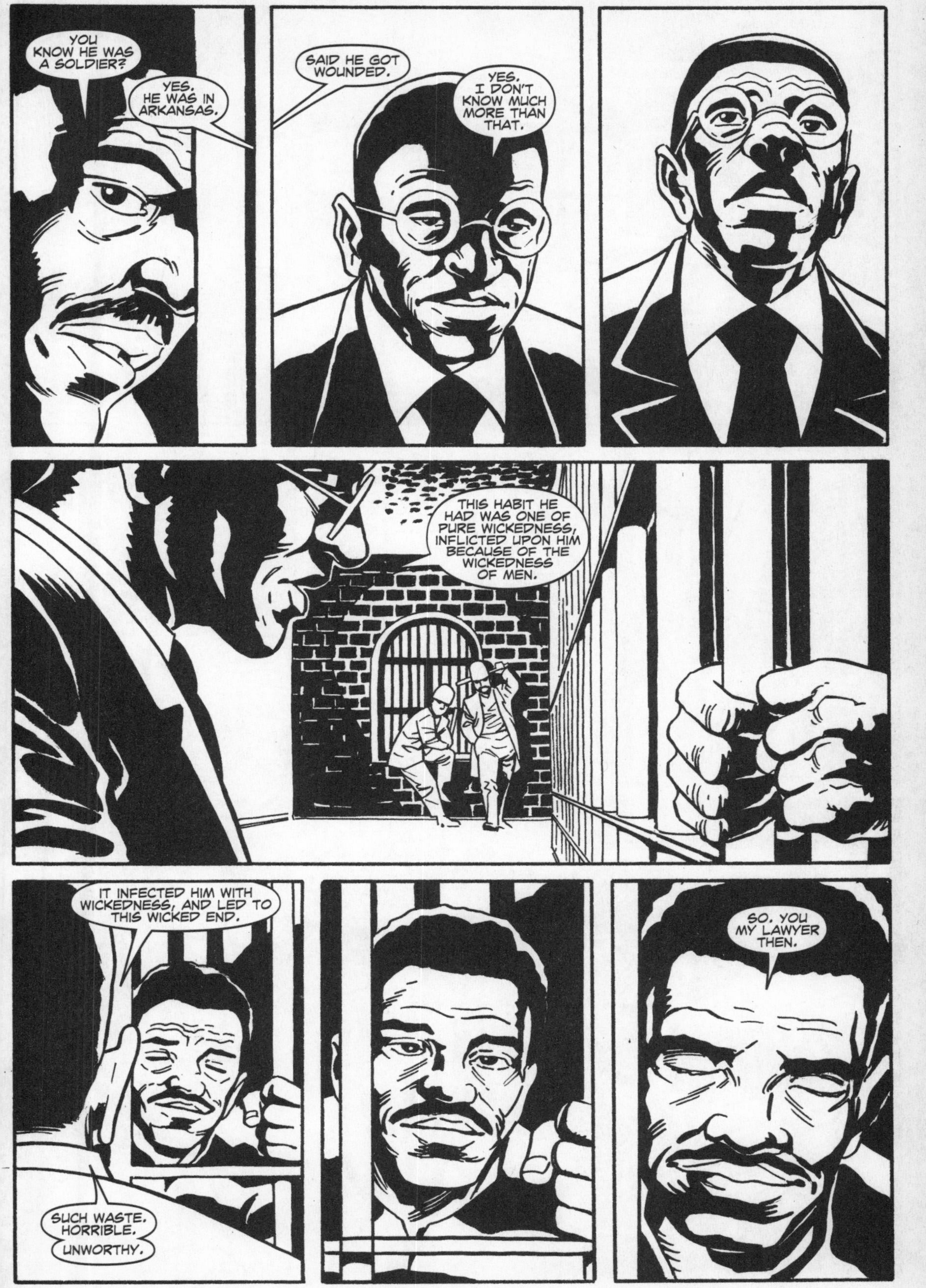
YOU KNOW HE WAS A SOLDIER?
YES. HE WAS IN ARKANSAS.
SAID HE GOT WOUNDED.
YES. I DON'T KNOW MUCH MORE THAN THAT.
THIS HABIT HE HAD WAS ONE OF PURE WICKEDNESS, INFLICTED UPON HIM BECAUSE OF THE WICKEDNESS OF MEN.
IT INFECTED HIM WITH WICKEDNESS, AND LED TO THIS WICKED END.
SUCH WASTE. HORRIBLE.
UNWORTHY.
SO. YOU MY LAWYER THEN.

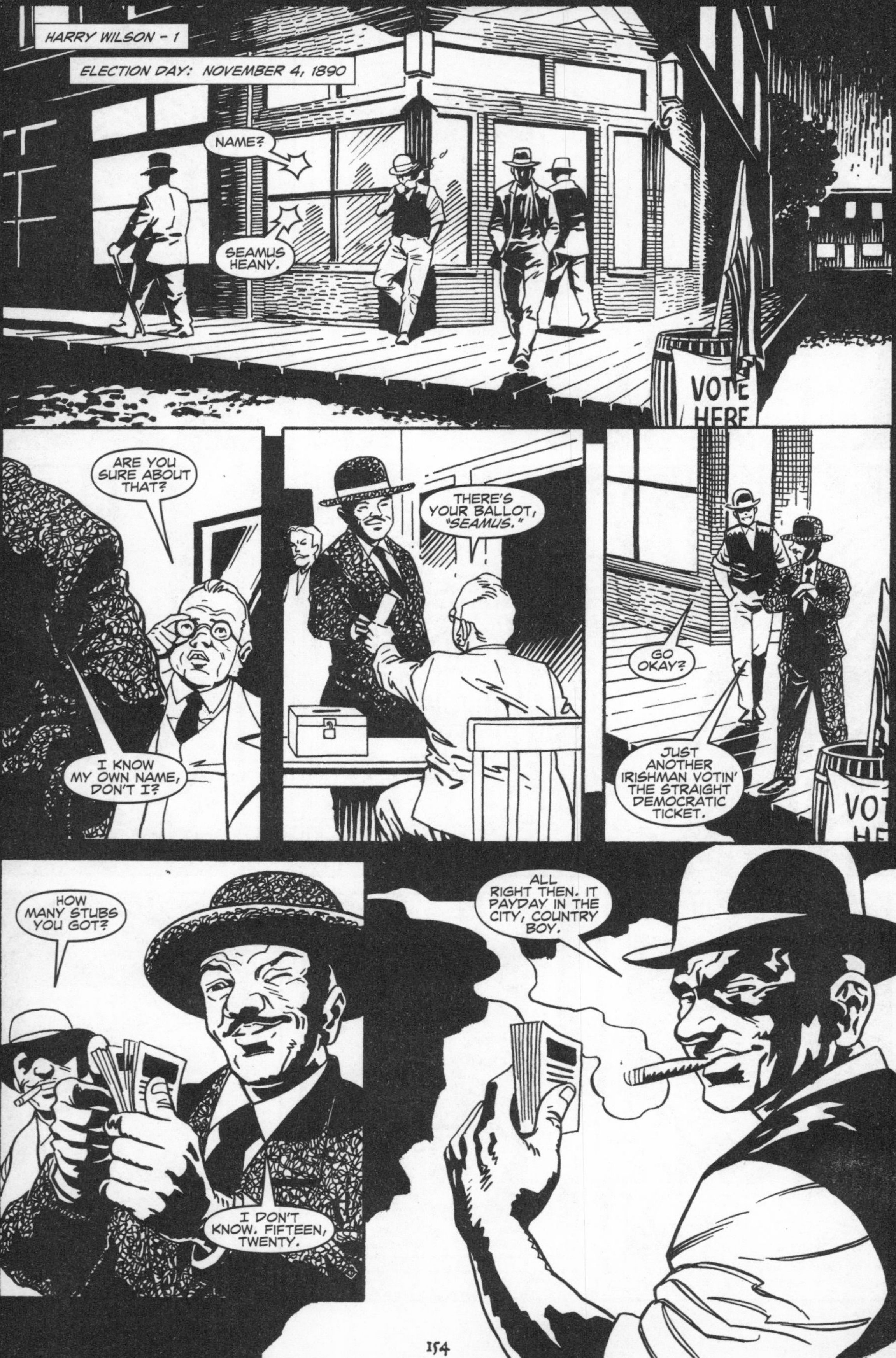
HARRY WILSON - 1
ELECTION DAY: NOVEMBER 4, 1890
NAME?
SEAMUS HEANY.
VOTE HERE
ARE YOU SURE ABOUT THAT?
I KNOW MY OWN NAME, DON'T I?
THERE'S YOUR BALLOT, "SEAMUS."
GO OKAY?
JUST ANOTHER IRISHMAN VOTIN' THE STRAIGHT DEMOCRATIC TICKET.
HOW MANY STUBS YOU GOT?
I DON'T KNOW. FIFTEEN, TWENTY.
ALL RIGHT THEN. IT PAYDAY IN THE CITY, COUNTRY BOY.

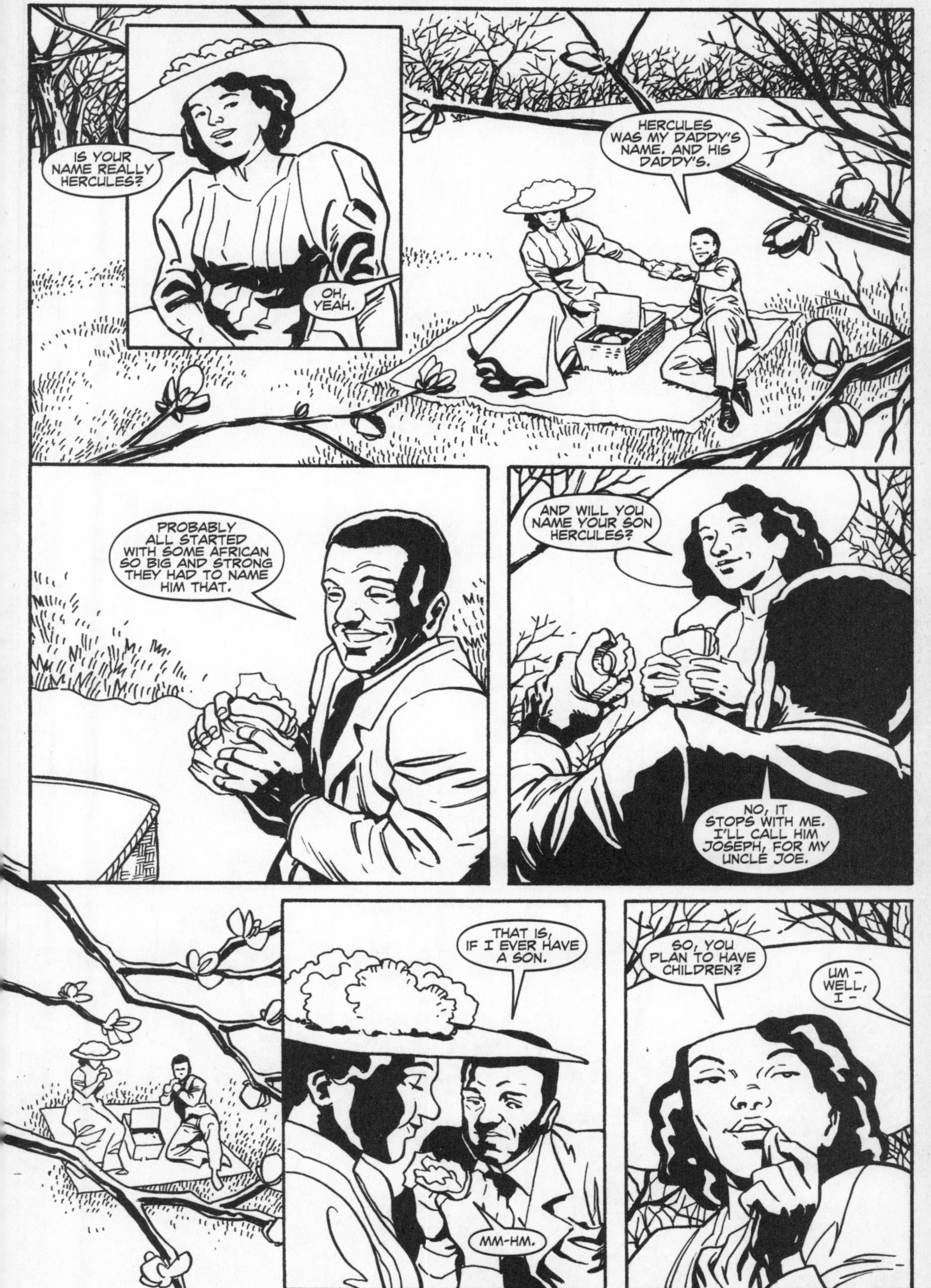
IS YOUR NAME REALLY HERCULES?
OH, YEAH.
HERCULES WAS MY DADDY'S NAME. AND HIS DADDY'S.
PROBABLY ALL STARTED WITH SOME AFRICAN SO BIG AND STRONG THEY HAD TO NAME HIM THAT.
AND WILL YOU NAME YOUR SON HERCULES?
NO, IT STOPS WITH ME. I'LL CALL HIM JOSEPH, FOR MY UNCLE JOE.
THAT IS, IF I EVER HAVE A SON.
MM-HM.
SO, YOU PLAN TO HAVE CHILDREN?
UM - WELL, I -

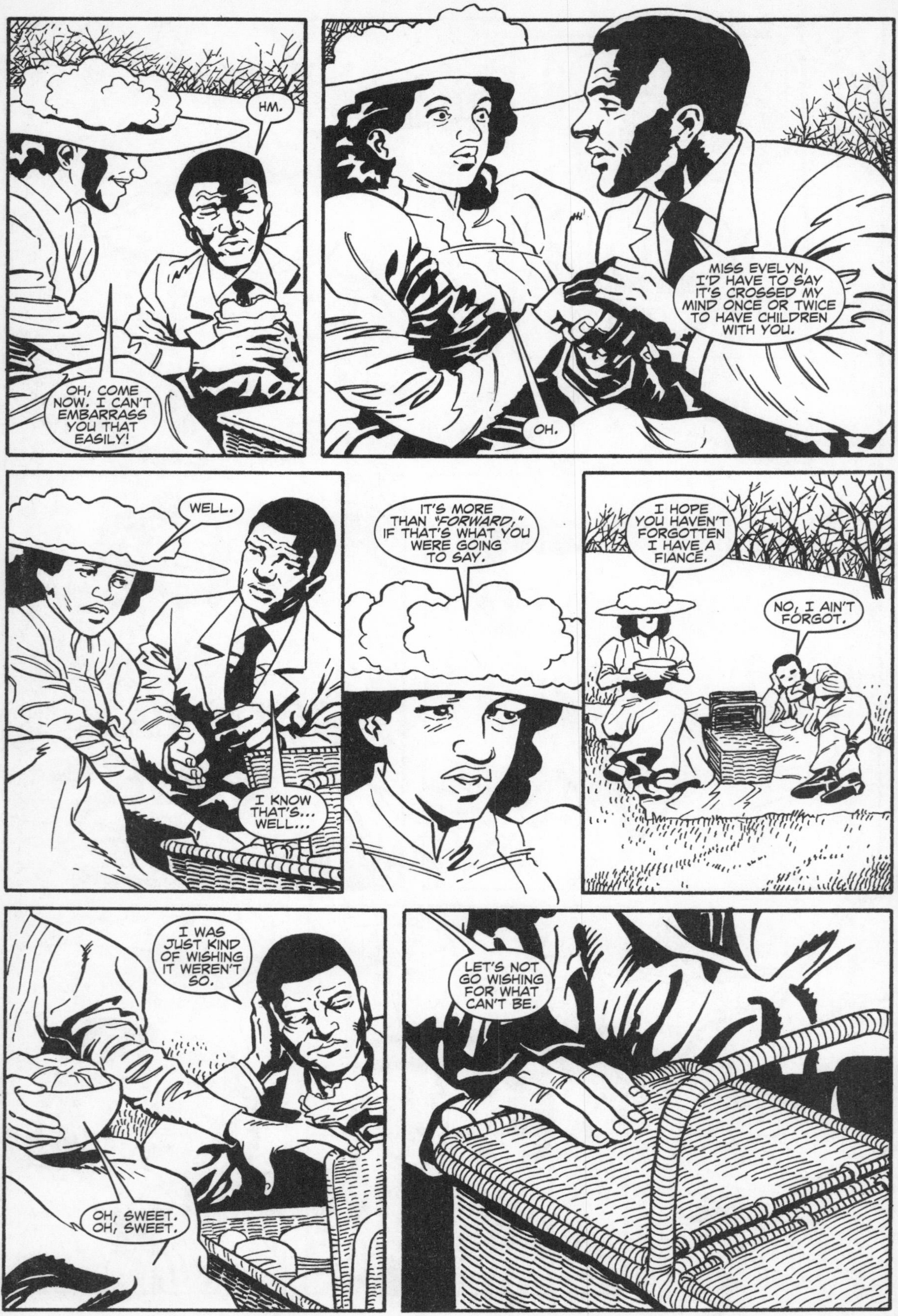
HM.
OH, COME NOW. I CAN'T EMBARRASS YOU THAT EASILY!
MISS EVELYN, I'D HAVE TO SAY IT'S CROSSED MY MIND ONCE OR TWICE TO HAVE CHILDREN WITH YOU.
OH.
WELL.
I KNOW THAT'S... WELL...
IT'S MORE THAN "FORWARD," IF THAT'S WHAT YOU WERE GOING TO SAY.
I HOPE YOU HAVEN'T FORGOTTEN I HAVE A FIANCE.
NO, I AIN'T FORGOT.
I WAS JUST KIND OF WISHING IT WEREN'T SO.
OH, SWEET. OH, SWEET.
LET'S NOT GO WISHING FOR WHAT CAN'T BE.

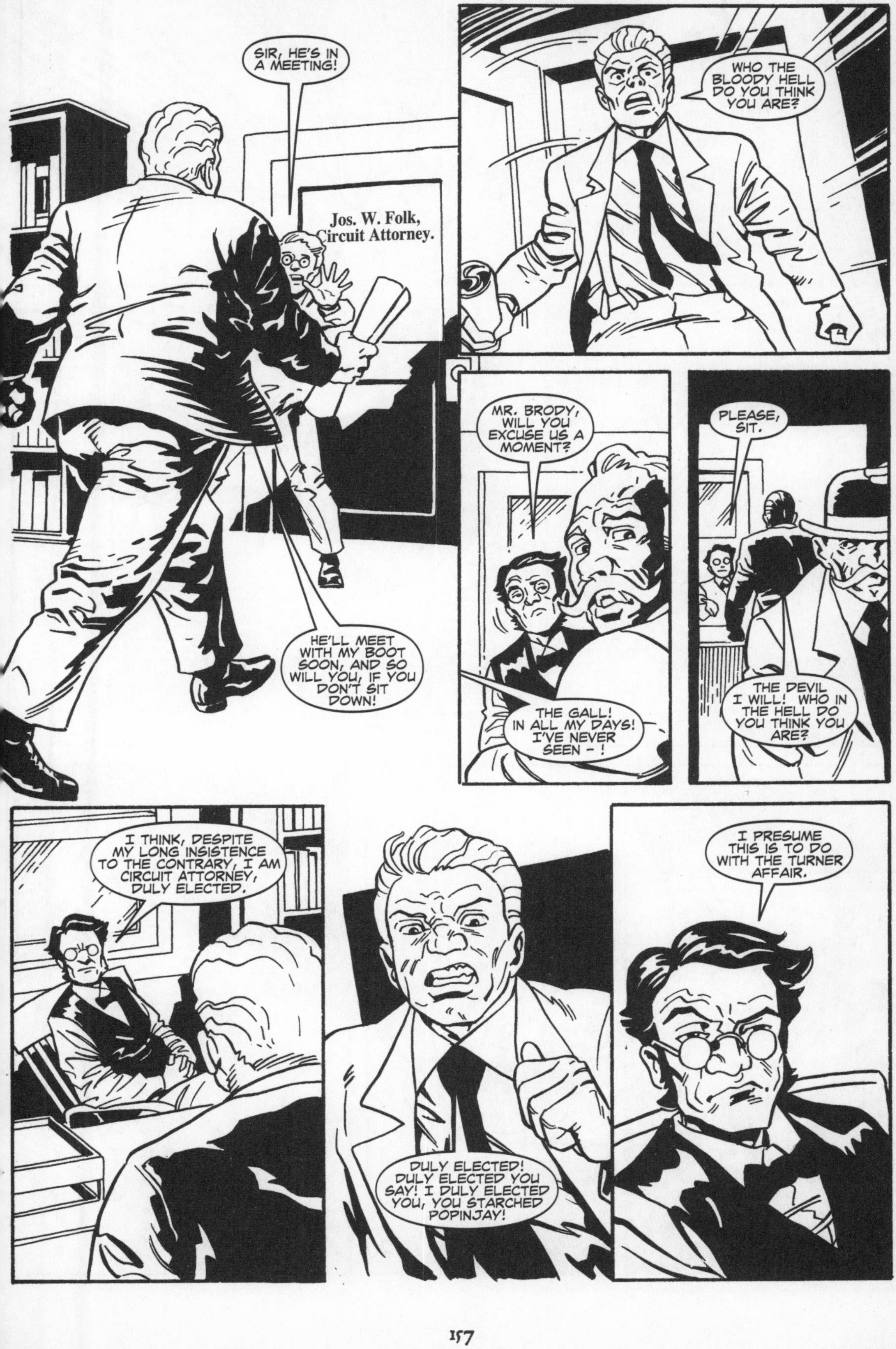
SIR, HE'S IN A MEETING!
Jos. W. Folk, Circuit Attorney.
HE'LL MEET WITH MY BOOT SOON, AND SO WILL YOU, IF YOU DON'T SIT DOWN!
WHO THE BLOODY HELL DO YOU THINK YOU ARE?
MR. BRODY, WILL YOU EXCUSE US A MOMENT?
THE GALL! IN ALL MY DAYS! I'VE NEVER SEEN - !
PLEASE, SIT.
THE DEVIL I WILL! WHO IN THE HELL DO YOU THINK YOU ARE?
I THINK, DESPITE MY LONG INSISTENCE TO THE CONTRARY, I AM CIRCUIT ATTORNEY, DULY ELECTED.
DULY ELECTED! DULY ELECTED YOU SAY! I DULY ELECTED YOU, YOU STARCHED POPINJAY!
I PRESUME THIS IS TO DO WITH THE TURNER AFFAIR.

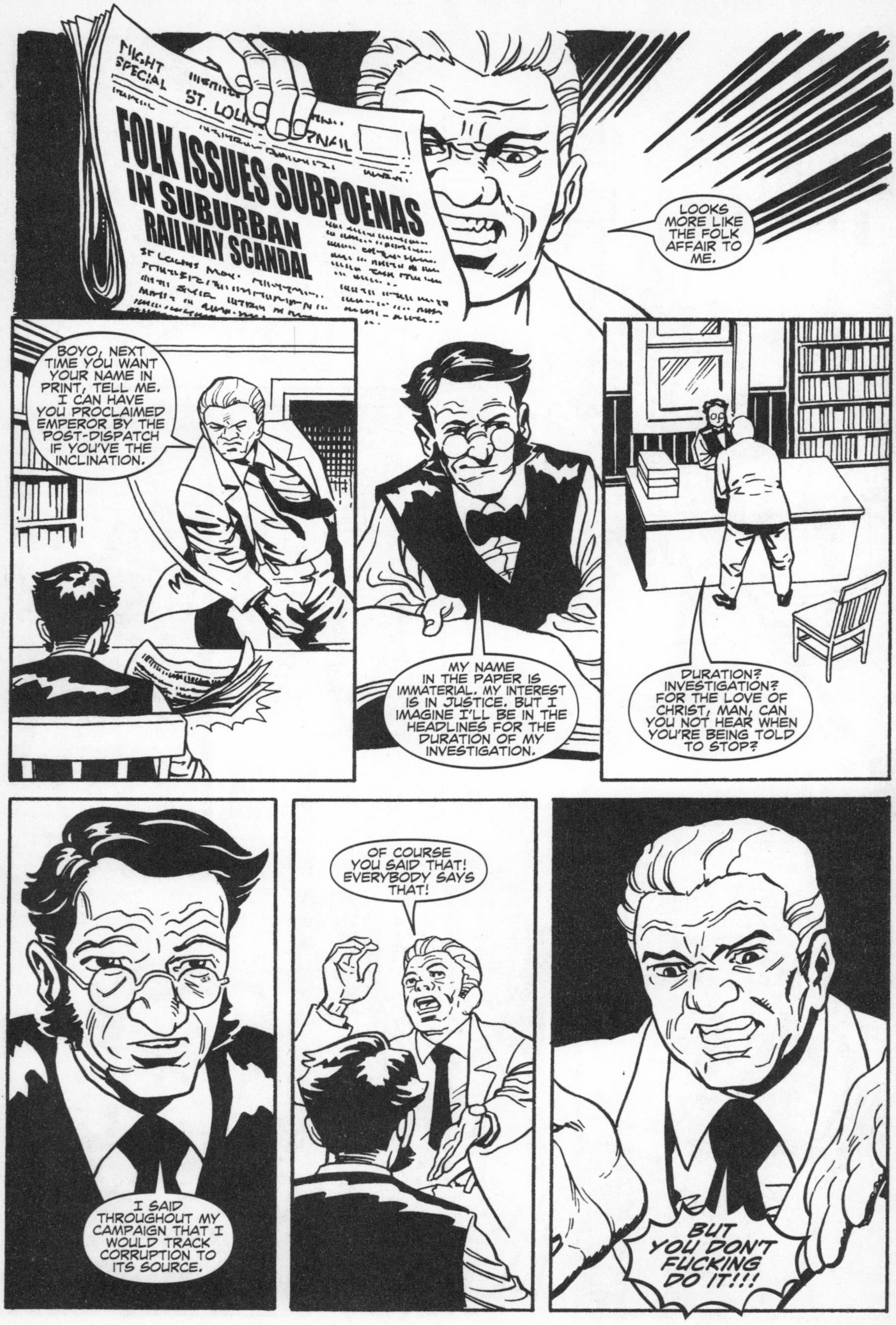
NIGHT SPECIAL
ST. LOUIS JOURNAL
FOLK ISSUES SUBPOENAS IN SUBURBAN RAILWAY SCANDAL
LOOKS MORE LIKE THE FOLK AFFAIR TO ME.
BOYO, NEXT TIME YOU WANT YOUR NAME IN PRINT, TELL ME. I CAN HAVE YOU PROCLAIMED EMPEROR BY THE POST-DISPATCH IF YOU'VE THE INCLINATION.
MY NAME IN THE PAPER IS IMMATERIAL. MY INTEREST IS IN JUSTICE. BUT I IMAGINE I'LL BE IN THE HEADLINES FOR THE DURATION OF MY INVESTIGATION.
DURATION? INVESTIGATION? FOR THE LOVE OF CHRIST, MAN, CAN YOU NOT HEAR WHEN YOU'RE BEING TOLD TO STOP?
I SAID THROUGHOUT MY CAMPAIGN THAT I WOULD TRACK CORRUPTION TO ITS SOURCE.
OF COURSE YOU SAID THAT! EVERYBODY SAYS THAT!
BUT YOU DON'T FUCKING DO IT!!!

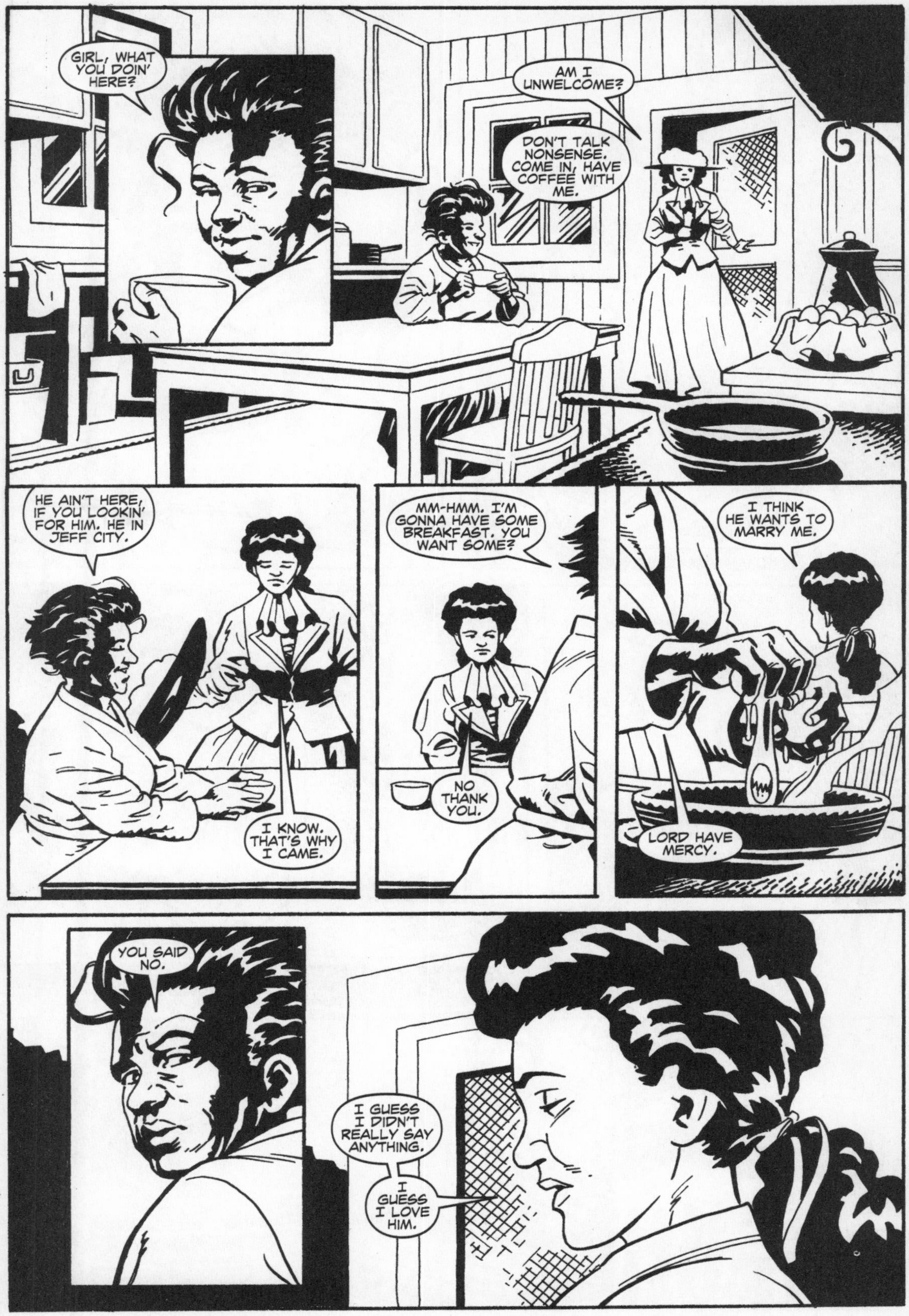

GIRL, WHAT YOU DOIN' HERE?
AM I UNWELCOME?
DON'T TALK NONSENSE. COME IN, HAVE COFFEE WITH ME.
HE AIN'T HERE, IF YOU LOOKIN' FOR HIM. HE IN JEFF CITY.
I KNOW. THAT'S WHY I CAME.
MM-HMM. I'M GONNA HAVE SOME BREAKFAST. YOU WANT SOME?
NO THANK YOU.
I THINK HE WANTS TO MARRY ME.
LORD HAVE MERCY.
YOU SAID NO.
I GUESS I DIDN'T REALLY SAY ANYTHING.
I GUESS I LOVE HIM.

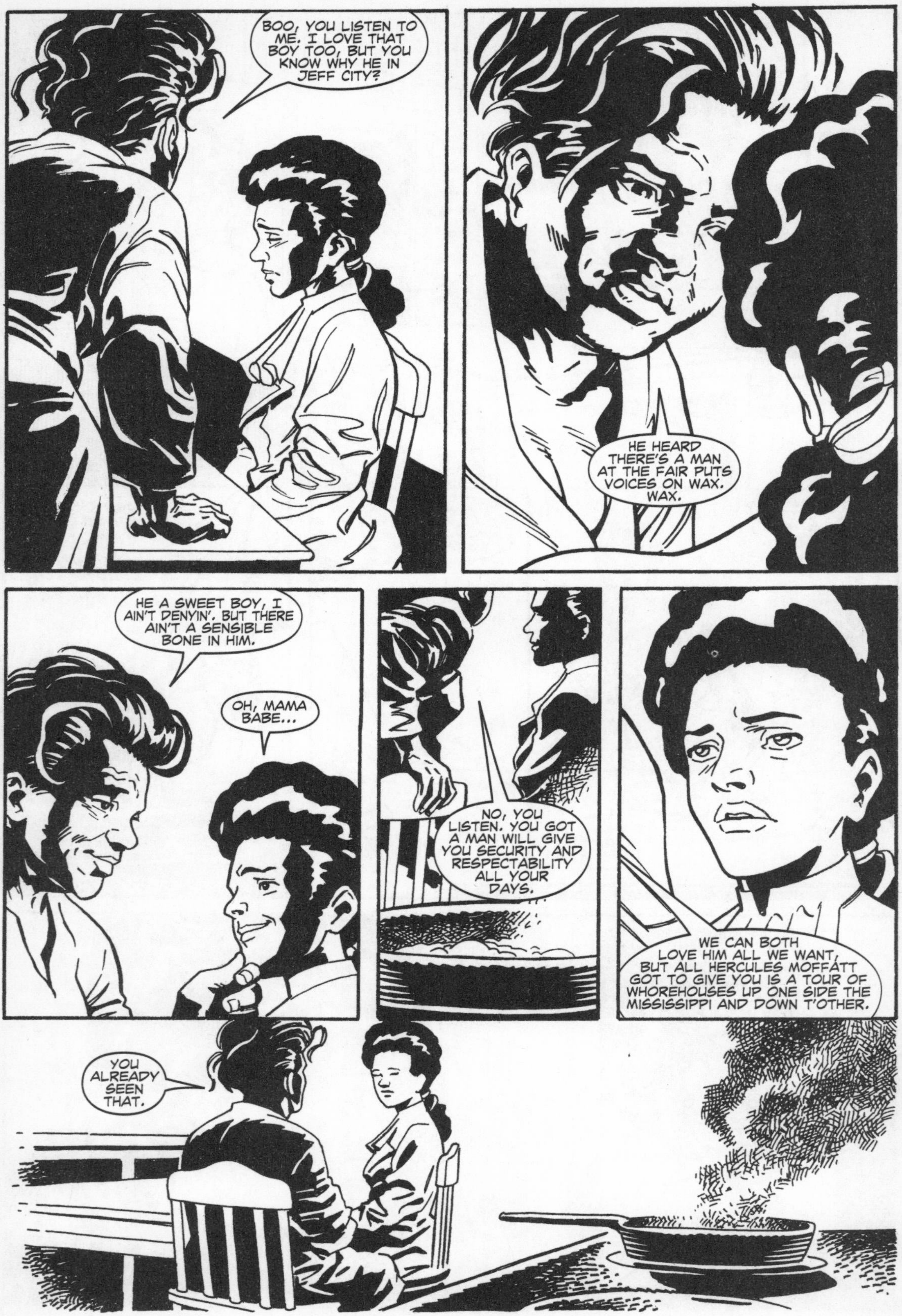
BOO, YOU LISTEN TO ME. I LOVE THAT BOY TOO, BUT YOU KNOW WHY HE IN JEFF CITY?
HE HEARD THERE'S A MAN AT THE FAIR PUTS VOICES ON WAX. WAX.
HE A SWEET BOY, I AIN'T DENYIN'. BUT THERE AIN'T A SENSIBLE BONE IN HIM.
OH, MAMA BABE...
NO, YOU LISTEN. YOU GOT A MAN WILL GIVE YOU SECURITY AND RESPECTABILITY ALL YOUR DAYS.
WE CAN BOTH LOVE HIM ALL WE WANT, BUT ALL HERCULES MOFFATT GOT TO GIVE YOU IS A TOUR OF WHOREHOUSES UP ONE SIDE THE MISSISSIPPI AND DOWN T'OTHER.
YOU ALREADY SEEN THAT.

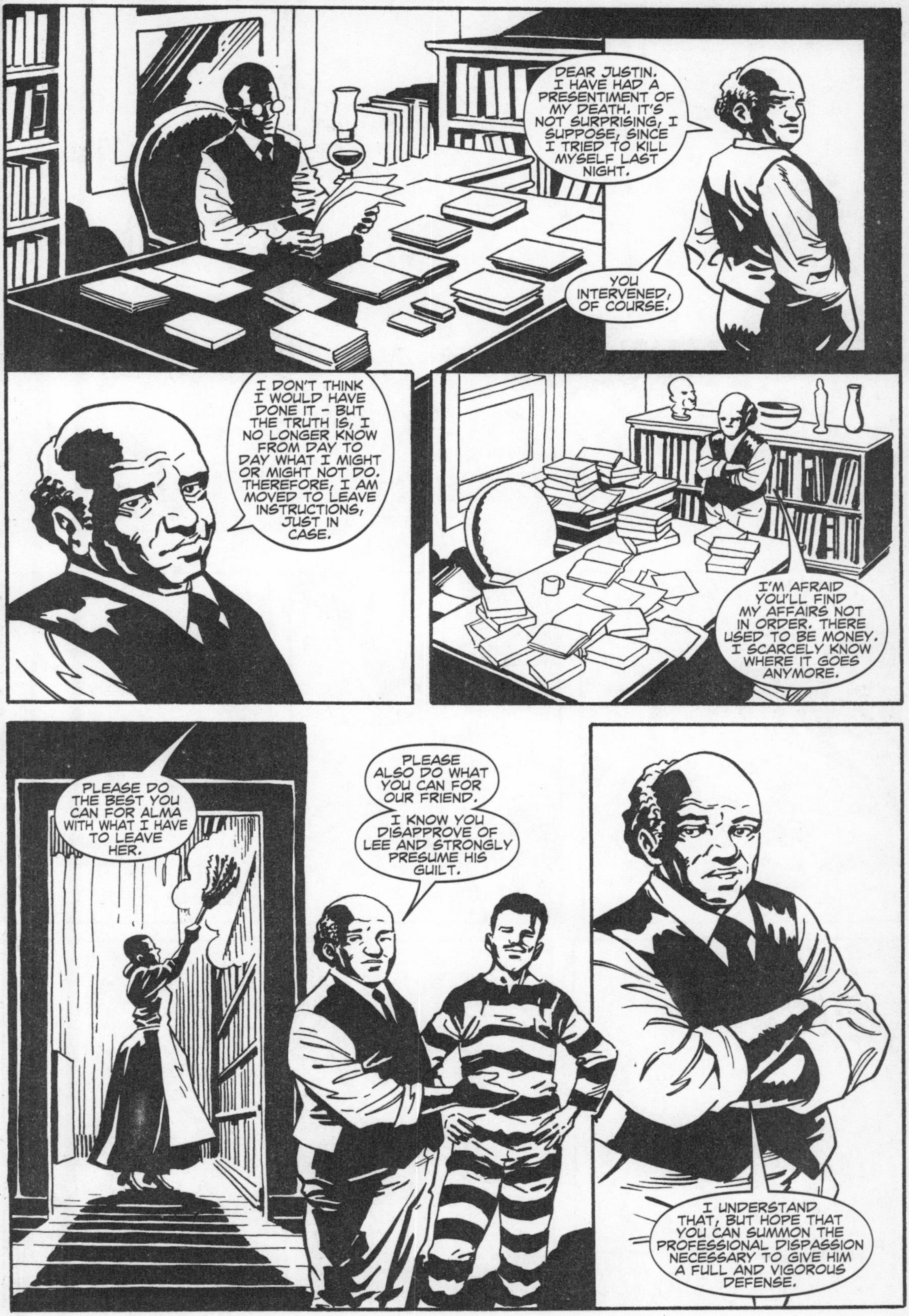

DEAR JUSTIN. I HAVE HAD A PRESENTIMENT OF MY DEATH. IT'S NOT SURPRISING, I SUPPOSE, SINCE I TRIED TO KILL MYSELF LAST NIGHT.
YOU INTERVENED, OF COURSE.
I DON'T THINK I WOULD HAVE DONE IT – BUT THE TRUTH IS, I NO LONGER KNOW FROM DAY TO DAY WHAT I MIGHT OR MIGHT NOT DO. THEREFORE, I AM MOVED TO LEAVE INSTRUCTIONS, JUST IN CASE.
I'M AFRAID YOU'LL FIND MY AFFAIRS NOT IN ORDER. THERE USED TO BE MONEY. I SCARCELY KNOW WHERE IT GOES ANYMORE.
PLEASE DO THE BEST YOU CAN FOR ALMA WITH WHAT I HAVE TO LEAVE HER.
PLEASE ALSO DO WHAT YOU CAN FOR OUR FRIEND.
I KNOW YOU DISAPPROVE OF LEE AND STRONGLY PRESUME HIS GUILT.
I UNDERSTAND THAT, BUT HOPE THAT YOU CAN SUMMON THE PROFESSIONAL DISPASSION NECESSARY TO GIVE HIM A FULL AND VIGOROUS DEFENSE.

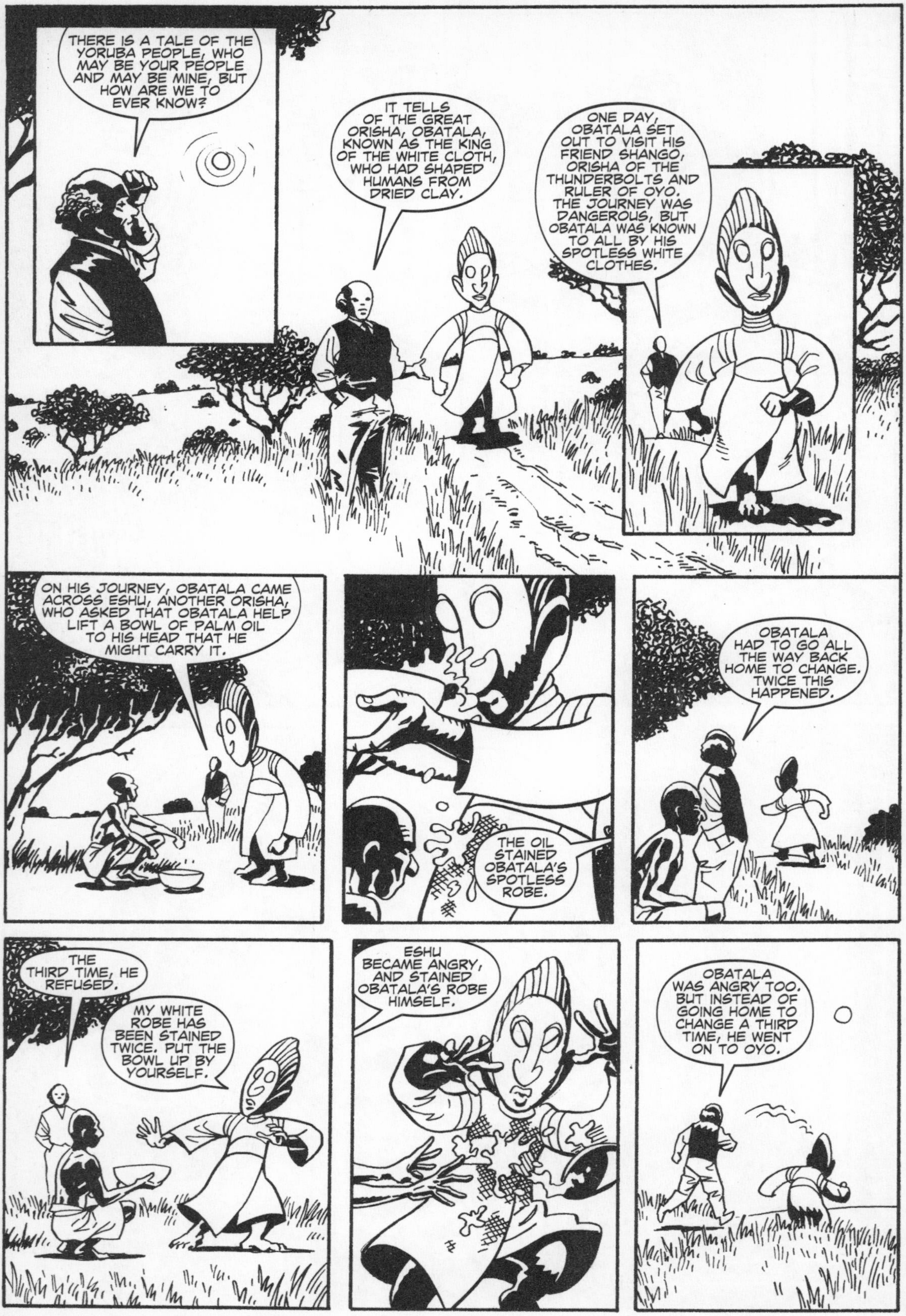
THERE IS A TALE OF THE YORUBA PEOPLE, WHO MAY BE YOUR PEOPLE AND MAY BE MINE, BUT HOW ARE WE TO EVER KNOW?
IT TELLS OF THE GREAT ORISHA, OBATALA, KNOWN AS THE KING OF THE WHITE CLOTH, WHO HAD SHAPED HUMANS FROM DRIED CLAY.
ONE DAY, OBATALA SET OUT TO VISIT HIS FRIEND SHANGO, ORISHA OF THE THUNDERBOLTS AND RULER OF OYO. THE JOURNEY WAS DANGEROUS, BUT OBATALA WAS KNOWN TO ALL BY HIS SPOTLESS WHITE CLOTHES.
ON HIS JOURNEY, OBATALA CAME ACROSS ESHU, ANOTHER ORISHA, WHO ASKED THAT OBATALA HELP LIFT A BOWL OF PALM OIL TO HIS HEAD THAT HE MIGHT CARRY IT.
THE OIL STAINED OBATALA'S SPOTLESS ROBE.
OBATALA HAD TO GO ALL THE WAY BACK HOME TO CHANGE. TWICE THIS HAPPENED.
THE THIRD TIME, HE REFUSED.
MY WHITE ROBE HAS BEEN STAINED TWICE. PUT THE BOWL UP BY YOURSELF.
ESHU BECAME ANGRY, AND STAINED OBATALA'S ROBE HIMSELF.
OBATALA WAS ANGRY TOO. BUT INSTEAD OF GOING HOME TO CHANGE A THIRD TIME, HE WENT ON TO OYO.

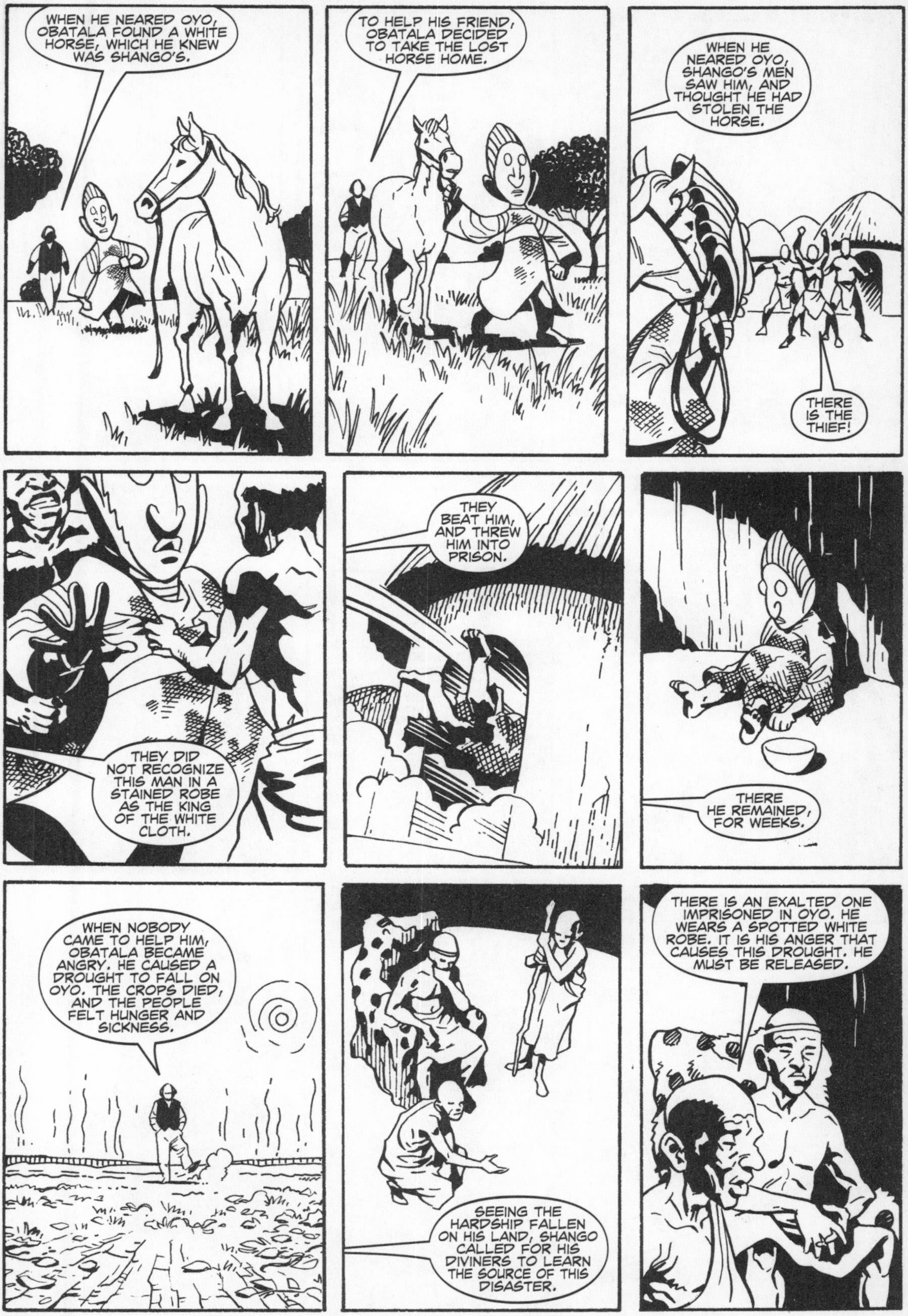
WHEN HE NEARED OYO, OBATALA FOUND A WHITE HORSE, WHICH HE KNEW WAS SHANGO'S.
TO HELP HIS FRIEND, OBATALA DECIDED TO TAKE THE LOST HORSE HOME.
WHEN HE NEARED OYO, SHANGO'S MEN SAW HIM, AND THOUGHT HE HAD STOLEN THE HORSE.
THERE IS THE THIEF!
THEY DID NOT RECOGNIZE THIS MAN IN A STAINED ROBE AS THE KING OF THE WHITE CLOTH.
THEY BEAT HIM, AND THREW HIM INTO PRISON.
THERE HE REMAINED, FOR WEEKS.
WHEN NOBODY CAME TO HELP HIM, OBATALA BECAME ANGRY. HE CAUSED A DROUGHT TO FALL ON OYO. THE CROPS DIED, AND THE PEOPLE FELT HUNGER AND SICKNESS.
SEEING THE HARDSHIP FALLEN ON HIS LAND, SHANGO CALLED FOR HIS DIVINERS TO LEARN THE SOURCE OF THIS DISASTER.
THERE IS AN EXALTED ONE IMPRISONED IN OYO. HE WEARS A SPOTTED WHITE ROBE. IT IS HIS ANGER THAT CAUSES THIS DROUGHT. HE MUST BE RELEASED.

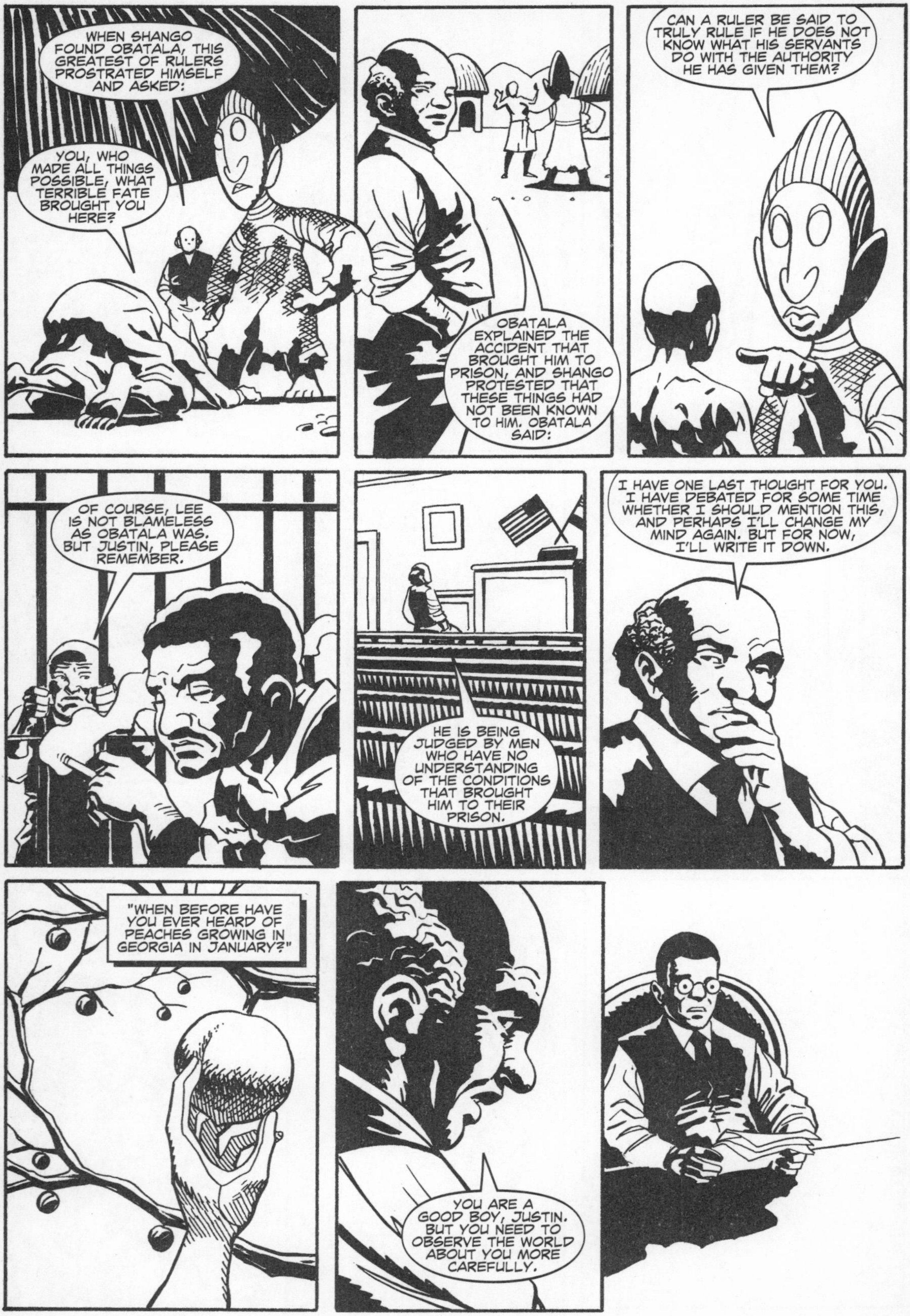
WHEN SHANGO FOUND OBATALA, THIS GREATEST OF RULERS PROSTRATED HIMSELF AND ASKED:
YOU, WHO MADE ALL THINGS POSSIBLE, WHAT TERRIBLE FATE BROUGHT YOU HERE?
OBATALA EXPLAINED THE ACCIDENT THAT BROUGHT HIM TO PRISON, AND SHANGO PROTESTED THAT THESE THINGS HAD NOT BEEN KNOWN TO HIM. OBATALA SAID:
CAN A RULER BE SAID TO TRULY RULE IF HE DOES NOT KNOW WHAT HIS SERVANTS DO WITH THE AUTHORITY HE HAS GIVEN THEM?
OF COURSE, LEE IS NOT BLAMELESS AS OBATALA WAS. BUT JUSTIN, PLEASE REMEMBER.
HE IS BEING JUDGED BY MEN WHO HAVE NO UNDERSTANDING OF THE CONDITIONS THAT BROUGHT HIM TO THEIR PRISON.
I HAVE ONE LAST THOUGHT FOR YOU. I HAVE DEBATED FOR SOME TIME WHETHER I SHOULD MENTION THIS, AND PERHAPS I'LL CHANGE MY MIND AGAIN. BUT FOR NOW, I'LL WRITE IT DOWN.
"WHEN BEFORE HAVE YOU EVER HEARD OF PEACHES GROWING IN GEORGIA IN JANUARY?"
YOU ARE A GOOD BOY, JUSTIN. BUT YOU NEED TO OBSERVE THE WORLD ABOUT YOU MORE CAREFULLY.

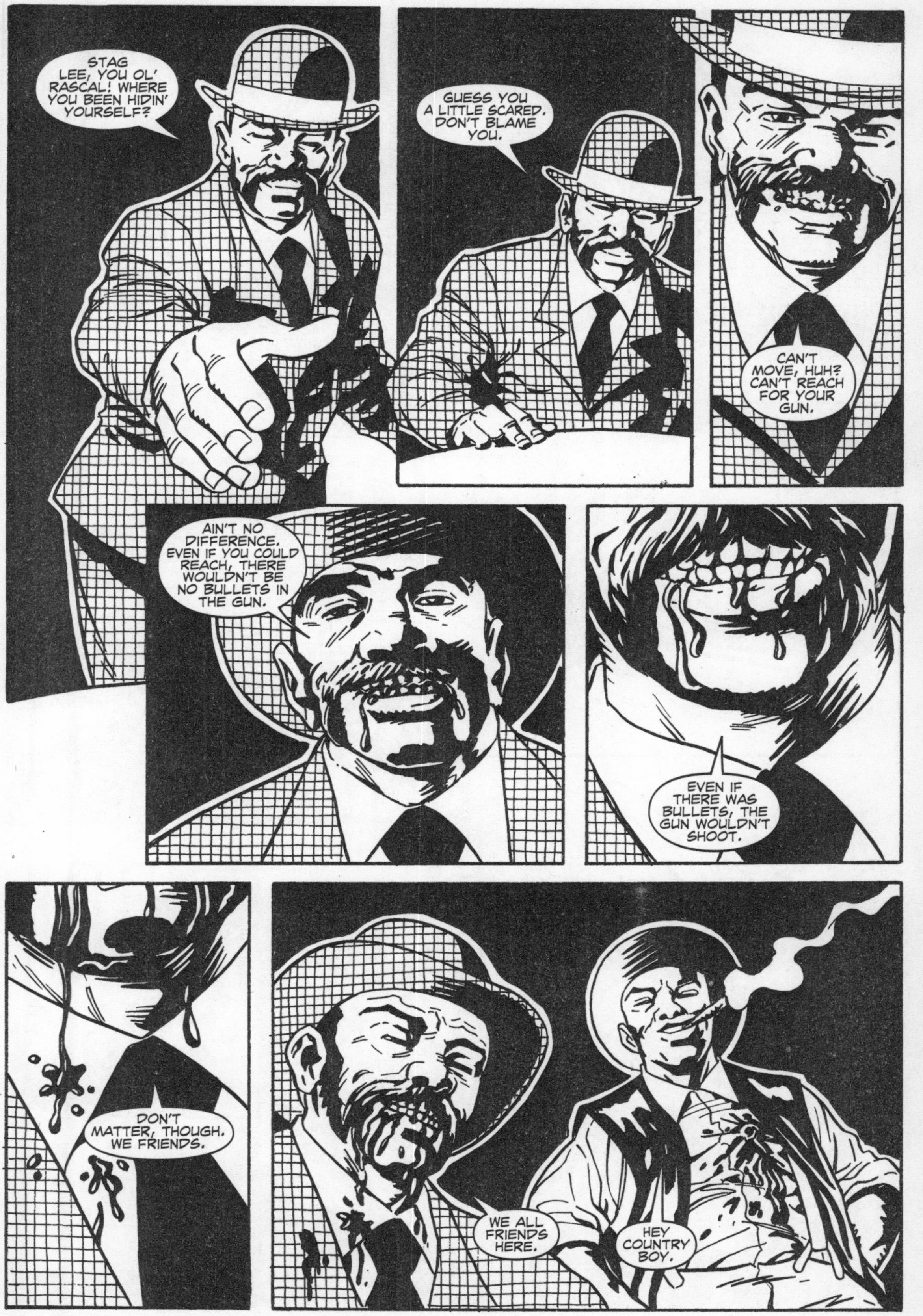
STAG LEE, YOU OL' RASCAL! WHERE YOU BEEN HIDIN' YOURSELF?
GUESS YOU A LITTLE SCARED. DON'T BLAME YOU.
CAN'T MOVE, HUH? CAN'T REACH FOR YOUR GUN.
AIN'T NO DIFFERENCE. EVEN IF YOU COULD REACH, THERE WOULDN'T BE NO BULLETS IN THE GUN.
EVEN IF THERE WAS BULLETS, THE GUN WOULDN'T SHOOT.
DON'T MATTER, THOUGH. WE FRIENDS.
WE ALL FRIENDS HERE.
HEY COUNTRY BOY.

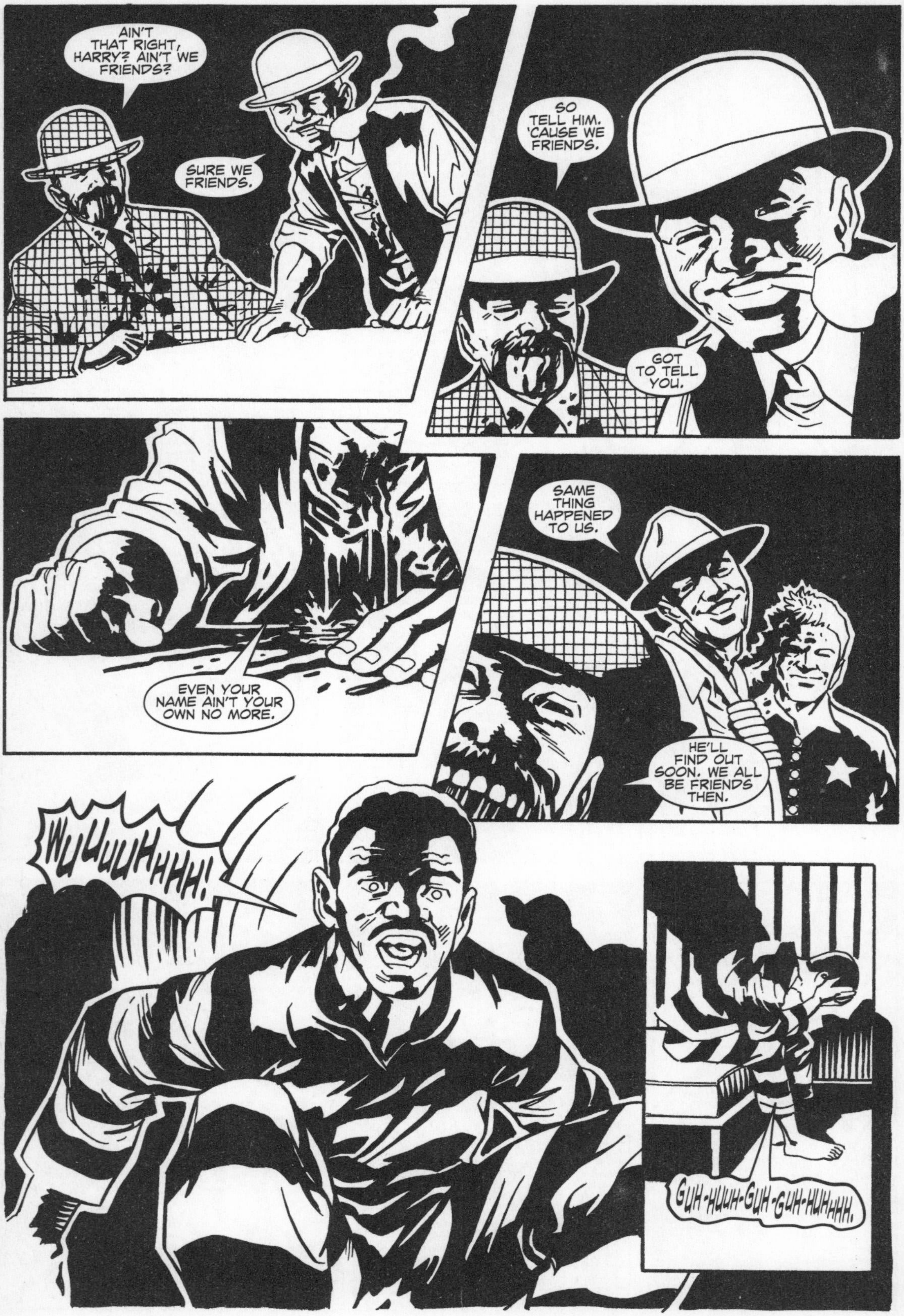
AIN'T THAT RIGHT, HARRY? AIN'T WE FRIENDS?
SURE WE FRIENDS.
SO TELL HIM. 'CAUSE WE FRIENDS.
GOT TO TELL YOU.
EVEN YOUR NAME AIN'T YOUR OWN NO MORE.
SAME THING HAPPENED TO US.
HE'LL FIND OUT SOON. WE ALL BE FRIENDS THEN.
WUUUUHHHH!
GUH-HUUH-GUH-GUH-HUHHHH.

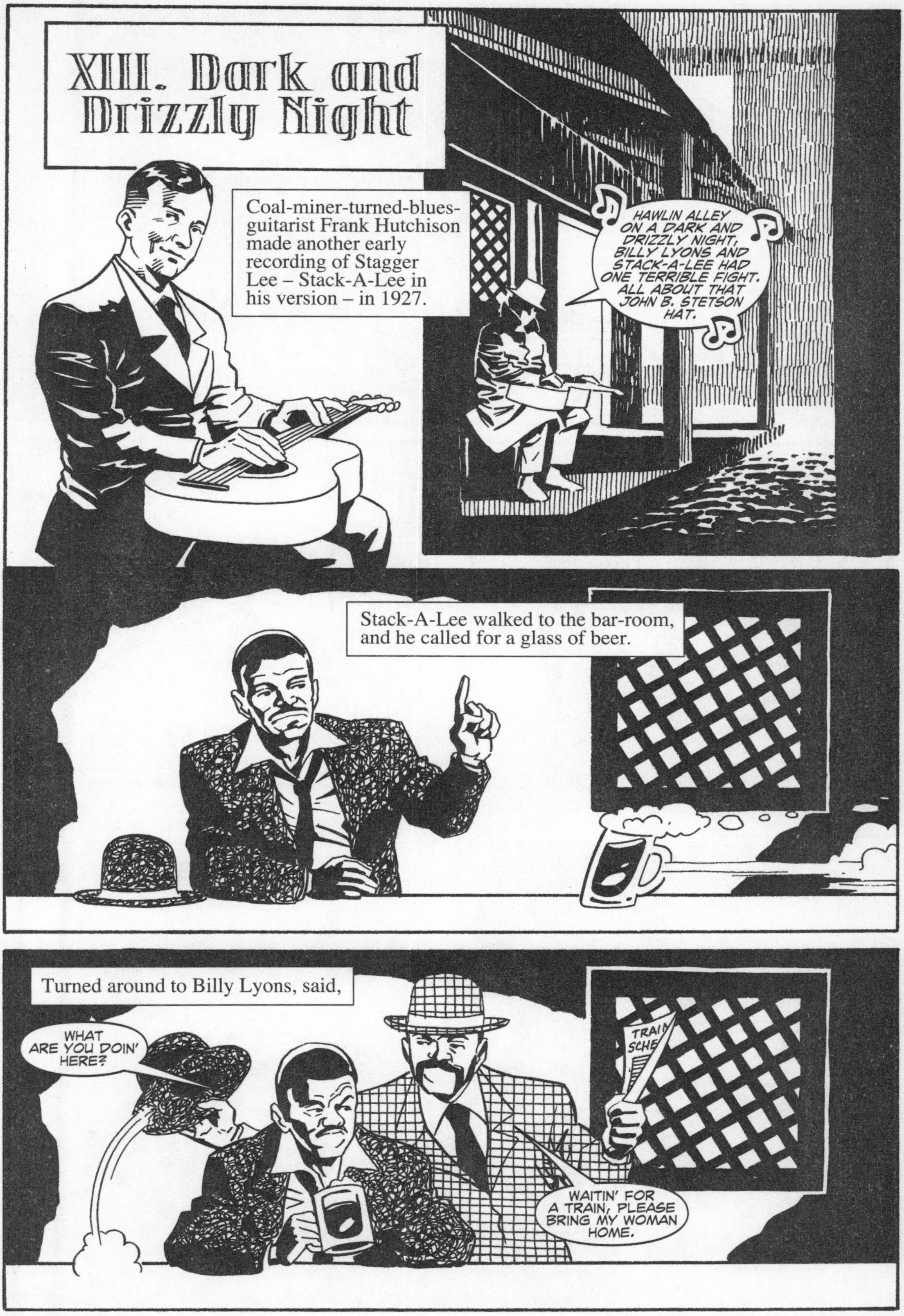
XIII. Dark and Drizzly Night
Coal-miner-turned-blues-guitarist Frank Hutchison made another early recording of Stagger Lee – Stack-A-Lee in his version – in 1927.
HAWLIN ALLEY ON A DARK AND DRIZZLY NIGHT, BILLY LYONS AND STACK-A-LEE HAD ONE TERRIBLE FIGHT. ALL ABOUT THAT JOHN B. STETSON HAT.
Stack-A-Lee walked to the bar-room, and he called for a glass of beer.
Turned around to Billy Lyons, said,
WHAT ARE YOU DOIN' HERE?
WAITIN' FOR A TRAIN, PLEASE BRING MY WOMAN HOME.

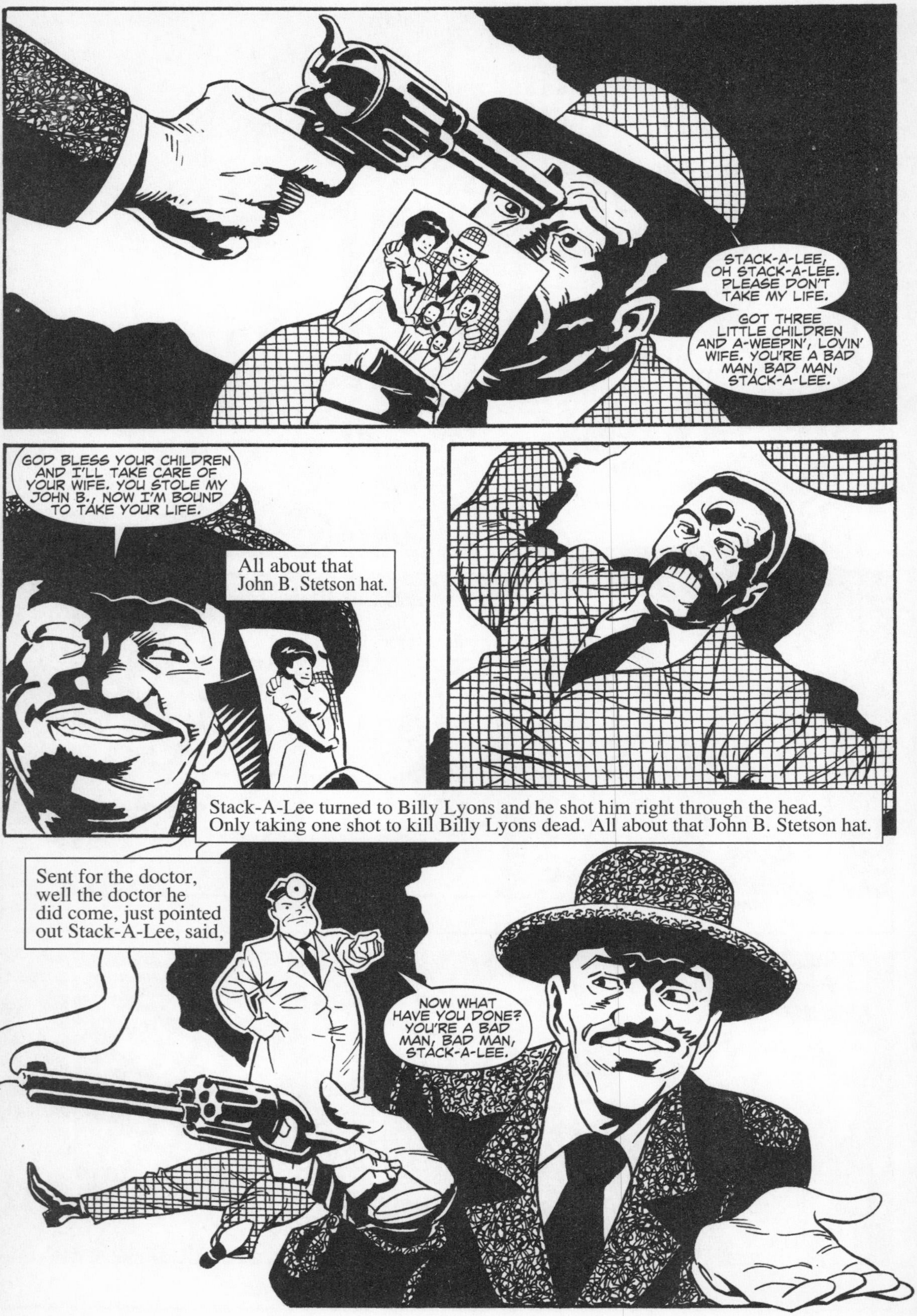
STACK-A-LEE, OH STACK-A-LEE. PLEASE DON'T TAKE MY LIFE.
GOT THREE LITTLE CHILDREN AND A-WEEPIN', LOVIN' WIFE. YOU'RE A BAD MAN, BAD MAN, STACK-A-LEE.
GOD BLESS YOUR CHILDREN AND I'LL TAKE CARE OF YOUR WIFE. YOU STOLE MY JOHN B., NOW I'M BOUND TO TAKE YOUR LIFE.
All about that John B. Stetson hat.
Stack-A-Lee turned to Billy Lyons and he shot him right through the head, Only taking one shot to kill Billy Lyons dead. All about that John B. Stetson hat.
Sent for the doctor, well the doctor he did come, just pointed out Stack-A-Lee, said,
NOW WHAT HAVE YOU DONE? YOU'RE A BAD MAN, BAD MAN, STACK-A-LEE.

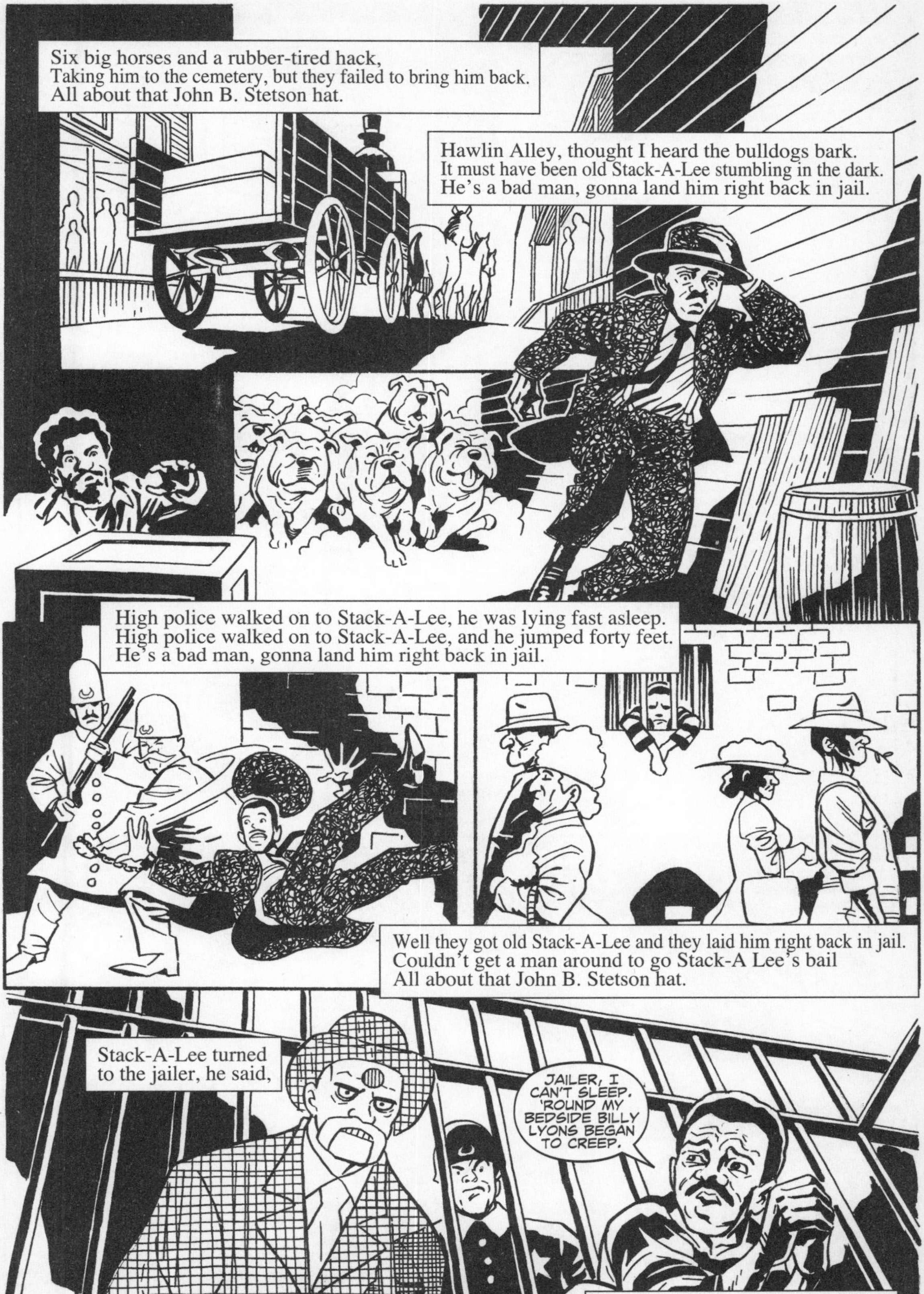
Six big horses and a rubber-tired hack,
Taking him to the cemetery, but they failed to bring him back.
All about that John B. Stetson hat.
Hawlin Alley, thought I heard the bulldogs bark.
It must have been old Stack-A-Lee stumbling in the dark.
He's a bad man, gonna land him right back in jail.
High police walked on to Stack-A-Lee, he was lying fast asleep.
High police walked on to Stack-A-Lee, and he jumped forty feet.
He's a bad man, gonna land him right back in jail.
Well they got old Stack-A-Lee and they laid him right back in jail.
Couldn't get a man around to go Stack-A Lee's bail
All about that John B. Stetson hat.
Stack-A-Lee turned to the jailer, he said,
JAILER, I CAN'T SLEEP. 'ROUND MY BEDSIDE BILLY LYONS BEGAN TO CREEP.
All about that John B. Stetson hat.

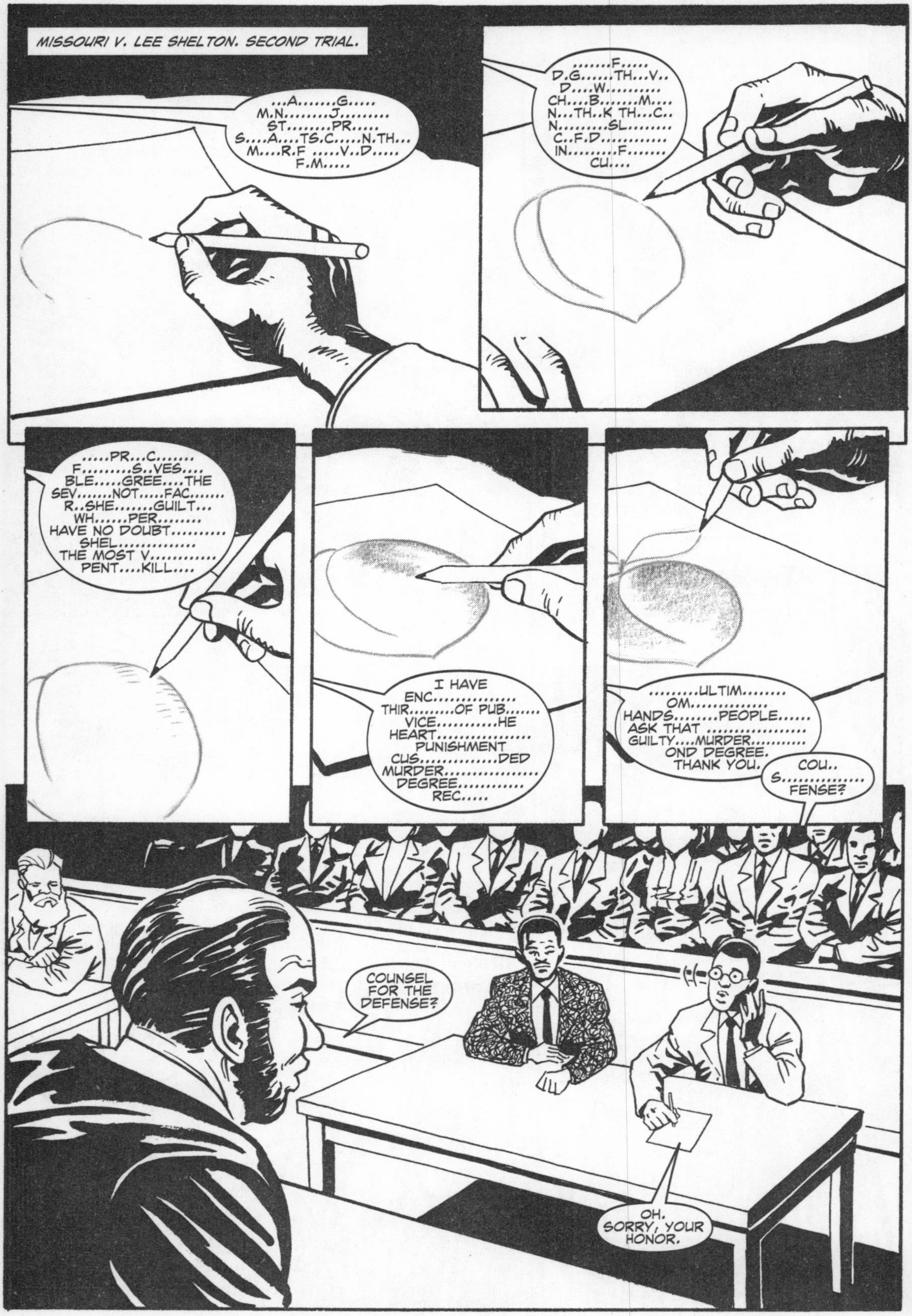
MISSOURI V. LEE SHELTON. SECOND TRIAL.
...A......G.... M.N.........J......... ST.........PR..... S...A....TS.C......N.TH... M....R.F ......V..D...... F.M.....
......F..... D.G.......TH...V.. D....W.......... CH....B........M.... N...TH..K TH...C.. N.........SL....... C..F.D............ IN...........F....... CU....
.....PR...C....... F..........S..VES.... BLE.....GREE....THE SEV........NOT.....FAC....... R..SHE........GUILT... WH.......PER........ HAVE NO DOUBT.......... SHEL............ THE MOST V........... PENT....KILL....
I HAVE ENC............... THIR.........OF PUB...... VICE............HE HEART................. PUNISHMENT CUS..............DED MURDER................ DEGREE............... REC.....
.........ULTIM........ OM.............. HANDS.........PEOPLE...... ASK THAT .... GUILTY....MURDER.............. OND DEGREE. THANK YOU.
COU.. S............... FENSE?
COUNSEL FOR THE DEFENSE?
OH. SORRY, YOUR HONOR.

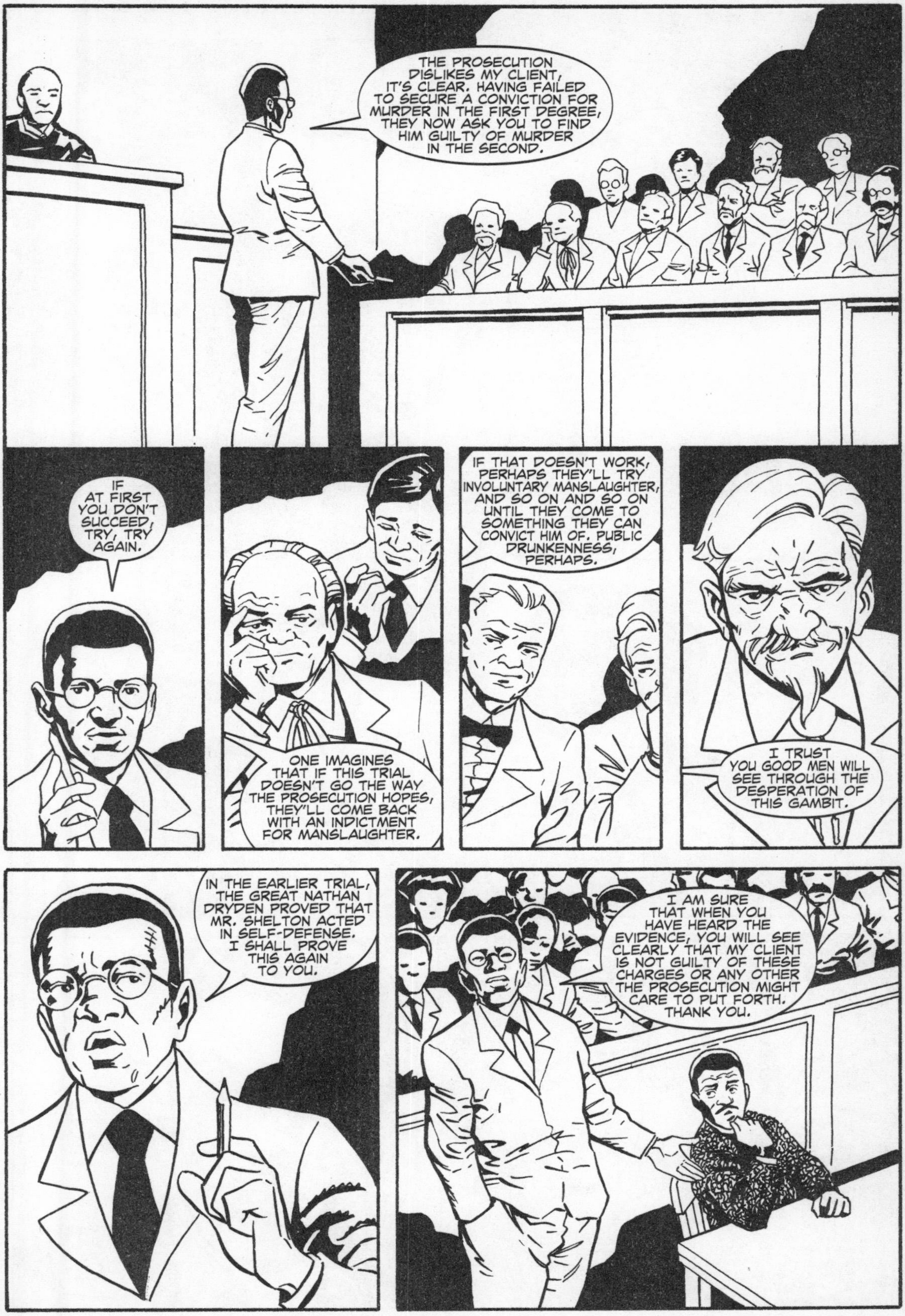
THE PROSECUTION DISLIKES MY CLIENT, IT'S CLEAR. HAVING FAILED TO SECURE A CONVICTION FOR MURDER IN THE FIRST DEGREE, THEY NOW ASK YOU TO FIND HIM GUILTY OF MURDER IN THE SECOND.
IF AT FIRST YOU DON'T SUCCEED, TRY, TRY AGAIN.
ONE IMAGINES THAT IF THIS TRIAL DOESN'T GO THE WAY THE PROSECUTION HOPES, THEY'LL COME BACK WITH AN INDICTMENT FOR MANSLAUGHTER.
IF THAT DOESN'T WORK, PERHAPS THEY'LL TRY INVOLUNTARY MANSLAUGHTER, AND SO ON AND SO ON UNTIL THEY COME TO SOMETHING THEY CAN CONVICT HIM OF. PUBLIC DRUNKENNESS, PERHAPS.
I TRUST YOU GOOD MEN WILL SEE THROUGH THE DESPERATION OF THIS GAMBIT.
IN THE EARLIER TRIAL, THE GREAT NATHAN DRYDEN PROVED THAT MR. SHELTON ACTED IN SELF-DEFENSE. I SHALL PROVE THIS AGAIN TO YOU.
I AM SURE THAT WHEN YOU HAVE HEARD THE EVIDENCE, YOU WILL SEE CLEARLY THAT MY CLIENT IS NOT GUILTY OF THESE CHARGES OR ANY OTHER THE PROSECUTION MIGHT CARE TO PUT FORTH. THANK YOU.

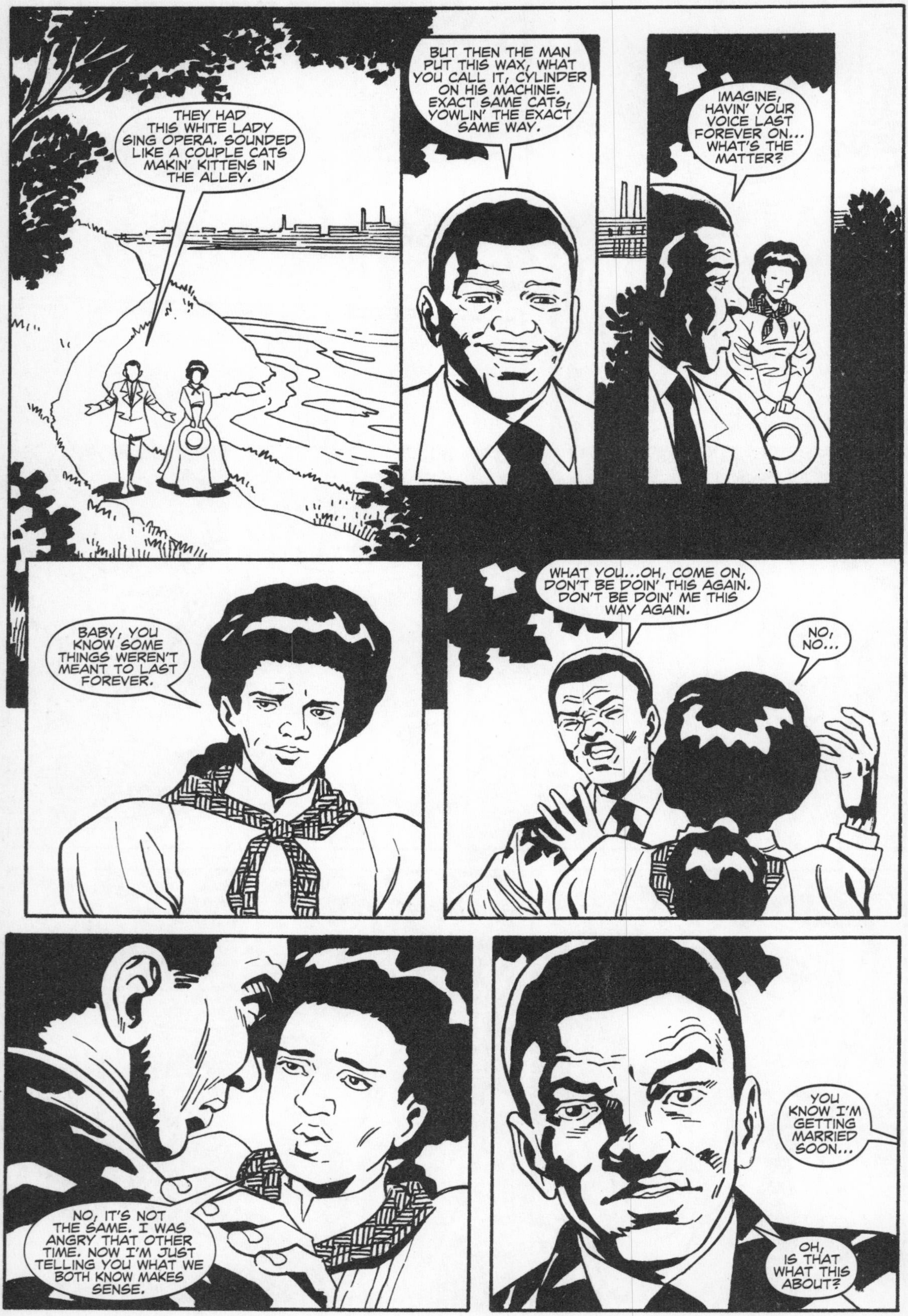
THEY HAD THIS WHITE LADY SING OPERA. SOUNDED LIKE A COUPLE CATS MAKIN' KITTENS IN THE ALLEY.
BUT THEN THE MAN PUT THIS WAX, WHAT YOU CALL IT, CYLINDER ON HIS MACHINE. EXACT SAME CATS, YOWLIN' THE EXACT SAME WAY.
IMAGINE, HAVIN' YOUR VOICE LAST FOREVER ON... WHAT'S THE MATTER?
BABY, YOU KNOW SOME THINGS WEREN'T MEANT TO LAST FOREVER.
WHAT YOU...OH, COME ON, DON'T BE DOIN' THIS AGAIN. DON'T BE DOIN' ME THIS WAY AGAIN.
NO, NO...
NO, IT'S NOT THE SAME. I WAS ANGRY THAT OTHER TIME. NOW I'M JUST TELLING YOU WHAT WE BOTH KNOW MAKES SENSE.
YOU KNOW I'M GETTING MARRIED SOON...
OH, IS THAT WHAT THIS ABOUT?

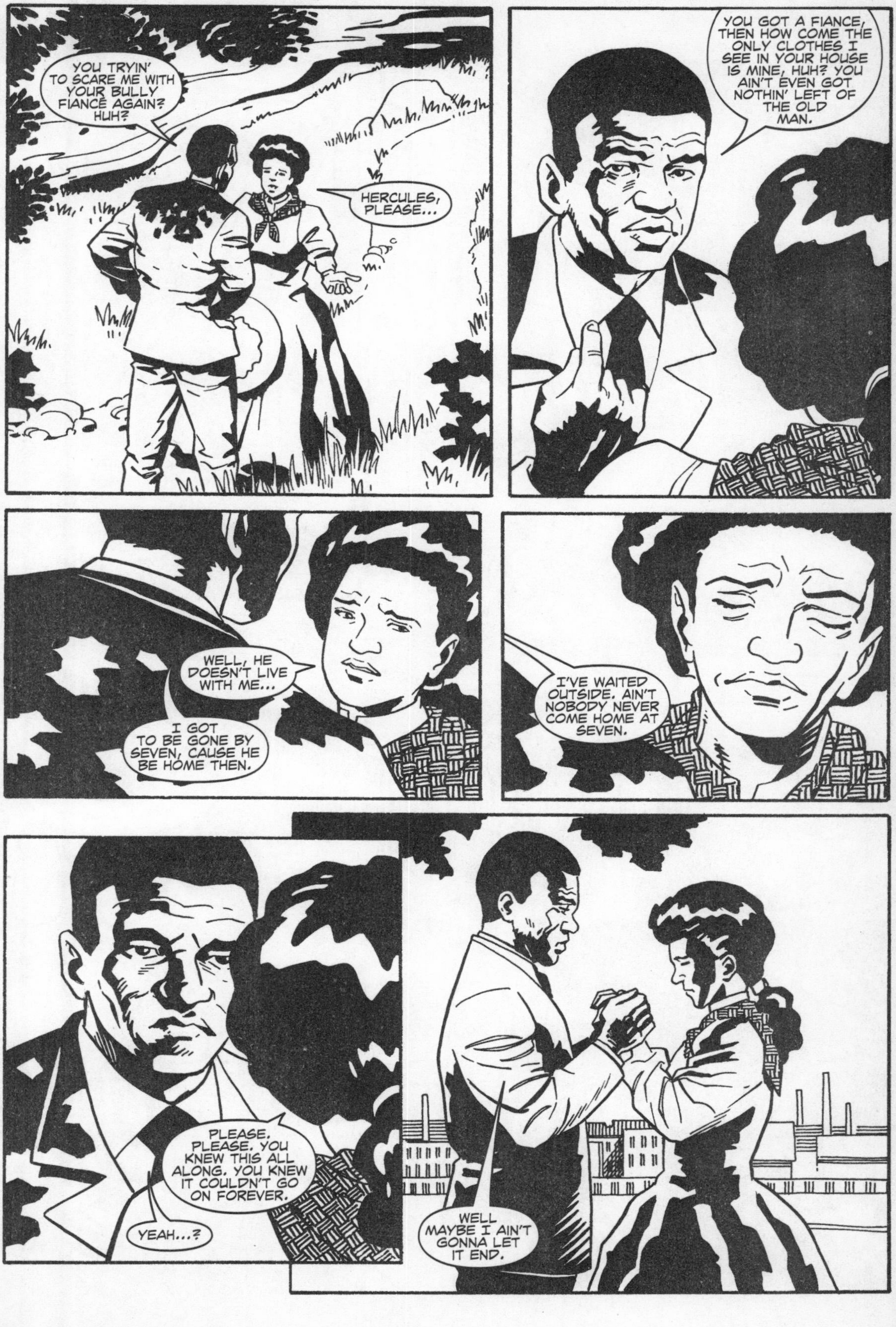
YOU TRYIN' TO SCARE ME WITH YOUR BULLY FIANCÉ AGAIN? HUH?
HERCULES, PLEASE...
YOU GOT A FIANCE, THEN HOW COME THE ONLY CLOTHES I SEE IN YOUR HOUSE IS MINE, HUH? YOU AIN'T EVEN GOT NOTHIN' LEFT OF THE OLD MAN.
WELL, HE DOESN'T LIVE WITH ME...
I GOT TO BE GONE BY SEVEN, CAUSE HE BE HOME THEN.
I'VE WAITED OUTSIDE. AIN'T NOBODY NEVER COME HOME AT SEVEN.
PLEASE. PLEASE. YOU KNEW THIS ALL ALONG. YOU KNEW IT COULDN'T GO ON FOREVER.
YEAH...?
WELL MAYBE I AIN'T GONNA LET IT END.

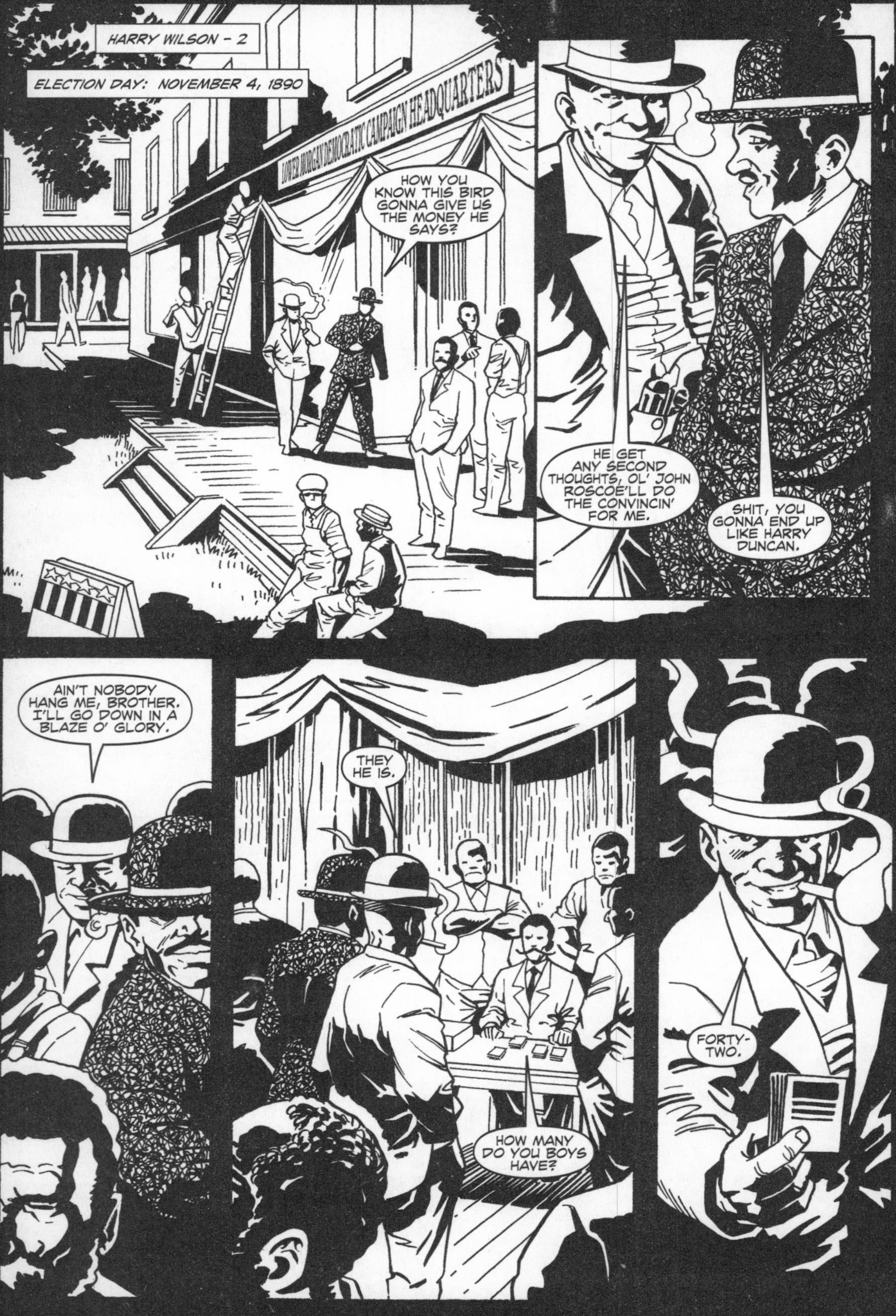
HARRY WILSON - 2
ELECTION DAY: NOVEMBER 4, 1890
LOWER MORGAN DEMOCRATIC CAMPAIGN HEADQUARTERS
HOW YOU KNOW THIS BIRD GONNA GIVE US THE MONEY HE SAYS?
HE GET ANY SECOND THOUGHTS, OL' JOHN ROSCOE'LL DO THE CONVINCIN' FOR ME.
SHIT, YOU GONNA END UP LIKE HARRY DUNCAN.
AIN'T NOBODY HANG ME, BROTHER. I'LL GO DOWN IN A BLAZE O' GLORY.
THEY HE IS.
HOW MANY DO YOU BOYS HAVE?
FORTY-TWO.

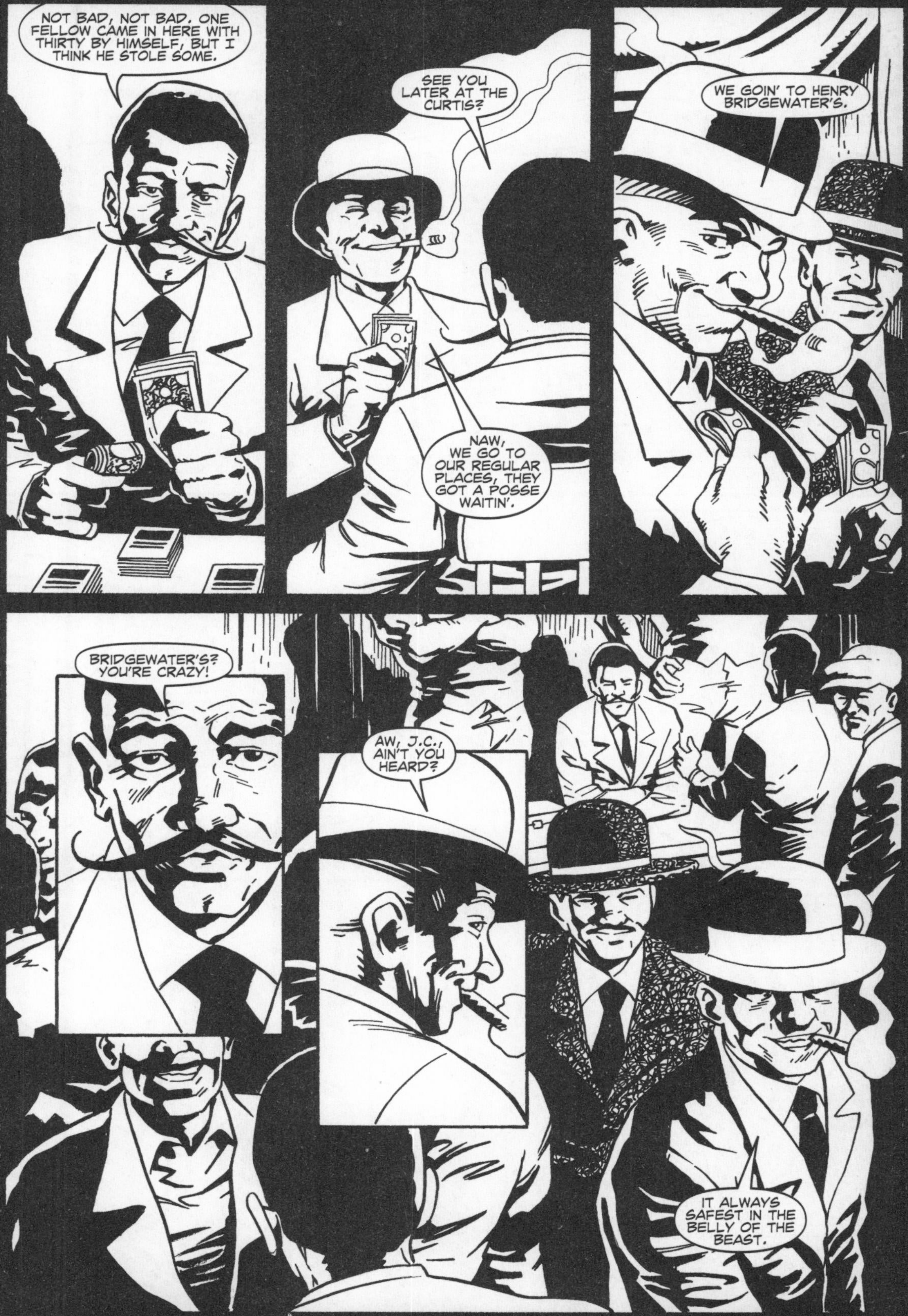
NOT BAD, NOT BAD. ONE FELLOW CAME IN HERE WITH THIRTY BY HIMSELF, BUT I THINK HE STOLE SOME.
SEE YOU LATER AT THE CURTIS?
NAW, WE GO TO OUR REGULAR PLACES, THEY GOT A POSSE WAITIN'.
WE GOIN' TO HENRY BRIDGEWATER'S.
BRIDGEWATER'S? YOU'RE CRAZY!
AW, J.C., AIN'T YOU HEARD?
IT ALWAYS SAFEST IN THE BELLY OF THE BEAST.

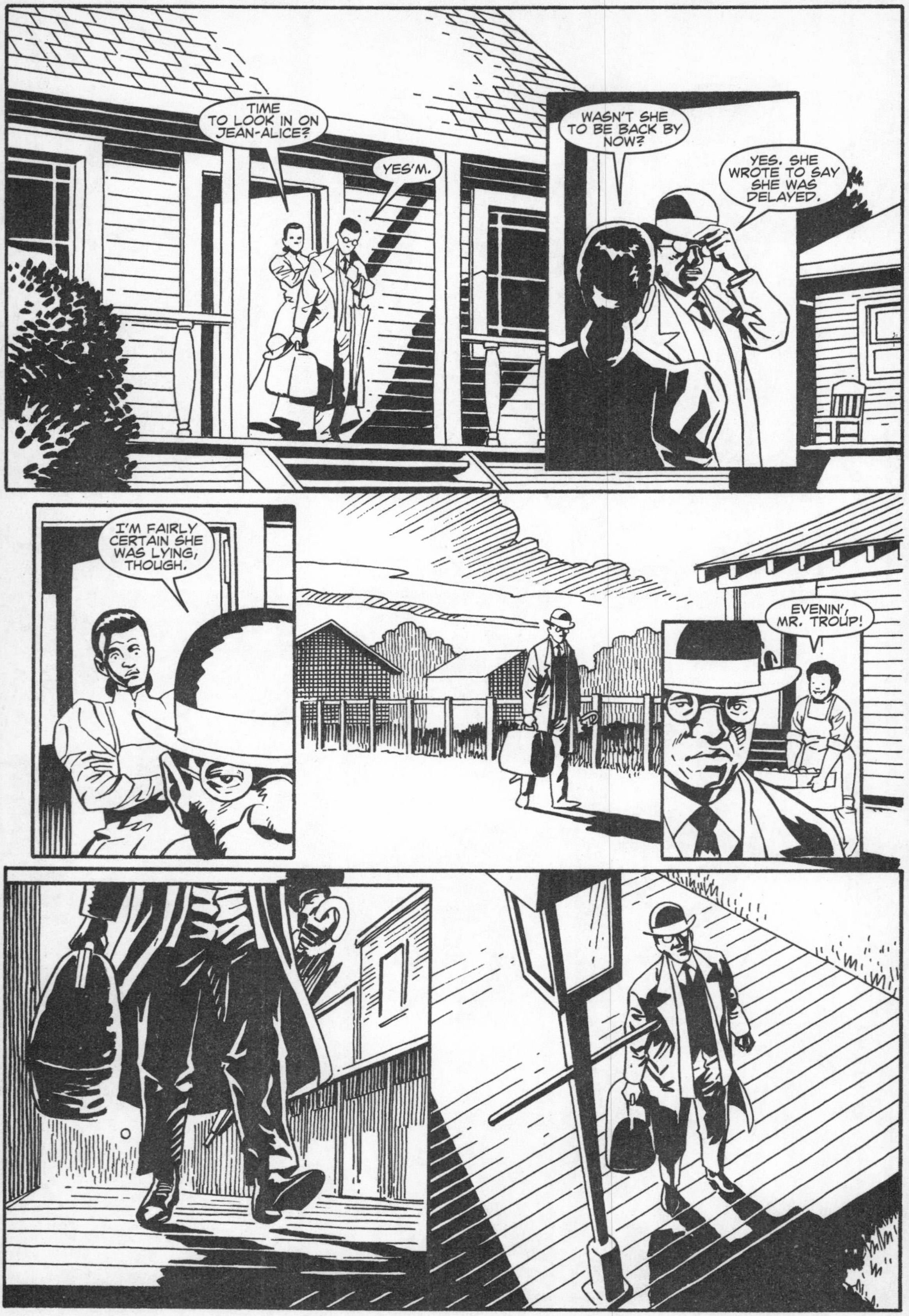
TIME TO LOOK IN ON JEAN-ALICE?
YES'M.
WASN'T SHE TO BE BACK BY NOW?
YES. SHE WROTE TO SAY SHE WAS DELAYED.
I'M FAIRLY CERTAIN SHE WAS LYING, THOUGH.
EVENIN', MR. TROUP!

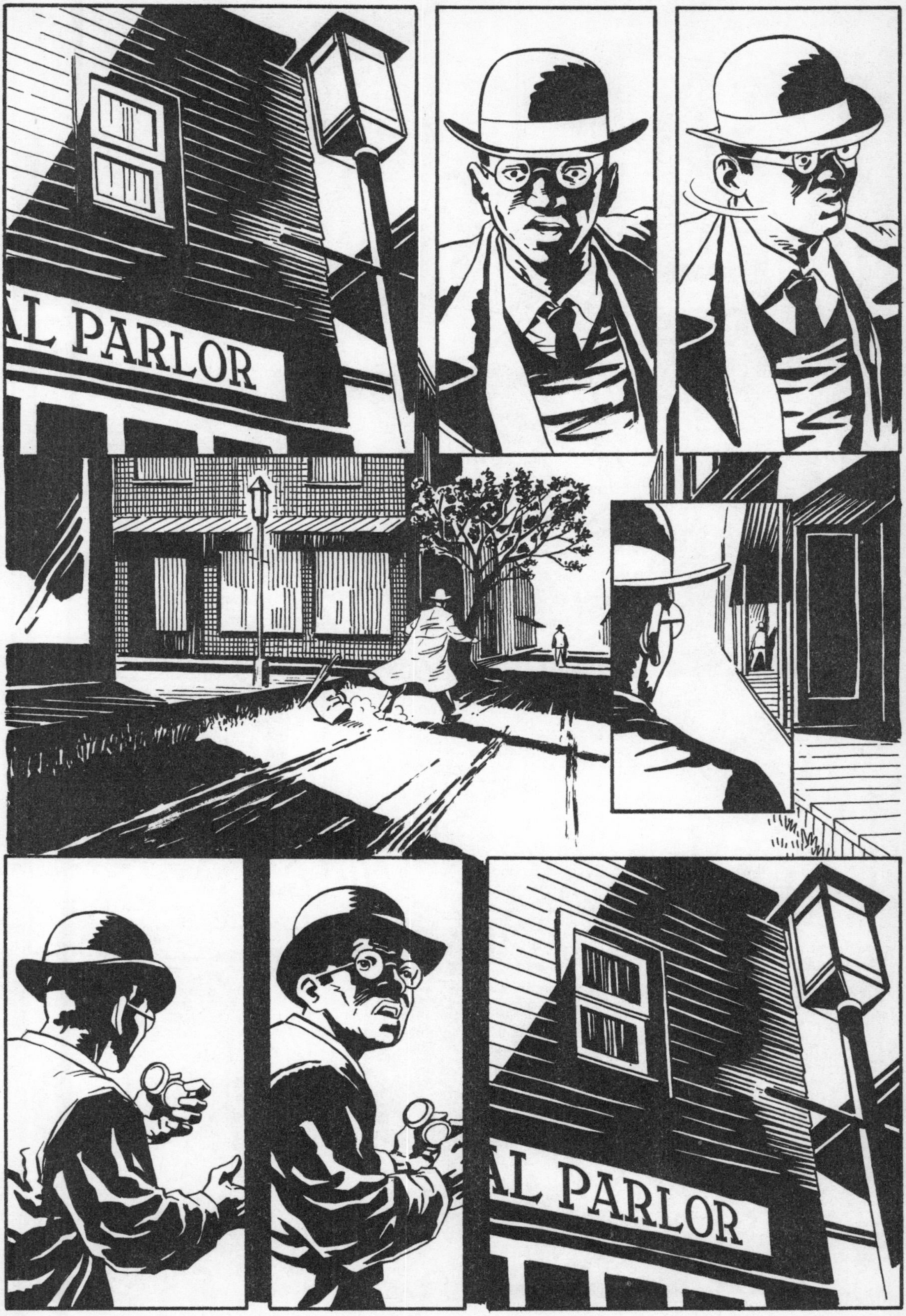
AL PARLOR
AL PARLOR

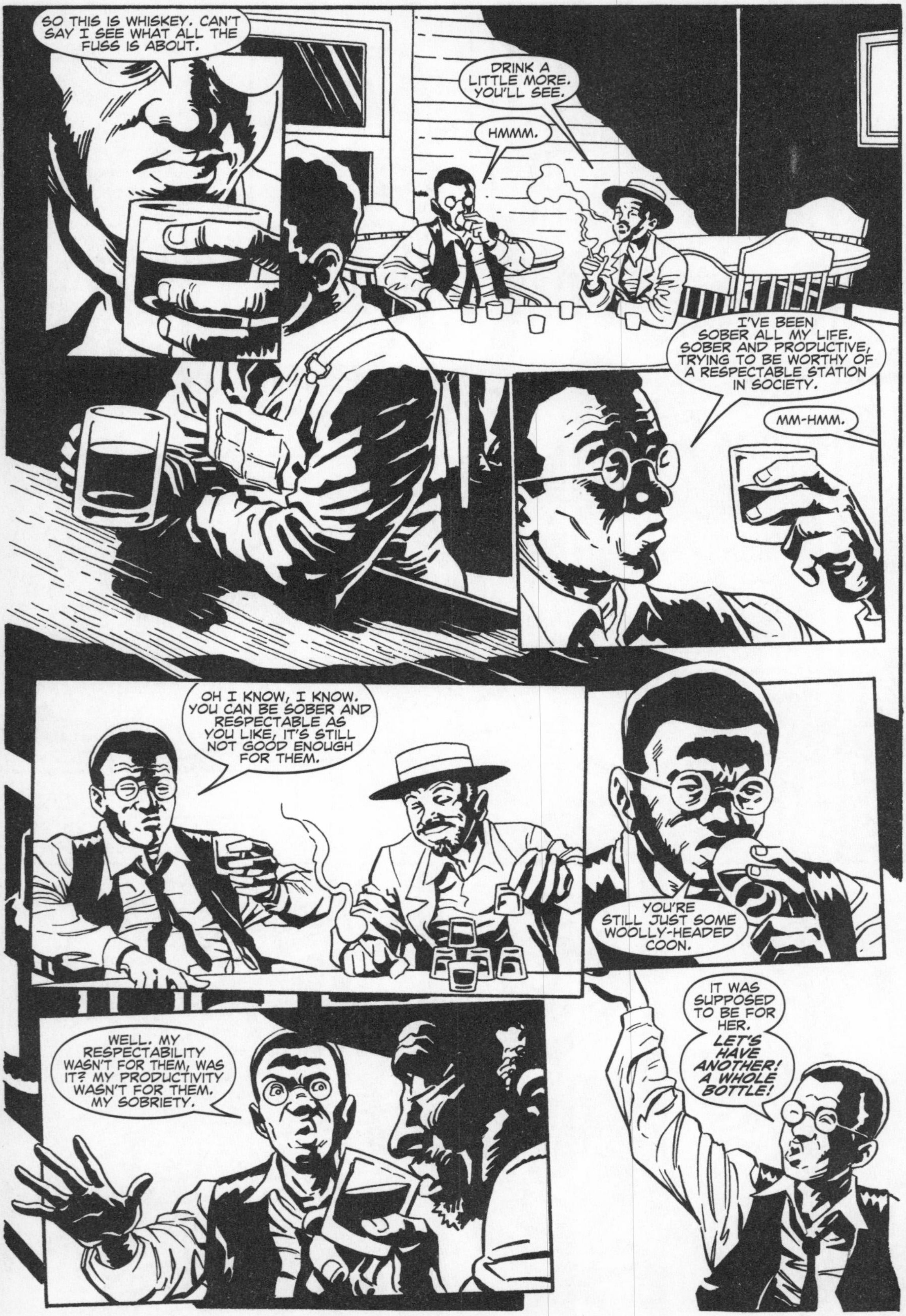

SO THIS IS WHISKEY. CAN'T SAY I SEE WHAT ALL THE FUSS IS ABOUT.
DRINK A LITTLE MORE. YOU'LL SEE.
HMMM.
I'VE BEEN SOBER ALL MY LIFE. SOBER AND PRODUCTIVE, TRYING TO BE WORTHY OF A RESPECTABLE STATION IN SOCIETY.
MM-HMM.
OH I KNOW, I KNOW. YOU CAN BE SOBER AND RESPECTABLE AS YOU LIKE, IT'S STILL NOT GOOD ENOUGH FOR THEM.
YOU'RE STILL JUST SOME WOOLLY-HEADED COON.
WELL. MY RESPECTABILITY WASN'T FOR THEM, WAS IT? MY PRODUCTIVITY WASN'T FOR THEM. MY SOBRIETY.
IT WAS SUPPOSED TO BE FOR HER. *LET'S HAVE ANOTHER! A WHOLE BOTTLE!*

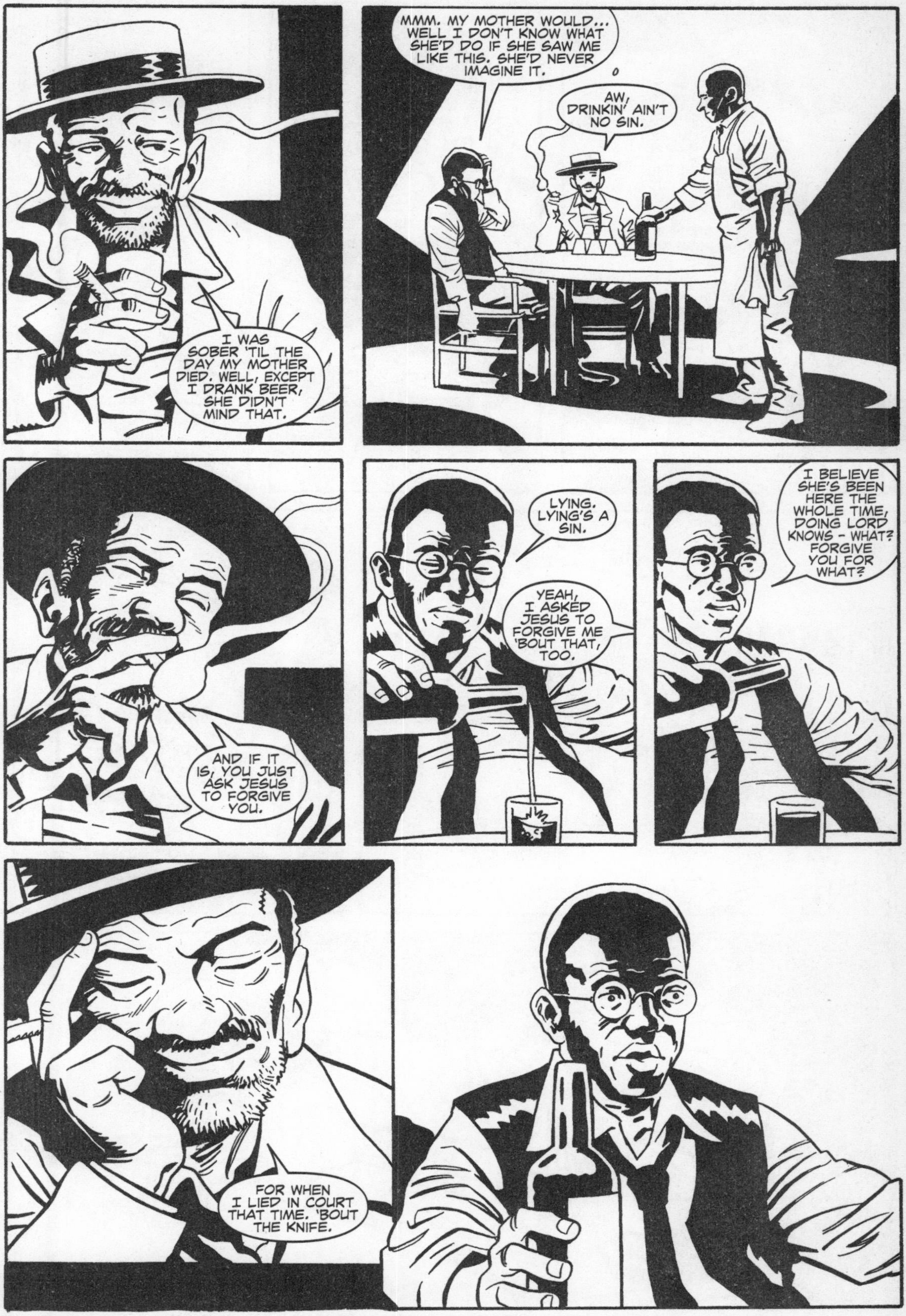
I WAS SOBER 'TIL THE DAY MY MOTHER DIED. WELL, EXCEPT I DRANK BEER, SHE DIDN'T MIND THAT.
MMM. MY MOTHER WOULD... WELL I DON'T KNOW WHAT SHE'D DO IF SHE SAW ME LIKE THIS. SHE'D NEVER IMAGINE IT.
AW, DRINKIN' AIN'T NO SIN.
AND IF IT IS, YOU JUST ASK JESUS TO FORGIVE YOU.
LYING. LYING'S A SIN.
YEAH, I ASKED JESUS TO FORGIVE ME 'BOUT THAT, TOO.
I BELIEVE SHE'S BEEN HERE THE WHOLE TIME, DOING LORD KNOWS - WHAT? FORGIVE YOU FOR WHAT?
FOR WHEN I LIED IN COURT THAT TIME. 'BOUT THE KNIFE.

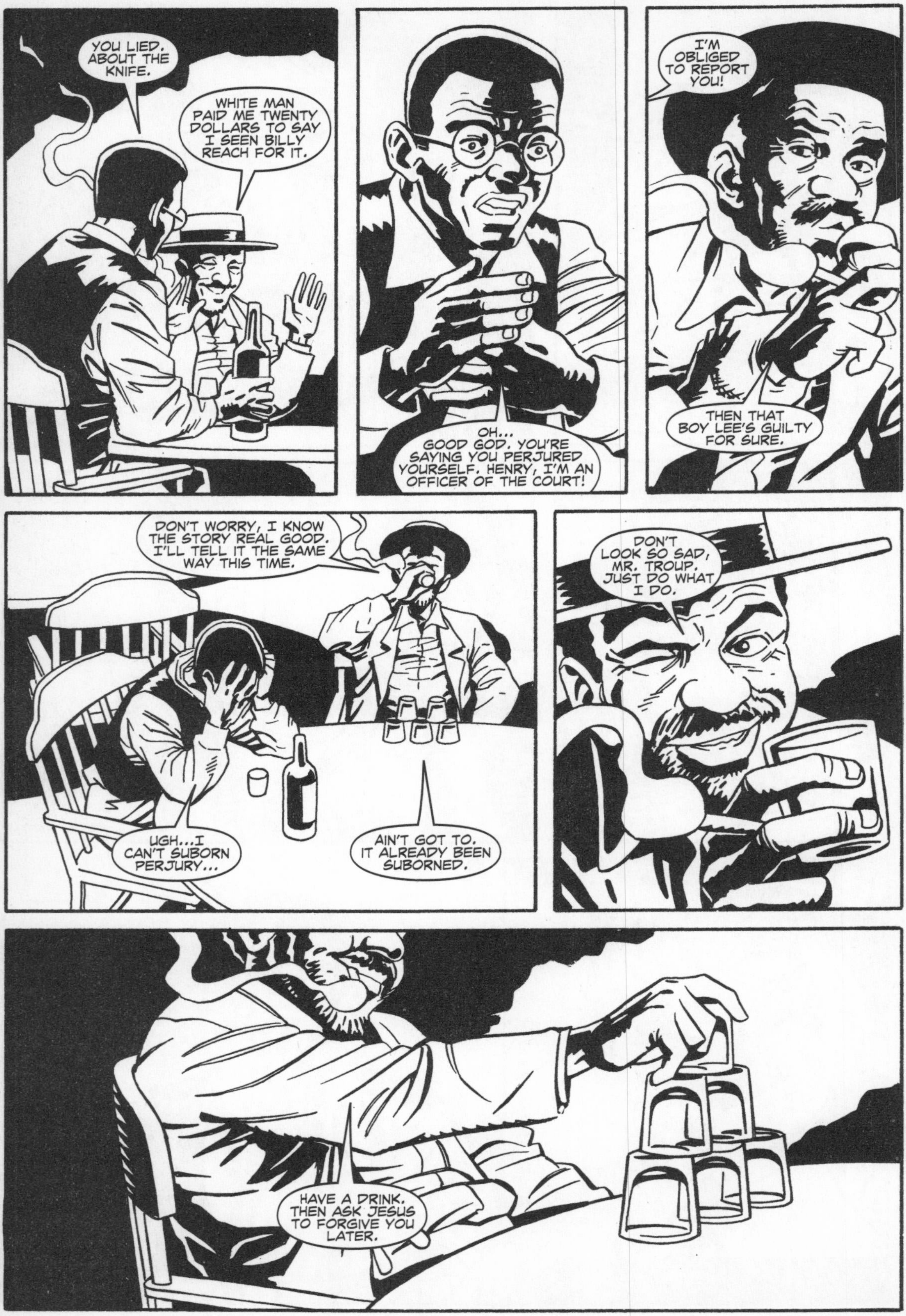
YOU LIED. ABOUT THE KNIFE.
WHITE MAN PAID ME TWENTY DOLLARS TO SAY I SEEN BILLY REACH FOR IT.
OH... GOOD GOD. YOU'RE SAYING YOU PERJURED YOURSELF. HENRY, I'M AN OFFICER OF THE COURT!
I'M OBLIGED TO REPORT YOU!
THEN THAT BOY LEE'S GUILTY FOR SURE.
DON'T WORRY, I KNOW THE STORY REAL GOOD. I'LL TELL IT THE SAME WAY THIS TIME.
UGH...I CAN'T SUBORN PERJURY...
AIN'T GOT TO. IT ALREADY BEEN SUBORNED.
DON'T LOOK SO SAD, MR. TROUP. JUST DO WHAT I DO.
HAVE A DRINK. THEN ASK JESUS TO FORGIVE YOU LATER.

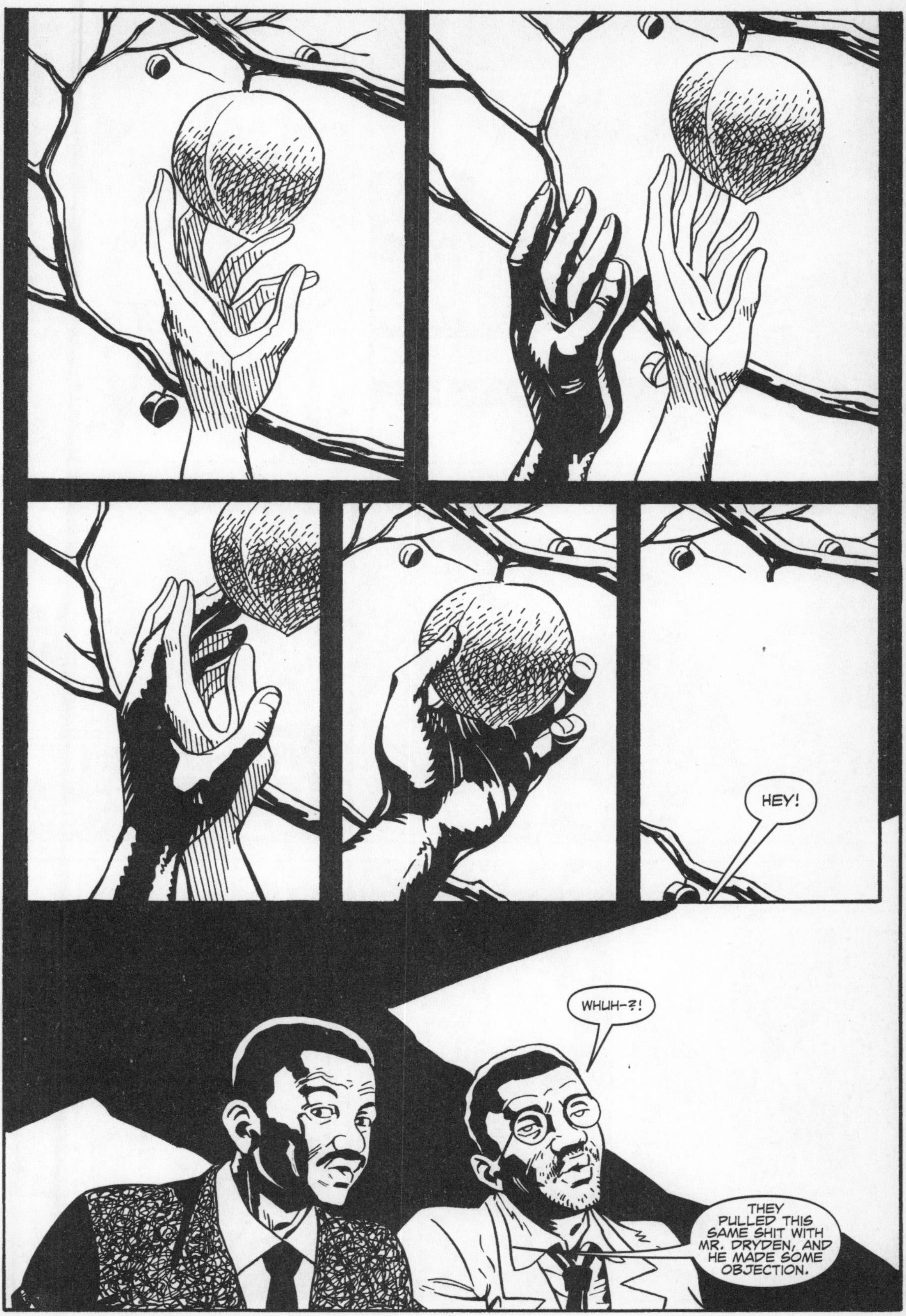
HEY!
WHUH-?!
THEY PULLED THIS SAME SHIT WITH MR. DRYDEN, AND HE MADE SOME OBJECTION.

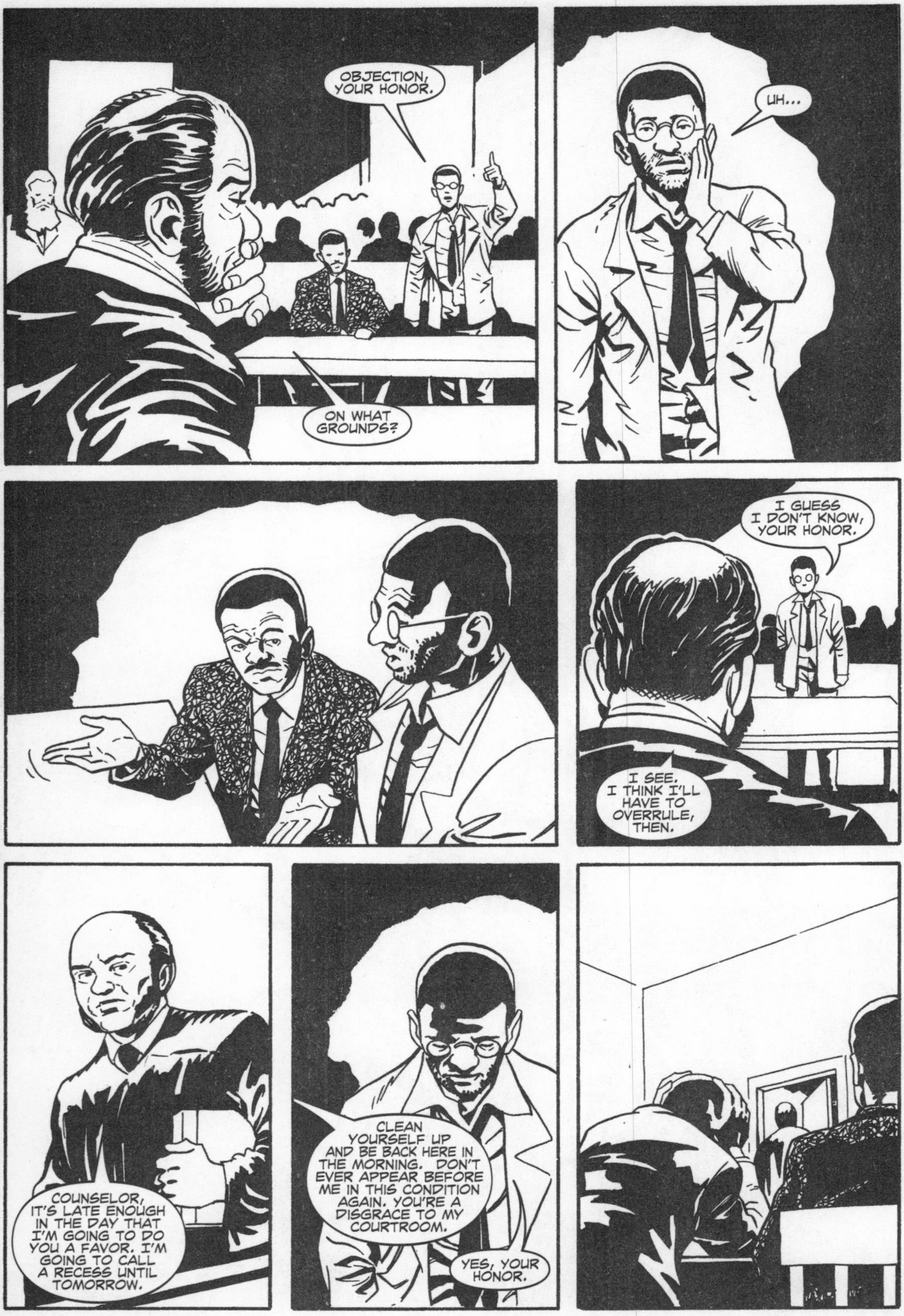
OBJECTION, YOUR HONOR.
ON WHAT GROUNDS?
UH...
I GUESS I DON'T KNOW, YOUR HONOR.
I SEE. I THINK I'LL HAVE TO OVERRULE, THEN.
COUNSELOR, IT'S LATE ENOUGH IN THE DAY THAT I'M GOING TO DO YOU A FAVOR. I'M GOING TO CALL A RECESS UNTIL TOMORROW.
CLEAN YOURSELF UP AND BE BACK HERE IN THE MORNING. DON'T EVER APPEAR BEFORE ME IN THIS CONDITION AGAIN. YOU'RE A DISGRACE TO MY COURTROOM.
YES, YOUR HONOR.

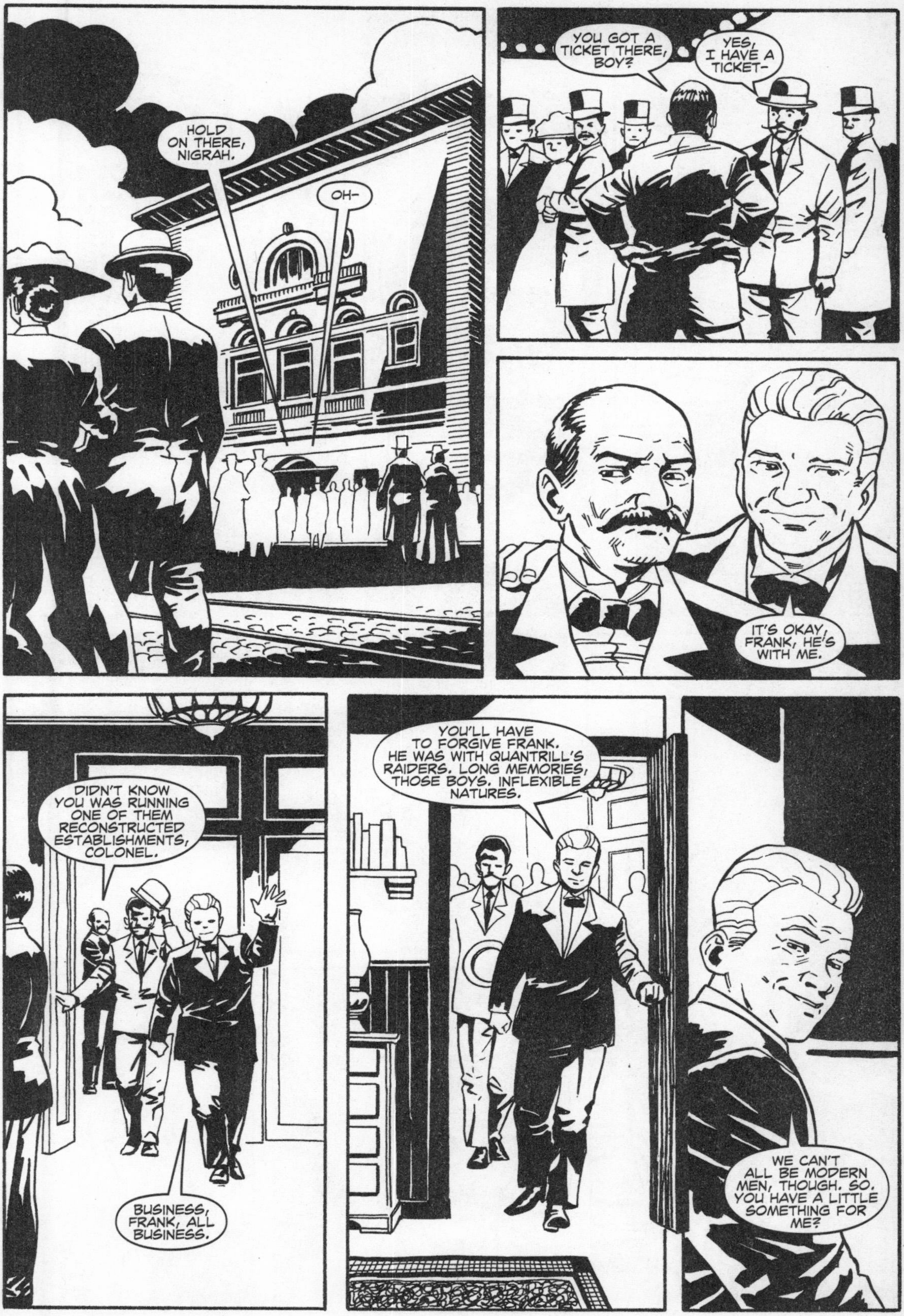
HOLD ON THERE, NIGRAH.
OH-
YOU GOT A TICKET THERE, BOY?
YES, I HAVE A TICKET-
IT'S OKAY, FRANK, HE'S WITH ME.
DIDN'T KNOW YOU WAS RUNNING ONE OF THEM RECONSTRUCTED ESTABLISHMENTS, COLONEL.
BUSINESS, FRANK, ALL BUSINESS.
YOU'LL HAVE TO FORGIVE FRANK. HE WAS WITH QUANTRILL'S RAIDERS. LONG MEMORIES, THOSE BOYS. INFLEXIBLE NATURES.
WE CAN'T ALL BE MODERN MEN, THOUGH. SO. YOU HAVE A LITTLE SOMETHING FOR ME?

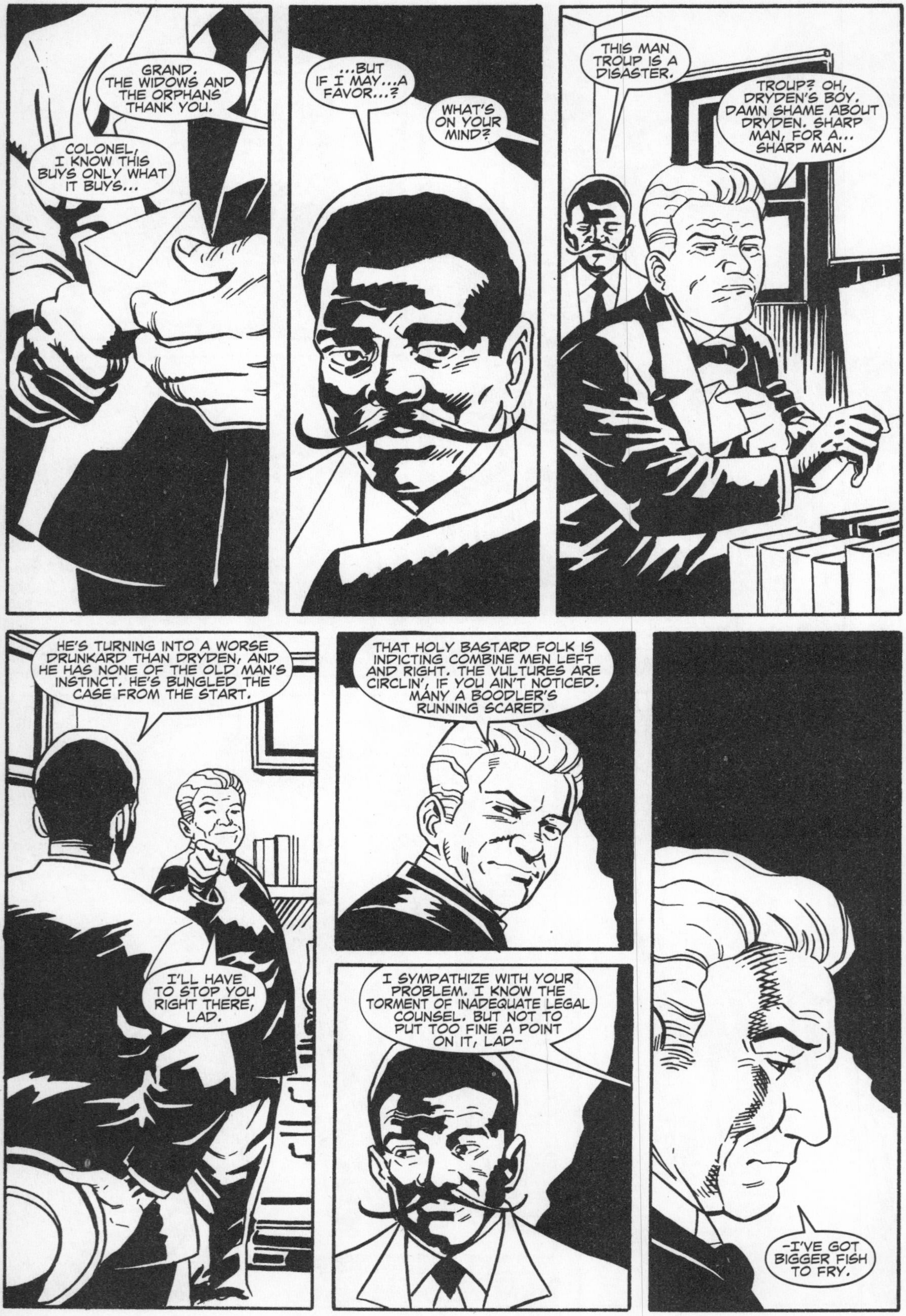
GRAND. THE WIDOWS AND THE ORPHANS THANK YOU.
COLONEL, I KNOW THIS BUYS ONLY WHAT IT BUYS...
...BUT IF I MAY...A FAVOR...?
WHAT'S ON YOUR MIND?
THIS MAN TROUP IS A DISASTER.
TROUP? OH, DRYDEN'S BOY. DAMN SHAME ABOUT DRYDEN. SHARP MAN, FOR A... SHARP MAN.
HE'S TURNING INTO A WORSE DRUNKARD THAN DRYDEN, AND HE HAS NONE OF THE OLD MAN'S INSTINCT. HE'S BUNGLED THE CASE FROM THE START.
I'LL HAVE TO STOP YOU RIGHT THERE, LAD.
THAT HOLY BASTARD FOLK IS INDICTING COMBINE MEN LEFT AND RIGHT. THE VULTURES ARE CIRCLIN', IF YOU AIN'T NOTICED. MANY A BOODLER'S RUNNING SCARED.
I SYMPATHIZE WITH YOUR PROBLEM. I KNOW THE TORMENT OF INADEQUATE LEGAL COUNSEL. BUT NOT TO PUT TOO FINE A POINT ON IT, LAD-
-I'VE GOT BIGGER FISH TO FRY.

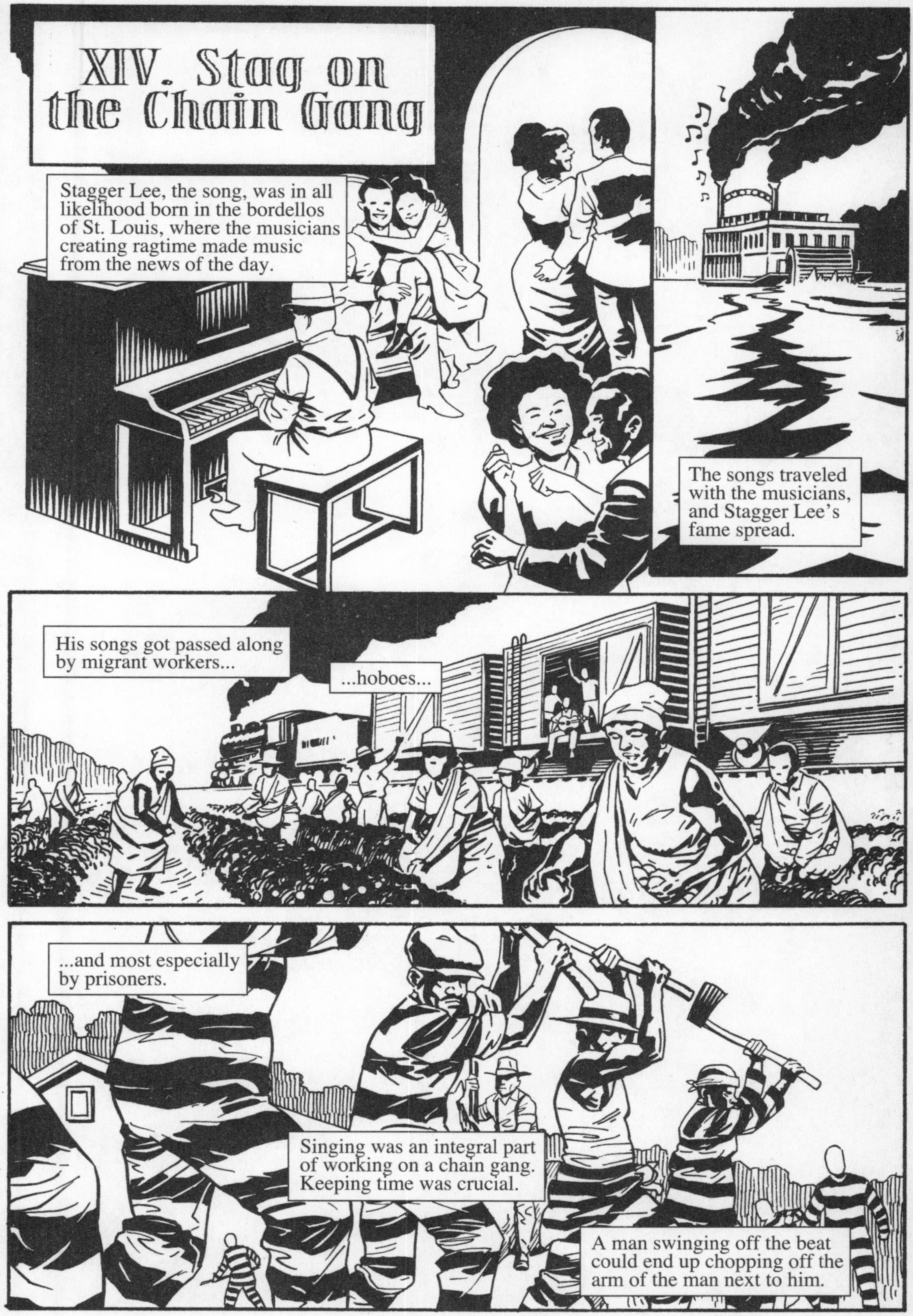

XIV. Stag on the Chain Gang
Stagger Lee, the song, was in all likelihood born in the bordellos of St. Louis, where the musicians creating ragtime made music from the news of the day.
The songs traveled with the musicians, and Stagger Lee's fame spread.
His songs got passed along by migrant workers...
...hoboes...
...and most especially by prisoners.
Singing was an integral part of working on a chain gang. Keeping time was crucial.
A man swinging off the beat could end up chopping off the arm of the man next to him.

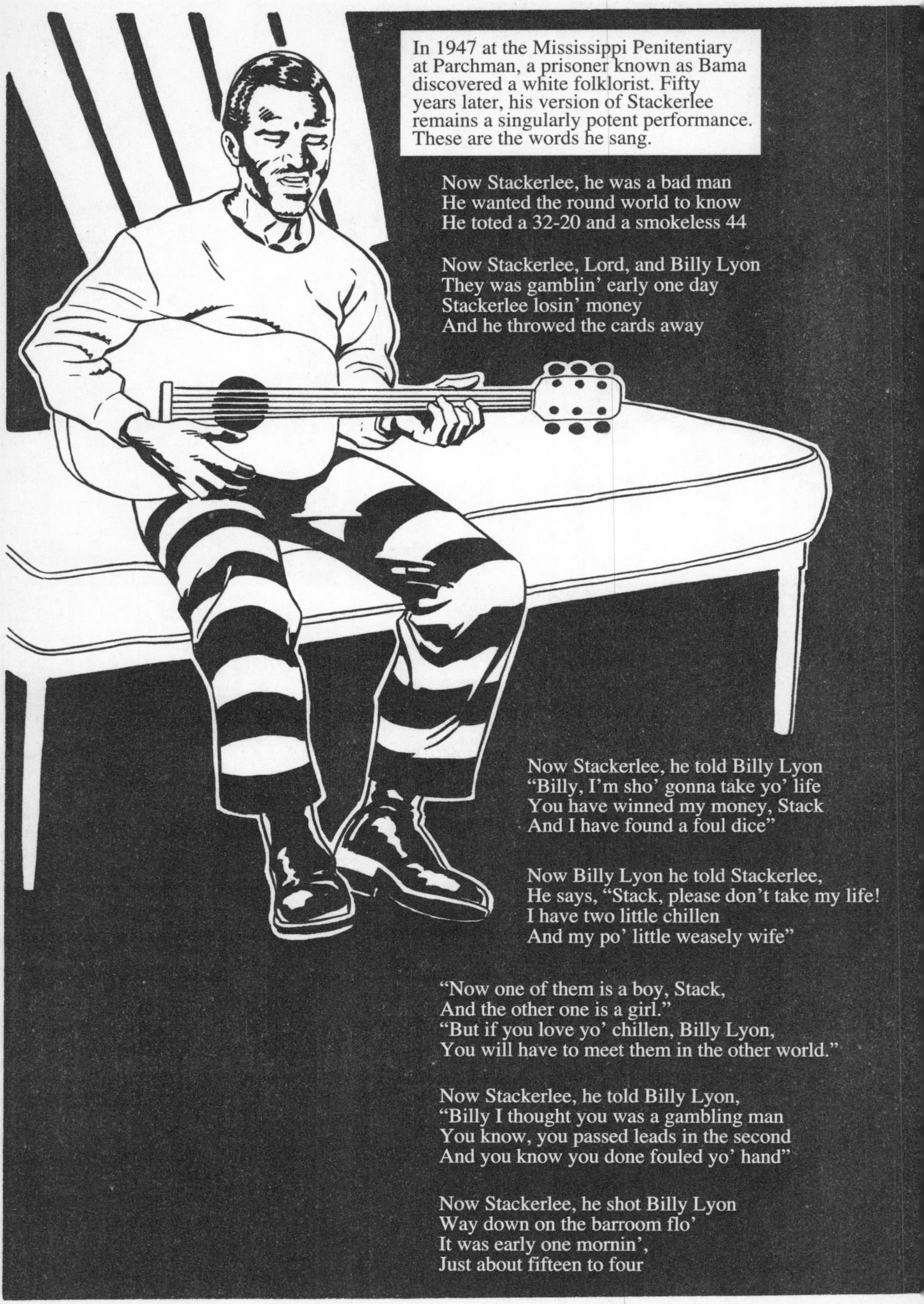
In 1947 at the Mississippi Penitentiary at Parchman, a prisoner known as Bama discovered a white folklorist. Fifty years later, his version of Stackerlee remains a singularly potent performance. These are the words he sang.

Now Stackerlee, he was a bad man
He wanted the round world to know
He toted a 32-20 and a smokeless 44

Now Stackerlee, Lord, and Billy Lyon
They was gamblin' early one day
Stackerlee losin' money
And he throwed the cards away

Now Stackerlee, he told Billy Lyon
"Billy, I'm sho' gonna take yo' life
You have winned my money, Stack
And I have found a foul dice"

Now Billy Lyon he told Stackerlee,
He says, "Stack, please don't take my life!
I have two little chillen
And my po' little weasely wife"

"Now one of them is a boy, Stack,
And the other one is a girl."
"But if you love yo' chillen, Billy Lyon,
You will have to meet them in the other world."

Now Stackerlee, he told Billy Lyon,
"Billy I thought you was a gambling man
You know, you passed leads in the second
And you know you done fouled yo' hand"

Now Stackerlee, he shot Billy Lyon
Way down on the barroom flo'
It was early one mornin',
Just about fifteen to four

Now Billy Lyon mother, she come runnin'
She said, "Lord, have mercy on my son
Po' Billy Lyon done got murdered
And I know he didn't have his gun!"

Alberta, Lord, Alberta
Baby don't you hear me calling you?
But you three times seven, Alberta,
And you know what you want to do

I'm going to call up the undertaker
Lord, I'm going to ring up Mr. Moss
I'm going to ask those people
What will Alberta funeral cost

I wants a two hundred dollar coffin
Lord, I wants a hundred dollar hearse
And that will put Alberta, I know
Six feet in the earth

Now give me water, Lord, when I'm thirsty,
Honey, give me whiskey when I'm dry
Give me Alberta when I need her
And Heaven when I die

Now when I gets all up in Glory
Lord I'm gonna sit down on the golden stool
And I'm going to ask St. Gabriel
To blow me the "Worried Blues."

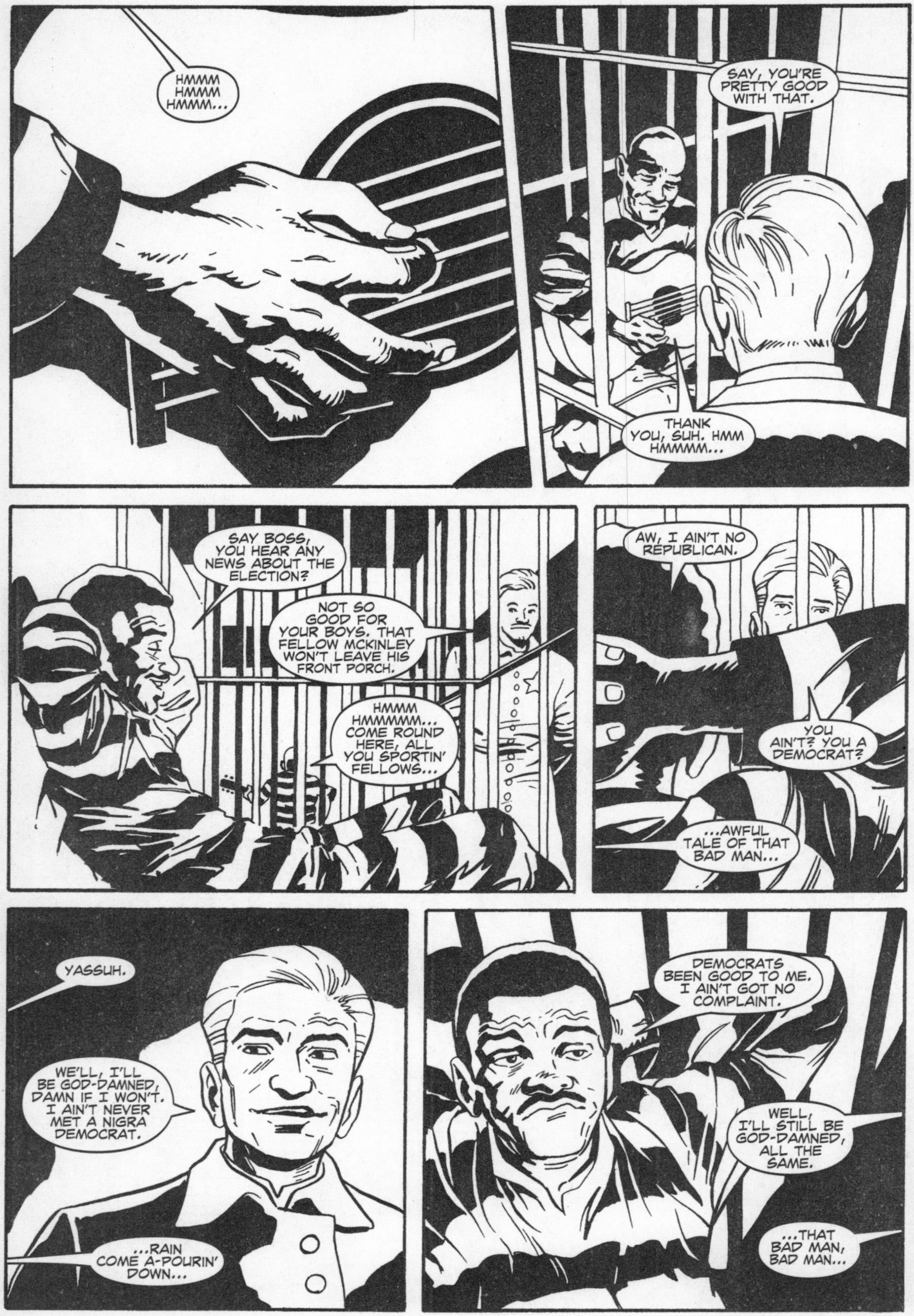
HMMM HMMM HMMM...
SAY, YOU'RE PRETTY GOOD WITH THAT.
THANK YOU, SUH. HMM HMMMM...
SAY BOSS, YOU HEAR ANY NEWS ABOUT THE ELECTION?
NOT SO GOOD FOR YOUR BOYS. THAT FELLOW MCKINLEY WON'T LEAVE HIS FRONT PORCH.
HMMM HMMMMM... COME ROUND HERE, ALL YOU SPORTIN' FELLOWS...
AW, I AIN'T NO REPUBLICAN.
YOU AIN'T? YOU A DEMOCRAT?
...AWFUL TALE OF THAT BAD MAN...
YASSUH.
WE'LL, I'LL BE GOD-DAMNED, DAMN IF I WON'T. I AIN'T NEVER MET A NIGRA DEMOCRAT.
...RAIN COME A-POURIN' DOWN...
DEMOCRATS BEEN GOOD TO ME. I AIN'T GOT NO COMPLAINT.
WELL, I'LL STILL BE GOD-DAMNED, ALL THE SAME.
...THAT BAD MAN, BAD MAN...

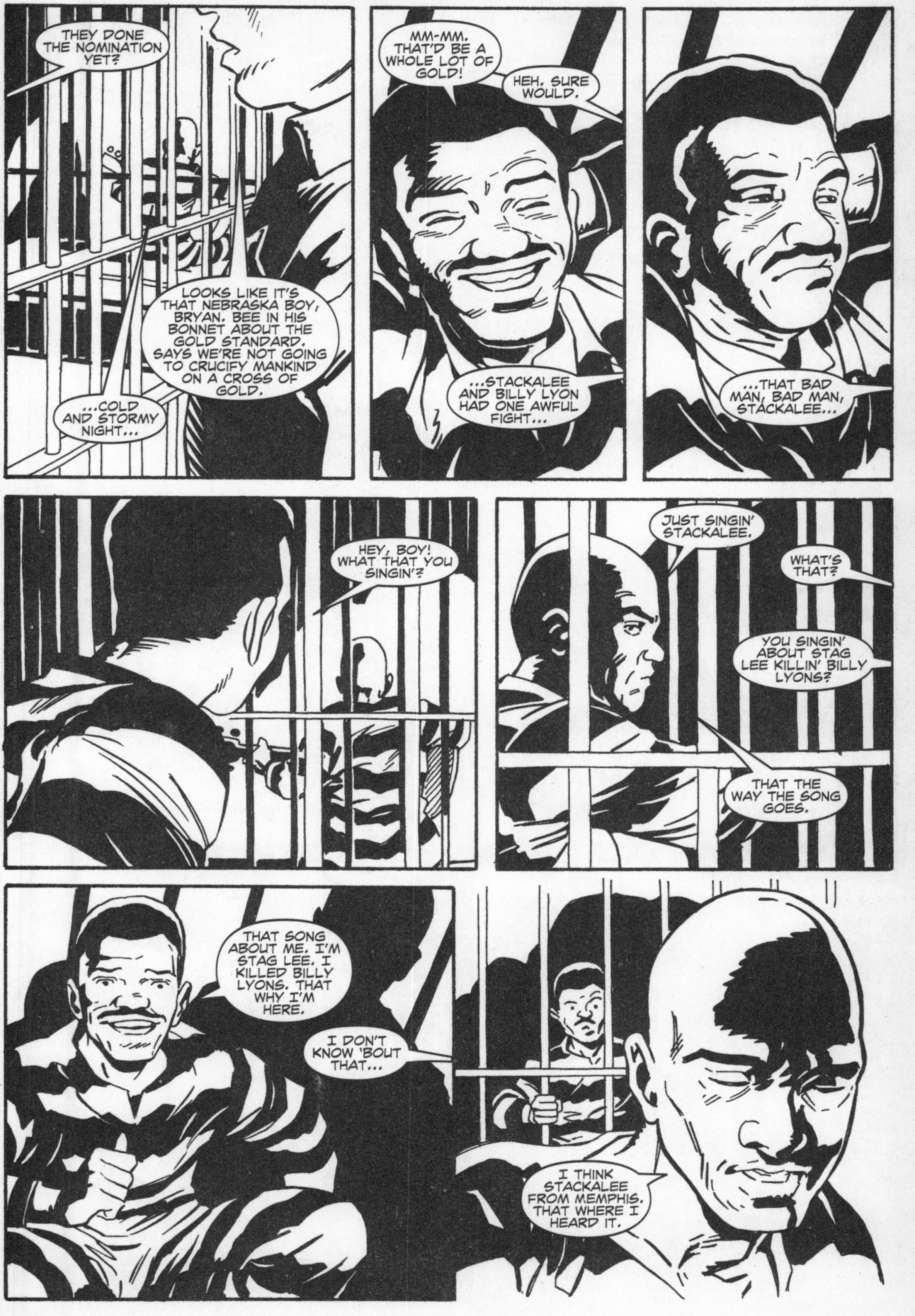
THEY DONE THE NOMINATION YET?
LOOKS LIKE IT'S THAT NEBRASKA BOY, BRYAN. BEE IN HIS BONNET ABOUT THE GOLD STANDARD. SAYS WE'RE NOT GOING TO CRUCIFY MANKIND ON A CROSS OF GOLD.
...COLD AND STORMY NIGHT...
MM-MM. THAT'D BE A WHOLE LOT OF GOLD!
HEH. SURE WOULD.
...STACKALEE AND BILLY LYON HAD ONE AWFUL FIGHT...
...THAT BAD MAN, BAD MAN, STACKALEE...
HEY, BOY! WHAT THAT YOU SINGIN'?
JUST SINGIN' STACKALEE.
WHAT'S THAT?
YOU SINGIN' ABOUT STAG LEE KILLIN' BILLY LYONS?
THAT THE WAY THE SONG GOES.
THAT SONG ABOUT ME. I'M STAG LEE. I KILLED BILLY LYONS. THAT WHY I'M HERE.
I DON'T KNOW 'BOUT THAT...
I THINK STACKALEE FROM MEMPHIS. THAT WHERE I HEARD IT.

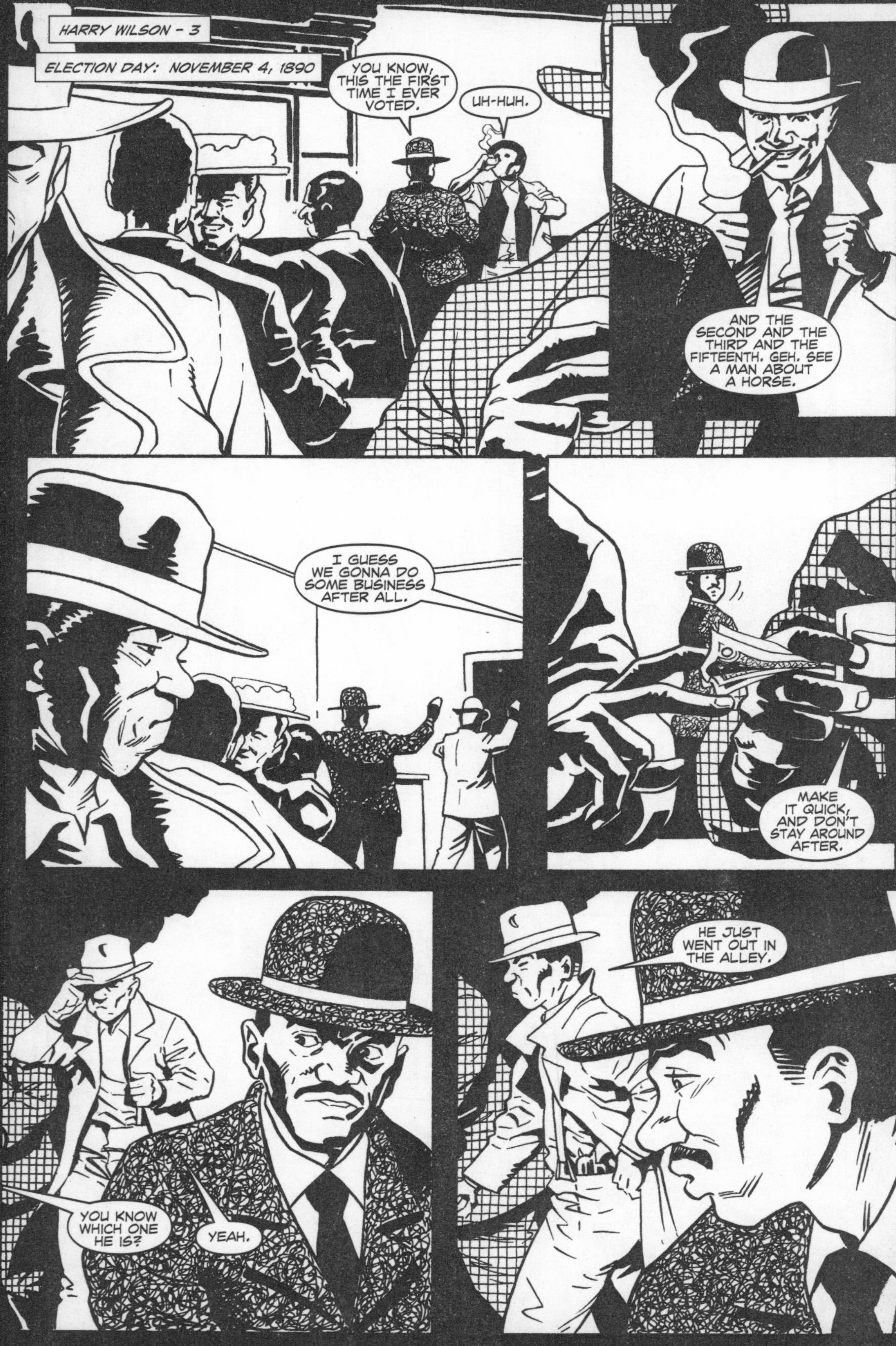

HARRY WILSON - 3
ELECTION DAY: NOVEMBER 4, 1890
YOU KNOW, THIS THE FIRST TIME I EVER VOTED.
UH-HUH.
AND THE SECOND AND THE THIRD AND THE FIFTEENTH. GEH. SEE A MAN ABOUT A HORSE.
I GUESS WE GONNA DO SOME BUSINESS AFTER ALL.
MAKE IT QUICK, AND DON'T STAY AROUND AFTER.
YOU KNOW WHICH ONE HE IS?
YEAH.
HE JUST WENT OUT IN THE ALLEY.

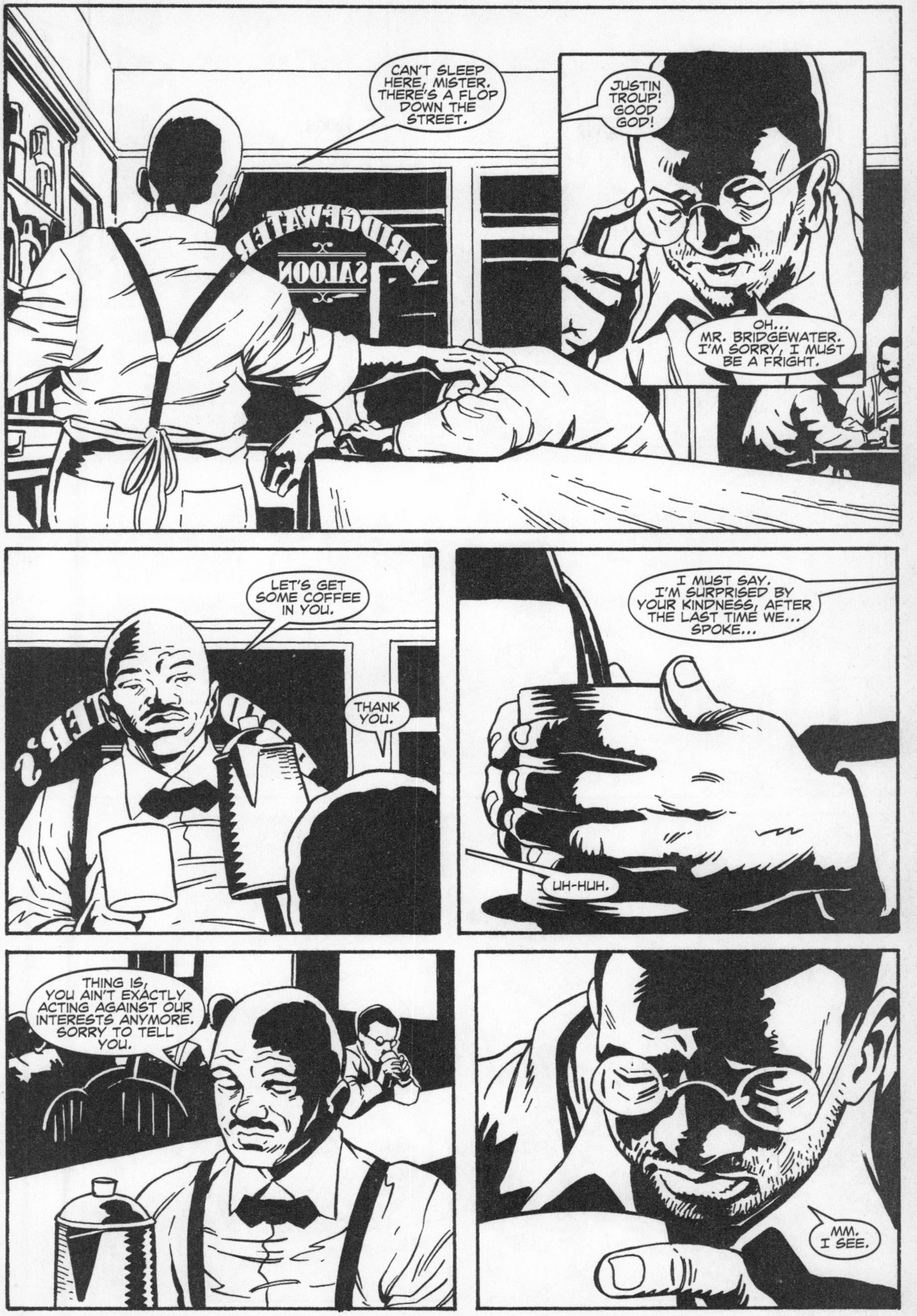
CAN'T SLEEP HERE, MISTER. THERE'S A FLOP DOWN THE STREET.
BRIDGEWATER SALOON
JUSTIN TROUP! GOOD GOD!
OH... MR. BRIDGEWATER. I'M SORRY, I MUST BE A FRIGHT.
LET'S GET SOME COFFEE IN YOU.
THANK YOU.
I MUST SAY. I'M SURPRISED BY YOUR KINDNESS, AFTER THE LAST TIME WE... SPOKE...
UH-HUH.
THING IS, YOU AIN'T EXACTLY ACTING AGAINST OUR INTERESTS ANYMORE. SORRY TO TELL YOU.
MM. I SEE.

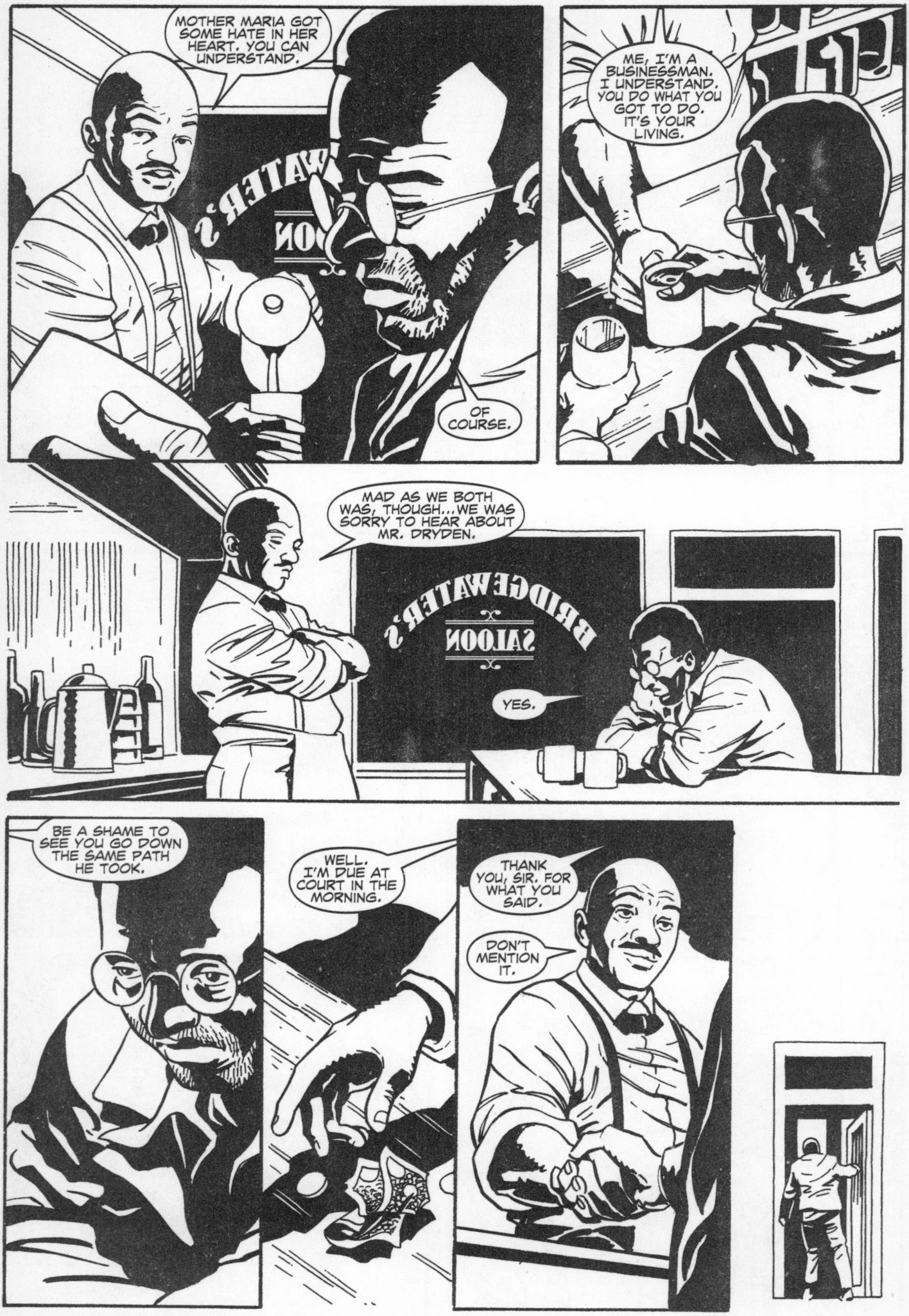
MOTHER MARIA GOT SOME HATE IN HER HEART. YOU CAN UNDERSTAND.
WATER'S
OON
OF COURSE.
ME, I'M A BUSINESSMAN. I UNDERSTAND. YOU DO WHAT YOU GOT TO DO. IT'S YOUR LIVING.
MAD AS WE BOTH WAS, THOUGH...WE WAS SORRY TO HEAR ABOUT MR. DRYDEN.
BRIDGEWATER'S
SALOON
YES.
BE A SHAME TO SEE YOU GO DOWN THE SAME PATH HE TOOK.
WELL. I'M DUE AT COURT IN THE MORNING.
THANK YOU, SIR. FOR WHAT YOU SAID.
DON'T MENTION IT.

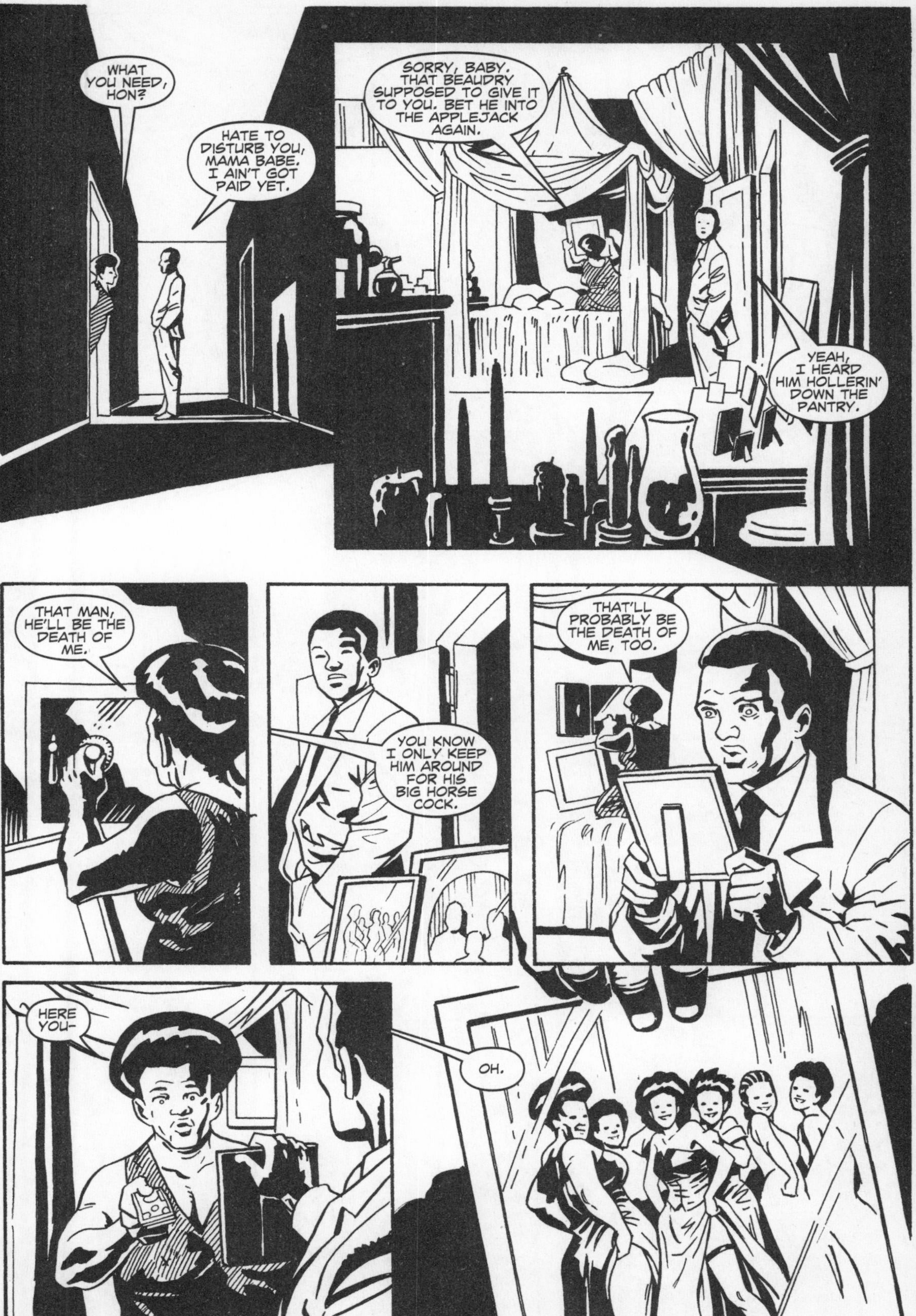
WHAT YOU NEED, HON?
HATE TO DISTURB YOU, MAMA BABE. I AIN'T GOT PAID YET.
SORRY, BABY. THAT BEAUDRY SUPPOSED TO GIVE IT TO YOU. BET HE INTO THE APPLEJACK AGAIN.
YEAH, I HEARD HIM HOLLERIN' DOWN THE PANTRY.
THAT MAN, HE'LL BE THE DEATH OF ME.
YOU KNOW I ONLY KEEP HIM AROUND FOR HIS BIG HORSE COCK.
THAT'LL PROBABLY BE THE DEATH OF ME, TOO.
HERE YOU-
OH.

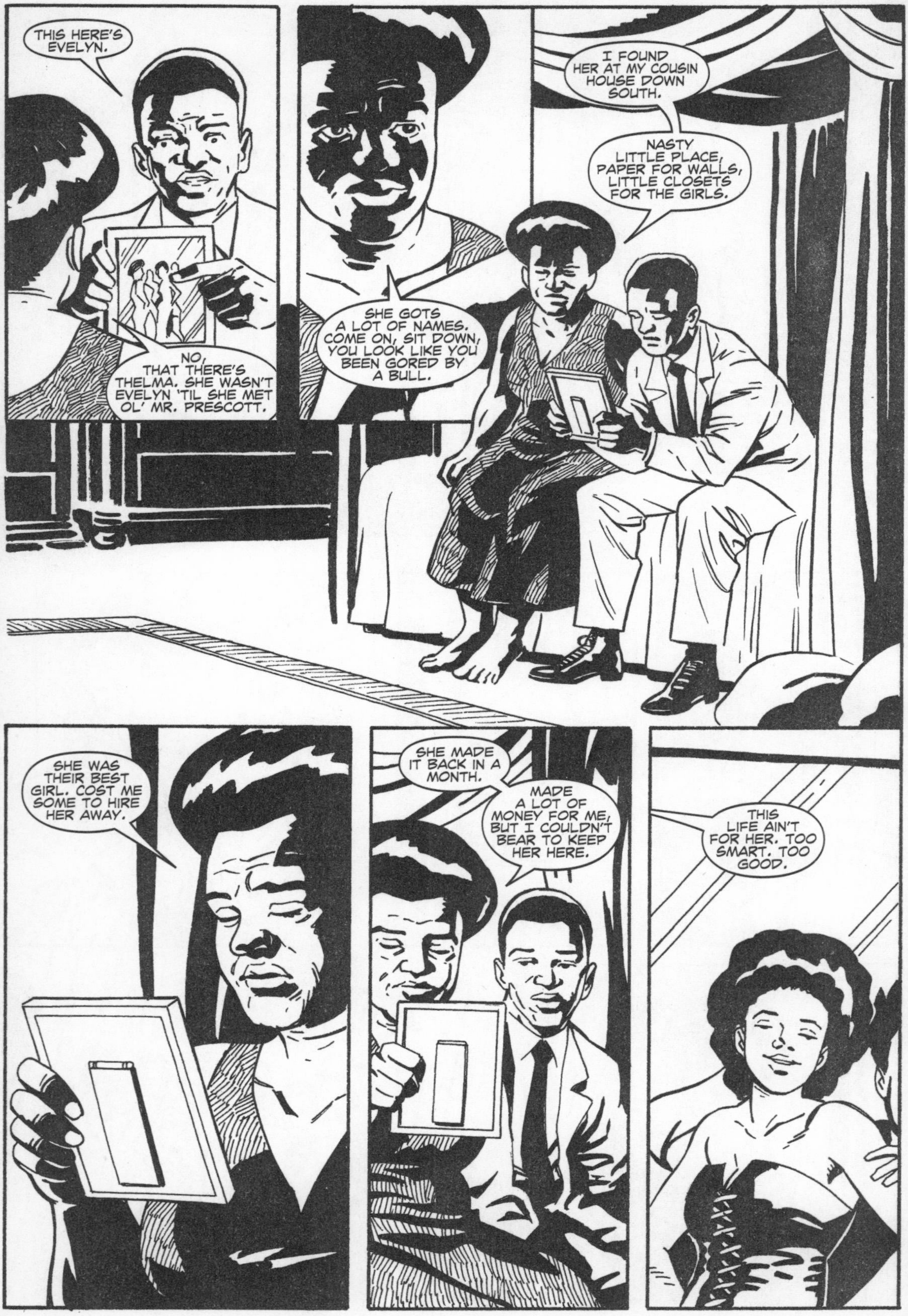
THIS HERE'S EVELYN.
NO, THAT THERE'S THELMA. SHE WASN'T EVELYN 'TIL SHE MET OL' MR. PRESCOTT.
SHE GOTS A LOT OF NAMES. COME ON, SIT DOWN, YOU LOOK LIKE YOU BEEN GORED BY A BULL.
I FOUND HER AT MY COUSIN HOUSE DOWN SOUTH.
NASTY LITTLE PLACE, PAPER FOR WALLS, LITTLE CLOSETS FOR THE GIRLS.
SHE WAS THEIR BEST GIRL. COST ME SOME TO HIRE HER AWAY.
SHE MADE IT BACK IN A MONTH.
MADE A LOT OF MONEY FOR ME, BUT I COULDN'T BEAR TO KEEP HER HERE.
THIS LIFE AIN'T FOR HER. TOO SMART. TOO GOOD.

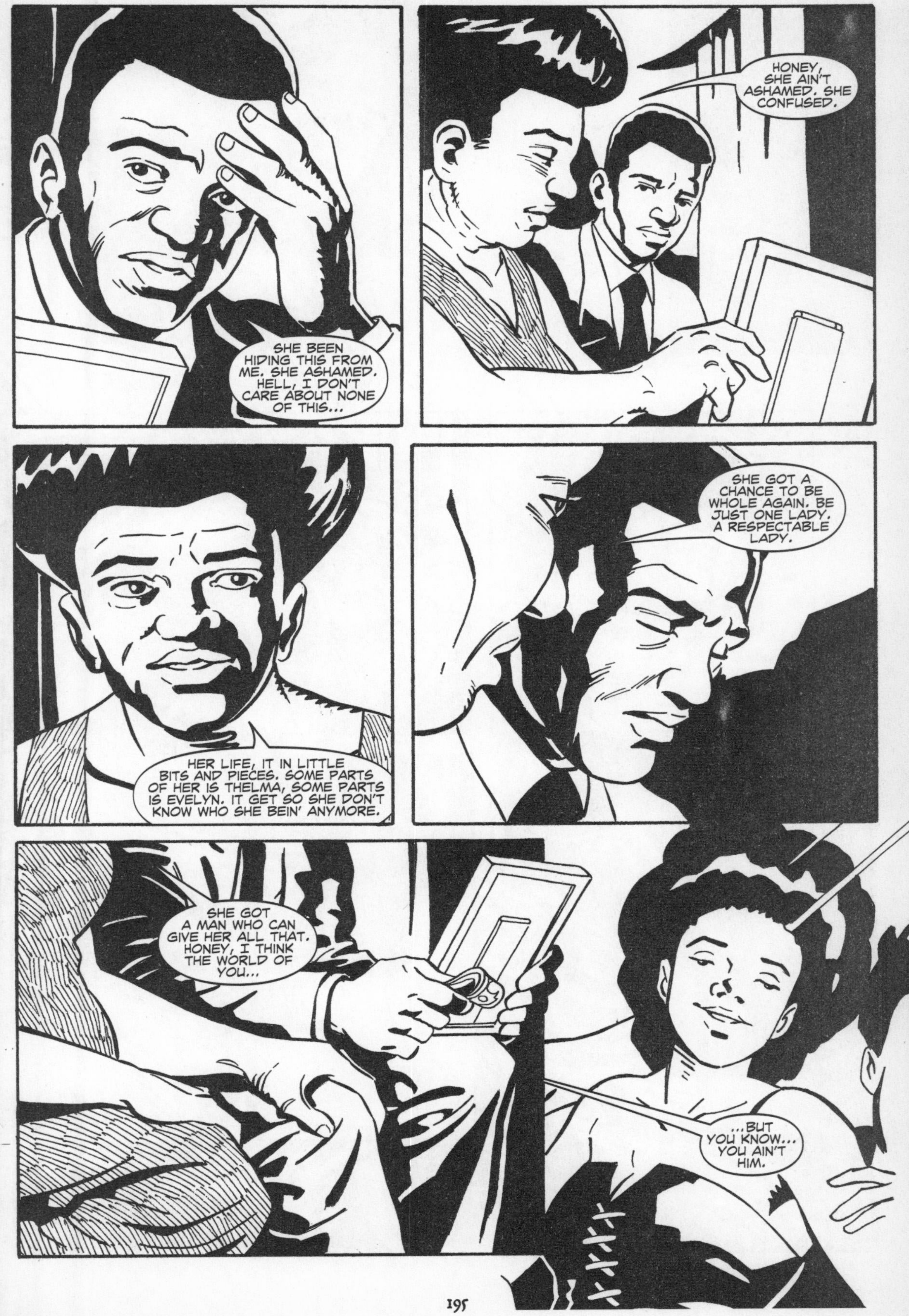
SHE BEEN HIDING THIS FROM ME. SHE ASHAMED. HELL, I DON'T CARE ABOUT NONE OF THIS...
HONEY, SHE AIN'T ASHAMED. SHE CONFUSED.
HER LIFE, IT IN LITTLE BITS AND PIECES. SOME PARTS OF HER IS THELMA, SOME PARTS IS EVELYN. IT GET SO SHE DON'T KNOW WHO SHE BEIN' ANYMORE.
SHE GOT A CHANCE TO BE WHOLE AGAIN. BE JUST ONE LADY. A RESPECTABLE LADY.
SHE GOT A MAN WHO CAN GIVE HER ALL THAT. HONEY, I THINK THE WORLD OF YOU...
...BUT YOU KNOW... YOU AIN'T HIM.

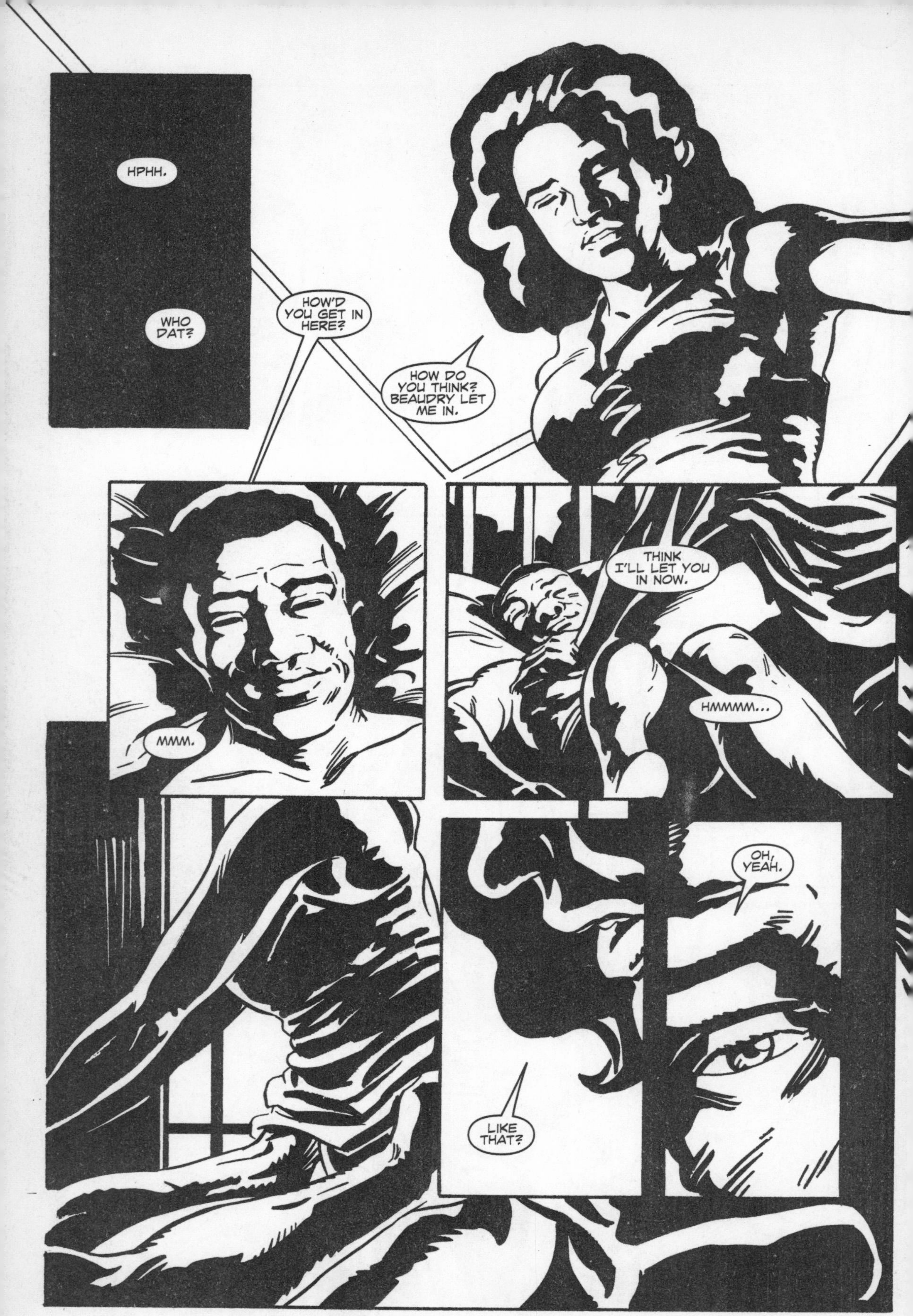
HPHH.
WHO DAT?
HOW'D YOU GET IN HERE?
HOW DO YOU THINK? BEAUDRY LET ME IN.
MMM.
THINK I'LL LET YOU IN NOW.
HMMMM...
OH, YEAH.
LIKE THAT?

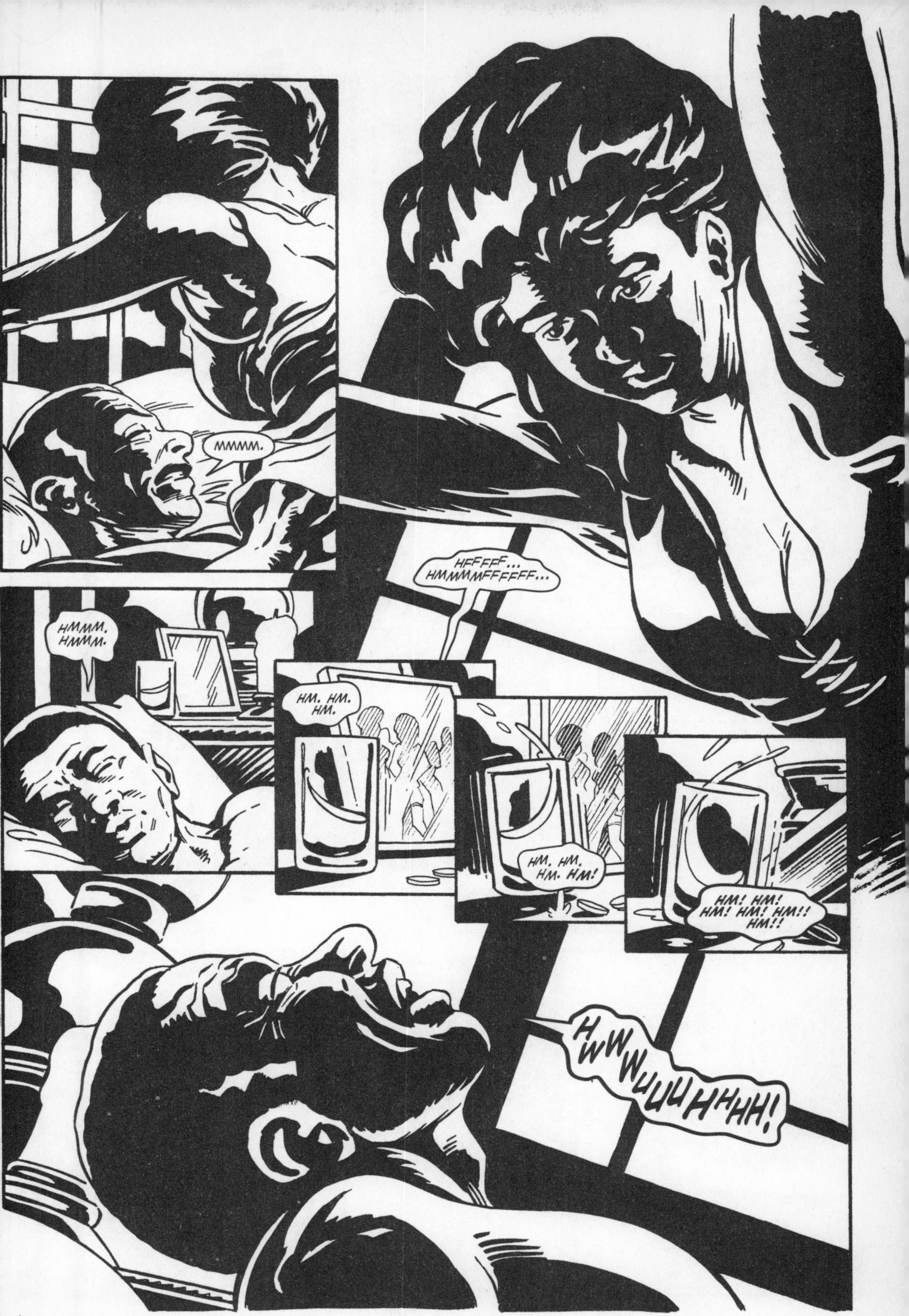
MMMM.
HFFFFF...
HMMMMFFFFFF...
HMMM.
HMMM.
HM. HM.
HM.
HM. HM.
HM. HM!
HM! HM!
HM! HM! HM!!
HM!!
HWWWUUUHHHH!

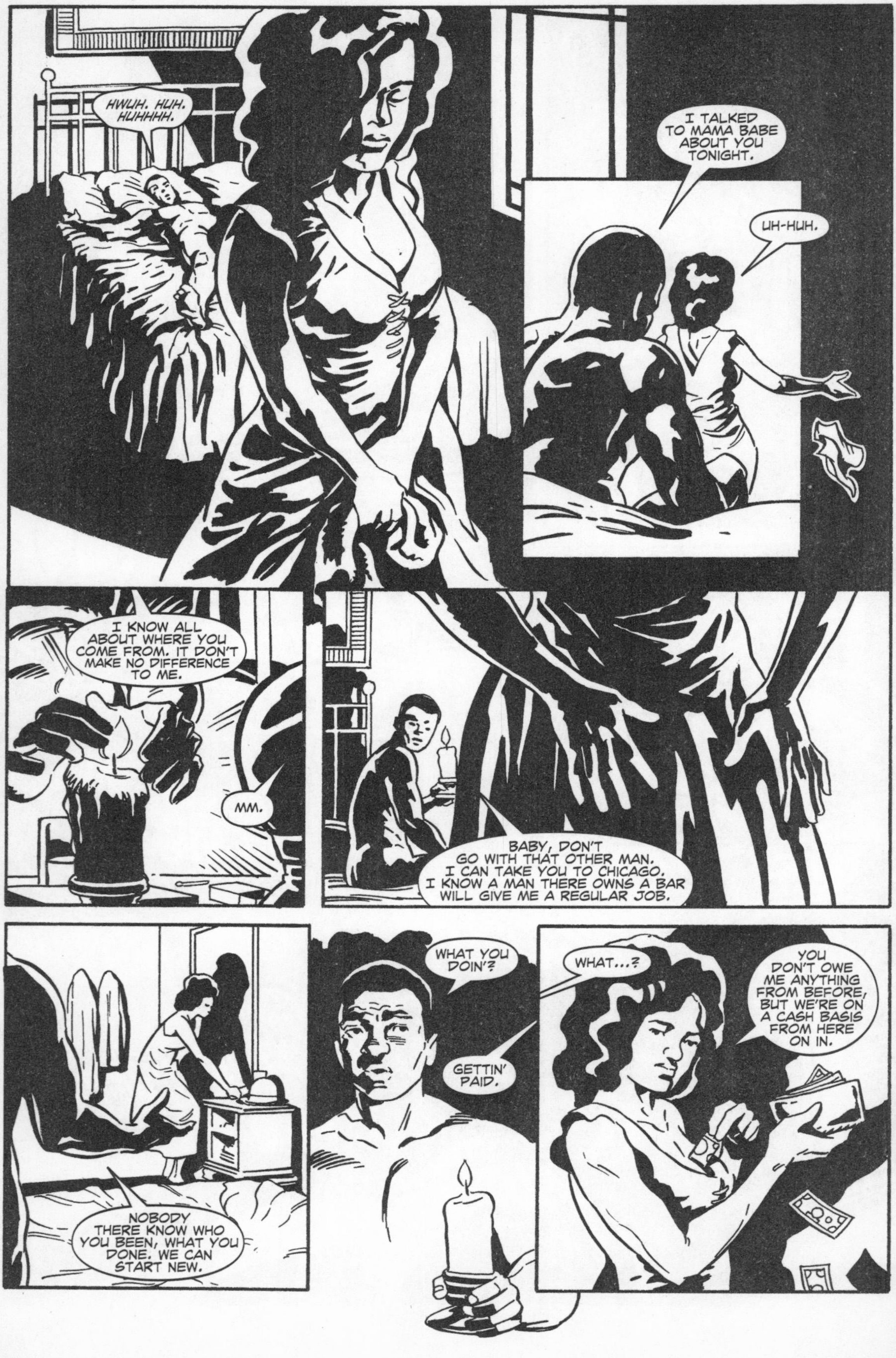
HWUH. HUH. HUHHHH.
I TALKED TO MAMA BABE ABOUT YOU TONIGHT.
UH-HUH.
I KNOW ALL ABOUT WHERE YOU COME FROM. IT DON'T MAKE NO DIFFERENCE TO ME.
MM.
BABY, DON'T GO WITH THAT OTHER MAN. I CAN TAKE YOU TO CHICAGO. I KNOW A MAN THERE OWNS A BAR WILL GIVE ME A REGULAR JOB.
NOBODY THERE KNOW WHO YOU BEEN, WHAT YOU DONE. WE CAN START NEW.
WHAT YOU DOIN'?
GETTIN' PAID.
WHAT...?
YOU DON'T OWE ME ANYTHING FROM BEFORE, BUT WE'RE ON A CASH BASIS FROM HERE ON IN.

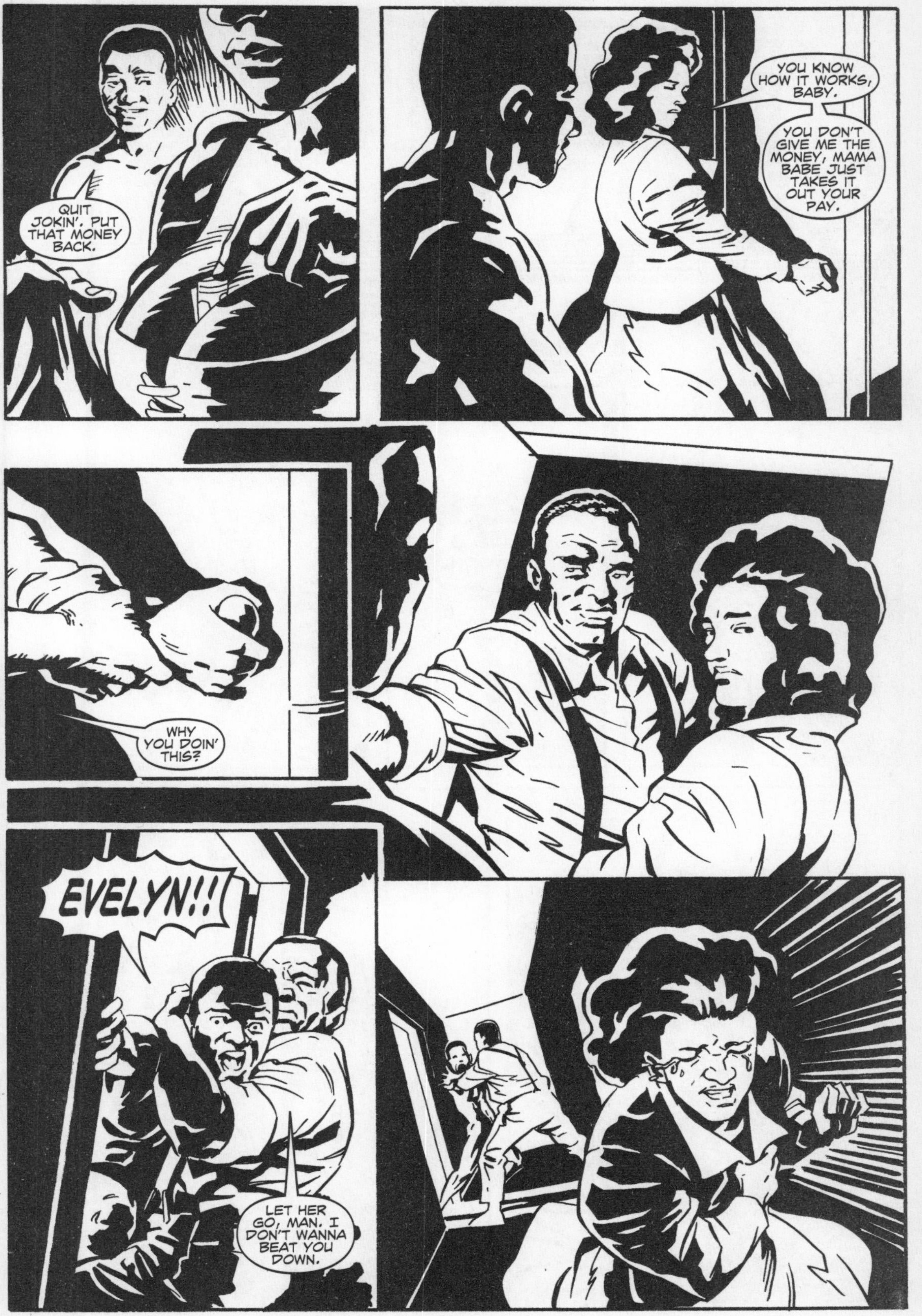
QUIT JOKIN'. PUT THAT MONEY BACK.
YOU KNOW HOW IT WORKS, BABY.
YOU DON'T GIVE ME THE MONEY, MAMA BABE JUST TAKES IT OUT YOUR PAY.
WHY YOU DOIN' THIS?
EVELYN!!
LET HER GO, MAN. I DON'T WANNA BEAT YOU DOWN.

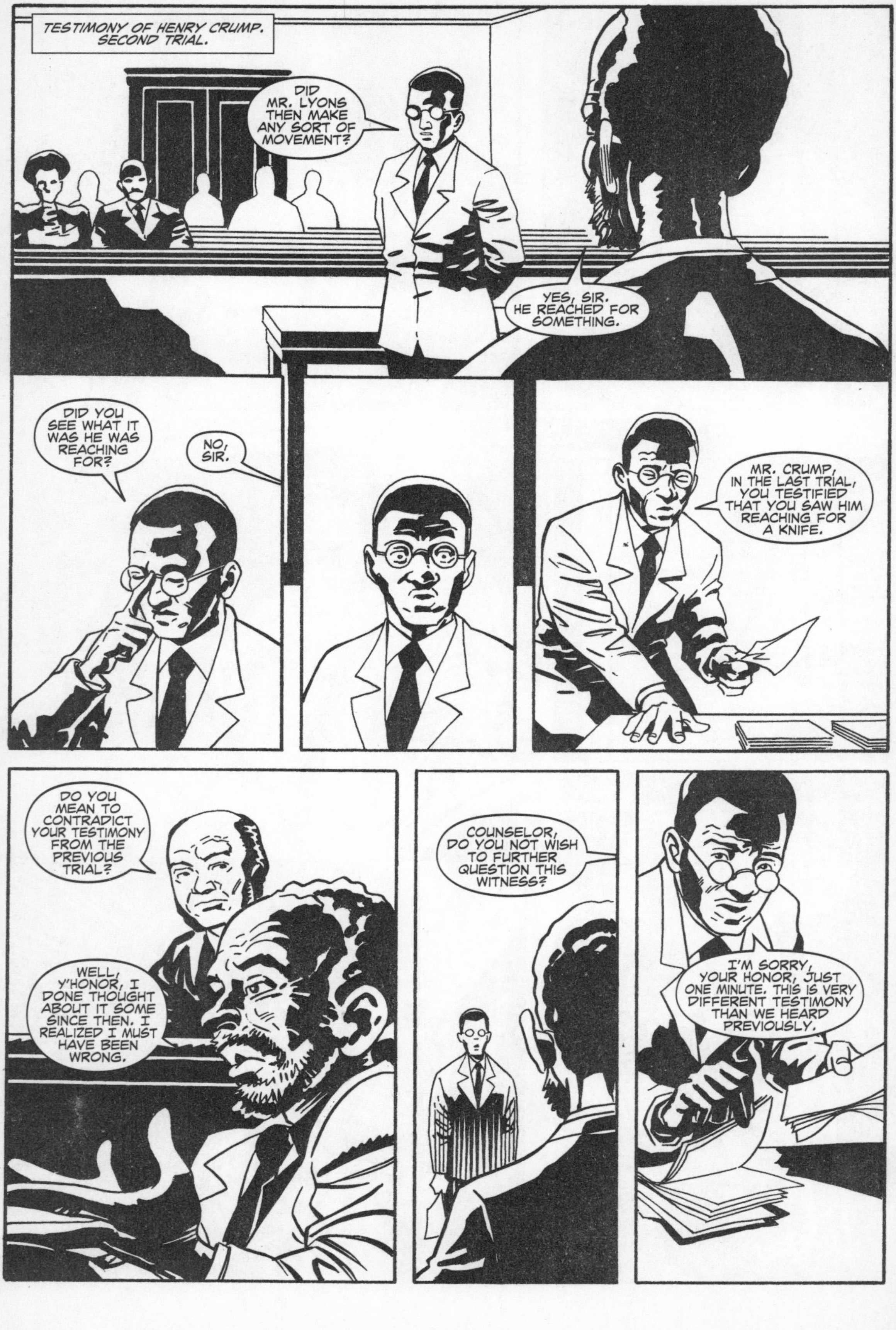
TESTIMONY OF HENRY CRUMP. SECOND TRIAL.
DID MR. LYONS THEN MAKE ANY SORT OF MOVEMENT?
YES, SIR. HE REACHED FOR SOMETHING.
DID YOU SEE WHAT IT WAS HE WAS REACHING FOR?
NO, SIR.
MR. CRUMP, IN THE LAST TRIAL, YOU TESTIFIED THAT YOU SAW HIM REACHING FOR A KNIFE.
DO YOU MEAN TO CONTRADICT YOUR TESTIMONY FROM THE PREVIOUS TRIAL?
WELL, Y'HONOR, I DONE THOUGHT ABOUT IT SOME SINCE THEN. I REALIZED I MUST HAVE BEEN WRONG.
COUNSELOR, DO YOU NOT WISH TO FURTHER QUESTION THIS WITNESS?
I'M SORRY, YOUR HONOR, JUST ONE MINUTE. THIS IS VERY DIFFERENT TESTIMONY THAN WE HEARD PREVIOUSLY.

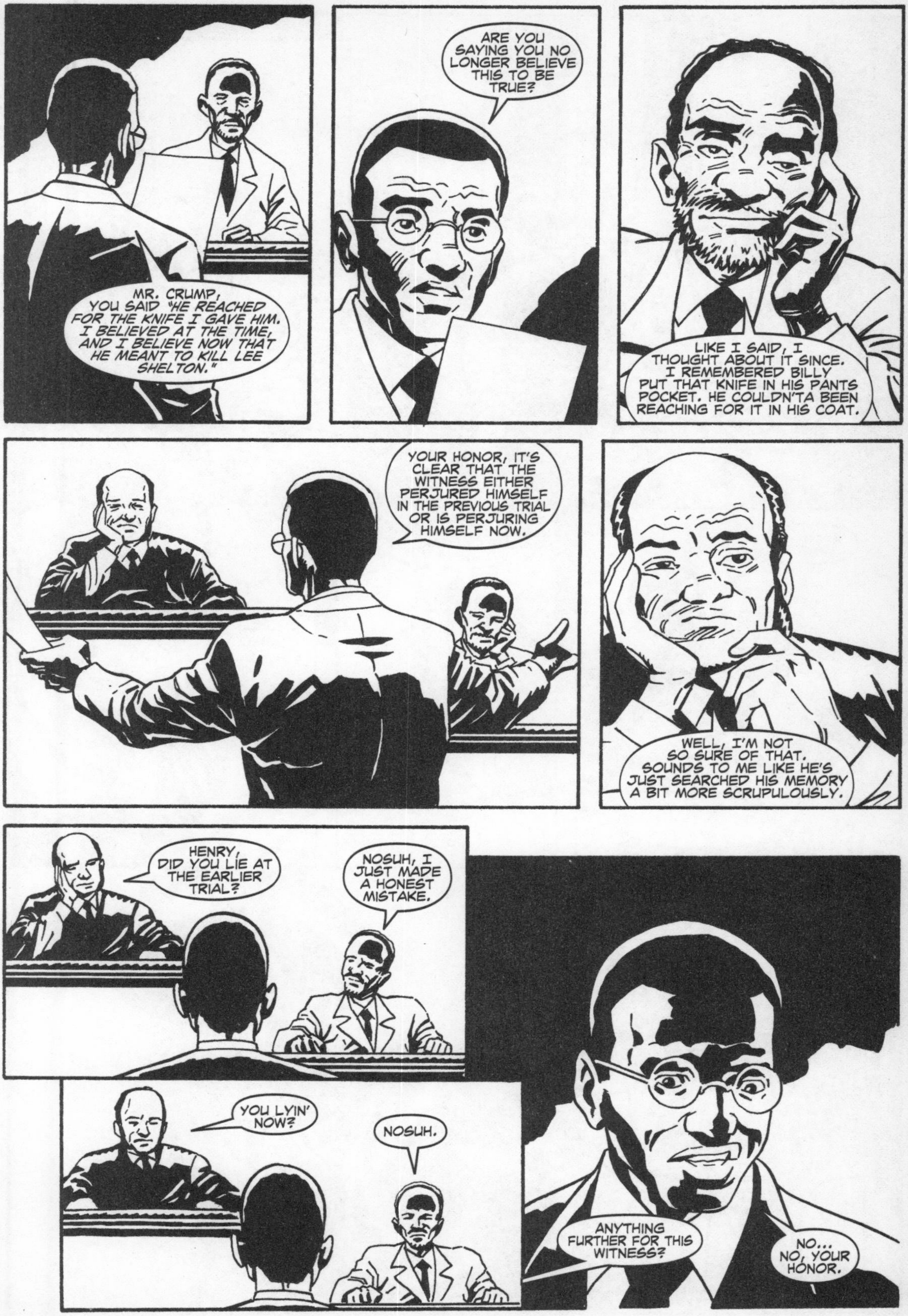
MR. CRUMP, YOU SAID "HE REACHED FOR THE KNIFE I GAVE HIM. I BELIEVED AT THE TIME, AND I BELIEVE NOW THAT HE MEANT TO KILL LEE SHELTON."
ARE YOU SAYING YOU NO LONGER BELIEVE THIS TO BE TRUE?
LIKE I SAID, I THOUGHT ABOUT IT SINCE. I REMEMBERED BILLY PUT THAT KNIFE IN HIS PANTS POCKET. HE COULDN'TA BEEN REACHING FOR IT IN HIS COAT.
YOUR HONOR, IT'S CLEAR THAT THE WITNESS EITHER PERJURED HIMSELF IN THE PREVIOUS TRIAL OR IS PERJURING HIMSELF NOW.
WELL, I'M NOT SO SURE OF THAT. SOUNDS TO ME LIKE HE'S JUST SEARCHED HIS MEMORY A BIT MORE SCRUPULOUSLY.
HENRY, DID YOU LIE AT THE EARLIER TRIAL?
NOSUH, I JUST MADE A HONEST MISTAKE.
YOU LYIN' NOW?
NOSUH.
ANYTHING FURTHER FOR THIS WITNESS?
NO... NO, YOUR HONOR.

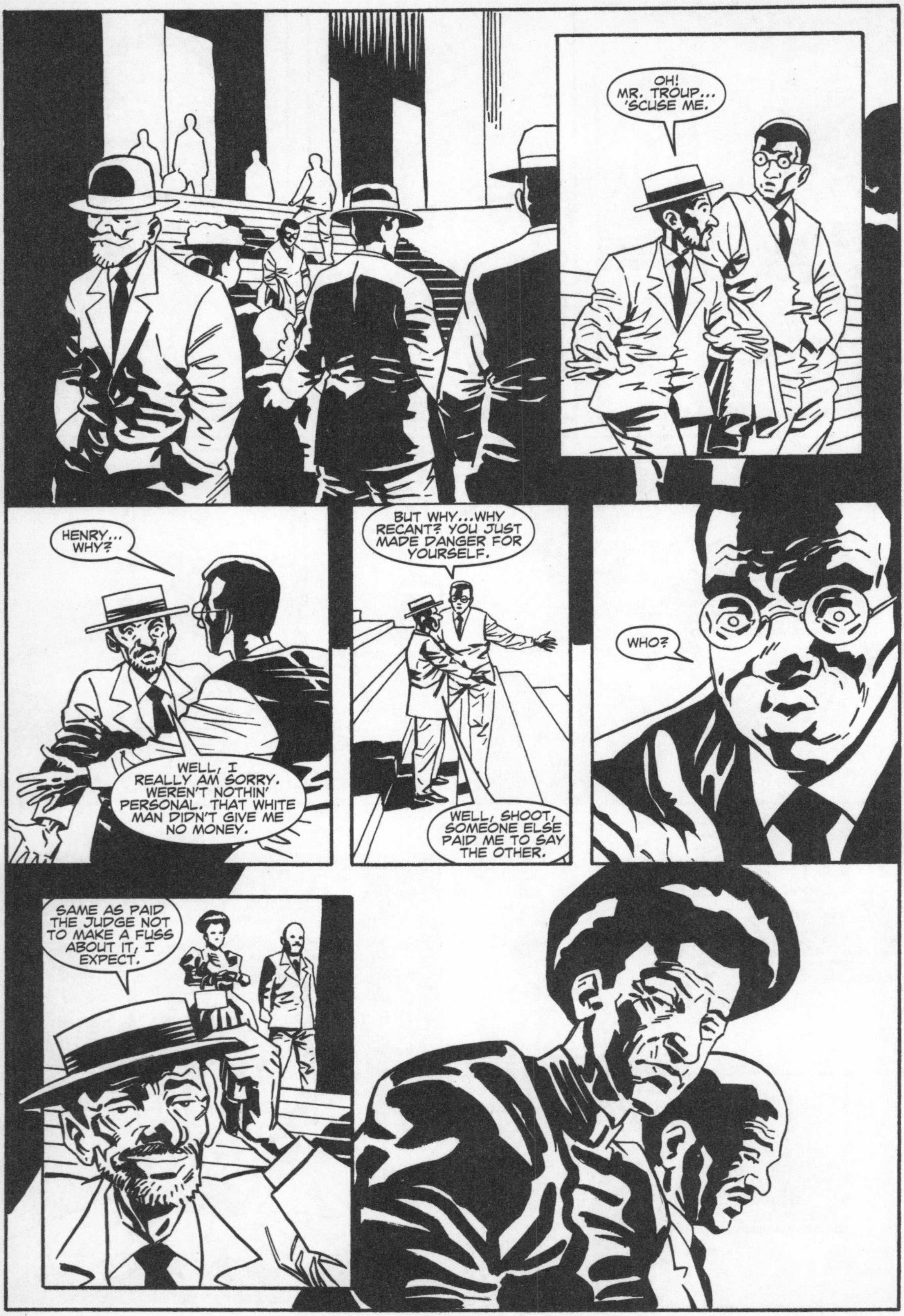
OH! MR. TROUP... 'SCUSE ME.
HENRY... WHY?
WELL, I REALLY AM SORRY. WEREN'T NOTHIN' PERSONAL. THAT WHITE MAN DIDN'T GIVE ME NO MONEY.
BUT WHY...WHY RECANT? YOU JUST MADE DANGER FOR YOURSELF.
WELL, SHOOT, SOMEONE ELSE PAID ME TO SAY THE OTHER.
WHO?
SAME AS PAID THE JUDGE NOT TO MAKE A FUSS ABOUT IT, I EXPECT.

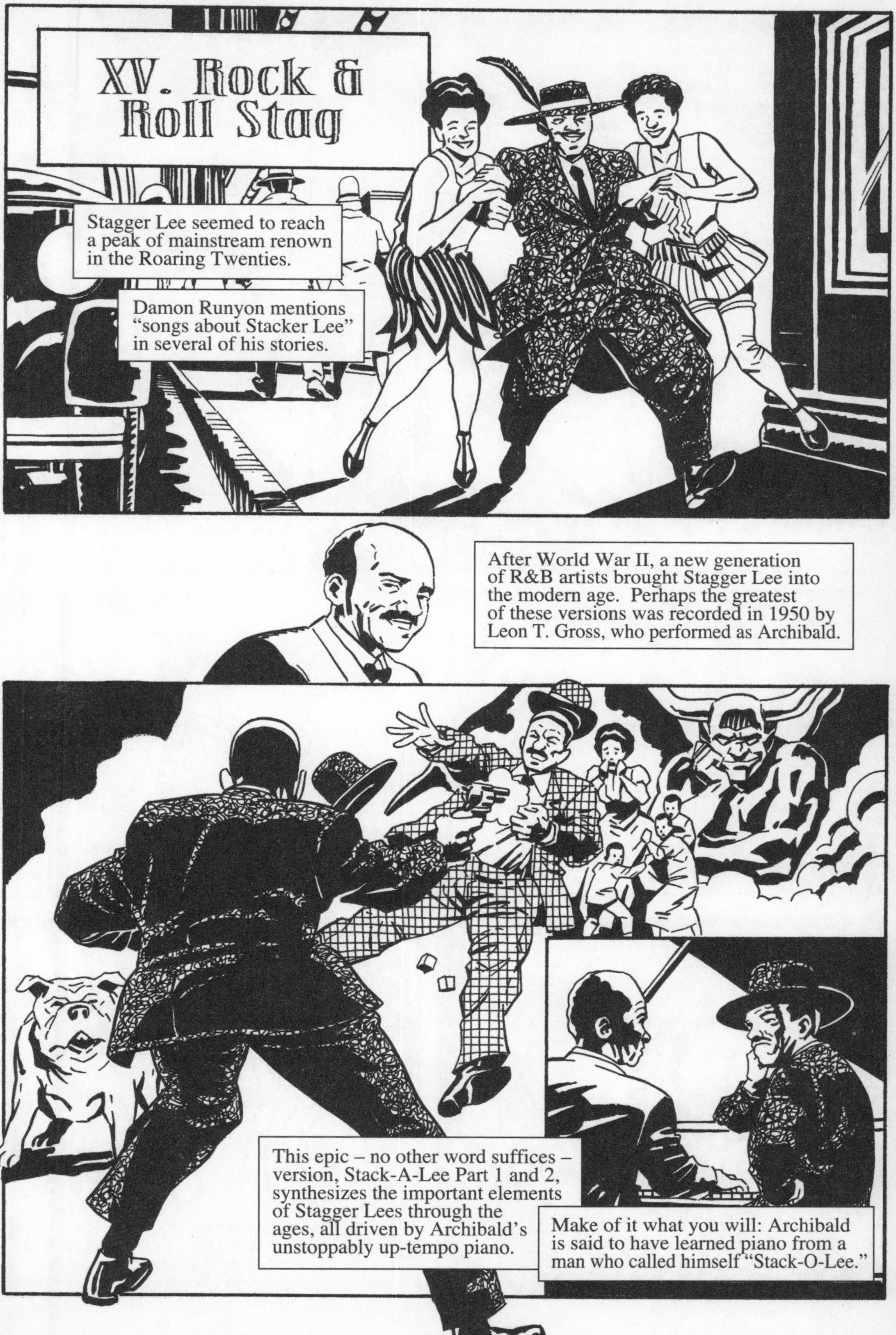
XV. Rock & Roll Stag
Stagger Lee seemed to reach a peak of mainstream renown in the Roaring Twenties.
Damon Runyon mentions "songs about Stacker Lee" in several of his stories.
After World War II, a new generation of R&B artists brought Stagger Lee into the modern age. Perhaps the greatest of these versions was recorded in 1950 by Leon T. Gross, who performed as Archibald.
This epic – no other word suffices – version, Stack-A-Lee Part 1 and 2, synthesizes the important elements of Stagger Lees through the ages, all driven by Archibald's unstoppably up-tempo piano.
Make of it what you will: Archibald is said to have learned piano from a man who called himself "Stack-O-Lee."

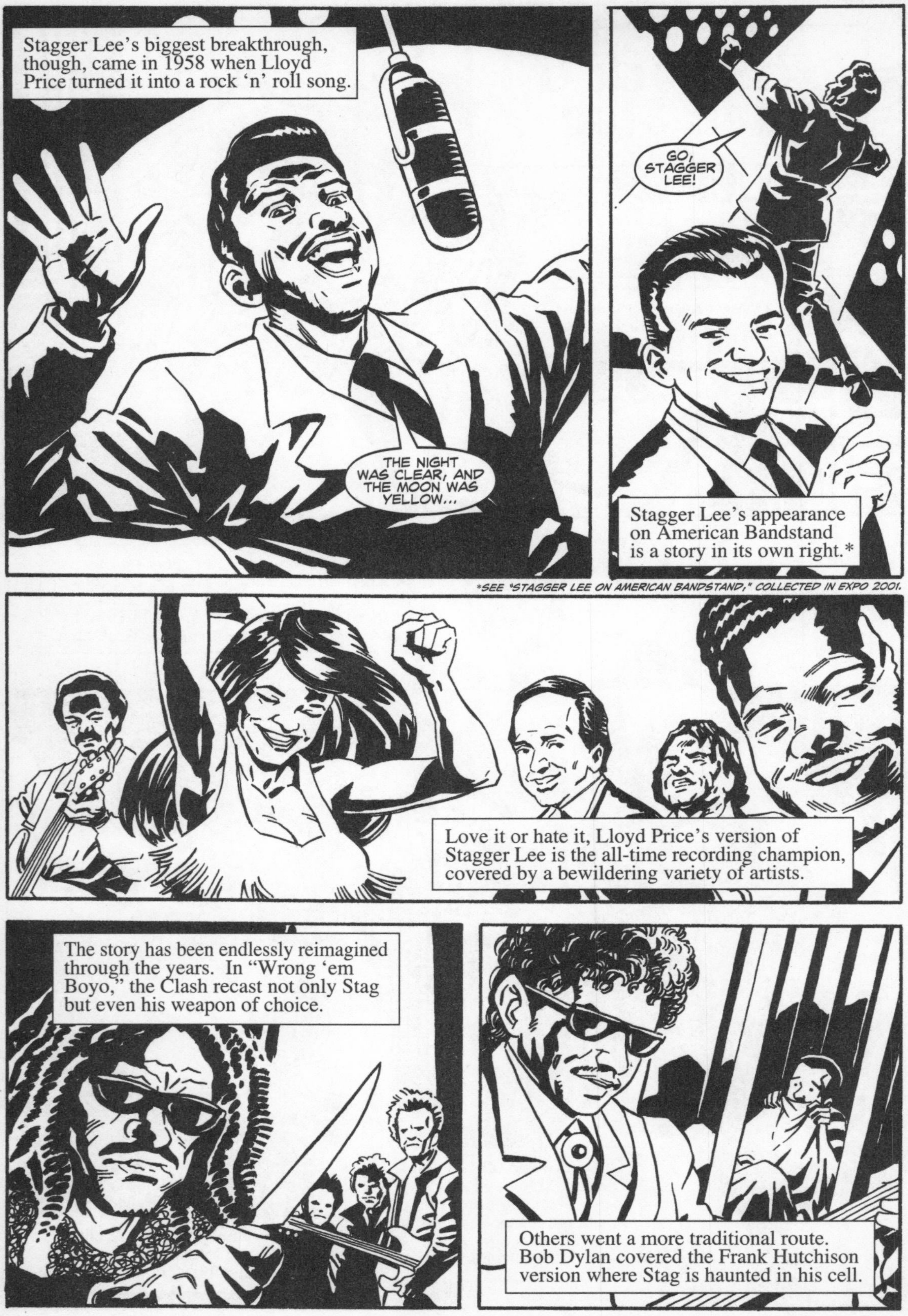
Stagger Lee's biggest breakthrough, though, came in 1958 when Lloyd Price turned it into a rock 'n' roll song.
THE NIGHT WAS CLEAR, AND THE MOON WAS YELLOW...
GO, STAGGER LEE!
Stagger Lee's appearance on American Bandstand is a story in its own right.*
*SEE "STAGGER LEE ON AMERICAN BANDSTAND," COLLECTED IN EXPO 2001.
Love it or hate it, Lloyd Price's version of Stagger Lee is the all-time recording champion, covered by a bewildering variety of artists.
The story has been endlessly reimagined through the years. In "Wrong 'em Boyo," the Clash recast not only Stag but even his weapon of choice.
Others went a more traditional route. Bob Dylan covered the Frank Hutchison version where Stag is haunted in his cell.

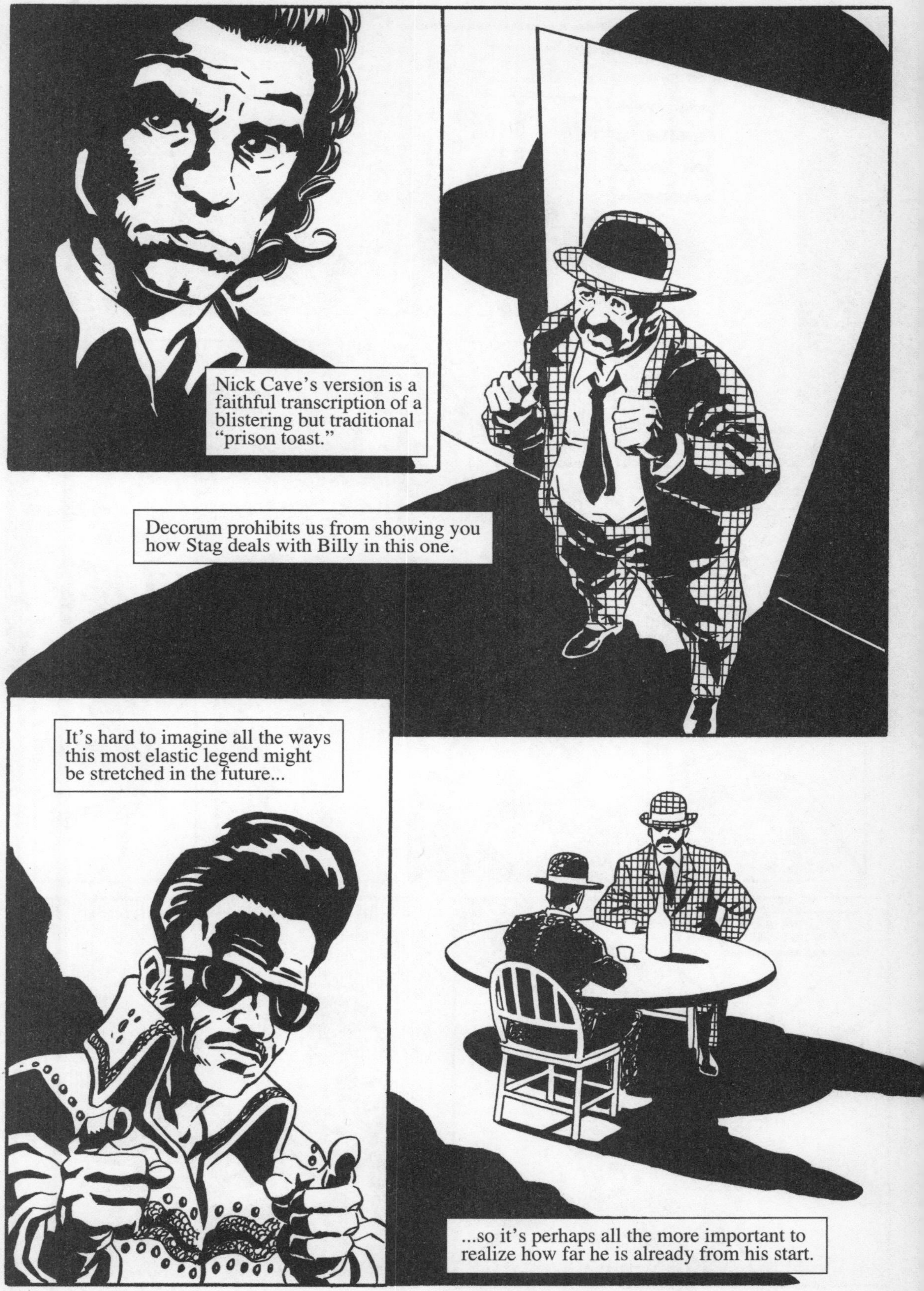
Nick Cave's version is a faithful transcription of a blistering but traditional "prison toast."
Decorum prohibits us from showing you how Stag deals with Billy in this one.
It's hard to imagine all the ways this most elastic legend might be stretched in the future...
...so it's perhaps all the more important to realize how far he is already from his start.

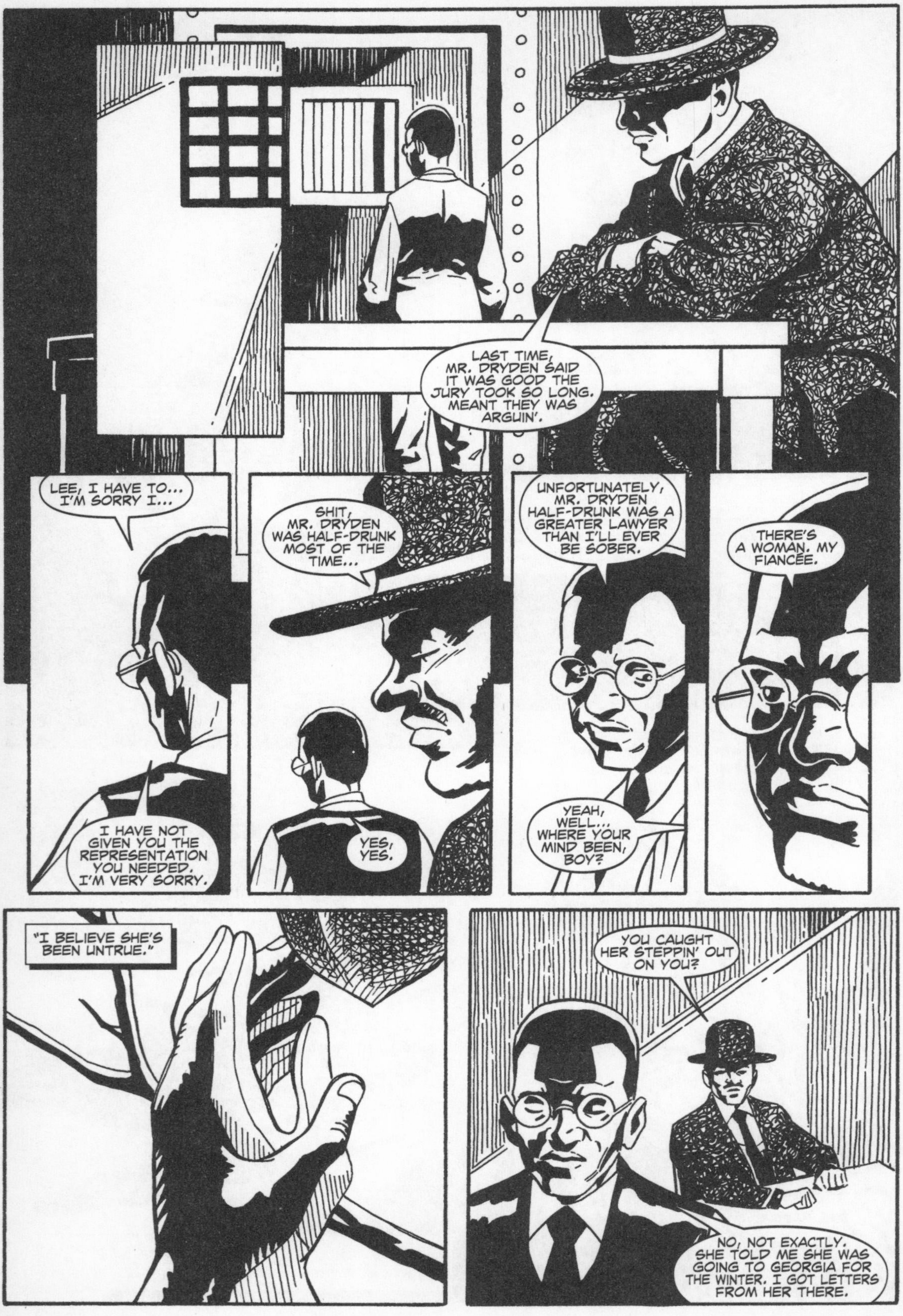
LAST TIME, MR. DRYDEN SAID IT WAS GOOD THE JURY TOOK SO LONG. MEANT THEY WAS ARGUIN'.
LEE, I HAVE TO... I'M SORRY I...
I HAVE NOT GIVEN YOU THE REPRESENTATION YOU NEEDED. I'M VERY SORRY.
SHIT, MR. DRYDEN WAS HALF-DRUNK MOST OF THE TIME...
YES, YES.
UNFORTUNATELY, MR. DRYDEN HALF-DRUNK WAS A GREATER LAWYER THAN I'LL EVER BE SOBER.
YEAH, WELL... WHERE YOUR MIND BEEN, BOY?
THERE'S A WOMAN. MY FIANCÉE.
"I BELIEVE SHE'S BEEN UNTRUE."
YOU CAUGHT HER STEPPIN' OUT ON YOU?
NO, NOT EXACTLY. SHE TOLD ME SHE WAS GOING TO GEORGIA FOR THE WINTER. I GOT LETTERS FROM HER THERE.

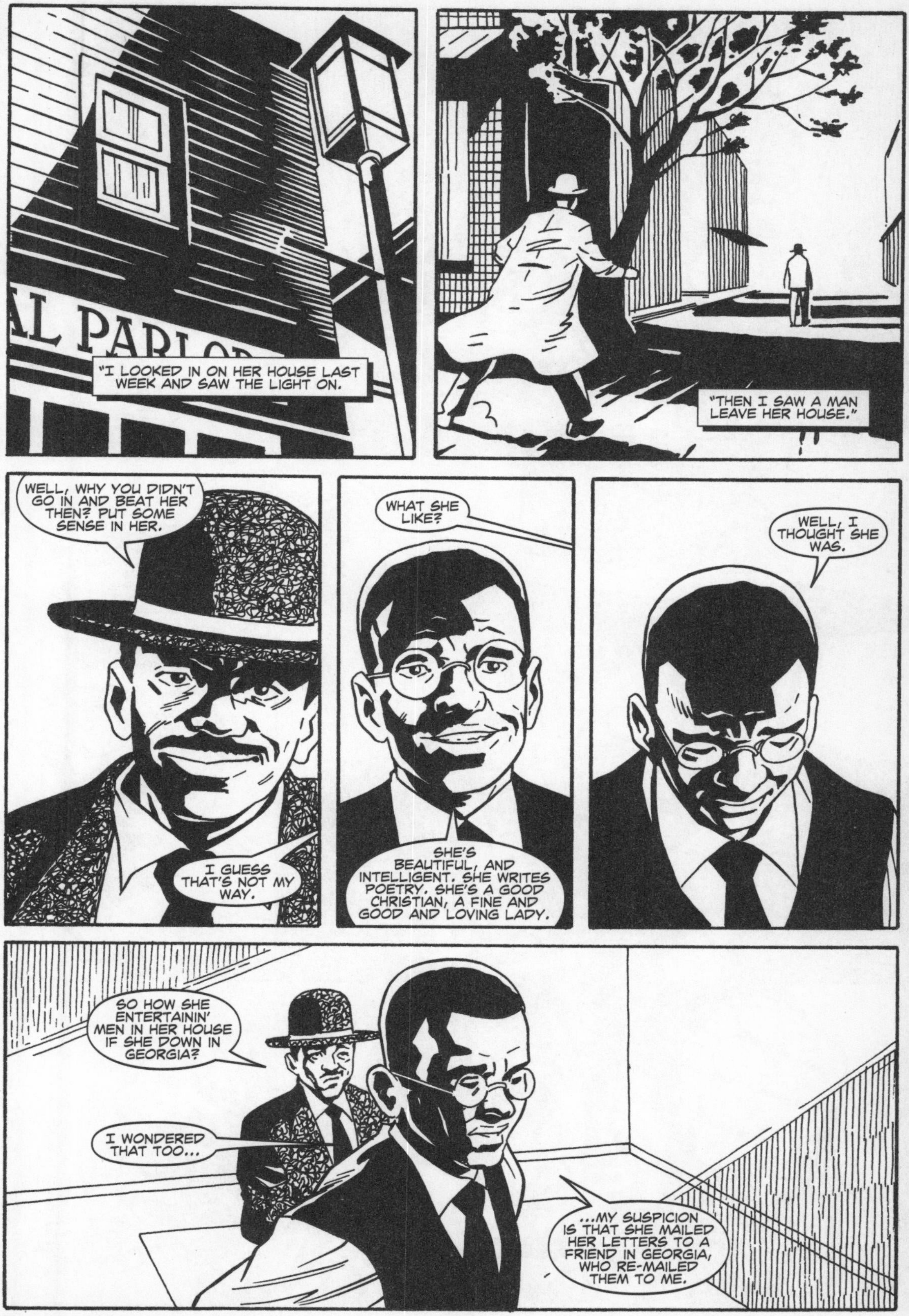

AL PARLO
"I LOOKED IN ON HER HOUSE LAST WEEK AND SAW THE LIGHT ON.
"THEN I SAW A MAN LEAVE HER HOUSE."
WELL, WHY YOU DIDN'T GO IN AND BEAT HER THEN? PUT SOME SENSE IN HER.
I GUESS THAT'S NOT MY WAY.
WHAT SHE LIKE?
SHE'S BEAUTIFUL, AND INTELLIGENT. SHE WRITES POETRY. SHE'S A GOOD CHRISTIAN, A FINE AND GOOD AND LOVING LADY.
WELL, I THOUGHT SHE WAS.
SO HOW SHE ENTERTAININ' MEN IN HER HOUSE IF SHE DOWN IN GEORGIA?
I WONDERED THAT TOO...
...MY SUSPICION IS THAT SHE MAILED HER LETTERS TO A FRIEND IN GEORGIA, WHO RE-MAILED THEM TO ME.

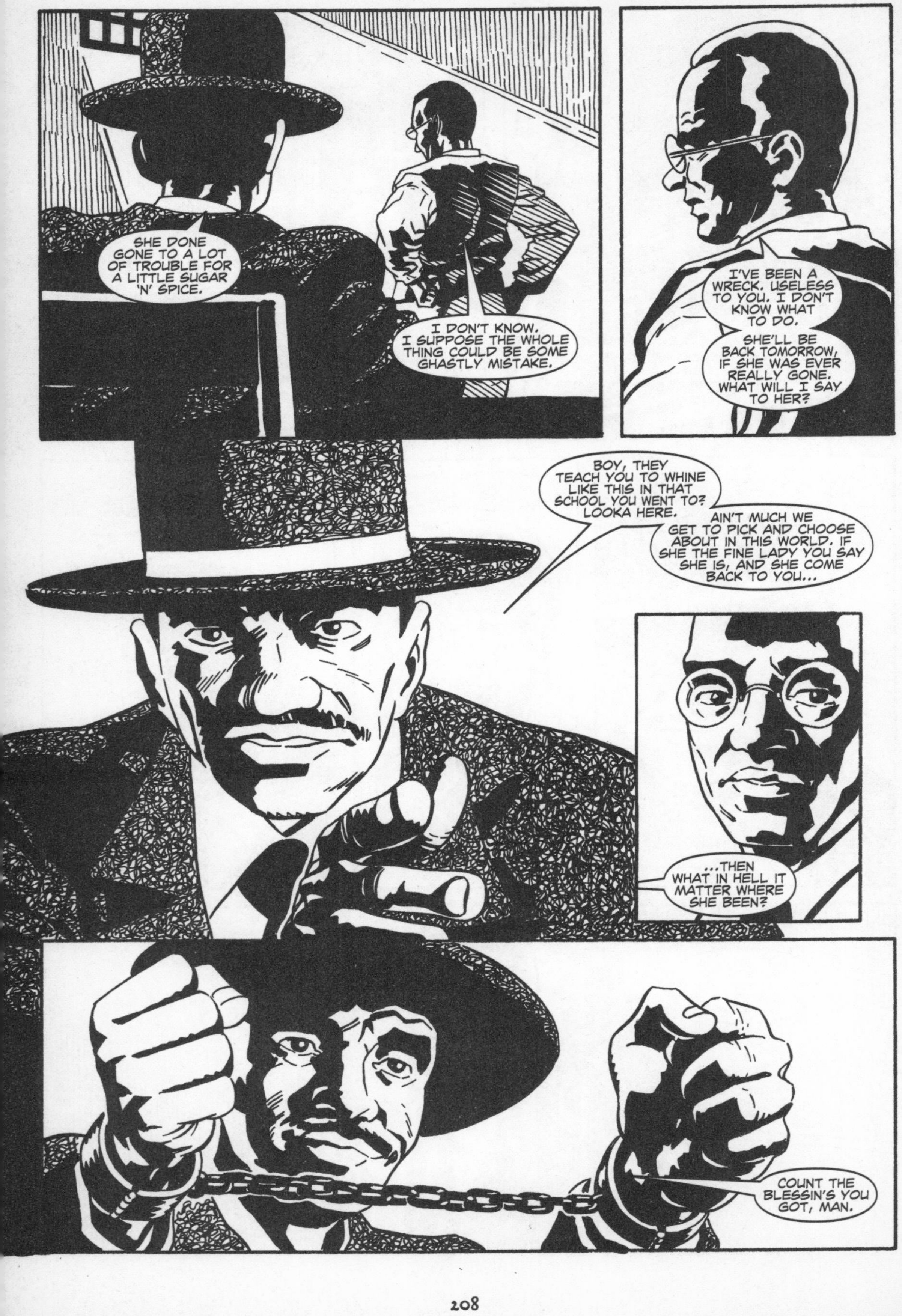
SHE DONE GONE TO A LOT OF TROUBLE FOR A LITTLE SUGAR 'N' SPICE.
I DON'T KNOW. I SUPPOSE THE WHOLE THING COULD BE SOME GHASTLY MISTAKE.
I'VE BEEN A WRECK. USELESS TO YOU. I DON'T KNOW WHAT TO DO.
SHE'LL BE BACK TOMORROW, IF SHE WAS EVER REALLY GONE. WHAT WILL I SAY TO HER?
BOY, THEY TEACH YOU TO WHINE LIKE THIS IN THAT SCHOOL YOU WENT TO? LOOKA HERE.
AIN'T MUCH WE GET TO PICK AND CHOOSE ABOUT IN THIS WORLD. IF SHE THE FINE LADY YOU SAY SHE IS, AND SHE COME BACK TO YOU...
...THEN WHAT IN HELL IT MATTER WHERE SHE BEEN?
COUNT THE BLESSIN'S YOU GOT, MAN.

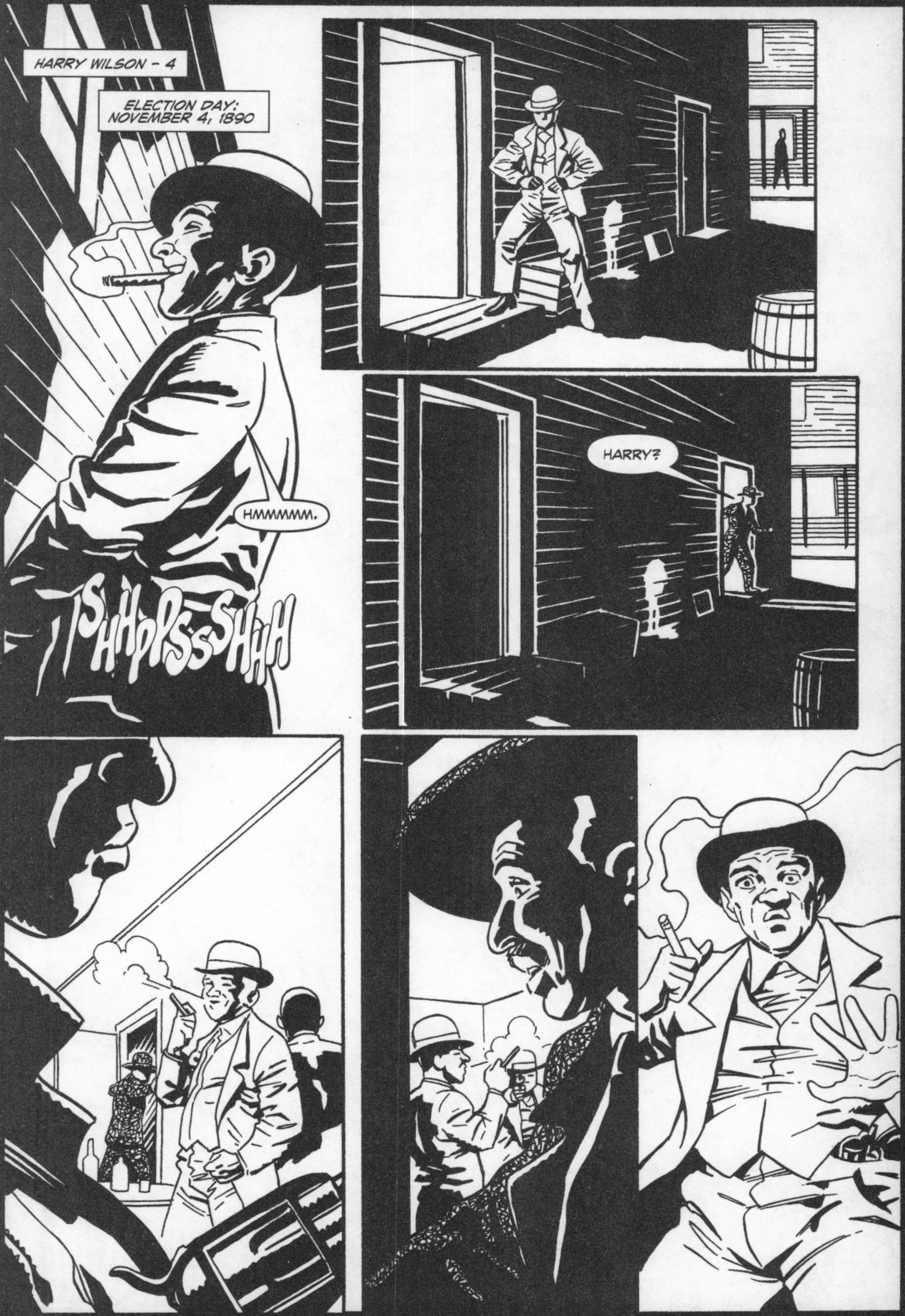
HARRY WILSON - 4
ELECTION DAY:
NOVEMBER 4, 1890
HMMMMM.
SHHPSSSHHH
HARRY?

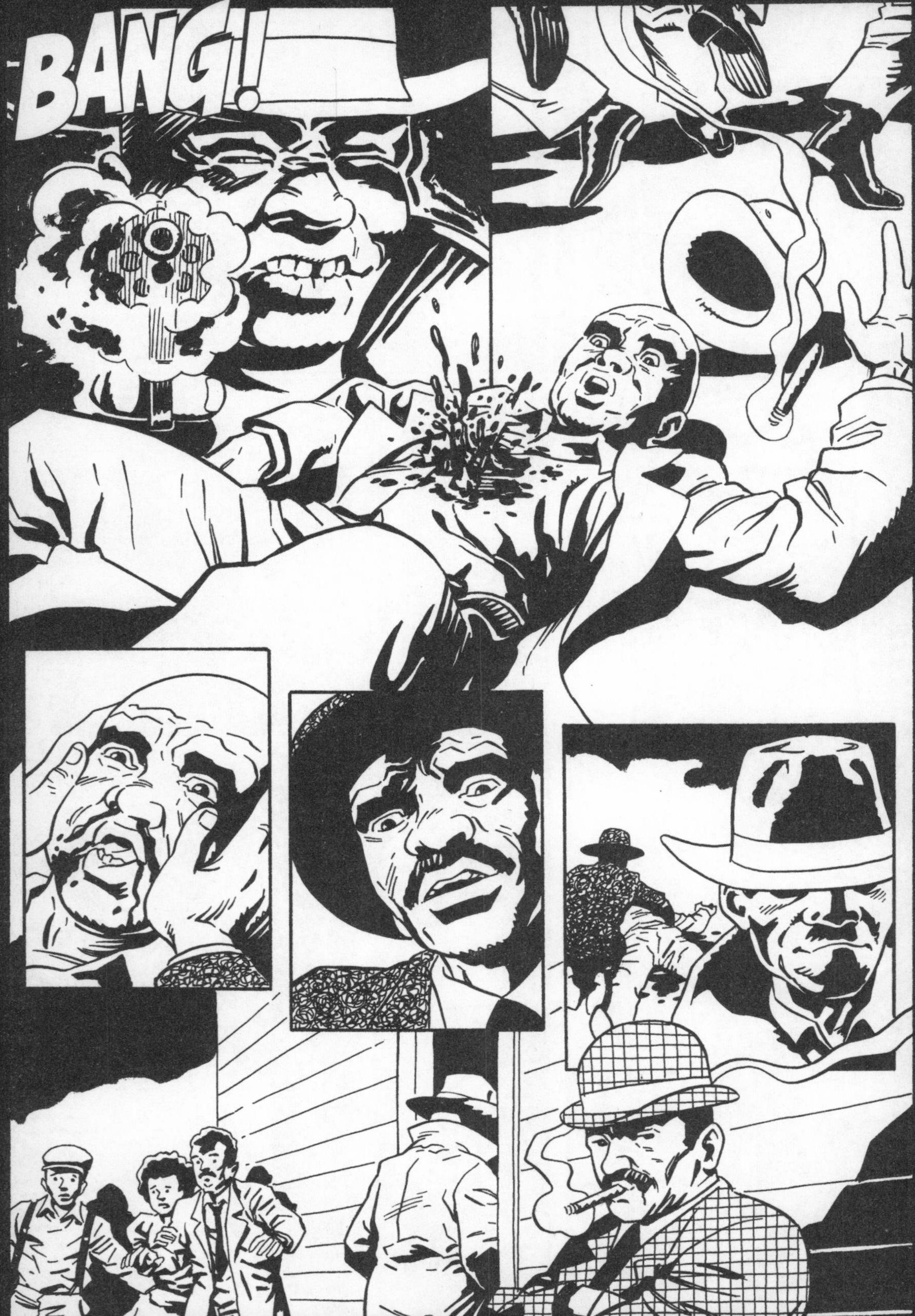
BANG!

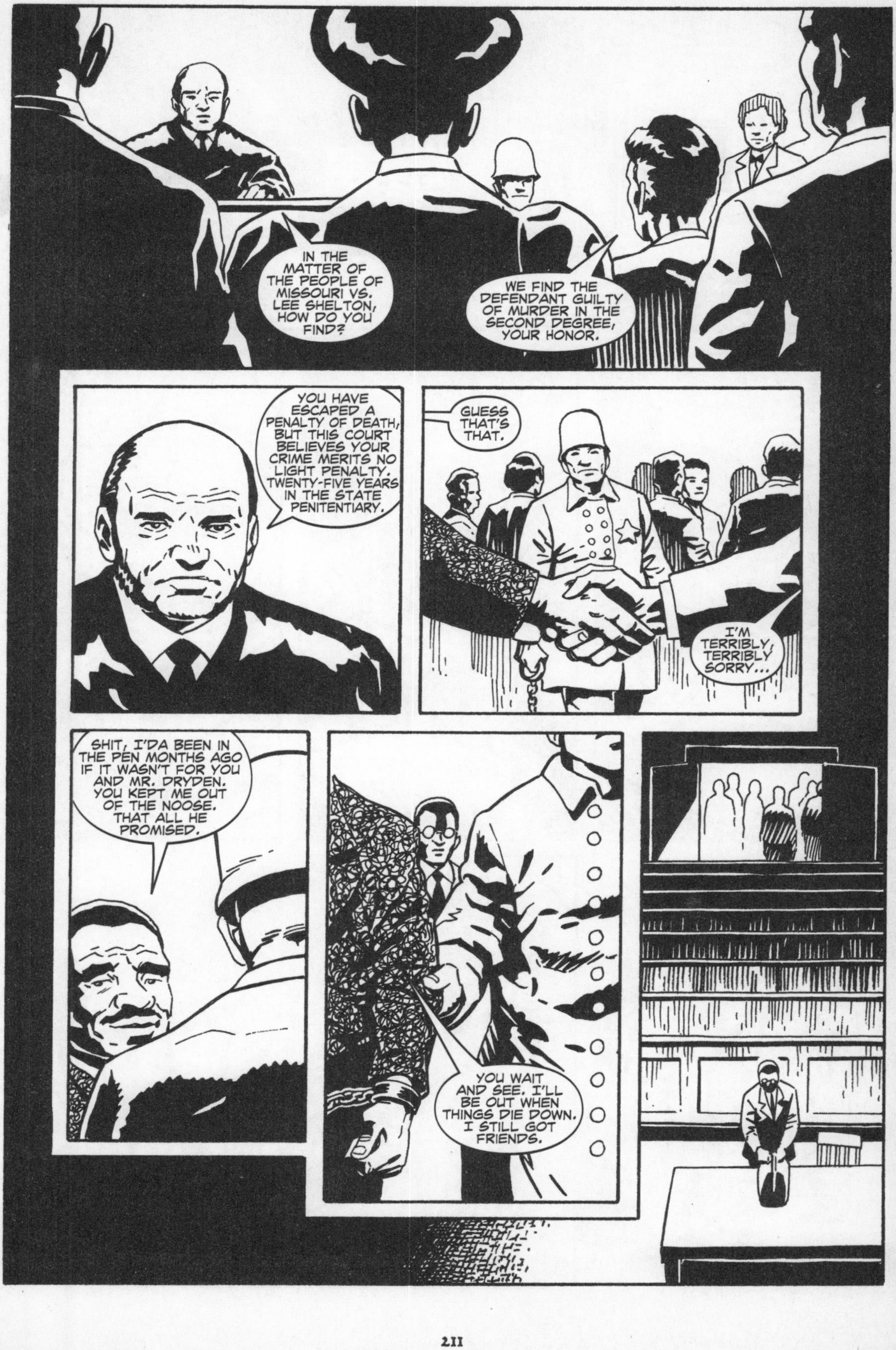
IN THE MATTER OF THE PEOPLE OF MISSOURI VS. LEE SHELTON, HOW DO YOU FIND?
WE FIND THE DEFENDANT GUILTY OF MURDER IN THE SECOND DEGREE, YOUR HONOR.
YOU HAVE ESCAPED A PENALTY OF DEATH, BUT THIS COURT BELIEVES YOUR CRIME MERITS NO LIGHT PENALTY. TWENTY-FIVE YEARS IN THE STATE PENITENTIARY.
GUESS THAT'S THAT.
I'M TERRIBLY, TERRIBLY SORRY...
SHIT, I'DA BEEN IN THE PEN MONTHS AGO IF IT WASN'T FOR YOU AND MR. DRYDEN. YOU KEPT ME OUT OF THE NOOSE. THAT ALL HE PROMISED.
YOU WAIT AND SEE. I'LL BE OUT WHEN THINGS DIE DOWN. I STILL GOT FRIENDS.

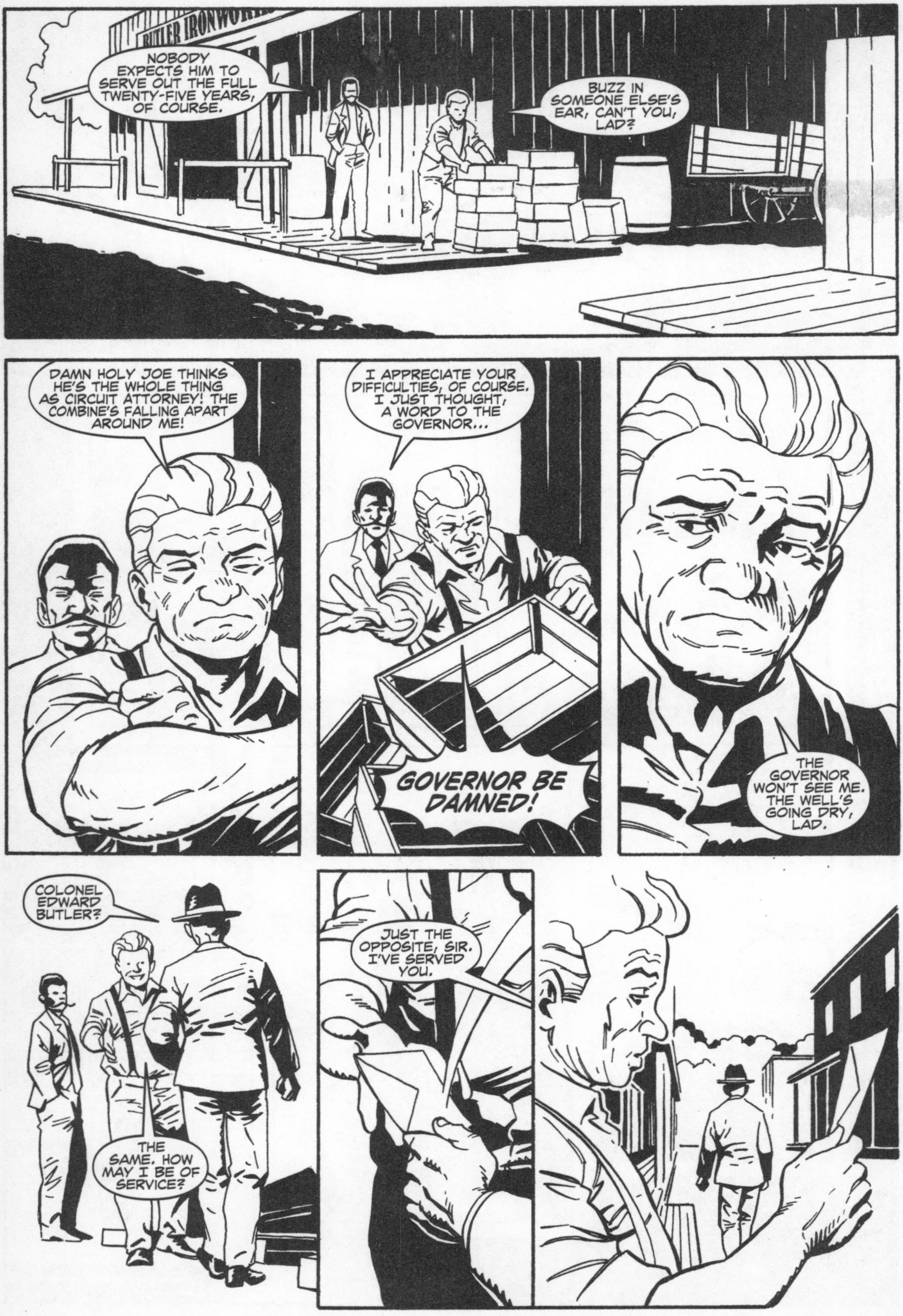
BUTLER IRONWORKS
NOBODY EXPECTS HIM TO SERVE OUT THE FULL TWENTY-FIVE YEARS, OF COURSE.
BUZZ IN SOMEONE ELSE'S EAR, CAN'T YOU, LAD?
DAMN HOLY JOE THINKS HE'S THE WHOLE THING AS CIRCUIT ATTORNEY! THE COMBINE'S FALLING APART AROUND ME!
I APPRECIATE YOUR DIFFICULTIES, OF COURSE. I JUST THOUGHT, A WORD TO THE GOVERNOR...
GOVERNOR BE DAMNED!
THE GOVERNOR WON'T SEE ME. THE WELL'S GOING DRY, LAD.
COLONEL EDWARD BUTLER?
THE SAME. HOW MAY I BE OF SERVICE?
JUST THE OPPOSITE, SIR. I'VE SERVED YOU.

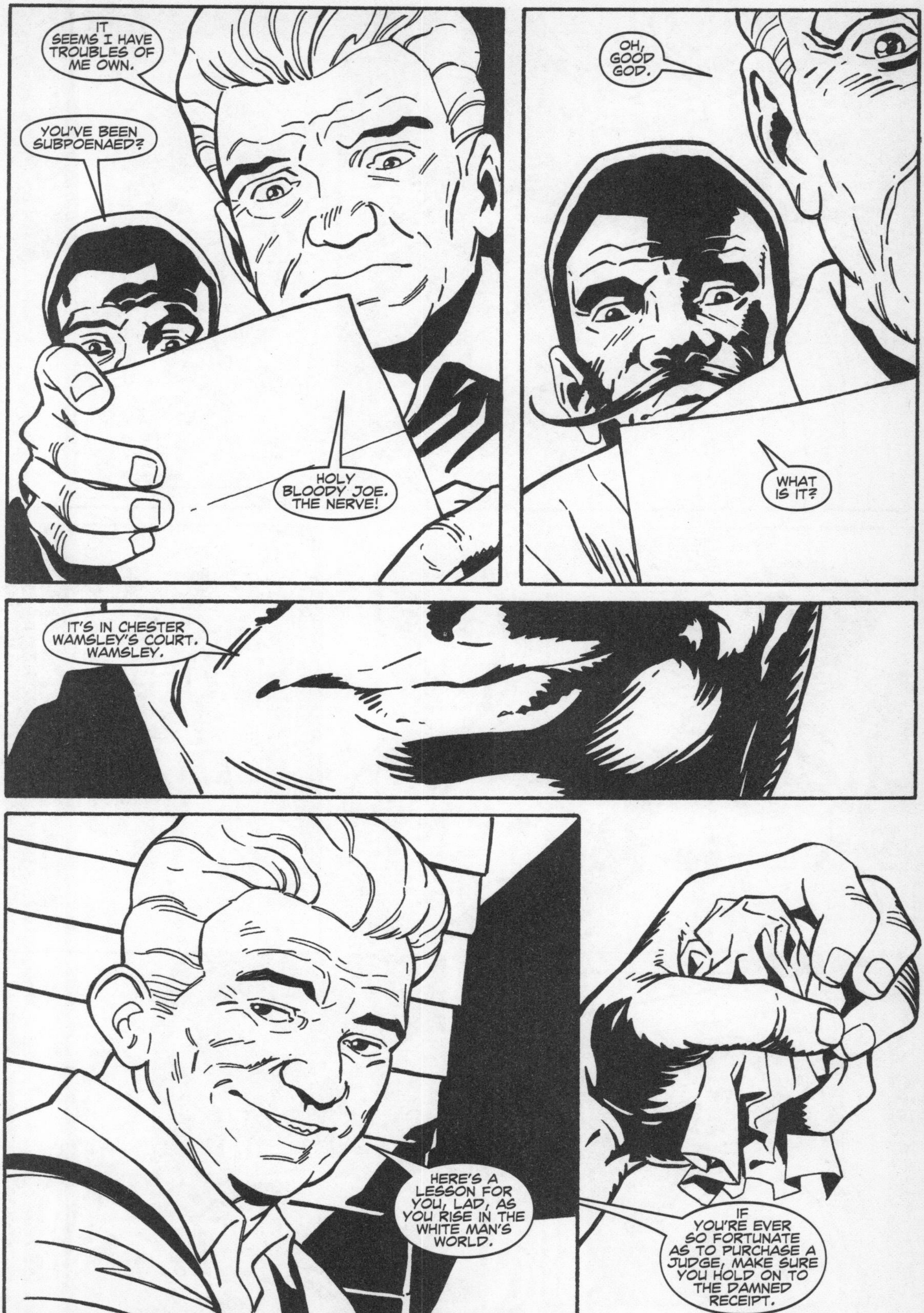
IT SEEMS I HAVE TROUBLES OF ME OWN.
YOU'VE BEEN SUBPOENAED?
HOLY BLOODY JOE. THE NERVE!
OH, GOOD GOD.
WHAT IS IT?
IT'S IN CHESTER WAMSLEY'S COURT. WAMSLEY.
HERE'S A LESSON FOR YOU, LAD, AS YOU RISE IN THE WHITE MAN'S WORLD.
IF YOU'RE EVER SO FORTUNATE AS TO PURCHASE A JUDGE, MAKE SURE YOU HOLD ON TO THE DAMNED RECEIPT.

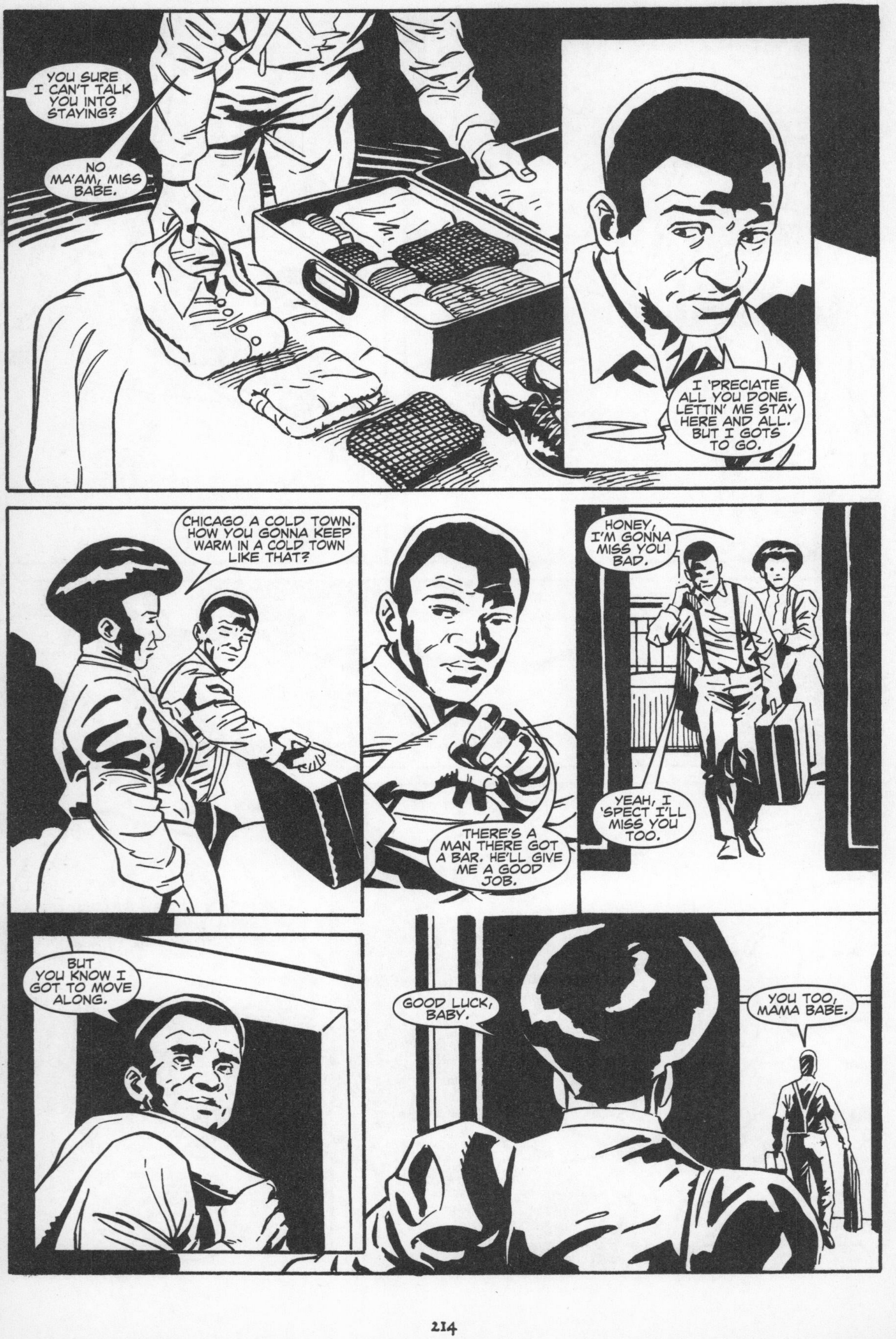
YOU SURE I CAN'T TALK YOU INTO STAYING?
NO MA'AM, MISS BABE.
I 'PRECIATE ALL YOU DONE. LETTIN' ME STAY HERE AND ALL. BUT I GOTS TO GO.
CHICAGO A COLD TOWN. HOW YOU GONNA KEEP WARM IN A COLD TOWN LIKE THAT?
THERE'S A MAN THERE GOT A BAR. HE'LL GIVE ME A GOOD JOB.
HONEY, I'M GONNA MISS YOU BAD.
YEAH, I 'SPECT I'LL MISS YOU TOO.
BUT YOU KNOW I GOT TO MOVE ALONG.
GOOD LUCK, BABY.
YOU TOO, MAMA BABE.

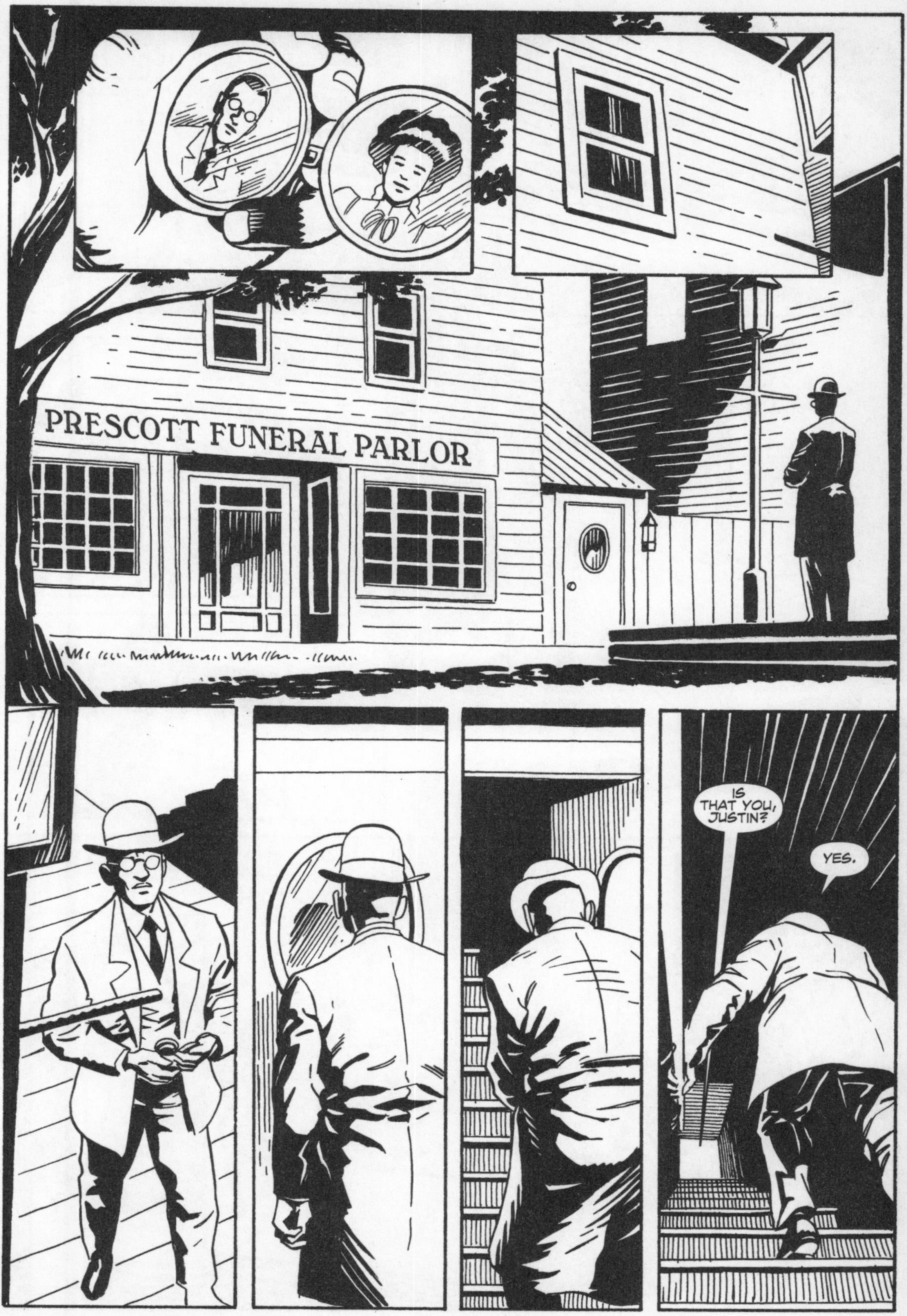
1907
PRESCOTT FUNERAL PARLOR
IS THAT YOU, JUSTIN?
YES.

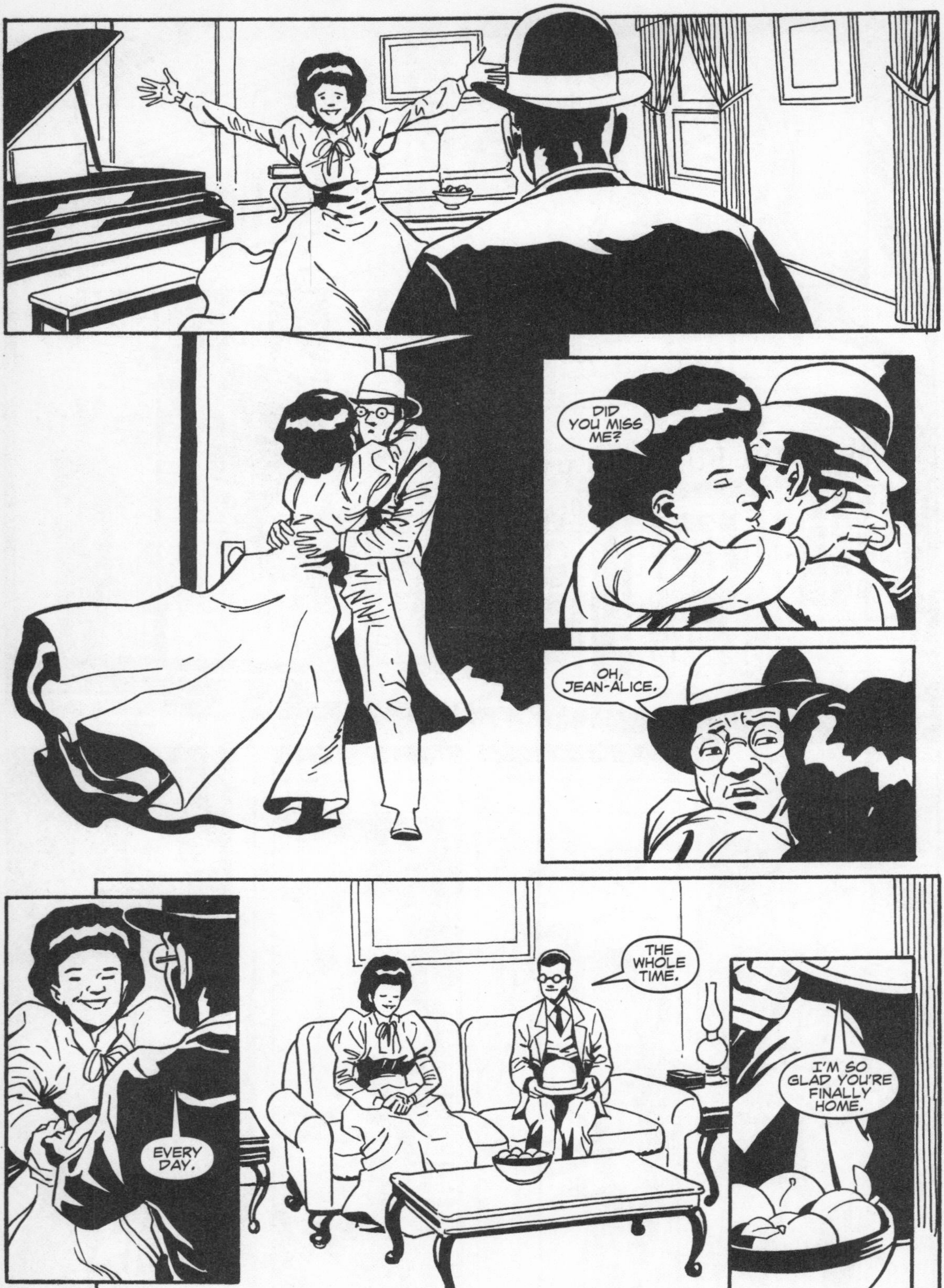
DID YOU MISS ME?
OH, JEAN-ALICE.
EVERY DAY.
THE WHOLE TIME.
I'M SO GLAD YOU'RE FINALLY HOME.

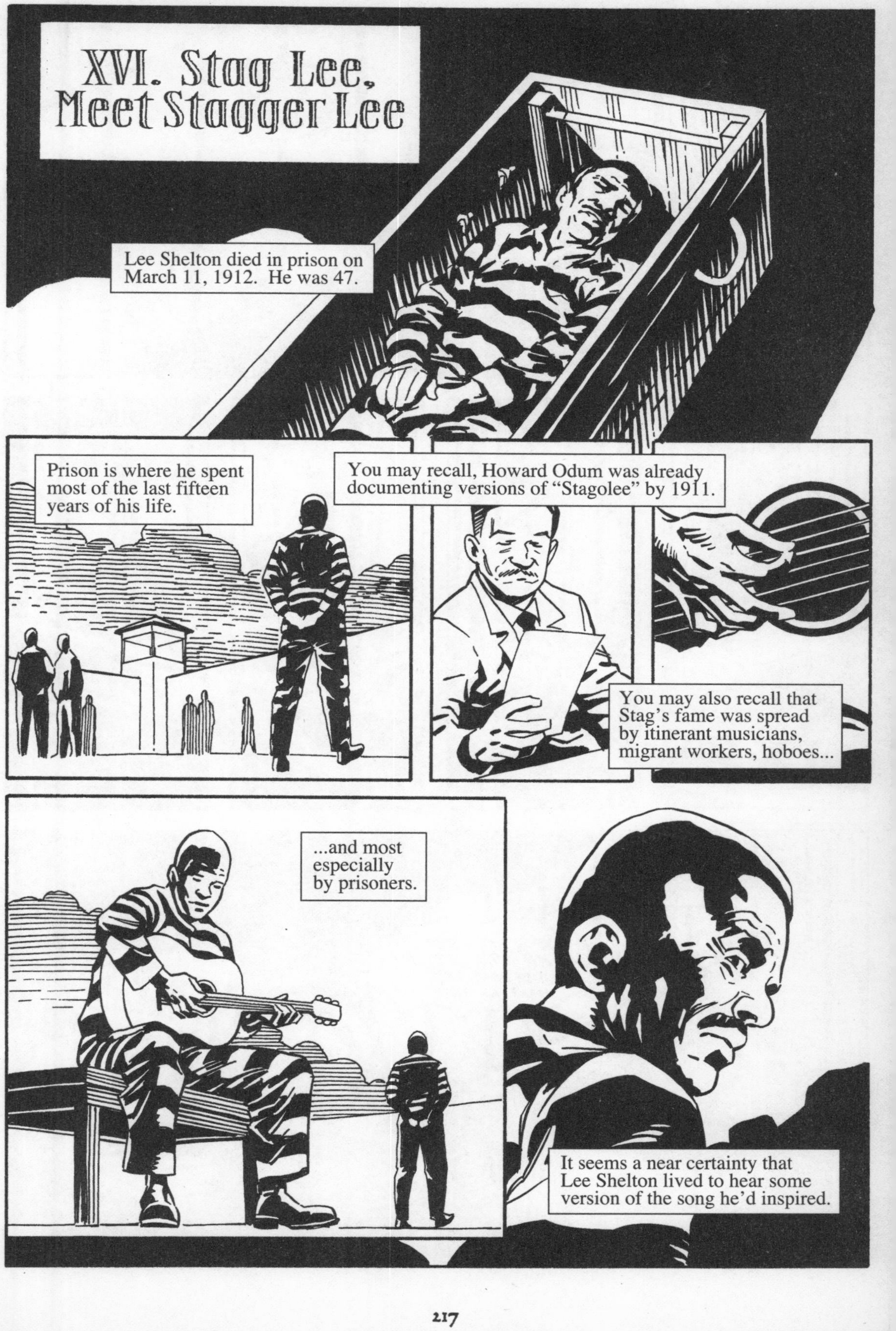
XVI. Stag Lee, Meet Stagger Lee
Lee Shelton died in prison on March 11, 1912. He was 47.
Prison is where he spent most of the last fifteen years of his life.
You may recall, Howard Odum was already documenting versions of "Stagolee" by 1911.
You may also recall that Stag's fame was spread by itinerant musicians, migrant workers, hoboes...
...and most especially by prisoners.
It seems a near certainty that Lee Shelton lived to hear some version of the song he'd inspired.

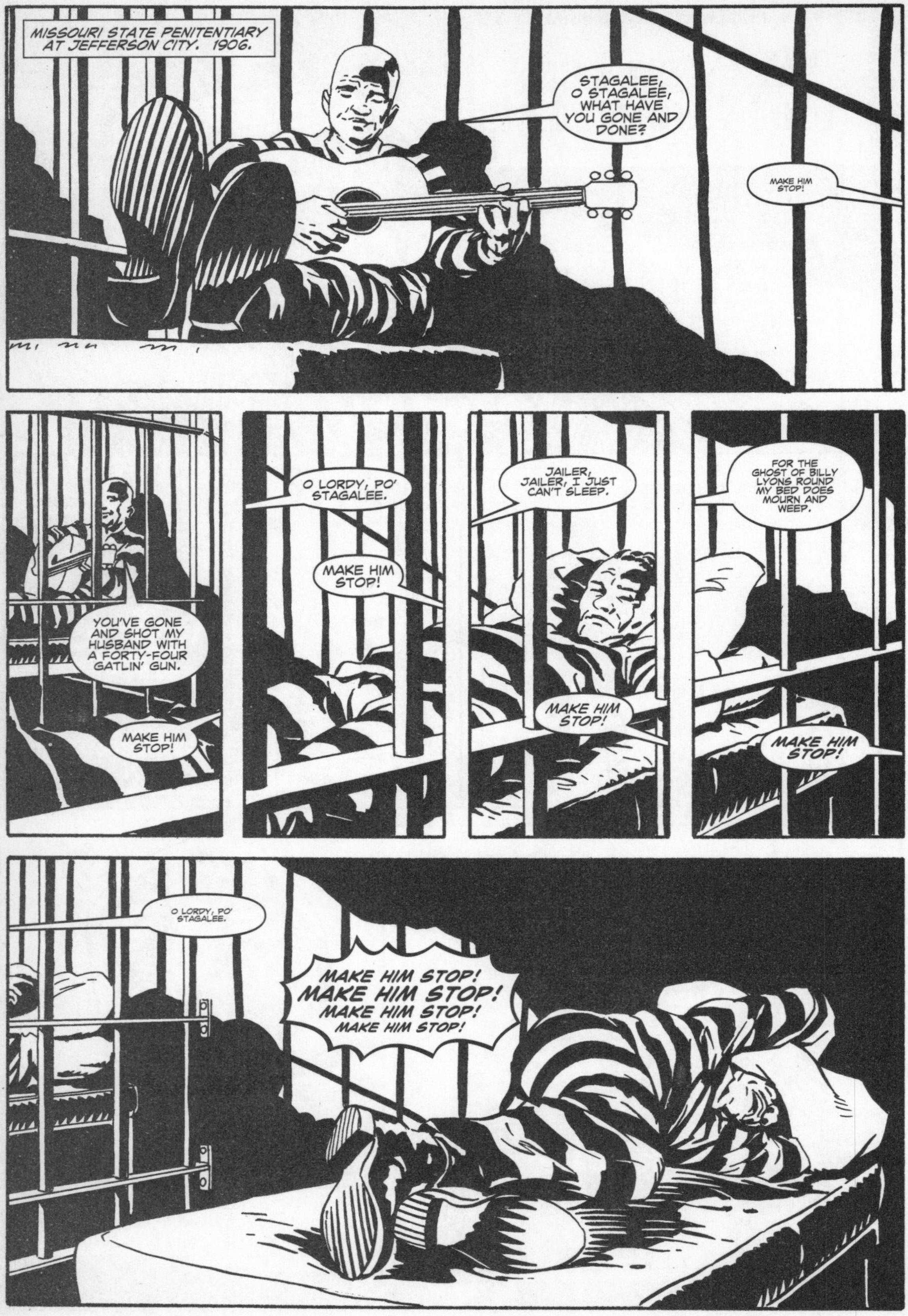
MISSOURI STATE PENITENTIARY AT JEFFERSON CITY. 1906.
STAGALEE, O STAGALEE, WHAT HAVE YOU GONE AND DONE?
MAKE HIM STOP!
YOU'VE GONE AND SHOT MY HUSBAND WITH A FORTY-FOUR GATLIN' GUN.
MAKE HIM STOP!
O LORDY, PO' STAGALEE.
MAKE HIM STOP!
JAILER, JAILER, I JUST CAN'T SLEEP.
MAKE HIM STOP!
FOR THE GHOST OF BILLY LYONS ROUND MY BED DOES MOURN AND WEEP.
MAKE HIM STOP!
O LORDY, PO' STAGALEE.
MAKE HIM STOP! MAKE HIM STOP! MAKE HIM STOP! MAKE HIM STOP!

EPILOGUE

,THEY CARRIED HIM to the CEMETERY, BUT THEY DID NOT BRING HIM BACK

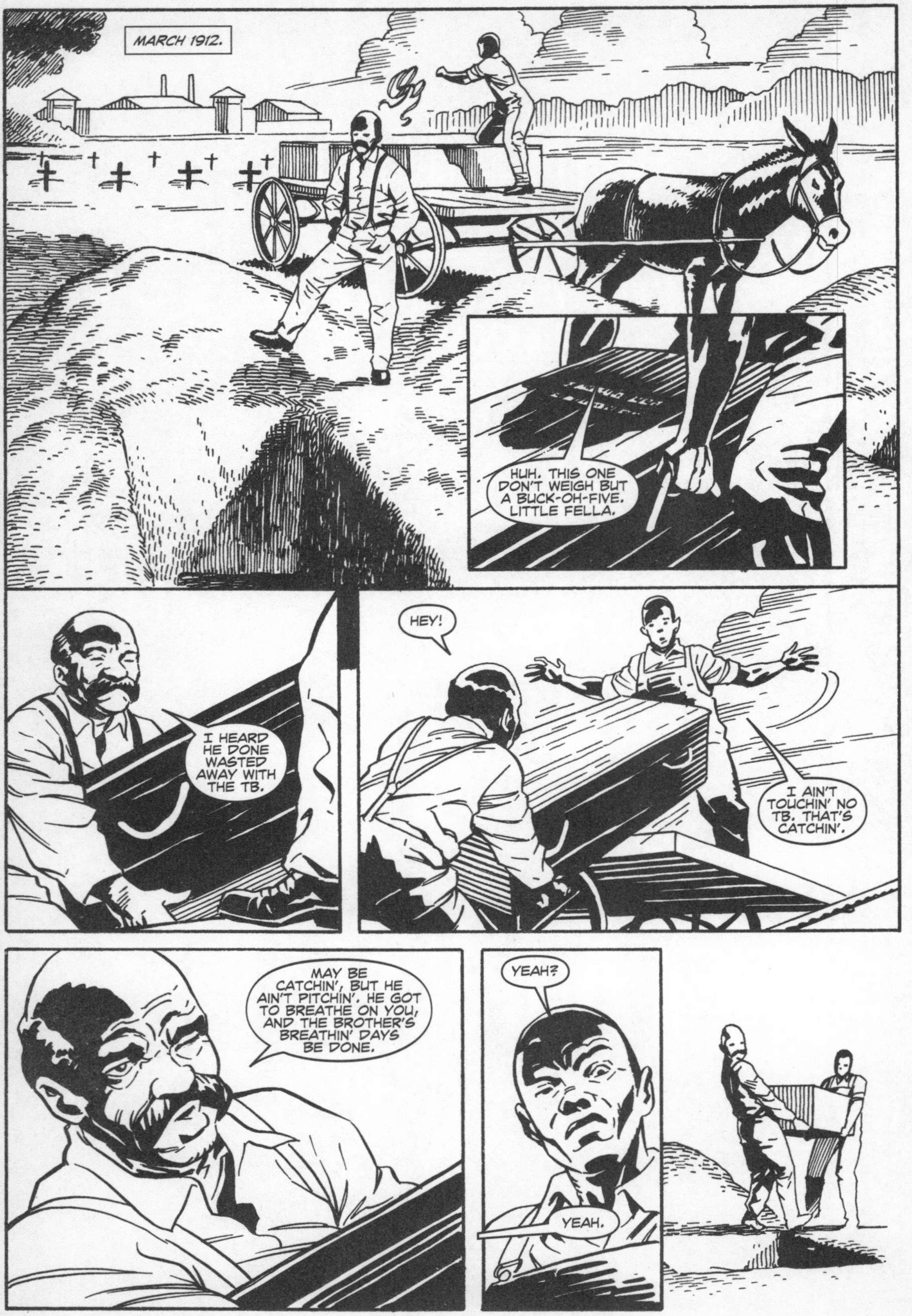
MARCH 1912.
HUH. THIS ONE DON'T WEIGH BUT A BUCK-OH-FIVE. LITTLE FELLA.
I HEARD HE DONE WASTED AWAY WITH THE TB.
HEY!
I AIN'T TOUCHIN' NO TB. THAT'S CATCHIN'.
MAY BE CATCHIN', BUT HE AIN'T PITCHIN'. HE GOT TO BREATHE ON YOU, AND THE BROTHER'S BREATHIN' DAYS BE DONE.
YEAH?
YEAH.

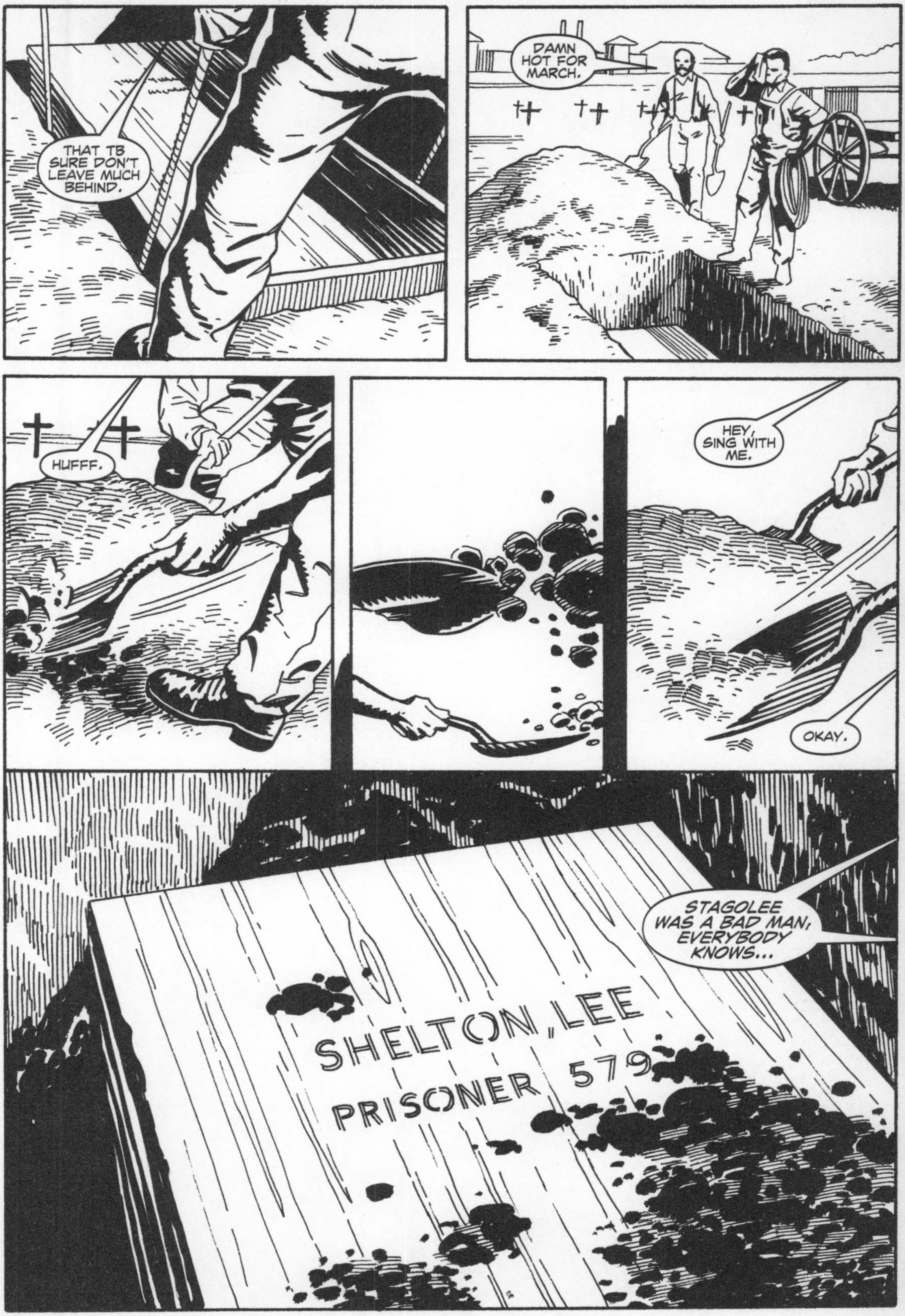
THAT TB SURE DON'T LEAVE MUCH BEHIND.
DAMN HOT FOR MARCH.
HUFFF.
HEY, SING WITH ME.
OKAY.
STAGOLEE WAS A BAD MAN, EVERYBODY KNOWS...
SHELTON LEE
PRISONER 579

ACKNOWLEDGMENTS

DEREK SAYS:

Writing and drawing are solitary arts, but publishing is collaborative. No book of any size is ever completed by the authors alone, and this is not a small book. Stagger Lee would not be reaching you in this form without the efforts of three men in particular:

Charles Brownstein can't be thanked enough for his advice, encouragement, and help from inception through publication. If it had not been for his prodding, I would probably still be thinking about maybe self-publishing this book someday.

Carl V. Harris, professor of history at UC Santa Barbara, provided historical insight and advice throughout the writing of the manuscript. Professor Harris, who specializes in race relations in the post-reconstruction South, helped me resolve countless narrative dilemmas and historical uncertainties. Not least of his contributions was tracking down the 1895 Sears catalog that gave us the model for Stagger Lee's hat: the Stetson Dakota.

Rik Livingston was my original collaborator, illustrating the short piece "Stagger Lee on American Bandstand," which appeared in SPX's Expo 2001 book. You can see Rik's work online at http://www.demolitionkitchen.com/zono/.

Also, this book would never have existed without the efforts of three men I've never met: Greil Marcus, whose book MYSTERY TRAIN introduced me to the story behind the song; and John David and Cecil Brown, whose scholarship on both the history of the song and the history behind the song uncovered the truth of Stagger Lee.

An unpayable debt is owed to the hundreds and probably thousands of musicians who composed and performed different versions of Stagger Lee over the last hundred-plus years. This book was entirely written and largely drawn to a soundtrack we called (more accurately for some tracks than others) "The Best of Stagger Lee." The play list included, in the following order:

"Stagger Lee," by Lloyd Price
"Stackalee," by Bama (Alan Lomax field recording)
"Wrong 'Em Boyo," by The Clash
"Stack-O-Lee (1960s live version)," by Mississippi John Hurt
"Stagger Lee (Bandstand Version)," by Lloyd Price
"Stack O'Lee Blues," by Ma Rainey
"Stagger Lee," by Nick Cave
"Stagger Lee," by Neil Diamond
"Stackolee," by Woody Guthrie
"Stack A Lee," by Bob Dylan
"Old Stack O'Lee Blues," by Sidney Bechet (instrumental)
"Stack O'Lee (1928 version)," by Mississippi John Hurt
"Stack-A-Lee," by Dr. John
"Stack-O-Lee," by Professor Longhair
"Billy Lyons and Stack O'Lee," by Furry Lewis
"Stagger Lee," by The Grateful Dead
"Stagger Lee," by Taj Mahal
"Stagolee," by Jesse Fuller
"Stagolee," by Hogman Maxey
"Stackalee," by Frank Hutchison (instrumental)
"Stack Lee's Blues," by Steve James
"Stagger Lee," by Fats Domino (live)
"Stackalee," by Frank Hutchison
"Stack O Lee Aloha," by Bob Brozman (instrumental)
"Stackalee," by Dave Van Ronk
"Stack-A-Lee Part 1 & 2," by Archibald
"Stack and Billy," by Fats Domino
"Stagger Lee," by Ike and Tina Turner
"Stackolee," by Sonny Terry (with Woody Guthrie)
"Stagger Lee," by Wilson Pickett
"Stagger Lee," by Johnny Moeller
"Stagger Lee," by the Isley Brothers
"Stagger Lee and Billy," by Ike and Tina Turner
"Stack-A-Lee," by Johnny Otis
"Stack-O-Lee," by Tennessee Ernie Ford
and "Stagger Lee," by Jerry Lee Lewis (live).

The "Stagger Lee Focus Group" is sincerely thanked for their early reading of the manuscript and their thoughtful comments thereon: Barbara Dunn, Michael Jay Forrester, Jean Lewis, Lisa Marie Minella, Lex O'Brien, Matt Pico, Michelle Pierce, Jimmie! Robinson, Lothar Tuppan, and Charlene Upshaw.

Additionally, for advice, assistance, and encouragement of various kinds, I thank: Kristine Anstine, Colleen Bray, Duncan Brown, Greg Espinoza, David Harris, Kathleen Hunt, Tom Diamant, Mark "El Dingo" Maggi, and Mike Patchen. Also, a second round of thanks goes to Jean Lewis for copyediting the manuscript and these text pages, and for not taking offense when this sentence wasn't originally included.

And, of course, not a word of this would have been possible without the constant love, support, and understanding of Tara Horton McCulloch.

Shepherd Says:

A big tip of the shout-out hat to Charles Brownstein and Tara Horton McCulloch for their packaging advice; a big shower of confetti to Eric Stephenson and the Image crew for taking us under their wing; a deep bow and curtsy to those who provided moral support along the way; a big Huzzah! to those-not-known-yet who will support us after this book is released; a big hug to Rochon Perry for her promotional advice; a big hug and kiss to Barbara Dunn (she's my mom—what more reason do I need?); and finally—crushing hugs, sloppy kisses, and undying gratitude to Gail Follansbee, Arielle Jones, and Edgar P. Philpott for putting up with the late nights and missed weekends and whose love sustained me while I was working on this book.

Thanks, all!

Primary Sources

Cecil Brown, 1993. "Stagolee: From Shack Bully to Culture Hero," Ph.D. Dissertation, Graduate Division, University of California, Berkeley. Available from UMI Dissertation Services at www.bellhowell.infolearning.com. In this paper, Cecil Brown builds on John David's historical research and provides the most thorough cultural context and analysis of Stagolee archetypes available.

Cecil Brown, 2003. STAGOLEE SHOT BILLY. Harvard University Press. Brown revises and expands on his dissertation. This book stands as the definitive examination of all things Stagolee.

Harold Courlander, 1973. TALES OF YORUBA GODS AND HEROES. Original Publications, New York. This was my source for the tale of Obatala and Shango.

John Russell David, 1976. "Tragedy in Ragtime: Black Folktales from St. Louis," Ph.D. Dissertation, Graduate School of Saint Louis University. Available from UMI Dissertation Services at www.bellhowell.infolearning.com. John David was the first researcher to connect the historical Lee Shelton with the legend of Stagger Lee. In addition to Stagger Lee, his paper also discusses the historic antecedents behind the songs "Duncan and Brady" and "Frankie and Johnny." All three songs are based on murders that took place within a decade and a few short blocks of one another.

Greil Marcus, 1997. MYSTERY TRAIN. 4th Revised Edition. Plume. This revision of Marcus' classic series of essays on "Images of America in Rock 'n' Roll Music" includes an extensive discussion on the history of Stagger Lee, culled largely from the dissertations by David and Brown.

Lincoln Steffens, 1904. THE SHAME OF THE CITIES. Hill and Wang American Century Series Edition, 29th printing, 1995. Steffens' classic contemporary muckraking helped bring down Ed Butler's Combine and shot Joseph Folk to national prominence. The details of various relevant political scandals are to be found in two essays, "Tweed Days in St. Louis" and "The Shamelessness of St. Louis."

Notes on the Historical Characters

By Derek McCulloch

Like any version of Stagger Lee, this book is a mixture of fact and fiction. While its wholly fictional characters are a distinct minority, it should not be confused with a work of history. Hercules Moffatt, Evelyn Prescott, Justin Troup, and Zell Baxley have never existed anywhere but in the mind of the author. All of the other major characters and virtually all of the minor characters, though, have antecedents in history. There is only scant historical record about most of these people, and in the case of the barroom witnesses I had little to work with but names. Furthermore, the demands of the fictional narrative occasionally made it necessary to fudge timelines, conflate episodes, or sneak in small anachronisms. Readers interested in a more historically sound treatment of this subject are encouraged to seek out the primary sources listed in the acknowledgments.* For those who'd rather just read the Cliff's Notes, here is a little further information about the key figures.

*The book contains other intentional anachronisms and omissions of too minor a nature to go into here. The curious can email me at badmanstaggerlee@sbcglobal.net for a more complete list of known errors. Anyone with expertise in this period of history is invited to add to my list.

LEE ("STAG LEE") SHELTON

Lee Shelton's year of birth is given in various sources as either 1861 or 1865. When he entered Missouri State Prison in 1897, his age was listed as 32, so I've chosen to view the later date as correct. It's known that he was born in Texas and that he was living in St. Louis probably no later than 1887. For the purposes of this book, I've placed Lee's arrival in St. Louis a bit later, in 1890, to coincide with the murder of policeman James Brady which, like Shelton's later murder of Billy Lyons, was immortalized in song ("Duncan and Brady"). Although in legend he becomes a hulking bully figure, Lee Shelton stood only 5'7" and weighed no more than 120 pounds. As he observes towards the end of this book, Lee did still have friends after his conviction in the second trial, many of whom wrote to successive governors urging a parole or pardon. In 1909 those pleas were heard, and on Thanksgiving day Governor Herbert Hadley commuted Lee's sentence. Lee found his return to society problematic. By this time his old political allies were either dead or deposed and he himself was in poor health (a major contributing factor to his parole). After fewer than two years of freedom, he was arrested and convicted of robbery and returned to the State Prison, where he commenced to waste away from tuberculosis. In January of 1912, the prison's physician wrote to the State's Pardon Attorney, describing Lee's poor health and urging clemency. On March 11, 1912, with the governor leaning towards a second commutation, Lee Shelton died in the prison hospital.

BILLY LYONS, MARIA BROWN & HENRY BRIDGEWATER

B illy Lyons was born in Missouri in 1864. By all accounts, he more closely fit the Stagger Lee archetype than Lee Shelton did. A big man with a violent temper, he was a member of a family with great political power in St. Louis' "Bloody Third" district. At that time, it was common for African-American saloonkeepers to wield considerable political power in their communities. Billy Lyons' stepmother, Maria Brown, was such a figure, as was his brother-in-law, Henry Bridgewater. Individually, Maria Brown or Henry Bridgewater would have had significant political sway with the city's white power structure. Together, they formed a formidable political partnership in seeing to the prosecution of Lee Shelton for the murder of their kin.

NATHAN DRYDEN

The character of Nathan Dryden marks this book's greatest deviation from historical fidelity, though it was (at least initially) an error in good faith. Dryden was a remarkable and colorful figure. It is true, as Ed Butler observes, that Dryden was the first prosecutor to secure a conviction of a white man for killing a black man in the state of Missouri. It is also true that he drank to excess and was addicted to morphine. He was known as an uncommonly eloquent attorney and a thorough bohemian. As depicted herein, he secured a hung jury for Lee Shelton in his first trial but died before the second trial.

In writing this book, I took at face value references in two sources to Dryden as "the most brilliant black lawyer of his time." Long after the script was completed, a source became available that included a photo of Nathan Dryden – who was very clearly Caucasian. Obviously, this created some issues of authenticity for the story. After much agonized thought, I decided to leave our fictional Nathan Dryden a black man. For one thing, the artwork was by this time well underway. More crucially, though, changing the race of Nathan Dryden meant rethinking the entire book; if our Nathan Dryden was white, then the reality of racial politics of the time would dictate that his clerk be white as well. If Justin Troup is white, his position as the lynchpin between all three stories is compromised. The deciding factor, though, is that Nathan Dryden is simply a more engaging character as a black man.

The most peculiar irony of all this is that before seeing the photograph of Nathan Dryden, I pursued a hunch of my own. Given the time period and the fact of his morphine addiction, it seemed likely that Dryden served in the Civil War and gained his dependence after treatment for a wound. Searching an online database of Civil War veterans, I found an entry for "Nat Dryden, 83rd Regiment, United States Colored Infantry." Since Dryden was known familiarly as "Nat," the matter seemed to be clinched, and I included that service record in my story. My apologies to the descendants of either Nat Dryden for the confusion, but I stand by the result. I think our amalgamation of Drydens has resulted in a compelling fictional character.

"COLONEL" ED BUTLER

"Colonel" Ed Butler was a minor political boss compared to other notorious figures such as New York's Boss Tweed or Boss Pendergast of Kansas City, but he is notable for having run a truly bipartisan political operation. Nominally a Democrat, he was willing to collaborate with representatives of any political stripe in the cause of mutually beneficial pocket-lining. A blacksmith by trade, he found his path to wealth and political power by gaining a monopoly on horseshoeing for St. Louis' streetcar lines. From there, he branched into garbage collection, real estate, and political influence.

Although it's strongly implied in this book that Colonel Butler took $145,000 from Charles Turner of the Suburban Railway Company to make the necessary bribes for the passage of a House Bill, this is not actually the case. Mr. Turner balked at Butler's price and found someone who would do it cheaper – for $75,000. Butler was guilty of no wrongdoing in this particular scandal, though not for lack of trying. I also place the meeting between Turner and Butler several years earlier than was actually the case.

The Suburban Railway scandal, though, was a focal point of the investigations by Circuit Attorney Joseph Folk that led to the eventual dismantling of Butler's "Combine." Folk successfully prosecuted Butler for bribing members of the Board of Health to benefit his own garbage collection operation. The Missouri Supreme Court eventually overturned the conviction, but by then the damage to Butler's political power was done, and his Combine was broken for good.

BABE CONNORS

HENRY CRUMP

Sarah "Babe" Connors, the mistress of the Castle Club, was a flamboyant and bawdy presence in 1890s St. Louis, the sort of woman Mae West later made a career of impersonating. In effect she was also a patron of the arts. The town's best musicians played the Castle Club, and it's more than likely that early versions of Stagger Lee were first performed there in the days after Billy Lyons' murder. Babe died wealthy in 1899. Readers who may think I'm indulging in a "whore with a heart of gold" stereotype in depicting Babe's donation to the orphanage may be assured that I'm merely reporting historical fact. Her obituary in the St. Louis Post-Dispatch read: "No one ever went hungry from this woman's door. Freely she received; freely she gave.... Certain sisters of certain holy orders in this town have a long list of items to enter on the credit side of her life's ledger; sums given them in secret, money handed them hidden in a napkin. Many a poor wretch has had cause to be glad for the day he found her door."

Henry Crump did indeed accompany Billy Lyons to Bill Curtis' saloon on the night of the murder, and it is reported that Billy requested and took from him a knife. This apparently was important testimony but since no transcript of either trial survives, one can only speculate on its significance. Given that Henry Crump's testimony reveals a weapon in Billy Lyons' possession, though, self-defense seems the likely argument. The notion depicted in this book that Henry Crump changed his testimony is a complete invention to help explain the different outcomes of the two trials. Again, my apologies to Mr. Crump's descendants for this capricious historical slander.

J.C. COVINGTON

JOSEPH FOLK

All I know about J.C. Covington is that his name appeared on a letter sent to the St. Louis Star Sayings disclaiming the theory that Billy Lyons was killed in revenge for the death of Harry Wilson, and that he signed the letter "Financial Secretary of the Colored 500." Since he listed Lee Shelton as "Captain" of this same group, I've chosen to depict him as the liaison between Lee and the city's white power structure, represented here by Ed Butler. There are other figures who might have fit this bill as well; Jim Ray, for example, a notorious casino owner who was Butler's political ally. I confess I made Covington the key political fixer in this story simply because I was charmed by the flowery prose style in his letter. His use of the term "pure bosh" to describe the Harry Wilson revenge theory stuck in my head throughout the years I was researching and preparing for the book, and I wanted to make sure I included his voice in my version of the story.

In a fine example of stuff I couldn't have made up, Joseph Folk (1869-1923) really was recruited for Circuit Attorney by the same people he later prosecuted from that office. Throughout his campaign, he promised to seek out and punish corruption in city government, but his backers heard it merely as a campaign song they'd heard before. Folk won national fame for his dismantling of the Combine, and sailed on the tide of reform to the governorship of Missouri in 1905. The same actions that brought him to the governorship ensured that he would hold that office only briefly. Having made powerful enemies in big business and both major political parties, he was beholden to none but could count on nobody for support. He served a single term as governor, failed twice to be elected to the Senate, and though his fame earned him consideration as a Presidential nominee in 1912, his limited electoral track record made it impossible for him to garner the necessary support. In another bit of historical legerdemain, I place Folk's run for Circuit Attorney concurrent with Lee's trials. In actuality, Folk was elected several years later, in 1900.

MORE GREAT BOOKS FROM IMAGE COMICS

For a comic shop near you carrying graphic novels from Image Comics, please call toll free: 1-888-COMIC-BOOK

A DISTANT SOIL
VOL. 1: THE GATHERING ,TP
ISBN# 1887279512
$19.95
VOL. 2: THE ASCENDANT ,TP
ISBN# 1582400180
$28.95
VOL. 3: ARIA ,TP
ISBN# 1582403619
$16.95
VOL. 4: GODA ,TP
ISBN# 158240478x
$17.99

AGE OF BRONZE
VOL. 1: A THOUSAND SHIPS ,TP
ISBN# 1582402000
$19.95
VOL. 2: SACRIFICE HG
ISBN# 1582403600
$29.95

,THE AMAZING JOY BUZZARDS,
VOL. 1 ,TP
ISBN# 1582404984
$11.95

BAD IDEAS COLLECTED: ,TP
ISBN# 158240531x
$12.99

,THE BLACK FOREST
VOL. 1 GN
ISBN# 1582403503
$9.95
VOL. 2: CASTLE OF SHADOWS GN
ISBN# 1582405611
$6.99

CREASED
ISBN# 1582404216
$9.95

DAWN
VOL. 1:
LUCIFER'S HALO NEW ED ,TP
ISBN# 1582405689
$17.99
VOL. 1: LUCIFERS HALO
SUPPLEMENTAL BOOK ,TP
ISBN# 1582405697
$12.99

DEATH, JR ,TP
ISBN# 1582405263
$14.99

EARTHBOY JACOBUS GN
ISBN# 1582404925
$17.95

FLIGHT
VOL. 1 GN
ISBN# 1582403816
$19.95
VOL. 2 GN
ISBN# 1582404771
$24.95

FOUR-LETTER WORLDS
ISBN# 1582404399
$12.95

GIRLS, VOL 1: CONCEPTION ,TP
ISBN# 1582405298
$14.99

GRRL SCOUTS
VOL. 1 ,TP
ISBN# 1582403163
$12.95
VOL. 2: WORK SUCKS ,TP
ISBN# 1582403430
$12.95

GUN FU, VOL 1 ,TP
ISBN# 1582405212
$14.95

HAWAIIAN DICK, VOL. 1:
BYRD OF PARADISE ,TP
ISBN# 1582403171
$14.95

HEAVEN, LLC GN
ISBN# 1582403511
$12.95

KANE
VOL. 1:
GREETINGS FROM NEW EDEN ,TP
ISBN# 1582403406
$11.95
VOL. 2: RABBIT HUNT ,TP
ISBN# 1582403554
$12.95
VOL. 3: HISTORIES ,TP
ISBN# 1582403821
$12.95
VOL. 4: THIRTY NINTH ,TP
ISBN# 1582404682
$16.95
VOL. 5: UNTOUCHABLE RICO
COSTAS & OTHER STORIES ,TP
ISBN# 1582405514
$13.99

LONG HOT SUMMER GN
ISBN# 158240559x
$7.99

MIDNIGHT NATION ,TP
ISBN# 1582404607
$24.99

MINISTRY OF SPACE
ISBN# 1582404232
$12.99

PUT ,THE BOOK BACK ON ,THE
SHELF: A BELLE & SEBASTIAN
ANTHOLOGY
ISBN# 1582406006
$19.99

PvP
,THE DORK AGES ,TP
ISBN# 1582403457
$11.95
VOL. 1: PVP AT LARGE ,TP
ISBN# 1582403740
$11.95
VOL. 2: PVP RELOADED ,TP
ISBN# 158240433X
$11.95
VOL. 3: PVP RIDES AGAIN ,TP
ISBN# 1582405530
$11.99

RIDE, VOL. 1 ,TP
ISBN# 1582405220
$9.99

RONIN HOOD OF ,THE 47
SAMURAI
ISBN# 1582405557
$9.99

SEA OF RED
VOL. 1:
NO GRAVE BUT ,THE SEA ,TP
ISBN# 1582405379
$8.95
VOL. 2: NO QUARTER
ISBN# 1582405417
$11.99

SHANGRI-LA GN
ISBN# 158240352x
$7.95

,TOMMYSAURUS REX GN
ISBN# 1582403953
$11.95

ULTRA: SEVEN DAYS ,TP
ISBN# 1582404836
$17.99

,THE WICKED WEST GN
ISBN# 1582404143
$9.95